INSIDE
SCIENTOLOGY

INSIDE
SCIENTOLOGY

The Story of **AMERICA'S MOST SECRETIVE RELIGION**

Janet Reitman

HOUGHTON MIFFLIN HARCOURT | Boston | New York
2011

For information about permission to reproduce selections from this book,
write to Permissions, Houghton Mifflin Harcourt Publishing Company,
215 Park Avenue South, New York, New York 10003.

www.hmhbooks.com

Library of Congress Cataloging-in-Publication Data
Reitman, Janet.
Inside scientology: the story of America's most secretive religion / Janet Reitman.
p. cm.
Includes bibliographical references and index.
ISBN 978-0-618-88302-8
1. Scientology — United States. 2. United States — Religion. I. Title.
BP605.S2R45 2011
299'.936 — dc22   2010049837

Book design by Melissa Lotfy

Printed in the United States of America

DOC 10 9 8 7 6 5 4 3 2 1

For my father, and for Lee
with love . . .

CONTENTS

INTRODUCTION

The World's Fastest-Growing Religion

THE LIMESTONE AND granite Church of Scientology in midtown Manhattan is located just northwest of Times Square, at 227 West 46th Street. Blending in seamlessly amid Broadway theaters, restaurants, and hotels, the place is very easy to miss, though it is seven stories tall and marked with a large metal awning proclaiming SCIENTOLOGY in gold letters. At various times during the year, clusters of attractive young men and women are posted on nearby street corners, where they offer free "stress tests" or hand out fliers. Ranging in age from the late teens to the early twenties, they are dressed as conservatively as young bank executives.

On a hot July morning several years ago, I was approached by one of these clear-eyed young men. "Hi!" he said, with a smile. "Do you have a minute?" He introduced himself as Emmett. "We're showing a film down the street," he said, casually pulling a glossy, postcard-sized flier from the stack he held in his hand. "It's about Dianetics — ever heard of it?"

I looked at the handout, which featured a large, exploding volcano, instantly familiar from the Dianetics commercials that played on local television stations when I was a teenager. The flier, which invited me to come and see the free introductory film ("Showing Now! Bring Your Friends!"), proclaimed that *Dianetics: The Modern Science of Mental Health* was "the most popular book on the mind ever written" and a bestseller for over fifty years, with "over 25 million copies in circulation in 50 languages on Earth."

"Okay," I said.

"Great!" A huge grin spread across Emmett's face. He escorted me across the street.

Inside the church, two young women in long skirts stood by the reception desk. Like Emmett, they seemed to be about twenty, had blond hair, and looked freshly scrubbed, reminding me of Mormon missionaries. They led me down a set of marble steps, and we entered the main lobby, a large glossy space with lighting that bathed everything in a pinkish-golden glow. Aside from my guides and me, it was completely empty.

The room appeared to be set up as a Scientology museum. Books by Scientology's founder L. Ron Hubbard — more than fifty of them — lined the walls, as did black-and-white photos of the man, all presenting him as a robust patriarch with graying sideburns and a benevolent smile, dressed in a sports jacket and ascot.

But far more prominent than Hubbard was Tom Cruise. Projected on a large video panel, his image dominated the space: earnest, handsome, dressed in a black turtleneck, looking directly into a camera and apparently giving a testimonial to the faith. What Cruise was actually saying, however, I couldn't tell. His words were almost completely drowned out by the sound of myriad other videos playing simultaneously nearby. The Church of Scientology, unlike other houses of worship, did not invite somber reflection on its beliefs but rather offered a technological wonderland: music videos promoting the group's Youth for Human Rights campaign played alongside infomercials extolling the wonders of Dianetics, which appeared alongside videos and documentary-style reports on the great work of Scientology's "volunteer ministers" at Ground Zero, which played next to a video of Tom Cruise receiving an award for outstanding service.

I was escorted into a small screening room to watch the free introductory film. This turned out to be a high-quality, rather long infomercial featuring a cast of ostensibly real people who explained how Dianetics had changed their lives and improved their health dramatically, curing them of ailments ranging from brain cancer to depression. It was fifteen minutes of fantastic and totally outlandish claims, and yet each testimonial was presented in such a reasonable way that in spite of myself, I felt kind of hopeful.

After the film, a woman came into the screening room and told me that she'd like me to fill out a questionnaire. Laurie, as she introduced herself, was a matronly woman of about fifty. She began her pitch gently. "Tell me about yourself," she said. "What made you interested in Scientology?"

Over the next hour or so, Laurie asked me a series of questions: Was I married? Was I happy? What were my goals? Did I feel like I was living up to my potential? She exuded warmth and was resolutely nonaggressive. And to my amazement, I began to open up to her, telling her about my relationship with my boyfriend and my desire to quit smoking.

In response, Laurie delivered a soft sell for Scientology's "introductory package": a four-hour seminar and twelve hours of Dianetics auditing, a form of counseling that cost $50. "You don't have to do it," Laurie said. "It's just something I get the feeling might help you." She patted my arm.

Laurie also had me take the two-hundred-question Oxford Capacity Analysis, Scientology's well-known personality test, which poses such questions as "Do you often sing or whistle just for the fun of it?" and "Do you sometimes feel that your age is against you (too young or too old)?" After looking at my test, Laurie told me that I had "blocks" in communication but was basically confident, though I did seem to suffer from nonspecific anxiety. "These are *all* things we can help you with," she said, and smiled. "It's really such a good thing you came in," she added, as she took my credit card. "You'll see."

On Monday, I returned to the church to begin my $50 package. My partner in auditing was named David. Sitting down across from me, he asked me to "relive" a moment of physical pain. "Don't choose something that's too stressful," he suggested.

I closed my eyes and concentrated, but try as I might, I could not relive much of anything. After fifteen minutes, I gave up.

Waiting just outside the room was Jane, a Scientology registrar who told me she was now handling my "case." A redhead dressed in jeans and a lightweight blouse, she asked me how it went. "I'm not sure this is for me," I told her.

"A lot of people feel that way when they first start auditing; it's not unusual," Jane said soothingly, all the while steering me away from the exit. She walked me down a long hall and into her office, where, on her desk, lay the results of my personality test. Jane studied them a bit. "What you need is something more personal," she said. She suggested Life Repair, a $2,000 package of one-on-one private auditing sessions, which she said would help me handle my everyday problems. Then, after I finished Life Repair, which could take a month or so, I could get right to The Bridge to Total Freedom, which, Jane explained, was how people really made gains, or had "wins," as she called them.

"How much do you think people spend on psychotherapy?" Jane asked me. I replied that it varied: in New York, $150–$250 could be standard for a forty-five-minute session. Auditing, she said, was much cheaper. Auditing sessions were sold in 12.5-hour blocks, known as intensives; one intensive, she said, cost $750 — half the price of therapy, hour for hour. "It's worth it, I promise you," she said.

"I'll think about it," I told her.

Jane seemed disappointed. "We should get you going as soon as possible," she said. "I really want you to have a win."

Scientology — the term means "the study of truth" — calls itself the "fastest-growing religion in the world." Born in 1954, the group now claims millions of members in 165 different countries and eighty-five hundred Scientology churches, missions, and outreach groups across the globe. Its holdings, which include real estate on several continents, are widely assumed to be worth billions of dollars. Its missionaries, known as "volunteer ministers," tour the developing world and are sent, en masse, to deliver aid in familiar disaster zones such as earthquake-ravaged Port-au-Prince or New Orleans after Hurricane Katrina. Wherever large groups of people are circulating — in city centers, on street corners, in subway stations, at shopping malls, and on college campuses — you can find Scientologists offering free "stress tests" and distributing leaflets. Like members of another homegrown American faith, the Church of Jesus Christ of Latter-day Saints, Scientologists live in virtually every major city in America and in numerous smaller cities and suburbs as well; they can be found in every age group and vocation. Each year, according to the church's estimates, fifty to sixty thousand people sign up for a Scientology course or buy a book about the faith for the first time.

Take a look at these statistics, and you might easily assume that Scientology is one of the most successful new religious movements in America. Certainly it is among the most recognizable, thanks to its most famous, not to mention outspoken, member, Tom Cruise. The creation of the late science fiction writer L. Ron Hubbard, Scientology is considered by some academics within the field of comparative religion to be one of the most significant faiths born in the past century. But type the word *Scientology* into Google, and it becomes immediately clear that it is also America's most controversial religion. It has been referred to as a "cult," a "dangerous cult," and an "evil cult." There are websites declaring that "Scientology kills" and "Scientology lies." Others are dedicated to exposing Scientology's "secret documents," its "secret teachings," and "what Scientology won't tell you." On message boards, former members post stories about their "escape" from the Church of Scientology, their "recovery" from the Church of Scientology, and their "life after" Scientology. It is a church that, over the past fifty years, has been the subject of more than half a dozen wide-scale government investigations around the world, and thousands of lawsuits, many of which center on its controversial doctrine and practices. Scientology, as its critics point out, is unlike any other Western religion in that it withholds key aspects of its central theology from all but its most exalted followers. This would be akin to the Catholic Church telling only a select number of the faithful that Jesus Christ died for their sins.

Whether or not Scientology *is* a religion is a matter of enduring debate. In Germany, where the church has been described as a "totalitarian" organization, Scientology has been roundly condemned as a cult, and its members have been barred from holding public office or even joining some political parties. In Great Britain, Scientology is also viewed as something other than a religion, but it is nonetheless protected by a statute that criminalizes hate speech and threatening actions directed against religious groups (in May 2008, for example, a fifteen-year-old boy was arrested in London for holding a picket sign denouncing Scientology). Australia banned the practice of Scientology in the 1960s but reversed this decision and recognized it as a religion in 1983; yet one outspoken member of the Australian government, Senator Nick Xenophon, has denounced Scientology as a "criminal organization." The French Church of Scientology has been under investigation for more than a decade. In October 2009, a French court found Scientology guilty of fraud and imposed a fine of nearly a million dollars. But the judge stopped short of banning Scientology from France, as the prosecution had requested. Scientology celebrated this decision as a victory. "I don't think that's going to have any lasting impact," the former inspector general of the Church of Scientology, Marty Rathbun, told a Canadian radio interviewer, in response to the verdict. The fine, he explained, was "like chump change" to the church.

The United States, where Scientology was born and where a majority of Scientologists live, has legitimized Scientology as a religion and granted it all of the legal protections that such a status confers, including tax exemption. But within the church itself, Scientology is usually defined as an "applied religious philosophy" — a "spiritual science" offering practical solutions to the problems of everyday life. Within every individual, it asserts, is a happier, purer, better self — a "perfect" self — waiting to be realized. Scientology claims that this idealized self can be realized today, in real time, and what's more, that this self can be godlike, immortal, and marked by supernatural powers. The traditional religious bedrock — worship, God, love and compassion, even the very concept of faith — is wholly absent from its precepts. And, unique among modern religions, Scientology charges members for every service, book, and course offered, promising greater and greater spiritual enlightenment with every dollar spent. People don't "believe" in Scientology; they buy into it.

This is a story about a global spiritual enterprise that trades in a product called "spiritual freedom." It is, on many levels, a story about the buying and selling of self-betterment: an elusive but essentially American concept that has never been more in demand than it is today. As far back as the mid-nineteenth century, when a New England hypnotist named Phineas Quimby popularized a form of healing he called "mind cure," Americans have yearned for a quick fix for their physical, psychological, and spiritual imperfections. The Church of Scientology is a shape-shifting and powerful organization that promises that fix.

The Scientologists you will read about in these pages are members, or former members, of a wealthy and mysterious organization whose goal, like that of most religions, is to improve human society. The church also aspires to greatly increase its global footprint and, finally, to make money, though members will never say this specifically. Rather, if you were to ask, they would tell you that they want to "clear the planet" — to remove, in a literal sense, the stain of war, insanity, and disease from the world — which, like all worthwhile endeavors, comes at a cost.

The church claims that more than half of its members were introduced to Scientology through family or friends. Indeed, at this point in its development, many current members are second- or even third-generation Scientologists. For example, the actress Priscilla Presley, who joined Scientology in the 1970s, raised her daughter, Lisa Marie, in the church; the British writer and graphic novelist Neil Gaiman, who currently maintains that he is not a practicing Scientologist, was nonetheless brought up in Scientology, at the church's worldwide headquarters. Other famous second-generation Scientologists include the actors Juliette Lewis, Elizabeth Moss, Giovanni Ribisi, and Danny Masterson, who introduced the faith to his girlfriend, the model Bijou Phillips, and to his former costar on *That Seventies Show*, Lauren Prepon. Sky Dayton, the founder of Earthlink, one of the first Internet service providers, also grew up in Scientology, as did the church's current spokesman, Tommy Davis, the son of the actress and longtime Scientologist Anne Archer.

But the vast majority of Scientologists are people you have never heard of. Many work in various parts of the entertainment industry, but still more of them write, teach, create art, build houses, trade stock, manage hedge funds, own businesses, and invent new forms of technology. They run schools and drug rehabilitation programs, work in prisons and inner cities, and lobby Congress and federal regulators. Roughly a quarter of them, according to church figures, were raised Catholic, another quarter Protestant; the rest come from Jewish, Mormon, Hindu, and even Muslim backgrounds. As for education, some Scientologists hold professional or advanced degrees; others are high school graduates; some never finished school.

What unites all of these individual Scientologists is a belief in their inherent spiritual imperfection, which can be rectified — if not totally reversed — only through intense study of, and rigid adherence to, the teachings of a single man: Scientology's founder, L. Ron Hubbard. Though he has been dead some twenty years, Hubbard's followers regard him as a living, vital entity — a personal Jesus of sorts. They refer to him, often in the present tense, as LRH or Ron, as if he were a friend. Hubbard's writings are known as "technology" or "tech" and are considered infallible doctrine. "If it isn't written, it isn't true," Hubbard once said. For a Scientologist to question the efficacy of anything Hubbard wrote is to question the very foundations of his or her belief.

Right now, church officials claim, Scientology is experiencing unprecedented expansion, its worldwide membership "growing faster now than at any time in its history." This is a claim the organization has made for many years. And to be sure, Scientology has expanded its reach in the developing world, where the church is opening missions in such far-flung locales as Kazakhstan. As a corporation, the Church of Scientology owns tremendous quantities of real estate virtually everywhere, for which it paid cash. Its holdings include a 55-acre Georgian estate in Sussex, England; a 64,000-square-foot medieval-style castle and resort in South Africa; more than a dozen architectural landmarks in the United States and Europe; and a cruise ship. Since 2004, the church has purchased seventy buildings in cities around the world, many of them faded gems that have been meticulously restored.

Some observers of the movement, however, contend that Scientology's new churches front an organization that is on the decline. In 2001, a survey conducted by the City University of New York found only fifty-five thousand people in the United States who claimed to be Scientologists; in 2008, a similar survey conducted by researchers at Trinity College in Hartford, Connecticut, determined that there might be only twenty-five thousand American Scientologists. And, even allowing for a significant margin of error, these figures fall in the same range as another measure of the movement's numbers: the International Association of Scientologists, to which virtually all dedicated Scientologists belong, reportedly has just forty thousand members. At most, experts say, there are probably no more than a quarter of a million practicing Scientologists in the world today.

But discerning what is true about the Church of Scientology is a challenge. Since it was granted tax-exempt status by the Internal Revenue Service in 1993, Scientology has not released any public information about its membership or finances. The church also has earned a reputation for harassing former church insiders and squelching critics through litigation. Those critics, who comprise an ever-growing network of ex-Scientologists (or "apostates," in church parlance), academics, and independent free-speech and human-rights activists, have fought back in recent years by blogging and posting a significant amount of information on the Internet: scans of controversial memos, photographs, legal briefs, and depositions, as well as written testimony and videotaped interviews with disillusioned former members, including some who were its highest-ranking officials. All paint the church in a negative light; some consider it abusive.

My own reporting on Scientology began in the summer of 2005, with an article for *Rolling Stone*. It was inspired, as were many of the pieces on the church assigned during that year, by Tom Cruise — or, more specifically, by the recent emergence of Tom Cruise as Scientology's most ardent proselytizer. This was a new role for the actor, who, until 2004, had been fiercely private about his faith, insisting that journalists stay off the topic entirely during interviews.

That was the news hook that first piqued my interest in Scientology. What sustained it was curiosity about a church that, for all of its notoriety, has remained America's least understood new faith, and seemingly an indelible one. The past fifty-odd years have seen the birth of dozens of religions; many have come and gone without a trace. The Church of Scientology has endured decades of scandal, litigation, government inquiry, exodus, street protest, and blistering media exposés in high-visibility venues such as the *Saturday Evening Post, Time,** and CNN. But unlike many alternative religions,

---

* The issue of *Time* published on May 6, 1991, bore the cover story "Scientology: The Thriving Cult of Greed and Power," which accused the church of "Mafia-like tactics"; it remains one of the most scathing exposés of the church ever written. In response, Scientology sued *Time* and the reporter Richard Behar for libel,

it has not died, or gone underground, or fled overseas. It has perse-vered.

And yet, for virtually all of its history, Scientology has maintained an aura of mystery. This holds true even today, when the church is in some ways more accessible than ever. Since 2009, the Church of Sci-entology has significantly upgraded its online presence, creating, for example, a flashy new website to explain its beliefs and its connec-tion to other religions and philosophies; it even offers a virtual tour of a Scientology organization. A separate Scientology video channel presents scores of testimonials to Scientology's effectiveness in han-dling life's problems, as well as slick advertisements featuring hip-looking young people promoting such themes as "life" and "purpose." In a recent online ad, "An Invitation to Freedom," a multiracial as-sortment of college-age men and women, standing atop skyscrap-ers, along beaches, and on oceanside cliffs, reach toward the sunrise. "You," proclaims one pretty girl, "are a spirit." "You are your own soul," the narration continues. "You are not mortal. You can be free."

It's not a bad pitch, immortality. And yet the ads stop short of pre-cise explanation. This is a central problem and in some ways the cen-tral genius of Scientology's presentation of its message. It is a church that deals in generalities: freedom, truth, immortality. Problems crop up when interested parties try to pin down the specifics. Scientology has always been hostile to serious journalistic inquiry and indepen-dent peer or academic review, and indeed has been so covetous of its doctrine that it has gone to court to keep its most exclusive teachings out of the public domain. The writer James R. Lewis, a philosophy professor and an expert in New Age and other new religious groups, has called Scientology "the most persistently controversial of all con-temporary new religious movements." Even today, with much of Sci-entology's doctrine freely available on the Internet, many academ-ics, well aware of Scientology's reputation for defensiveness, have avoided the subject entirely; the same has often held true for many news organizations. This situation has allowed Scientology, for good or for ill, to remain relatively inscrutable. It has also made under-

---

and lost, though the suit cost the publisher, Time Warner, millions of dollars.

standing Scientology, in any meaningful and balanced way, almost impossible.

This book, the culmination of a five-year journey, sets out to provide that understanding. It has been my goal to write the first objective modern history of the Church of Scientology. Much of the current Scientology canon — a relatively slender list — consists of memoirs and histories penned by former Scientologists, and they present some credibility problems. These accounts, while compelling, contain information that is hard to verify, and they are palpably hostile toward the organization. To make things even more complicated, a number of former church insiders who've given sworn testimony against Scientology have later changed their stories after allegedly receiving payoffs or other incentives. The church itself, while more open to speaking with reporters in recent years, has always balked at truly meaningful dialogue. In one stunning example of this, the Scientology spokesman Tommy Davis in 2009 walked off the set during an interview on ABC's *Nightline* after the reporter Martin Bashir dared to ask him about a controversial aspect of church doctrine.

How then to write about the church? Perhaps the most credible source is L. Ron Hubbard himself, whose voluminous "tech" in many ways tells the unvarnished story of both his ideology and his organization. But to glean the truth of Hubbard's church, in all its permutations, requires that one learn its language — the lingua franca of Hubbard's world.

It is the goal of *Inside Scientology* to translate this language and separate myth from fact. My reporting is based on the reading of thousands of pages of Scientology doctrine, including many confidential papers and memos that have never before been made available, and on personal interviews and e-mail exchanges with roughly one hundred former and current Scientologists, ranging from well-known critics of Scientology to church loyalists who, before being interviewed for this book, had never spoken to a reporter. It also draws on my conversations with a number of academics on both sides of the ideological spectrum, and, crucially, my talks with Scientology officials. Early in my reporting, in an unexpected moment of openness, the church granted me unprecedented access to its officials, schools, social programs, and key religious headquarters. This yielded a rare, and at times wholly uncensored, view into one of the most exclusive, and elusive, communities in the world.

Scientology is a faith that is both mainstream and marginal. Known for its Hollywood members, it is run by a uniformed set of believers who rarely, if ever, appear in the public eye. It is an insular society — one that exists, to a large degree, as something of a parallel universe to the secular world, with its own nomenclature, ethical code, and, most daunting to those who break its rules, its own rigorously enforced justice system. As an American subculture, it has been described to me, many times, as a subculture within a subculture within a subculture, whose outer layers appear harmless and even appealing, but which hides an inner stratum that reeks of authoritarian control.

For the past five years, I have sought to understand Scientology: not to judge, but simply to absorb. What I have found defies expectations, and even definition.

PART I

CHAPTER 1

The Founder

Adventure is the vitamizing element in histories, both individual and social . . . Its adepts are rarely chaste, or merciful, or even law-abiding at all, and any moral peptonizing, or sugaring, takes out the interest, with the truth, of their lives. And so it is with all great characters.

—WILLIAM BOLITHO, *TWELVE AGAINST THE GODS*

WHATEVER ELSE MIGHT be said about Lafayette Ron Hubbard, he undoubtedly had a strange and unique genius. One of the most effective hucksters of his generation, he understood the common American yearning for self-transformation and exploited it by connecting this impulse to two of the great American passions of the twentieth century: science and religion. He would remove all that was fuzzy and imprecise about religion. He would discard all that was cold and inhuman about science. And he'd sell the results like soap. Some people think he was the greatest con man of his time. Others believe he was a savior.

As a young man, Hubbard was a prolific writer of science fiction and fantasy, as well as an amateur explorer, magician, and hypnotist. At the age of forty, he came up with an alternative to psychotherapy that he called Dianetics, wrote a best-selling book about it, and became famous. Within a year he lost everything. In 1952, he started over, reimagining Dianetics as a spiritual science he called Scientology. Over the course of the next thirty-five years, he would be a salesman, guru, sea commodore, spymaster, poet, recluse, tyrant, and, last but not least, a very rich man.

When Hubbard died in 1985, the world took note, but he remained a mystery. Hubbard's official biography, which has been rigorously promoted by the Church of Scientology, presents him as a modern-day Ulysses: a restless explorer and spiritual seeker whose youthful adventures led him to the far corners of the Orient, where he visited Buddhist lamaseries, befriended Manchurian warlords, and even lived for a time with bandits in the hills of Tibet. Significantly less glowing assessments of Hubbard can be found in a number of court transcripts, affidavits, and even some of Hubbard's own early writings, which present the founder of Scientology as a fabulist whose claims contained certain embellishments, together with, in many cases, outright fabrications.

Hubbard was born in Tilden, Nebraska, on March 13, 1911. His father, Harry Ross "Hub" Hubbard, served in the navy; when he was promoted to lieutenant in 1921, the Hubbards embarked on a life of perpetual motion, relocating almost yearly to posts in Guam, San Diego, Seattle and Bremerton in the state of Washington, and Washington, D.C. For Ron, an only child, it was an exciting but alienating way to spend his childhood, and loneliness would remain an issue throughout his life. "When I was very young, I was pathetically eager for a home," Hubbard wrote in the early 1940s.

The itinerant nature of Hubbard's childhood stimulated a lifelong love for adventure and also fueled what by any estimation was a particularly rich and detailed inner life. He grew up thrilling to the stories told by the men in his father's naval circles, and had particularly romantic notions of the sea, "a lovely, vicious lonely thing," as he conceived of it. A restless boy with an isolationist streak, he harbored dreams of commanding his own ship — though he had no intention of winding up like his father, a naval supply officer who spent most of his career behind a desk. Harry Hubbard, as the journalist Russell Miller noted in his critical yet comprehensive biography of Hubbard, *Barefaced Messiah,* was "a deeply conservative plodder, a man ruled by routine and conformity." Ron Hubbard, by contrast, was a dreamer who saw himself as the hero of his own adventure story. Though his real-life exploits were limited — routine Boy Scout hikes*

---

* Hubbard, an avid Boy Scout, became an Eagle Scout at the age of twelve, making him the youngest Eagle Scout in the country at the time, according to the Church of Scientology.

and swimming expeditions were interspersed with a few exotic trips with one or both of his parents through the Panama Canal and eventually parts of Asia and the South Pacific — Hubbard viewed himself as a young Jack London; he penned swashbuckling accounts of his (greatly embellished) heroics in his journal, and later projected his fantasies onto fictional (and often, like him, redheaded) heroes: sailors, spies, pilots, soldiers of fortune. He had a sponge-like ability to absorb facts and details about the places he'd visited, no matter how briefly, and he wrote breezily, "as if he was a well-traveled man of the world," Miller noted, and "a carefree, two-fisted, knockabout adventurer," not the gawky, freckled teenager he actually was.

In 1929, Hubbard entered Swavely, a preparatory school in Manassas, Virginia, in anticipation of what his parents hoped would be his next step: the U.S. Naval Academy. But appointment to Annapolis was not to be — terrible at math, Hubbard failed that portion of his entrance exam and was also discovered to be nearsighted, instantly disqualifying him from becoming a cadet. Faced with life as a civilian, Hubbard enrolled at George Washington University in the fall of 1930 with a major in civil engineering. But while exceedingly bright, Hubbard was a diffident student and had no more interest in engineering than he'd had in mathematics.

Hubbard's destiny, he felt certain, lay in more exciting realms. Fascinated by the concept of "motorless flight," he'd earned a commercial glider pilot's license in 1931 and also learned how to fly a small stunt plane. That summer, he and a friend took off to "barnstorm" around the Midwest. It was a rather hapless adventure; the stunt plane, "which had a faculty for ground-looping at sixty miles an hour," Hubbard later said, by turns sank into mud, went off course, and nearly plowed into a fence. But it was a genuine adventure nonetheless. Hubbard returned to college that fall with a new self-coined nickname: L. Ron "Flash" Hubbard, "daredevil speed pilot and parachute artist."

The following summer, Hubbard chartered an aged four-mast schooner, intending to lead an expedition around the Caribbean in search of pirate treasure. He promoted the trip as a research and motion-picture voyage — he dubbed it the Caribbean Motion Picture Expedition. Placing an ad in local college newspapers for "adventurous young men with wanderlust," he managed to recruit some fifty other students to go with him, at the cost of $250 per person. The trip was a bust: not only did the expedition fail to explore or film a single pirate haunt, but, plagued first by bad weather and then by financial difficulties, the men made it only as far as Martinique before the captain, who would later call the voyage "the worst trip I ever made," decided to turn back. Hubbard, however, maintained that the trip had been a great success, even telling his college newspaper that the *New York Times* had agreed to buy some of the group's photographs.*

The ability to spin a setback as a triumph was a quality that would define Hubbard throughout his life. He was an immensely charming young man whose stories, while sometimes dubious, were often, by virtue of his own salesmanship, utterly convincing. Garrulous, with self-deprecating humor and a ready wit, he attracted people like a magnet and made them believe in his dreams. What's more, he seemed to believe in them himself. A naval commander named Joseph Cheesman "Snake" Thompson had imparted to the youthful Hubbard a crucial bit of wisdom: "If it's not true for you, it's not true." Hubbard took that as a motto. "If there is anyone in the world calculated to believe what he wants to believe," he later said, "it is I."

By 1938, L. Ron Hubbard was twenty-seven years old, a tall, strapping young man with a head of thick, fiery red hair and one of those unforgettable faces: pale, long-nosed, a bit fleshy around the lips, and frequently flushed — all of which, as one acquaintance noted, gave him "the look of a reincarnated Pan who'd been a bit too long on the ambrosia." But he also had tremendous self-confidence, which had served him well through the hardest years of the Great Depression. "I seem to have a sort of personal awareness which only begins to come alive when I begin to believe in a destiny," he wrote to his wife, Polly, a flying enthusiast he'd met on a Maryland airfield in 1932 and married the following year.

Hubbard had dropped out of college in 1932, having spent two

---

* Staff at the *New York Times* would later tell the biographer Russell Miller that they had no record of ever buying any photographs from Hubbard or making any agreement to do so.

unimpressive years there. With neither a job nor a college degree, he tried his hand at freelance journalism but soon gave it up for mass-market fiction, action-packed stories that constituted one of the most popular forms of entertainment in the 1930s — a precursor, in many ways, to TV. Published in cheap, dime-store magazines known as "pulps," the narratives generally featured hearty, adventurous men who'd fly spy missions over occupied Germany, engage in battle on the high seas, or romance weak-kneed women held captive in enemy forts — a perfect format, in other words, for Hubbard to express his own lusty sensibilities.

Within a year of embarking on this career, he'd found success, largely due to his journeyman's approach. Tremendously prolific, he wrote westerns, detective stories, adventure tales, and mysteries, churning out thousands of words every day and sending his stories, one after another, to New York City publishers. This entrepreneurial spirit seemed at odds with Hubbard's more fanciful, decidedly impractical side. But Hubbard was an interesting paradox: a man who not only dreamed improbably large, but also recognized the bottom line. "My writing is not a game," he wrote in an essay entitled "The Manuscript Factory" in 1936. "It is a business, a hardheaded enterprise which fails only when I fail."

There were roughly three hundred pulp fiction writers in New York during the 1930s, and most, if not all of them, knew of L. Ron Hubbard. He'd emerged on the scene in 1934 and joined the American Fiction Guild, which counted numerous pulp fiction writers as members. Every week, a number of guild members would meet for lunch at a midtown cafeteria, where Hubbard, a night owl who wrote in frenzied bursts and thought nothing of interrupting a colleague's sleep to discuss a story, or some other revelation, soon developed a reputation as a champion raconteur. In his memoir *The Pulp Jungle*, Frank Gruber, a writer of western and detective stories, recalled one New York get-together during which Hubbard, then twenty-three, regaled a group of writers with tales of his adventure-filled life. Fascinated, Gruber took notes. "He had been in the United States Marines for seven years, he had been an explorer on the upper Amazon for four years, he'd been a white hunter in Africa for three years . . .

After listening for a couple of hours, I said, 'Ron, you're eighty-four years old, aren't you?'"

It was a joke, but Hubbard, as Gruber recalled, "blew his stack." Most pulp fiction writers told tall tales — virtually everyone in the New York pulp world had a story, usually wholly made-up — but Hubbard regarded his own as gospel truth. His tall tales were part of his image, a self-created mythology that made him just as much a product of his imagination as his stories were. This seemed to suit his editors just fine. Beleaguered by the Depression, Americans were looking for heroes, and the editors of magazines like *Thrilling Wonder Stories* or *Adventure* were all too happy to publish the work of "one of aviation's most distinguished hell raisers," as Hubbard was described in one magazine; it went on to state that Hubbard, at various times in his life, had been a "Top Sergeant in the Marines, radio crooner, newspaper reporter, gold miner in the West Indies, and movie director–explorer."

But Hubbard's efforts did not transfer into monetary success: the average pulp fiction writer earned just a penny per word, and even the most prolific among them often found it hard to make a living. Hoping to break into the far more lucrative business of screenwriting, Hubbard moved to Hollywood in 1935 but produced just one script, an adaptation of his story "The Secret of Treasure Island," which was purchased as a Saturday morning serial by Columbia Pictures. In 1936, Hubbard moved with Polly and their two young children, L. Ron Hubbard Jr., known as "Nibs," and Katherine, to South Colby, Washington, near Hubbard's parents. There, Hubbard set out to work on a novel.

He also studied the world of popular advertising and at one point in the 1930s wrote a long letter to the head of Kellogg's Foods, proposing his ideas for new, more artistic packaging for breakfast cereal. He suggested that the lyrics to popular ballads, accompanied by watercolor pictures, be printed on cereal boxes; even short illustrated stories might be published on them. These innovations could, he believed, have a profound effect, making a functional box not only decorative but also a symbol of positive cultural values. "Corn flakes could, in no better way, become synonymous for bravery and gallantry," Hubbard wrote. Kellogg's didn't respond — though in later years some of these ideas would, in fact, find their way onto cereal boxes.

Hubbard remained undeterred. "I have high hopes of smashing my name into history so violently that it will take a legendary form," he told Polly. "That goal is the real goal as far as I am concerned."

By 1939, L. Ron Hubbard had tired of writing western and adventure stories, and his screenwriting efforts had failed. He was looking for a new challenge and found it in an unexpected genre: science fiction. Until the late 1930s, science fiction had been one of the more obscure areas of the pulp market, dominated by hackneyed stories of alien invaders and bug-eyed monsters. This changed, however, with the ascension of John W. Campbell to editor of *Astounding Science Fiction* magazine, the most popular science fiction magazine of the day. A fast-talking, chain-smoking, twenty-eight-year-old graduate of Duke University, Campbell saw science fiction as a metaphor, and under his exacting eye, the genre was radically transformed. Gone were the stock characters and formulaic plots. Campbell wanted fictional stories whose characters seemed human and whose plots reflected actual scientific discovery. He required that his writers gain a detailed knowledge of science and didn't hesitate to correct them if they were wrong.

Out of Campbell's vision came science fiction's golden age, during which some of the great technological advances of the future were first anticipated. Robert Heinlein, for example, wrote of waterbeds, moving sidewalks, moon landings, and the coming space race. Arthur C. Clarke predicted the birth of telecommunications satellites. Jack Williamson invented the term *genetic engineering* and, in the early 1940s, also explored the concept of anti-matter, a realm of physics that would not be fully realized until the advent of the particle accelerator in 1954. The moon landing, space shuttles, high-powered weapons, satellites, robotics, automated surveillance systems — all were predicted by science fiction writers informed by the scientific theories and developments of the day. *Astounding* brought these two worlds together. "We were all exploring possible human futures — most of them still seeming splendid in those years before the [atomic] bomb," said Jack Williamson, who began writing for *As-*

tounding in 1939. Though they still made only a penny a word, writing for Campbell meant membership in a "gifted crew as important as the money," said Williamson. "The best stories in the competing magazines were often his rejects."

L. Ron Hubbard did not fit Campbell's idea of a science fiction writer. He had a rudimentary understanding of science and engineering, but he lacked the rigorous scientific grounding possessed by writers such as Heinlein or Isaac Asimov, a Columbia University-educated biochemist. But Hubbard did have tremendous intellectual curiosity and research skills — "Given one slim fact for a background, I have found it easy to take off down the channel of research and canal-boat out a cargo of stories," he once wrote — and he was fascinated by such themes as psychic phenomena and psychological control, which Campbell also found intriguing.

After assigning Hubbard a story for *Astounding*'s sister publication, *Unknown*, Campbell soon began to nurture Hubbard's talent as a fantasy writer. The heroes of his stories tended to reflect one of two distinct archetypes. One was the shy, wimpy, bookish sort who, through magic of his own or some other supernatural power, is transported to an alternate, somewhat parallel, universe, where he is transformed into a roguish adventurer. The other was the solitary loner type, hugely self-driven, often with autocratic leanings. "Some thought him a Fascist because of the authoritarian tone of certain stories," recalled the science fiction writer L. Sprague De Camp, who also remembered that Hubbard was careful not to admit to having any political ideology. "He gave wildly different impressions of himself . . . One science fiction writer, then an idealistic left-liberal, was convinced that Hubbard had profound liberal convictions. To others, Hubbard expressed withering disdain for politics and politicians." When asked whether he would fight in World War II, Hubbard balked. "Me? Fight for a political system?"

In fact, Hubbard wanted desperately to join the military. During the late 1930s, he'd tried to interest various branches of the service in his "research," and in 1939, he made a formal application to the War Department to "offer my services in whatever capacity they might be of the greatest use." Nothing came of these attempts. In March 1941, with America's entrance into the war almost certain, Hubbard applied once more to join the navy, providing letters of recommendation from a long list of contacts he'd cultivated. Four months later, on July 19, 1941, L. Ron Hubbard was commissioned as a lieutenant (junior grade) in the U.S. Naval Reserve.

For years, the Church of Scientology has maintained that Hubbard, who would later give himself the self-styled rank of Commodore, was a "master mariner" and a fearless war hero.* This was an image Hubbard carefully nurtured, boasting to fellow sailors of his lengthy experience on destroyers.

But Hubbard's naval records show that he had an inglorious wartime career. Boastful and often argumentative, with a propensity for having his "feelings hurt," as one superior noted, he was a behavior problem from day one. Though he did get the opportunity to take the helm of a submarine chaser in April 1943, he was relieved of that duty within a month after he (unwittingly, he claimed) steered his ship into Mexican waters and took target practice by firing on the Los Coronados Islands.

Depressed and suffering from ulcers, Hubbard spent the rest of the war drifting from post to post, taking part in various training programs, serving as the navigator of a cargo ship, and studying for several months at the School of Military Government at Princeton. For the first time in his life, he seemed utterly lost. "The Great Era of Adventure is over," he wrote in his journal, sounding decades older than his thirty-three years. "I feel a little like a child who tries to see romance in an attic and holds tenaciously as long as he can to his conception, though he well recognizes the substance . . . as a disinteresting tangle of old cloth and dust.

"Money, a nice car, good food and a 'good job' mean nothing to me when compared to being able to possess the thought that there is a

---

* The Church of Scientology has long held that L. Ron Hubbard had two war records, one possibly used as a front. In the official record released by the U.S. Department of the Navy, Hubbard's achievements are meager. But church officials have explained this by stating that most of what is in the record is falsified to cover up Hubbard's more sensitive and covert activities as a member of naval Intelligence.

surprise over the horizon," he added. "[But] I have come to that state of mind, that supreme disillusion of knowing that nothing waits, that the horizon never seen does not exist. I am restless still."

The city of Los Angeles lives in the American imagination as a realm of fresh beginnings and limitless possibility. That this is something of a hollow promise has never mattered all that much; southern California, as the writer Carey McWilliams reflected, was built on artifice, "conjured into existence" by its founders in the late nineteenth century and enduring ever since as a city of hope, though, as is often the case, that hope may be utterly false.

It was here that L. Ron Hubbard found himself at the end of World War II. On leave, and with no apparent desire to see Polly and the children, Hubbard followed the path of numerous science fiction writers, including Robert Heinlein, who'd moved to southern California, as had myriad other authors, scientists, and intellectuals since the start of the war. Low on cash and looking for a cheap place to stay, Hubbard found it within a sprawling Craftsman-style house at 1003 South Orange Grove Avenue, in Pasadena, the home of the enigmatic, brilliant rocket scientist John Whiteside Parsons.

The scion of a wealthy Pasadena family, Jack Parsons was a self-taught chemist and explosives expert and a leader of the fledgling rocket program at the California Institute of Technology. The intellectual hub of the California aerospace industry, Caltech was also the birthplace of American rocket science, a discipline that seemed to merge the worlds of science and fantasy and might pave the way for the "promising new futures" foretold in magazines like *Astounding Science Fiction*. It would also give birth to an entire sector of the California economy, for nowhere else in America did the dreams of amateurs dovetail so neatly with the needs of both the U.S. government and private industry.

A stellar assortment of Nobel laureates and other geniuses had wandered the elegant grounds of Caltech's Pasadena campus over the years, among them Albert Einstein, Edwin Hubble, J. Robert Oppenheimer, and Linus Pauling. Parsons was a protégé of the great aeronautics expert Theodore von Kármán, with whom he'd conducted secret experiments during the war. Though still in his early thirties, Parsons helped invent a new form of solid jet fuel that, in years to come, helped NASA start the U.S. space program. There is a crater on the moon named after Parsons.

Unbeknownst to most of his colleagues, Parsons was also an occultist; a devotee of the British writer and black magician Aleister Crowley, or the "Great Beast," as he liked to be known. Crowley was the founder of a school of esoteric thought he called Thelema. His most famous work, a lengthy prose poem entitled *The Book of the Law,* laid out its central, hedonistic doctrine: "Do what thou wilt shall be the whole of the law."

To disseminate Thelema, Crowley took over an already-existing mystical society called the Ordo Templi Orientis, or OTO, whose Los Angeles branch was known as the Agape Lodge. Parsons, who'd been inducted into the lodge in 1940, soon became OTO's Los Angeles leader.

Parsons brought an air of glamour to the underground world of Thelema. Witty and sophisticated, he was a lover of music and poetry, a sexual libertine, and a ladies' man whose dark wavy hair and good looks lent him an air of danger. At his twenty-five-acre Pasadena estate, which became the Agape Lodge's home, Parsons hosted regular parties where he would discuss literature and mysticism while members of the lodge wandered the garden paths, consorting with a variety of free spirits: chemists, poets, artists, engineers, nuclear physicists, Caltech grad students. A large structure known as the Tea House became the site of secret rendezvous. Partner swapping and general sexual debauchery were the rule, as were all-night bacchanals in which Parsons, dressed in a three-piece suit, would engage his friends in fencing duels or recite Crowley's poem "Hymn to Pan."

By 1944, Parsons had turned his eleven-bedroom home into a boarding house for the eccentrics of Los Angeles, placing an ad urging "artists, musicians, atheists, anarchists, or other exotic types" to apply for a room. Among those who won a spot were a professional fortuneteller, a onetime organist for Hollywood's great silent-movie palaces, and an aging courtesan. Other less flamboyant boarders at the Parsonage, as the house was known, included Nieson Himmel, then a twenty-three-year-old journalist who would later become one of the most prominent crime reporters at the *Los Angeles Times*, and the physicist Robert Cornog, chief engineer of the Manhattan Project's ordnance division and a creator of the atom bomb.

One August day in 1945, Lieutenant Commander L. Ron Hubbard, on leave from the navy, came to lunch at the Parsonage as the guest of another boarder. Parsons had never met Hubbard, though as a dedicated science fiction fan he had read most of his stories in *Unknown* and *Astounding,* and was no doubt thrilled to have the writer at his table. After lunch, Parsons invited him to spend the rest of his leave at the Parsonage. Hubbard moved in that afternoon.

Now sporting a pair of horn-rimmed glasses, Hubbard cut a dashing figure at 1003 South Orange Grove Avenue. He'd arrived in full military regalia, his lieutenant's bars gleaming on the shoulders of his navy whites. Within a day or two, he was dominating the conversation around the communal dinner table, telling his housemates how he'd narrowly escaped from Japanese-occupied Java by making off on a raft after suffering bullet wounds and broken bones in his feet. He also claimed to have been involved in a variety of counterintelligence activities,* to have commanded ships in both the Atlantic and the Pacific theaters, to have battled a polar bear in the Aleutians, and, while in England, to have had his skull measured by scientists at the British Museum.

---

* In 1969, in response to an investigation by the London *Sunday Times* into Hubbard's relationship with Parsons, the Church of Scientology issued a statement explaining that Hubbard had been sent to 1003 South Orange Grove Avenue by U.S. Naval Intelligence, assigned to infiltrate and break up a so-called black magic cult. The church gave as evidence the fact that the Agape Lodge ultimately dissolved and that a number of high-ranking physicists associated with Parsons were ultimately put on a U.S. "enemies list" and stripped of security clearance. A few historical facts support this claim: by the 1940s, a widespread anti-cult campaign was sweeping the country, and numerous groups and individuals suspected of cult activity, including Parsons, had been investigated by the FBI. But, as many of Hubbard's critics have pointed out, no evidence substantiates the claim that he was assigned intelligence work, and though, because of his odd activities, Parsons's FBI file had grown quite thick, he retained top-secret security clearance until his death in 1952. Hubbard is not mentioned in connection to Parsons in any FBI papers.

"He was a fascinating storyteller," recalled Nieson Himmel, who was Hubbard's roommate at the Parsonage. "Everyone believed him." Himmel, however, recognized the polar bear story as an old folk legend and recalled the skull-measuring tale as part of a story by George Bernard Shaw. "He was so obviously a phony. But he was not a dummy," said Himmel. "He was very sharp and very quick . . . he could charm the shit out of anybody."

Perhaps the person Hubbard charmed most was Parsons, who saw a kindred spirit in the young naval officer, and Hubbard thought the same of him. As the author George Pendle pointed out in his fascinating biography of Parsons, *Strange Angel,* Parsons was in many ways the embodiment of the man Hubbard wanted to be. Sophisticated, well connected, with impeccable bona fides, Parsons was both an intellectual and a serious scientist, and had no need to lie or embellish his credentials. Though his family had lost much of its fortune in the Depression, Parsons had made a substantial amount as one of the founders of the Aerojet Engineering Corporation, an aerospace company that benefited substantially from government sponsorship during World War II. Prior to that, he'd gained entrance to the rarefied world of Caltech by impressing the Hungarian-born von Kármán with his innate intelligence and enthusiasm for scientific experimentation, which seemed to override his lack of formal training. (Parsons, like Hubbard, lacked a college degree.)

Soon, Hubbard and Parsons were fencing, without masks, in the living room of the Parsonage. Afterward, often with Robert Heinlein, a frequent guest, they'd engage in lively discussions about science and science fiction. Parsons ultimately began to reveal to Hubbard the secrets of Thelema. This of course involved breaking the sacred code — Hubbard was not even an initiate of the Agape Lodge. But he seemed intrinsically capable of understanding esoteric principles, and, to Parsons's surprise, he was already familiar with Crowley's writing. He also had an impressive grasp of the field of magic, no doubt acquired from the years he spent writing fantasy for John W. Campbell. "From some of his experiences, I deduce he is in direct touch with some higher intelligence, probably his Guardian Angel," Parsons wrote to Crowley. "He is the most Thelemic person I have ever met and is in complete accord with our own principles."

Hubbard also seemed enamored of Parsons, though self-interest motivated him as much as a sense of fellowship did. Soon after he arrived at the Parsonage, Hubbard succeeded in stealing away Parsons's mistress, Sara Northrup, a seductive and spirited twenty-one-year-old blonde known by house members as "Betty." Just about every man at 1003 South Orange Grove Avenue was in love with Betty, recalled Nieson Himmel, but only Hubbard had the audacity to act on it. Hubbard was still married to Polly, though he'd seen her only sporadically since the late 1930s and had left his family behind upon settling in Pasadena. "He was irresistible to women, swept girls off their feet," said Himmel. "There were other girls living there with guys and he went through them one by one." Finally he set his sights on Betty, and the two began a passionate affair. Parsons did nothing; challenging Hubbard and making a stand against free love would have defied his own Thelemic principles.

Nieson Himmel recalled that Hubbard, on at least one occasion at the Parsonage, talked about his desire to start his own religion. Certainly many others had done it. During the 1920s and 1930s in particular, Los Angeles teemed with new or offbeat religions, from the Theosophists to the Mighty "I Am" to the Church of Divine Science and the yoga-inspired Vedanta Society. There were also many prophets in residence, notably the evangelist Aimee Semple McPherson, whose International Church of the Foursquare Gospel was one of the country's first mega churches — at its peak, McPherson's Angelus Temple in Echo Park attracted crowds of well over five thousand people, and it had its own Bible school, radio station, and publishing house, as well as numerous bands and choirs. It was also a lucrative business. H. L. Mencken once called McPherson "the most profitable ecclesiastic in America."

As Hubbard kept scant records during this time, we will never know his precise ideas on the matter, nor what he might have learned or assimilated from Aleister Crowley's Thelema. But Hubbard would later refer to Crowley as a "good friend," even though the two never met. Seizing upon this statement, numerous critics of Scientology have tried to establish a definite link between Crowley and Hubbard; religious scholars, however, differentiate Thelema from Scientology, pointing out that unlike Thelema, Scientology does not believe in "sex magick" or in many other occult practices. But certain tenets of Scientology echo Crowley's belief system, including the emphasis on finding "who, what, and why" one is and the assertion that "suppressives" of various sorts are hostile to one's success. Similarly, Scientology, like Thelema, is drawn from the Western esoteric tradition, which is also true of faiths like Theosophy or Rosicrucianism, in which secret knowledge and secret levels of enlightenment are core principles.

In September, Hubbard left the Parsonage and entered the Oak Knoll Naval Hospital in Oakland, California, to be treated for a recurrence of a duodenal ulcer. There, Hubbard would later claim, he healed himself of not just ulcers, but of war wounds that had left him "crippled and blinded."* He also, according to his later statements, did groundbreaking research into the workings of the human mind.

No evidence of this research has ever been found in Hubbard's hospital file. Instead, his chronic ulcers gave the navy cause to discharge him. This was not welcome news, as the navy had provided Hubbard with a steady income, the first he'd ever had. He sent an anxious telegram to his superiors, trying to downplay the seriousness of his ulcer — "Have served at sea with present symptoms much worse . . . without prejudice to duty and did not leave that duty because of present diagnosis," he said, imploring to be kept on — but it was to no avail. Two months later, on December 5, 1945, Hubbard was discharged from Oak Knoll and officially "detached" from the navy. Then, hitching a trailer to the back of his Packard, still dressed in his navy uniform, Hubbard drove south to Pasadena, where the next stage of his transformation awaited him.

During the months that Hubbard was gone, Parsons immersed himself in the practice of magic. He was set on conjuring up a woman — he would refer to her as his "elemental" — to be his new mate. Parsons was pleased when his friend returned to the Parsonage and asked him to be his assistant during a prolonged ritual that Parsons called his "magical working." Hubbard agreed, and after several weeks of their combined efforts, Parsons claimed to have summoned his el-

---

* No evidence has been found in Hubbard's medical records to suggest he was ever crippled or blinded in World War II, or at any other time.

emental, who appeared at his door a week later in the form of a very attractive young redhead named Marjorie Cameron (an artist, Cameron moved into the Parsonage almost immediately; soon after, the couple married).

As for Hubbard, when he wasn't serving as the sorcerer's apprentice, he was holed up in his bedroom, contending with what appeared to be a massive bout of writer's block. Having purchased a new Dictaphone, which he hoped would help speed his productivity, he'd written reassuringly to his agent that he was about to experience "a flood of copy" over the next few weeks. "You will have to hire squads of messengers just to get it around and an armored car just to pick up checks," Hubbard said. But he spent day after day staring at the wall.

It was during this period that Hubbard convinced Parsons that they should go into business together, with Betty as a silent third. The idea was to pool their resources in a venture called Allied Enterprises and then profit jointly off the "capabilities and crafts of each of the partners," on projects yet to be determined. Parsons put up most of the capital, investing nearly his entire savings of $21,000. Hubbard put in all of his money too — about $1,200 — but his primary job was to come up with ideas.

As their first venture, Hubbard suggested that Allied Enterprises go into the yachting business. He and Betty would withdraw $10,000 from the partnership's account and go to Miami, where they'd use the money to secure the boats. Then, he told Parsons, they would sail them back to California to be sold at a profit. Excited by the adventure of the business and confident that Hubbard's proficiency as a sailor and sea captain would stand them in good stead, Parsons readily agreed to the plan. Hubbard had meanwhile written to the chief of naval personnel,* requesting permission to leave the country in order to sail around the world collecting "writing material" under the patronage of Allied Enterprises. But Parsons had no knowledge of that proposal, and so it was that in April 1946, L. Ron Hubbard left Pasadena for Miami, spiriting away both Jack Parsons's onetime mistress and his money.

Parsons finally began to worry when a month went by without

---

*Though Hubbard had been discharged from active duty in the navy, he remained a commissioned officer until October 30, 1950.

hearing from his business partners. Chastened after several members of his household, and Aleister Crowley, warned him that he had been the victim of a confidence trick, Parsons flew to Miami in June, where he found that his fears were justified. Hubbard and Sara — she was called Betty only at 1003 South Orange Grove — had taken out a $12,000 mortgage and purchased the boats: two schooners, the *Harpoon* and the *Blue Water II*, and a yacht named the *Diane*. Now, having hired a crew with Parsons's money, they were preparing to sail away on the *Harpoon*. Quickly, Parsons secured an injunction to prevent them from leaving the country, and a week later, Allied Enterprises was formally dissolved. In exchange for Parsons's agreement not to press charges, Hubbard and Sara agreed to pay half of Parsons's legal fees and relinquish their right to the *Diane* and the *Blue Water II*. They were allowed to keep the *Harpoon*, which they ultimately sold, but they paid Parsons $2,900 to cover his interest in the ship. Parsons returned to Pasadena "near mental and financial collapse," as he said, and soon afterward sold 1003 South Orange Grove.* The era of the Parsonage was over.

But the era of L. Ron Hubbard had just begun. L. Sprague De Camp, Hubbard's colleague in science fiction, had attended Caltech and knew Jack Parsons. De Camp was aware of Hubbard's friendship with the scientist and also knew of his most recent escapade in Miami. De Camp, skeptical from the beginning, saw in Hubbard's activities a familiar pattern. Sometime soon, De Camp predicted in a letter to Isaac Asimov, Hubbard would arrive in Los Angeles "broke, working the poor-wounded-veteran racket for all it's worth, and looking for another easy mark. Don't say you haven't been warned. Bob [Robert Heinlein] thinks Ron went to pieces morally as a result of the war. I think that's fertilizer, that he always was that way, but when he wanted to conciliate or get something from somebody he could put on a good charm act. What the war did was to wear him down to where he no longer bothers with the act."

On August 10, 1946, L. Ron Hubbard, then thirty-five, and Sara

---

* With the halcyon days of the Parsonage at an end, Parsons and Marjorie Cameron moved into a smaller house in Pasadena. In 1952, at the age of thirty-six, Parsons was killed in a mysterious chemical explosion in his garage. It was, as many have noted, a fitting way for a black magician to die.

"Betty" Northrup, twenty-two, were married (bigamously, as Hubbard had never bothered to get a divorce from Polly).* They settled into a small cottage in Laguna Beach, where Hubbard, nearly penniless, tried to resume his writing career. True to De Camp's predictions, Hubbard started filing claims with the Veterans Administration, hoping to increase his disability pension. He complained of numerous ailments, including psychological problems, and in one letter appealed to the VA to help him pay for psychiatric counseling. In that letter, dated October 15, 1947, Hubbard complained of "long periods of moroseness" and "suicidal inclinations" — symptoms that, in more recent years, might suggest a form of posttraumatic stress disorder. But he'd "avoided out of pride" seeking help, or even confiding in a physician, in the hopes that "time would balance a mind which I had every reason to suppose was seriously affected [by the war]." But now, having tried and failed to regain his equilibrium, "I am utterly unable to approach anything like my own competence," he wrote. "My last physician informed me that it might be very helpful if I were to be examined and perhaps treated psychiatrically or even by a psychoanalyst . . . I cannot, myself, afford such treatment."

The Veterans Administration responded by urging Hubbard to report for a physical and ultimately did increase his pension. But Hubbard, by all accounts, never followed through with psychiatric counseling. Instead, he chose a more independent path, quietly writing a series of personal "affirmations" in his journal. It was an experiment, as he said, to "re-establish the ambition, willpower, desire to survive, the talent and confidence of myself." It would also be the most revealing psychological self-assessment, complete with exhortations to himself, that he had ever made.

In the affirmations, Hubbard confessed to deep anxiety about his writing as well as his struggles with impotence, which he blamed on steroid treatments he had received to treat his ulcers. He also acknowledged his compulsion toward lying and exaggeration. Despite frequent exhortations to the contrary, his war record, he admitted,

---

* Polly filed for divorce in 1947, still unaware that Hubbard had remarried. Later that year, he scandalized his parents by bringing Sara to Washington, where they settled, briefly, into the house he and Polly, and their two children, had once shared. The divorce was finalized in 1948.

was "none too glorious," but he added that he must be convinced that he suffered no reaction from any disciplinary action. His service was honorable, he affirmed.

Hubbard's months under Jack Parsons's tutelage had led Hubbard to believe himself to be a "magus" or "adept," an enlightened, ethereal being who communicated through a human body. Since adepts exist on a higher spiritual plane than the rest of humanity, the standard rules of behavior, he reasoned, shouldn't apply to them. He could have anything he desired, Hubbard told himself. "Men are your slaves. Elemental spirits are your slaves. You are power among powers, light in the darkness, beauty in all."

The affirmations went on for pages, as Hubbard repeatedly avowed his magical power, sexual attractiveness, good health, strong memory, and literary talent. He would make fortunes in writing, he affirmed. "You understand all the workings of the minds of humans around you, for you are a doctor of minds, bodies and influences."

He would use his mind, in other words, to repair his soul. And soon, he would show others how to use their own minds to do exactly the same thing. "You have magnificent power," he wrote. "You need no excuses, no crutches. You need no apologies about what you have done or been . . . You start your life anew."

CHAPTER 2

Dianetics

E ARLY IN THE WINTER of 1949, L. Ron Hubbard wrote to his literary agent, Forrest Ackerman, to tell him that he was preparing a manuscript of brilliance. The book would be so powerful, Hubbard joked, that a reader would be able to "rape women without their knowing it, communicate suicide messages to [their] enemies as they sleep . . . evolve the best way of protecting or destroying communism, and other handy household hints." He wasn't sure what to title his book — perhaps something along the lines of *Science of the Mind*. "This has more selling and publicity angles than any book of which I have ever heard," he said.

Soon after, Hubbard sent a letter to the American Psychological Association, hoping to interest its leaders in his discoveries. Having studied the theories of Sigmund Freud, he wrote, he had come up with a "technology" that could erase painful experiences from one's past that were buried in the subconscious, and also help a person relive his or her own birth. Hubbard, like the Freudian disciple Otto Rank, believed that the "birth trauma" lay at the root of many contemporary neuroses and psychosomatic ills. Unlike anyone else, however, he claimed to have engineered a cure for these ills, which he had used successfully on more than two hundred people. Hubbard offered the APA a paper on his findings. The society turned him down.

The science fiction editor John Campbell was not nearly as dismissive. Urging Hubbard to visit him, he found Ron and Sara a cottage in the genteel New Jersey beach town of Bay Head, about an hour's drive from Campbell's own home in suburban Plainfield. A few weeks later, Hubbard arrived and offered his editor a demonstration of his techniques.

Over the past several years, Hubbard had become a skilled hypnotist, though he never explained where he learned the technique. In Los Angeles, he had demonstrated his skills to science fiction colleagues, often wearing a turban while putting people under. His new technology had many of the classic elements of hypnosis: Campbell lay on his couch, closed his eyes, and counted to seven. Then, with Hubbard guiding him, he tried to recall his earliest childhood experiences in as much detail as possible: What were the sights, sounds, smells, and other feelings associated with each event? Had something similar occurred at a previous time? Campbell found himself not just remembering but sensing that he was actually returning to long-ago times and places to again experience particular incidents; after a few sessions, he'd traveled far enough back on the "time track" of his life to reexperience his own birth. Afterward, to his great surprise he found that his sinus condition, a chronic annoyance, was much improved.

Convinced that Hubbard had made a truly groundbreaking discovery, Campbell eagerly began promoting Hubbard's work, alerting friends and colleagues in the science fiction world to an upcoming article on "the most important subject imaginable." "This is not a hoax article," Campbell wrote in his editor's letter in the December 1949 issue of *Astounding Science Fiction.* "It is an article on the science of the human mind, of human thought . . . Its power is almost unbelievable."

This was the first public mention of Dianetics, which Hubbard later explained was a combination of the Greek terms *dia* (through) and *nous* (the mind). Within a month, Walter Winchell, the powerful syndicated columnist of the New York *Daily Mirror,* had heard the rumors. "There is something new coming up in April called Dianetics," he wrote in his column on January 31, 1950. "From all indications it will prove to be as revolutionary for humanity as the first caveman's discovery and utilization of fire."

Hubbard had by now a small circle of disciples. The "Bayhead Circle," as they would be known, was led by Campbell and included Dr.

Joseph Winter, a Michigan physician and sometime contributor to *Astounding* who'd taken an interest in Dianetics after Campbell had told him that Hubbard had cured more than a thousand people with his techniques. "My response to this information was one of polite incredulity," said Winter. But he was sufficiently intrigued to visit Hubbard in New Jersey and also to submit himself to Dianetics therapy. Hubbard was then enlisting a number of his colleagues to give it a try, and, as Winter recalled, "the experience was intriguing." People went into a Dianetics session tense, depressed, and irritable; they'd come out cheerful and relaxed. Sometimes, while observing Hubbard use his techniques on another subject, Dr. Winter found himself experiencing sympathetic pain, exhaustion, or agitation. Winter also found that his memory greatly improved after Dianetics therapy. He was further impressed when his young son appeared cured of his crippling fear of the dark after a few sessions.

The Bayhead Circle also included Art Ceppos, the head of Hermitage House, a publisher of medical and psychiatric textbooks; Campbell had enlisted him to publish Hubbard's new book. The group spent the next several months refining Dianetics theory and coming up with much of its scientific-sounding terminology. By the end of December, Hubbard had extracted a sixteen-thousand-word manifesto from his larger manuscript. Entitled "Dianetics: The Evolution of a Science," it ran in the May 1950 issue of *Astounding Science Fiction*. It bore an introduction by Dr. Winter, who described Dianetics as "the greatest advance in mental therapy since man began to probe into his mental makeup."

On May 9, 1950, Hermitage House published Hubbard's book *Dianetics: The Modern Science of Mental Health*. Weighing in at a hefty 452 pages, it opened with a dramatic statement: "The creation of Dianetics is a milestone for Man comparable to his discovery of fire and superior to his inventions of the wheel and the arch."

Dianetics, which Scientologists often refer to today as simply *"Book One,"* portrays the mind not as the mysterious, complex labyrinth that many scientists made it out to be, but as a simple mechanism that works very much like a computer. Its main processor, called the *analytical mind,* is like Freud's conception of the conscious mind, in charge of daily events and decisions and the management of information: taking it in, sorting it, and filing it in the appropriate places. The mind also has a subprocessor, which Hubbard called the *reactive mind.* This tends to undermine the work of the analytical mind by promulgating system glitches, or "aberrations," which manifest as fear, inhibition, intense love and hate, and also various psychosomatic ills. Like the Freudian subconscious, the reactive mind is not capable of independent thought and in fact lies dormant until awakened by a jarring event: a moment of pain, unconsciousness, or trauma, the most significant of which is the moment of birth.

Painful or traumatic moments are recorded in the reactive mind as lasting scars, which Hubbard called "engrams."* These, Hubbard asserted, are the source of many present physical and psychological problems. To get rid of them he advocated a new therapeutic process called "auditing." In an auditing session, a patient was led through a series of commands intended to call up the minute details of an engramatic incident. The first questions might deal with a recent problem—an illness or injury, perhaps. But with each request for "the next incident needed to resolve this case," the patient, lying on a couch, eyes closed, would become aware of incidents farther and farther back in the past, all the way to what Hubbard called the "basic-basic," or prenatal incident. Once that had been identified, the subject would be asked to "run," or reexperience, the incident numerous times until its impact was neutralized.

This form of therapy was not new. In the late nineteenth century, Sigmund Freud and the psychoanalyst Josef Breuer had used similar techniques in their early treatment of hysteria, often hypnotizing patients to uncover buried memories and lead them to relive traumatic incidents, a process known as "abreaction" therapy. Freud ultimately abandoned it in favor of free association and, later, standard psychoanalysis. Carl Jung, another champion of abreaction, or what he called "trauma theory," also lost interest in the process, finding

---

* This is an actual scientific term defined by *Merriam-Webster's Medical Dictionary* as "a hypothetical change in neural tissue postulated in order to account for persistence of memory called also *memory trace*."

that most neuroses were not caused by trauma. "Many traumata were so unimportant, even so normal, that they could be regarded at most as a pretext for the neurosis," he'd later write. "But what especially aroused my criticism was the fact that not a few traumata were simply inventions of fantasy and had never happened at all."

Hubbard, however — who in early editions of *Dianetics* made sure to acknowledge his influences,* including Freud and Breuer, as well as Count Alfred Korzybski, the creator of general semantics — maintained that his therapy "cures and cures without failure." Hundreds of people, Hubbard said, had already been cured using Dianetics techniques.

For audiences of 1950, this claim was appealing on many levels. After World War II, the American system of mental health care was stretched as at no prior time in its history, the result, at least in part, of the tremendous psychological damage caused by the war and the specter of the atom bomb. In 1946, Veterans Administration hospitals had some forty-four thousand patients with mental disorders. By 1950, half a million people were being treated in U.S. mental institutions, a number that would increase dramatically by the middle part of the decade, when psychiatric patients were said to account for more beds than any other type of patient in U.S. hospitals.

Though psychiatry was not a new discipline, there were still only about six thousand psychiatrists in the United States in 1950, most working at mental hospitals. Few options existed outside these facilities for those needing mental health care. Only six hundred or so psychoanalysts (practitioners of the most popular form of outpatient

---

* In his first edition of *Dianetics*, Hubbard acknowledged "fifty thousand years of thinking men without whose speculations and observations the creation and construction of Dianetics would not have been possible," giving particular credit to "Anaxagoras, Thomas Paine, Aristotle, Thomas Jefferson, Socrates, René Descartes, Plato, James Clerk Maxwell, Euclid, Charcot, Lucretius, Herbert Spencer, Roger Bacon, William James, Francis Bacon, Sigmund Freud, Isaac Newton, van Leeuwenhoek, Cmdr. Joseph Thompson (MC) USN, William A. White, Voltaire, Will Durant, Count Alfred Korzybski, and my instructors in atomic and molecular phenomena, mathematics and the humanities at George Washington University and at Princeton." Later editions of the book, however, do not carry this acknowledgment.

therapy at the time) were available; they practiced psychoanalysis, a technique based on Freud's theories, which usually required a commitment to years of therapy involving multiple sessions per week, at a cost of time and money that most people could not afford. It was also markedly impersonal: analysts, working on the principle that they were the blank slate onto which a patient would transfer anger or other emotions, tended to sit quietly in a chair, taking notes, while the patient spoke.

Hubbard proposed Dianetics as an alternative. Done with a partner who, Hubbard suggested, could be a family member or a friend, it was interactive. It was also efficient — only a few sessions, he said, could rid a person of an engram. It was noninvasive, unlike the groundbreaking new psychiatric treatment of the time, the lobotomy; some twenty thousand had been performed by 1950 in the United States. And Dianetics was affordable: all it cost to get started with Dianetics, at least initially, was the money required to buy L. Ron Hubbard's book.

By the summer of 1950, *Dianetics* was making its way up the bestseller lists. College students were interested in it, as were their professors. In suburban living rooms, people began holding "Dianetics parties," auditing one another playfully, as if the activity was the equivalent of a game of charades. In southern California, home of all things new and experimental, it became particularly popular with avant-garde members of the Malibu Colony and other artistic enclaves. Some Los Angeles booksellers, in fact, reportedly had so much trouble keeping *Dianetics* in stock that, fearing a run on the books, they began to sell *Dianetics* under the counter, offering it only to those who asked for it by name.

"A new cult is smoldering across the U.S. underbrush," declared *Time* magazine on July 24, 1950. By August of that year, more than fifty-five thousand copies of *Dianetics* had been sold and more than five hundred "Dianetics clubs" had sprung up across the nation. (It held, for many, the same excitement that *The Secret* would hold for audiences more than fifty years later.) By the end of 1950, more than half a million people had bought *Dianetics*. "The trail is blazed, the routes are sufficiently mapped for you to voyage into safety in your own mind and recover your full potential," Hubbard wrote. "You are beginning an adventure. Treat it as an adventure. And may you never be the same again."

Certainly, L. Ron Hubbard never was.

Few books of the past sixty years — at least few that were so successful — have been as widely derided as *Dianetics: The Modern Science of Mental Health*. Within weeks of its publication, a score of physicians and psychologists rushed to point out that there was very little science in it: citing a lack of "empirical evidence of the sort required for the establishment of scientific generalizations," the American Psychological Association denounced the practice of Dianetics as dangerous. Some of Hubbard's key premises, including one that held that embryos had "cellular memory," were deemed unprovable. And so, in many respects, was Hubbard's overall view of human behavior.

The book *Dianetics* depicts most people as victims of their own unfortunate prenatal experiences. Hubbard wrote voluminously of life in the womb, a noisy and rather chaotic place, as he described it. The baby was captive to everything that happened outside the womb, all of which could prove engramatic. The most crucial engrams seemed to be the result of domestic violence — there are abundant examples in *Dianetics* of women being thrown down the stairs, pushed, shoved, kicked, or yelled at by angry husbands. But even worse were those caused by attempted abortions, or "AAs," as Hubbard called them. In an era preceding the birth control pill and legalized abortion, Hubbard made the astounding claim that twenty to thirty attempted abortions occurred *per woman*, effected by knitting needles or other devices.*

Numerous scientists, including readers of *Astounding*, were skep-

---

* In a 1983 interview with *Penthouse* magazine, Hubbard's eldest son, L. Ron Hubbard Jr., maintained that he was the result of a failed abortion, according to his father. "Nibs" — who would later change her son's name to "Ronald DeWolf" in an attempt to distance him from his father — also recalled that when he was six years old, he'd watched his father try to perform an abortion on his mother, using a coat hanger. "There was blood all over the place . . . A little while later a doctor came and took her off to the hospital. She didn't talk about it for quite a number of years. Neither did my father." Nibs later retracted these and many other denigrating statements he'd made about Hubbard Senior.

tical if not roundly condemning. *Newsweek,* calling it the "poor man's psychoanalysis," denounced the entire concept of Dianetics as "unscientific and unworthy of discussion or review." Some of Hubbard's own colleagues found the book's premise preposterous and its prose almost unreadable. "To me, it looked like a lunatic revision of Freudian psychology," said the writer Jack Williamson. Isaac Asimov was less generous. "I considered it gibberish," he said.

In his review of *Dianetics,* published on September 3, 1950, in the *New York Herald Tribune Book Review,* the psychologist and social theorist Erich Fromm raised a crucial distinction between Dianetics theory, which was in some ways a reduction of Freud's early work, and what could only be referred to as the "Dianetic spirit." Freud's aim, wrote Fromm, "was to help the patient to understand the complexity of his mind." Dianetics, by contrast, "has no respect for and no understanding of the complexities of personality. Man is a machine, and rationality, value judgments, mental health, happiness are achieved by an engineering job." Hubbard believed that those who rejected his thesis either had ulterior motives or were being controlled by what Hubbard called a "denyer," which he defined as "any engram command which makes the patient believe that the engram does not exist."

Fromm saw these ideas as misguided, even dangerous. But many others found them comforting. Perhaps the greatest attraction of Dianetics was that it offered concrete answers. The vastly complex problems of the human condition could be solved not through prayer, or politics, or through the work of great philosophical teachers, but through the application of a set of basic scientific techniques. The foggy, fuzzy precepts of psychoanalysis could be replaced by straightforward, foolproof actions that could be practiced at home, by anyone. The result of successful Dianetics therapy, Hubbard promised, would be a person liberated from all aberrations, infinitely more powerful and free; according to his system, this person was known as a Clear.

"For a world frightened by atomic-bomb destruction, with limited faith in the afterworld, no more hypnotic slogan could have been used to entrance people and allay their fears," wrote Milton Sapirstein in an essay printed in August 1950 in *The Nation.* "The real and, to me, inexcusable danger in Dianetics lies in its conception of the amoral, detached, 100 per cent efficient mechanical man — superbly free-floating, unemotional, and unrelated to anything. This is the authoritarian dream, a population of zombies, free to be manipulated by the great brains of the founder, the leader of the inner manipulative clique."

For a man with no prior business experience, L. Ron Hubbard proved very adept at turning *Dianetics* into a phenomenon. Weeks before the book was published, Hubbard and Campbell had set up a training school, the Hubbard Dianetic Research Foundation, across the Hudson River from Manhattan, in Elizabeth, New Jersey. As the book's popularity grew, devotees made the trek to the so-called Elizabeth Foundation to be trained as licensed Dianeticists, or practitioners, for which they received a certificate. Soon Hubbard had opened similar Dianetic Research Foundations in New York, Chicago, Los Angeles, Honolulu, and Washington, D.C. Each center offered a similar package. A five-week course, priced at $500, including lectures and demonstrations (often delivered by Hubbard personally), would turn a starry-eyed fan into a "professional auditor," as Hubbard called those who, having completed the course, often hung a shingle and began seeing clients. A one-on-one session at one of the foundations with a Dianeticist cost $25. More aggressive therapy, offered in ten-day processes known as "intensives," could be had for between $600 and $1,000, depending on the experience level of the auditor.

For all the talk about a "poor man's psychoanalysis," Dianetics was turning into a pricey undertaking. One $25 session with a Dianeticist cost $10 more than many psychiatrists at the time charged for a consultation. The ten-day intensive cost more than thirty times that amount. But Hubbard's therapy promised a cure. And, according to John Campbell, Dianetics delivered. Gushing in a letter to Jack Williamson that just "fifteen minutes of Dianetics can get more results than five years of psychoanalysis," Campbell, a board member of the Elizabeth Foundation, claimed that Hubbard's technology had cured homosexuals, asthmatics, arthritics, and nymphomaniacs. "It produces the sort of stability and sanity men have dreamed about for centuries. And a sort of physical vitality men didn't know they could have!" he said.

Such claims were very hard to verify. Though Hubbard craved the approval of the medical and psychological establishment — and indeed, a stated purpose of the Dianetic Research Foundations was to stimulate further research — he rejected numerous pleas by Dr. Winter, now the Elizabeth Foundation's medical director, to submit his findings for peer review.

Instead, Hubbard hit the lecture circuit, adopting the dignified mien of a professor while simultaneously holding large demonstrations at concert halls or on university campuses. The *Los Angeles Daily News* described him as "a personality, a national celebrity and the proprietor of the fastest-growing 'movement' in the United States." Gracious to the press and imbued with a huckster's exuberance, he posed for pictures and entertained reporters with stories of his life as an engineer, explorer, and nuclear scientist.

At times, Hubbard would fail to produce a promised result in front of an audience of thousands. For example, on one occasion he presented the "World's First Clear" — a woman, Hubbard claimed, who would be able to demonstrate "full and perfect recall of every moment of her life." Yet, as witnessed by the crowd, she couldn't even remember the color of Hubbard's tie. Nonetheless, Hubbard continued to pull in sellout audiences. "I thought he was a great man who had made a great discovery, and whatever his shortcomings they must be discounted because he had the answer," said Richard De Mille, the adopted son of the film director Cecil B. De Mille. Then just out of college, De Mille was present at the Shrine Auditorium in Los Angeles on August 10, 1950, the night of the Clear disaster. He'd brought his girlfriend, who dismissed Hubbard as a fraud; De Mille, though, was unswayed. "He promised heaven," he explained. "It did not matter that his qualifications were suspect; he held the key. People present new ideas that they say are going to change the world and there are always a certain number of people who believe them. Lenin was the Hubbard of 1917. Hubbard was the Madame Blavatsky of 1950."

Another person who believed in Hubbard was Helen O'Brien. She was a young, recently married housewife living in Philadelphia

when she read in the *New York Times* that the American Psychological Association had publicly condemned Dianetics. O'Brien didn't
pay much attention to fads, and the word *Dianetics* was new to her.
Nor did the article shed much light on the concept. What the article
revealed was what she later called the "immoderate, almost panicky
tone" that the psychological establishment took when discussing this
new therapy. Intrigued, O'Brien bought the book and read it in one
sitting.

Not long afterward, Dr. Joseph Winter came to Philadelphia to
lecture on Dianetics at a local church. O'Brien had read Winter's
glowing introduction to Hubbard's book, in which he stated that Dianetics was "the most advanced and most clearly presented method
of psychotherapy and self-improvement ever discovered."

But now, during the lecture, Winter seemed far less enthusiastic.
In the audience, O'Brien wasn't sure why. She guessed he was feeling pressure from the medical establishment. "You could practically
see the AMA reaching for the back of his neck," she told her husband later that night. In fact, Winter's equivocation was attributable
to his growing conviction that Dianetics should be in the hands of
people with at least a minimal amount of medical training. Since the
book's publication, he'd been bothered by the slapdash atmosphere
at the foundations and was frustrated by Hubbard's sloppy research
techniques. Two preclears he knew of had suffered nervous breakdowns as a result of auditing, a result that wasn't unusual. "People
had breakdowns quite often," Perry Chapdelaine, a former student
at the Elizabeth Foundation, told the biographer Russell Miller in
1986. "It was always hushed up before anyone found out about it. It
happened to a guy on my course, a chemical engineer. They wanted
to get him out of the school and I volunteered to stay with him in an
adjoining building. He never slept or ate and was in a terrible state,
no one could do anything with him, and in the end they took him off
to an asylum."

And yet new auditors were being certified every day. Winter was
also bothered by Hubbard's continued claim that he could produce
Clears — he once maintained he could produce this state in as little as
twenty hours of auditing. Winter felt sure that it was impossible. "I
know of persons who have had 1,500 to 2,000 hours of therapy and

do not approximate the state of 'clear' as defined," he later wrote. "I have not reached that state myself, nor have I been able to produce that state in any of my patients."

But O'Brien knew nothing about Winter's reservations, and not long after attending his lecture, she signed up to be audited by a man she had met there. "Looking back, it is hard to believe that I had no doubts or hesitation about entrusting myself to these unorthodox therapies," she wrote in her 1966 memoir, *Dianetics in Limbo*. "I became a Dianetic preclear by the simple actions of taking off my shoes and lying down on a cot."

Though she'd been raised a Christian, O'Brien had never been particularly devout. A generation later, she might have been called a "seeker," for she had studied Sanskrit and Chinese and was familiar with the *I Ching*, the *Tao Te Ch'ing*, and the *Rig-Veda*. Nothing she'd learned previously prepared her for Dianetics — in her very first auditing session, O'Brien felt she had returned to her mother's womb. On another occasion, she reexperienced her own birth. The event was so traumatic, she said, that she continued to experience it for a week between auditing sessions. "It nearly floored my auditor and it was a living nightmare to me," she said. "I can vividly recall how it felt to be smothered and helpless while being violently handled by the flesh, muscles, and bones of another human body."

Soon afterward, O'Brien was being audited when she found herself in another body. "I was a husky young woman wearing a rough-textured, full-skirted dress," she recalled. She was in Ireland, circa 1813. British soldiers had arrived in her barnyard, and a boy she recognized as her fourteen-year-old son lay on the ground, about to be bayoneted. "The violence of that sight was terrific. I literally shuddered with grief," she said. Moments later, O'Brien felt herself being thrown down onto a hillside, about to be raped by one of the soldiers. "I snapped into vivid awareness then, and spit into his face. His response was immediate. He picked up a loose cobblestone and crushed my skull." At that moment, O'Brien experienced her own earlier death.

The session lasted for three hours, with O'Brien continually reliving the violence and horror of the incident until its "charge," or emotional impact, was nullified. "By the end of it, I was luxuriously comfortable in every fiber, yawning and stretching and taking breaths in full, deep satisfaction that seemed to reach to the soles of my feet." When the sessions ended, she walked down the stairs into her living room, which was decorated with Christmas lights. O'Brien was dazzled. "I was freshly there from another age. For the first time in this lifetime, I knew I was beyond the laws of space and time," she said. "I never was the same again."

Hubbard's affirmations, it seemed, had paid off. No longer a struggling science fiction writer, he was flush with cash, and his Dianetic Research Foundations were thriving across the country. Sara Hubbard would later estimate that the foundations took in over $1 million in less than a year. The most successful branch stood in Los Angeles, housed in an elegant Spanish-style mansion once occupied by the governor of California. Known as the Casa, for its Mission architecture, the Los Angeles Foundation featured an auditorium big enough for five hundred people, and it was routinely full, according to the science fiction writer A. E. Van Vogt, whom Hubbard had enlisted to run the organization.

But the flourishing was brief. The revenues generated by the Los Angeles branch of the Hubbard Dianetic Research Foundation weren't enough to cover its expenses. Hubbard thought nothing of drawing cashier's checks against the proceeds of the foundation. "The organization spent $500,000 in nine months and went broke," Van Vogt later told the interviewer Charles Platt. By the spring of 1951, Van Vogt would have no choice but to fold the operation to avoid declaring bankruptcy.

Similar things were happening at Dianetic Research Foundations all over the country. One official of the Elizabeth Foundation later told Helen O'Brien that he'd resigned after watching the foundation take in $90,000 in a single month and account for only $20,000 of it. By the end of 1950, the income of the Elizabeth Foundation, as well as the Dianetic Research Foundations in Chicago, Miami, Washington, D.C., and virtually everywhere else, had dropped so significantly that they were unable to meet their payroll and other costs.

"The tidal wave of popular interest was over in a few months," O'Brien wrote in *Dianetics in Limbo*. "People began to see that although Dianetics worked, in the sense that individuals could cooperate in amateur explorations of buried memories, this only occasionally resulted in improved health and enhanced abilities, in spite of Hubbard's confident predictions." She recalled an empty fishbowl at one of the foundation's reception desks, placed there for people to discard their eyeglasses once Dianetics had "cured" them of nearsightedness. It remained empty. "The only thing I ever saw in it was a cigarette lighter left there by someone who had quit smoking," O'Brien said.

Now struggling to maintain control of a ship that was sinking fast, Hubbard grew intensely paranoid, sniping at foundation officials for minor infractions and accusing his staff of using irregular, non-Hubbard-approved methods, or "Black Dianetics," as he called them. The New Jersey Board of Medical Examiners began an inquiry into the activities of the Elizabeth Foundation, as it was apparently practicing medicine without a license. Feeling persecuted, Hubbard began to believe that some of his students might be spies. His fears worsened when *Look* magazine published a scathing article in December 1950, in which the head of the famous Menninger Clinic, a leading psychiatric hospital, denounced Hubbard as a charlatan and condemned his techniques as potentially harmful.

By then, Dr. Joseph Winter and another key figure, Arthur Ceppos, the man who'd published *Dianetics,* had resigned from the foundation; Winter, having concluded that Dianetics might be dangerous in the hands of those not licensed as health-care professionals, was dismayed that most practitioners had absolutely no medical training. In March 1951, Hubbard's most ardent disciple, John Campbell, unhappy with the general disorganization of the Dianetics movement, returned to editing science fiction.

Upset by the defection of these apostles, Hubbard accused Winter and Ceppos of trying to take over the foundation. He also accused Ceppos of being a Communist sympathizer. This was a serious matter, as the increasingly shrill anti-Communist rhetoric of Senator Joseph McCarthy made itself felt throughout the country. At the peak of this frenzy, in 1951, Hubbard wrote a letter to the FBI, denouncing more than a dozen members of his organization as suspected members of the Communist Party. They included leaders of both the Chicago Foundation and the New York Foundation, numerous figures in the Dianetics movement in California, and, most astoundingly, Sara Northrup, Hubbard's own wife.

Hubbard and Sara's marriage had grown increasingly strained after the publication of *Dianetics*, and they had been largely living apart. Both were having affairs, Sara with a handsome young member of the Los Angeles Foundation named Miles Hollister, and Hubbard with a twenty-year-old college student named Barbara Klowden, who'd been hired by the Los Angeles Foundation as a press agent. Klowden, who ultimately became a psychologist, believed that Hubbard suffered from manic depression with paranoiac tendencies. As she said, "Many manics are delightful, productive people with tremendous energy and self-confidence. He was like that in his manic stage — enormously creative, carried away by feelings of omnipotence and talking all the time of grandiose schemes."

At other points, Hubbard became extremely depressed, drinking heavily and sedating himself with drugs like phenobarbital. He had come to believe, as he told Klowden, that Sara had caused his most recent bout of writer's block, having hypnotized him in his sleep and "commanded" him not to write. And Sara wasn't the only one who was against him, he said. Officers of the Elizabeth Foundation had tried to "slip him a mickey" in a glass of milk; he claimed they had also attempted to "insert a fatal hypo[dermic needle] into his eye and heart to try and stop him from ever writing again."

During one of these episodes, Klowden was visiting Hubbard in Palm Springs when he suddenly announced that "something was brewing" in Los Angeles, and he needed to return home. A week later, he knocked on the door of her apartment, disheveled and pale, and announced that he'd discovered Sara and Miles Hollister in bed together. He was afraid they were plotting to have him committed.*

"Please don't ask me anything," Hubbard told her. "I'm in a very bad way."

The next evening, February 24, 1951, Hubbard took his one-year-old daughter, Alexis, from her crib at the Los Angeles Foundation

---

* Sara Hubbard had, in fact, written to the head of the Elizabeth Foundation, stating that she felt her husband was a paranoid schizophrenic and urging him to help get Hubbard psychiatric care.

and deposited her at a local nursing agency. A short while later, Richard De Mille, who was now working as Hubbard's personal assistant, arrived at Hubbard's apartment and took Sara by force into Hubbard's waiting Lincoln Continental.

Striking first, Hubbard had decided to declare his wife insane. De Mille sped the Lincoln out of Los Angeles toward San Bernardino as the couple argued venomously about their marriage. For an hour or so, Hubbard searched in vain for a psychiatrist who'd agree to commit his wife in the middle of the night; then he ordered De Mille to drive into the desert.

In Yuma, Arizona, Hubbard agreed to release Sara but had an aide take his infant daughter to Elizabeth, New Jersey, where her father joined her several days later. Then, together with De Mille and baby Alexis, Hubbard flew to Havana, Cuba, at that time a rum-soaked, anything-goes city where Americans were free to enter without a passport. There, he rented an apartment in a wealthy section of town and, putting Alexis into the care of a nanny, sat down to finish his next book, *Science of Survival*.

Sara meanwhile filed divorce proceedings against Hubbard, accusing him of kidnapping both her and their daughter and alleging physical and mental abuse. After a protracted battle, she finally regained custody of Alexis in June 1951 — though not before agreeing to drop her divorce suit, in which she'd asked for a portion of the $1 million she said the Dianetic Research Foundations had earned. Instead, Sara agreed to let Hubbard divorce *her* and then signed a statement retracting all of her prior attacks on her husband, which she said had been "grossly exaggerated or entirely false." Contrary to what she may have said before, she now asserted that "L. Ron Hubbard was a fine and brilliant man." She added that Dianetics "may be the only hope of sanity in future generations." With that, mother and daughter disappeared from his life.*

---

* In 1971, Alexis, now a twenty-one-year-old college student, went looking for her father. In response, Hubbard sent two church officials to visit her, with a letter asserting that he was not her real father. According to Hubbard, Sara had been his secretary in Savannah, Georgia, in 1948, and in 1949, "destitute and pregnant," had come to find him when he was living in Elizabeth, New Jersey, writing a movie. As Sara later testified in *Armstrong v. The Church of Scientol-*

Hubbard by now had many other problems to worry about. Because the existing foundations were in shambles, he had accepted the offer of a wealthy supporter named Don Purcell to leave Havana and start a new Dianetic Research Foundation in Wichita, Kansas, which he did. But Purcell was not prepared to assume the debts of the other foundations, particularly not the Elizabeth Foundation, which closed its doors for good at the end of 1951, hundreds of thousands of dollars in debt. In 1952, a court ruled that the Wichita Foundation was liable for the Elizabeth Foundation's debts. Purcell implored Hubbard to file for voluntary bankruptcy, which he refused to do. Left with no choice, Purcell held an emergency meeting of the Wichita Foundation's board of directors in February 1952, which voted to go ahead with the bankruptcy proceedings.

Furious, Hubbard resigned from the board and sued Purcell for mismanagement, breach of faith, and breach of contract. To no avail: the court auctioned off the foundation's assets, which Purcell bought for just over $6,000. Hubbard launched a bitter campaign to discredit Purcell, accusing him of accepting a $500,000 bribe from the American Medical Association to destroy Dianetics.

It was no use. Purcell owned Dianetics; Hubbard was left without rights to any part of his creation, including its name. His great scientific adventure, it appeared, was at an end. Hubbard needed to reinvent himself, once again.

---

ogy in 1984, Hubbard also told her daughter that Sara had been a Nazi spy and that the couple had never been legally married. As Jon Atack would later point out, the wording of the letter was crucial: "Hubbard did not deny his marriage to Sara, simply its legality. He was technically correct; the marriage, being bigamous, was illegal, but that was hardly the fault of either Alexis or Sara."

CHAPTER 3

The Franchised Faith

I N MARCH OF 1952, L. Ron Hubbard sent personal telegrams to about eighty loyal Dianeticists, his remaining followers. He had "important new material" to present, he said.

Hubbard didn't disappoint. Standing at the lectern in a hotel banquet room in Wichita, he unveiled, with theatrical flourish, a device he called an "electropsychometer," or E-meter. It had been developed by an inventor and Dianeticist named Volney Mathison; having heard Hubbard talk about the problems he was having with identifying incidents of heavy emotional charge by simply questioning a patient, Mathison came up with an apparatus that would give an auditor "deep and marvelous insight into the mind of his preclear," as Hubbard put it. This simple black box with adjustable knobs and a lit dial measured galvanic skin response — the tiny electrical fluctuations under the surface of the skin that occur at moments of excitement, stress, or physical pain.

It was, essentially, a lie detector, operating on many of the same principles. And it would be used, said Hubbard, in the practice of what he called a brand-new science: Scientology. According to Hubbard, the term derived from the Latin *scio*, meaning "study," and the Greek *logos*, meaning "knowing." *Scientology* is thereby defined as "the study of knowledge." Hubbard's followers would come to refer to it in slightly different terms: "Knowing How to Know."

If Dianetics had revealed "the exact anatomy of the human mind," Scientology went further, allowing its practitioners to discover the anatomy of the human soul. Hubbard called that entity the thetan (*theta*, Hubbard said, meant "life") and said it represented a person's "true," or innate, self, which was wholly separate from the body, the mind, and the physical world.

Thetans, Hubbard explained, existed long before the beginning of time and had drifted through the eons, picking up and then discarding physical bodies as if they were temporary shells. Bored, they created the universe. But after a while, they got trapped in that creation. During the lengthy course of their history, which Hubbard called the "whole track," they had been implanted, through electric shock, pain, or hypnotic suggestion, with a host of ideas, some positive, like love, and others contradictory or negative — such as the ideas of God, Satan, Jesus Christ, and political or bureaucratic government. Eventually they came to believe themselves to be no more than the bodies they inhabited — Hubbard called them "theta beings" — and their original power was lost.

The goal of Scientology, Hubbard said, was to restore that power, which was the purpose of Scientology auditing. Thanks to the E-meter,* which for starters would enable people to recover buried memories, this form of therapy would be far more precise than Dianetics auditing.

By the time Jana Daniels arrived in Phoenix, Arizona, in the summer of 1952, the Hubbard Association of Scientologists (founded that April as a training facility, book publisher, and exclusive seller of E-meters) was enjoying moderate success. Hubbard had left Wichita several months earlier and moved west, taking with him his adoring new bride, Mary Sue Whipp, an attractive nineteen-year-old former student of the University of Texas. To the delight of many male students, though not to the women ("She was a nothing," Helen O'Brien told Russell Miller; "Her favorite reading was *True Confessions*"), Mary Sue had been studying at the Wichita Foundation since the

---

* Contrary to Hubbard's claims, the E-meter was not a new invention. It was technically a variation of a Wheatstone Bridge, which is an electronic meter that measures resistance to various electrical flows. Constructed to measure the tiny electrical fluctuations under the surface of the skin, "psychogalvanometers," as they were called, were used as far back as the nineteenth century, and Carl Jung, for one, enthusiastically embraced the devices as a therapy tool.

summer of 1951. About thirty or so people soon gathered at the association in Phoenix: science fiction fans, musicians, artists, a few psychologists, and various young people — a scruffier and less professional crowd than those who'd surrounded Hubbard in Elizabeth and Los Angeles, but just as fascinated by what he had to sell.

Daniels, then twenty-two, had been a fan of Hubbard's since she'd first read *Dianetics*, in 1950. Like Helen O'Brien, she'd been a young housewife, somewhat bored, and she became curious about this new "science of the mind." Then living in Shreveport, Louisiana, she was also curious about Hubbard, whom a friend had described as "a Hollywood person who was an acolyte of Aleister Crowley and went about the streets dressed in white robes and wearing a turban."

But the L. Ron Hubbard whom Daniels met in Phoenix didn't live up to this exotic description. "My first impression of him was of a fairly tall, orange-haired, pink-skinned man who had lips that looked like raw liver and who appeared somehow moist," she said. "I considered him a singularly unattractive man. He was not a snappy dresser and often looked as if he had slept in his clothes." And yet something about Hubbard drew Daniels in. "He was immensely charismatic. He was *magnetic*," she said. He was also, Daniels added, "a man of many faces. He was who you wanted him to be. There were countless facets to his personality. He would put them on as if they were clothing."

Hubbard had begun to promote the myth that his life had been one of sober exploration. According to this revision of his biography, he had wandered the world to gain understanding of the human mind and spirit, and had written science fiction as a way to fund that extensive "research." He now claimed to have spent a full year at Oak Knoll Naval Hospital, where he had access to the whole medical library, including the records of former prisoners of war. He met these men and began to treat their psychological wounds, holding consultations on a park bench. He claimed that in 1949, while spending time in Savannah, Georgia, he had continued this research by volunteering at a psychiatric clinic.

In Arizona, however, Hubbard also played the role of Everyman. He and Mary Sue rented a small house near Camelback Mountain that maintained an open-door policy. "In those beginning days there was not so much a 'belief' in what Hubbard said and claimed, as there was hope that it was true," said Daniels. "We were more on a journey of discovery than following a belief system."

Having come up with the idea that thetans could move objects with their minds, Hubbard and some of his acolytes sat around the kitchen table, trying to remove the cellophane from a cigarette package by using their "intention beams." Now in her seventies, Daniels, who left Scientology in 1983, laughed to think of it. "We were not successful," she said. "At another time I was in his car with him and we went out into the desert and practiced pulling clouds from the sky. No dice. Pulling oranges from a tree. Fail." But nonetheless, Hubbard could make you feel as if anything you tried would be a success. "He could zap you with admiration, with affinity, with whatever suited him. He had a way of mesmerizing one with subtle repetitive gestures and repetition of words. I think his motivation was obvious — money," she said. "But there was a great deal of idol worship. Some thought him a god."

In Philadelphia, meanwhile, Helen O'Brien and her husband, John, had opened a branch of the Hubbard Association of Scientologists. By 1953, similar groups had formed in other cities, including London, where Hubbard began to spend an increasing amount of time. All of these organizations were bleeding money.

Perhaps it was time to try a different approach. They should create a company, independent of the Hubbard Association of Scientologists, but fed by the HAS, Hubbard suggested in a letter to O'Brien, dated April 10, 1953. This new organization, a "clinic" of sorts, would see clients and pay the HAS a percentage of its proceeds, which would go to cover costs. All they'd need to make "real money," he noted, was ten or fifteen preclears a week, who might easily be convinced to pay upwards of $500 for twenty-four hours of auditing. Shrewdly, Hubbard anticipated that the more they charged, the more popular they might become. Hubbard told O'Brien that he'd seen it happen. "Charge enough and we'd be swamped."

The failure of Dianetics, as Hubbard saw it, had been its democracy: he'd written a book and sold it to the people, and they had taken the techniques and done with them what they wanted. Even Hubbard's onetime lieutenant, A. E. Van Vogt, now had his own Dianetics practice in Los Angeles. Hubbard received none of the profits from this and other similar ventures; neither did he get any credit for coming up with the ideas. He wanted both. Now he could ensure that he got them by turning Scientology into a business. Perhaps the best way to do that was also to make it into a religion.

"Perhaps we could call it a Spiritual Guidance Center," he suggested to O'Brien. Hubbard described installing attractive desks, outfitting the staff in uniform, and hanging diplomas on the wall. With that, they could "knock psychotherapy into history," he said. A "religious charter" would be necessary to make it stick. "But I'm sure I could make it stick." After all, they were treating the spirit of a person, he said. "And brother, that's religion, not mental science."

The more he thought about it, Hubbard told O'Brien in his April 1953 letter, the more "the religion angle," as he put it, seemed to make sense. "It's a matter of practical business."

This reframing from the "mental science" of Dianetics to the religion of Scientology was a typically canny move by Hubbard, which picked up on the national mood. In 1950, more than half of the American population were members of one or another Christian congregation; by the end of the decade, that number had reached 69 percent. "Churches were by far the most trusted institution in American life [in the 1950s] — ahead of schools, radio and newspapers, and the government itself," the historian Stephen Whitfield noted in his book on 1950s America, *The Culture of the Cold War*. It was probably not lost on L. Ron Hubbard that the most popular therapist and self-help guru in America, Dr. Norman Vincent Peale, was also a minister. In an age of increasing anxiety and paranoia, faith was seen as a route to sound mental health. Peale's best-selling book, *The Power of Positive Thinking*, was published in 1952, the same year Hubbard announced the advent of Scientology; it would remain on bestseller lists for years. Cloaking Scientology in religious garb was practical on numerous levels. Certainly it would make the organization seem more respectable — "in my opinion, we couldn't get worse public opinion than what we have had, or less customers with what we've got to sell," Hubbard noted in his letter — it would also allow auditors to sidestep the rules regarding certification for psychological counseling. As practitioners of "mental science," Dianetics and Scientology auditors

had been scrutinized for lacking the appropriate medical or psychological licenses; as clergy, they could counsel whomever they wanted,
under the protection of a church. They could also claim tax-exempt
status,* which Hubbard would later explain to his flock was a fundamental reason for taking the religious route. "No one ever saw it as a
religion," Jana Daniels explained. "It was a most unpopular idea until
it was explained by Mr. Hubbard that for tax reasons, a church would
get a better shake."

Hubbard spent the next six months laying the groundwork for Scientology's evolution as a religion. On February 18, 1954, a Scientologist named Burton Farber filed incorporation papers in Los Angeles
for the Church of Scientology of California, considered by Scientologists to be the first official Scientologist church. L. Ron Hubbard, the
adventurer and science fiction writer turned scientist and philosopher, was now the founder of his own church.

Hubbard then set about creating a worldwide spiritual corporation. Individual Scientology organizations, or franchises, would become churches (though members would refer to them as "orgs").
Every church would cede 10 percent of its gross income to a larger organization, the Hubbard Association of Scientologists International
(HASI), also known as the Mother Church, a so-called religious fellowship, according to its incorporation papers, which also sold to the
franchises books, E-meters, and tapes of Hubbard's teachings. The
HASI was incorporated in England and controlled by L. Ron Hubbard — who also controlled every church of Scientology, in practice.
But each separate org had its own shadow president and board of directors, which allowed them to appear, at least on paper, independent. "Hubbard had learned from his mistakes," wrote the former
Scientologist Jon Atack in his 1990 history of the Church of Scien-

---

* In 1956, the Founding Church of Scientology, in Washington, D.C., was
granted tax-exempt status by the IRS; soon many other Scientology churches
would be granted similar exemptions. In 1959, the Washington church's tax exemption was revoked (though several other Scientology organizations would remain tax-exempt). Upon review, the U.S. Court of Claims found that Hubbard
was profiting from Scientology beyond what would have been considered standard remuneration.

tology, *A Piece of Blue Sky*. "He was not on the board of every corporation, so a check of records would not show his outright control. He did, however, collect signed, undated resignations from directors before their appointment." Perhaps more significant, Hubbard also controlled the bank accounts of these organizations.

Hubbard presented Scientology to the public as a true religious movement — complete with an eight-pointed Scientology cross, wedding and funeral rites, and an ever-growing catalog of "scripture," which according to Hubbard's decree was the true status of his writings. Auditing sessions were often referred to as "confessionals." In future years, Scientology officials would be referred to, and ordained, as "ministers," complete with clerical collars.

To sell his new faith, Hubbard used the techniques of modern marketing and advertising; from his newly created Hubbard Communication Office, he directed his followers to aggressively spread the word. "If advertised products don't have good word-of-mouth they don't sell," Hubbard admonished them. How that word-of-mouth was created changed, depending on the locale. To tap into the loneliness and disconnectedness of city dwellers, Hubbard instructed one of his British followers, Ray Kemp, to advertise this offer, together with a phone number, in the London evening newspapers: "I will talk to anyone about anything." "We were inundated with calls," Kemp later recalled. "Everyone from potential suicides to a girl who couldn't decide which of three men to marry."

In both England and the United States, Hubbard exploited fear and concern about polio by encouraging his followers to run ads in the paper stating that a "research foundation" was looking for polio victims willing to try out a new cure. A similar ad was used to attract those suffering from asthma and arthritis.

Another technique Hubbard advocated was scanning the daily papers to find anyone who'd been recently "victimized one way or the other by life" and then, "as speedily as possible [to make] a personal call on the bereaved or injured person." Auditors, Hubbard said, were perfectly within their rights to call themselves either "researchers" or "ministers."

Once a person arrived at the church, Scientologists presented themselves in one of two ways, depending on the nature of the potential recruit: as members of a humanitarian movement or as students of a new science that could expand the person's mind and horizons. Wishing to make sure that, unlike Dianetics, Scientology would never slip from his control, Hubbard created strict and aggressive policies to curtail the actions of independent operators, those who aimed to use Scientology outside the sanction of the organized church. There would be no negotiation with such "squirrels," as Hubbard called them. Instead, he recommended legal action as a way to shut them down. "The law can be used very easily to harass, and enough harassment on somebody who is simply on the thin edge anyway . . . will generally be sufficient to cause his professional decease," Hubbard explained. "If possible, of course, ruin him utterly."

The founder of Scientology earned a modest $125 per week for his labor. But he also earned a commission from the sale of E-meters and training manuals — sold through HASI — and received royalties from his books. Lectures also provided him with income. The Church of Scientology hosted weekend seminars, called "Congresses," at which Hubbard would give a talk and occasionally audit members of the audience. Congresses could be highly lucrative: one in the late 1950s was said to earn more than $100,000 in a single weekend. Whatever Hubbard made from these appearances was pure profit: the church paid his expenses and also provided him and his growing family — between 1952 and 1958, Mary Sue gave birth to Diana, Quentin, Suzette, and Arthur — with a house and a car.

In 1956, the Church of Scientology's gross receipts were just under $103,000. By 1959, the church was making roughly $250,000 per year. Hubbard received about $108,000 during the four-year period of 1955–59, much of it earned after he stopped drawing his $125 per week salary and was paid instead a percentage of the Church of Scientology's gross profits.

This exceeded the salary of the president of the United States at the time, and it also outstripped the earnings of many Fortune 500 executives. But Hubbard did not see wealth as inconsistent with righteousness, and the years he'd spent advancing his own interests now served him particularly well. Hubbard had always looked at his fiction writing with a commercial eye; early on he'd analyzed how much money could be earned from various genres and pursued the most lucrative course. Now he looked at Scientology through a similar lens.

Hubbard envisioned a church that was organized in a strictly top-down structure, which merged science, religion, and successful business practices. Efficiency would be the main marker of success. "The prosperity of any organization is directly proportional to the speed of its particles — goods, people, papers," Hubbard said. The standard method of therapy — namely, the spontaneous interaction of patient and therapist — was grossly inefficient, in Hubbard's view. Even Dianetics had relied too much on human interaction. Scientology would streamline the process of enlightenment.

The local org was, as Hubbard designed it, a full-service operation, tightly structured to facilitate the "processing" of clients as efficiently as possible. A sales team, known as registrars, met with clients (often simply called PCs, short for preclears), discussed their needs, and then recommended a product, usually an "intensive," a package of auditing sessions. The registrars procured payment on the spot. From there, the client moved to the service delivery team, led by a case supervisor who worked with the auditor to design and oversee the client's process. Ethics officers, who were responsible for disciplining and rehabilitating wayward clients, handled any problems within the organization. Another department, known as the "Public Division," would supervise outreach and fundraising.

Into this structure flowed the money received from paying customers, which in turn funded not only the smaller organizations but also the Mother Church, which licensed the orgs to sell and market Scientology services and also monitored their sales and membership statistics. From the 10 percent tithe that each franchise paid to the Mother Church, Hubbard took a 10 percent cut. How much the founder made from Scientology during this period was unknown to the membership at large. He often claimed to invest far more in Scientology than he earned; on the other hand, he boasted to friends that he had more than $7 million stashed in Swiss bank accounts.

With this structure in place, Scientology would grow into "the McDonald's hamburger chain of religion," as Jon Atack described it, with independent franchised churches springing up all over the world. Hubbard's doctrine, known as "standard tech," was marketed and ultimately trademarked. Church officials would later compare Scientology's trademarks (each one "a symbol which assures the public of a certain quality," in the words of one Scientology attorney) to Coca-Cola's.

While this might have been an off-the-cuff statement, Scientology did, in fact, mimic certain features of the Coca-Cola Company. Its orgs functioned as processing plants, churning out an identical product at every site worldwide. As the years went by, some of its core doctrine would be referred to not as sacred teachings but as "trade secrets." The Church of Scientology would go to court to protect its proprietary rights over this material: litigation, in fact, would become its hallmark.

When Scientology made its debut, few in the mainstream took it seriously. In one of the first articles about Hubbard's new spiritual science, published in *Time* on December 22, 1952, the magazine laid out the predominant view of the newly self-designated "Dr." Hubbard. "Now, the founder of still another cult, he claims to have discovered the ultimate secrets of life and the universe, and to be able to cure everything, including cancer," the article stated. "His latest ology is compounded of equal parts of science fiction, Dianetics (with 'auditing,' 'preclears' and engrams), and plain jabberwocky."

It did not help Hubbard's reputation that his latest books struck many as even more implausible than *Dianetics*. Hubbard's 1951 book, *Science of Survival*, laid out a theory of human behavior based on eighty emotional "tones," or levels, ranging from +40.0 (serenity of being) to −40 (total failure). The higher up the tone scale a person was positioned, the more emotionally and spiritually alive he or she would be. A tone, Hubbard said, affected a person's overall attitude or vibe, as well as the ability to communicate and to relate to others; it even determined a person's smell. People with body odor, Hubbard noted, were invariably lower on the tone scale than those with none; the same held true for those with bad breath. "The body is normally sweet-smelling down to 2.0" — the tone of "antagonism" — "but begins to exude chronically certain unpleasant effluvia from 2.0 down."

But as people were audited "up" the tone scale, they would most likely lose these embarrassing traits.*

In his 1952 book *The History of Man*, Hubbard ventured away from the psychological into what could easily be read as pure fantasy. But Hubbard began the book by telling readers it was "a cold-blooded and factual account" of the past sixty trillion years of their own existence. Homo sapiens had a genetic line that confirmed much of what Darwin laid out in his evolutionary theory, Hubbard said, but Scientology helped fill in the blanks by explaining the various phases of development through the prism of engrams. Some engrams on the evolutionary chain could be traced back to a mollusk-centered era, dominated by a deadly incident known as the Clam. Auditing a person on this incident could be dangerous; simply asking this question — "Can you imagine a clam sitting on the beach, opening and closing its shell very rapidly?" — could cause the person severe jaw pain. "One such victim, after hearing about a clam death, could not use his jaws for three days. Another 'had to have' two molars extracted because of the resulting ache."

Elsewhere in *The History of Man,* Hubbard described engrams that arose from traumas suffered during the Paleogene and Neanderthal eras, and finally, as they affected modern humans. He explained that thetans moved from body to body, arriving after the death of one body at a halfway house called an "implant station" where they were deluged with pictures — "stills of vacant lots, houses, backyards" — which served as what Hubbard called a "forgetter," erasing the thetan's past life and thus priming it to receive its next body. Some of these stations, Hubbard added, were on Mars.

The FBI was a recipient of another genre of Hubbard's writing.

---

* Even more controversial was Hubbard's assertion that low-toned individuals should be exiled from society. "The sudden and abrupt deletion of all individuals occupying the lower bands of the tone scale from the social order would result in an almost instant rise in the cultural tone and would interrupt the dwindling spiral into which any society may have entered," Hubbard wrote. "It is not necessary to produce a world of clears in order to have a reasonable and worthwhile social order; it is only necessary to delete those individuals who range from 2.0 down, either by processing them enough to get their tone level above the 2.0 line" — a task that might take as few as fifty hours or more than two hundred, according to Hubbard — "or simply quarantining them from the society."

The founder of Scientology had maintained his correspondence with the bureau since denouncing his associates and his wife as Communists in 1951. Though he continued to view attacks upon Scientologists as the defamations of "Communist-connected personnel," as he wrote in one letter, Hubbard had become increasingly antagonistic toward psychiatrists, who, he seemed to believe, were intent on destroying him. In one 1955 missive, he reported that several Scientologists had gone "suddenly and inexplicably insane," an event that he believed had nothing to do with Scientology counseling. Rather, an "LSD attack" launched by a psychiatrist intent on doing harm had caused this misfortune. LSD, Hubbard noted, was the "insanity producing drug so favored by the APA."

By the autumn of 1955, the FBI had received so many similar letters from Hubbard that they stopped responding. "Appears mental," one agent wrote on a rambling Hubbard missive of this kind. But Hubbard was undeterred and persisted in sharing with the U.S. government what he considered his groundbreaking discoveries.

In April 1956, the FBI received a pamphlet titled "Brain-Washing: A Synthesis of the Russian Textbook on Psychopolitics," which Hubbard told them was the Church of Scientology's reprinting of what "appeared to be a Communist manual." The bureau examined it and concluded that its authenticity was doubtful "since it lacks documentation of source material and Communist words and phrases." It was widely assumed that Hubbard had written the booklet himself. He was also thought to be the anonymous author of a pamphlet called "All About Radiation," signed by "a Nuclear Physicist and a Medical Doctor." The text promoted a vitamin product called Dianazene, claiming it could treat and prevent radiation sickness, as well as certain cancers. The Food and Drug Administration, having been given a copy, investigated these claims. In 1958 the FDA confiscated, and then destroyed, a shipment of twenty-one thousand Dianazene tablets, which Hubbard was selling as a substance that prevented radiation sickness.

In the wake of the Dianazene seizure, authorities increased their scrutiny of Hubbard's activities. As his FBI file thickened by the day, the CIA also decided to open a file on his burgeoning organization. But making their way through the tangled morass of ad hoc corporations and shell companies that composed the Church of Scientology proved daunting. In addition to more than a hundred churches of Scientology, various other groups existed as part of the web, with names like Hubbard Guidance Center, American Society for Disaster Relief, Society of Consulting Ministers, and Academy of Religious Arts and Sciences. By the end of the 1950s, Scientology had grown into a tremendously complex network of businesses, not all of which were churches; all, however, sent money to the Mother Church. Figuring out how the whole conglomerate worked was, then as now, nearly impossible.

After a year of investigation, the CIA had discovered no hard evidence of wrongdoing. Scientologists nonetheless felt under siege. Hubbard began spending an increasing amount of time in England, where both the HASI and the Hubbard Communications Office, the issuer of myriad memos and policies to organizations worldwide, were now based. In 1959, he decided to move there permanently and purchased a 225-year-old estate in the Sussex countryside known as the Saint Hill Manor. A weathered Georgian mansion with eleven bedrooms and an indoor swimming pool, it sat on fifty-five acres amid rolling hills and flowering rhododendrons. This, Hubbard decided, would be Scientology's new home.

Located just outside the tiny town of East Grinstead, Saint Hill was the former residence of the Maharaja of Jaipur. In a note published in the journal of the Explorer's Club, of which Hubbard was a member, the founder of Scientology said he had "sort of won" the estate in a poker game. In fact, the house had been up for sale for almost a decade before Hubbard abruptly purchased it for the fire-sale price of £14,000 (about $70,000). The people of East Grinstead had no idea that the founder of a religious movement had moved into their village. Most newspapers, in fact, ignored Hubbard's association with Scientology and described "Dr. L. Ron Hubbard" as a celebrated American scientist and humanitarian, who had moved with his wife and their four young children from America to conduct, among other things, horticultural experiments.

At Saint Hill, Hubbard was industrious and almost manically busy, spending his days conducting research, training and coaching new auditors, and lecturing several times a week. Hubbard also ran all of Scientology's organizations, which by the early 1960s were located in a dozen cities in the United States and in Canada, Mexico, and South America, as well as throughout Europe and in countries such as South Africa, Australia, New Zealand, and Rhodesia. "This was a guy working eighteen hours a day, seven days a week for years on end," said Alan Walter, who was one of a number of young people interested in Hubbard's theories who made the pilgrimage to Saint Hill. "Definitely not the Lord of the Manor."

Contrary to Scientology's later claims, L. Ron Hubbard did not single-handedly come up with all of Scientology's techniques. He was helped by scores of special assistants like Walter, who came to Saint Hill to attend the Special Briefing Course, in which the work, to a large degree, revolved around the creation of new processes or auditing techniques. "You had professors, doctors, paupers, multimillionaires — you name it," said Walter. "They were your students, your fellow classmates, your coaches. So the mixture of knowledge was enormous. There were a hundred students on the course at any given time at Saint Hill — the top processors from all over the world."

About half of these elite auditors were sponsored by a Scientology organization; the rest paid their own way. Walter, an Australian businessman and former professional Australian-rules soccer player, was part of the latter category. "I was between jobs and I didn't quite know what I was going to do with myself, which was a perfect way to go study something," said Walter. "I had no agenda other than to get knowledge."

Most of the students were seduced by Hubbard's charisma, though many remained skeptical of the leader's credentials. "We all saw him as a bullshit artist because you'd have to be forty people to have lived what he said he did," said Walter. Hubbard claimed to be a doctor of philosophy, having earned a degree from Sequoia University. "Everybody knew that had come out of a diploma mill. But that was accepted. Don't forget, we'd come out of the 1950s when everything was thought to be a façade. Just about everyone was pretending to be someone they weren't."

Hubbard's academic bona fides may have been suspect, but his focus on the technology and its results struck Walter as admirable. The criterion for success was easy to judge: a person's life improved after auditing. If auditing worked, "the guy became more alert, more aware, and life became easier. If he didn't, it was back to the drawing board."

A Scientology process, as it developed, was a formulaic type of therapy — Walter called it "structured therapy." A common "identity process," for example, might ask a subject to list all of his or her qualities to find out what aspects of the self the person might keep hidden. One item might have particular "charge," indicated by a jump of the needle on the E-meter, which would suggest to the auditor that a problem had been located. At that point, the auditor would dig deeper. "The idea was to find out what games you were playing without even realizing it, and what might be motivating you to act in certain ways," Walter said. Upon recognizing these hidden motivations or "games," the person would generally feel tremendous relief, followed by a sense of heightened self-knowledge and, ultimately, freedom. "The idea," he said, "was to come out of a session with all this awareness that you were a spiritual being."

New techniques were constantly being devised and refined by trial and error, with Hubbard serving as coach. "Hubbard would arrive early in the morning and pin the process up on the door, and then we'd come in and copy it down and run it on each other," said Walter. The teams kept track of everything that happened during these sessions and then submitted their notes for Hubbard's review. Each evening, Hubbard read these notes, made revisions, and then posted a new set of processes for the next morning. This is how, between 1962 and 1964, many of Scientology's core auditing procedures and many of its theoretical precepts were developed.

Walter was in awe of Hubbard's raw ability to dissect problems, and people. "He could tear you apart if he wanted to — just rip you to shreds, and then put you back together again." Having played sports his whole life, Walter saw that kind of process as proof of Hubbard's commitment to helping his students improve, and he gladly allowed himself to serve as test subject. "I loved it, and I got tremendous gains from that kind of coaching."

But as time went on, Walter's mind was slowly reshaped, though he wouldn't realize it for many years. Later he'd understand that this as a byproduct of other, less positive effects of Scientology's auditing processes and especially its particular use of language. Hubbard's word for *spirit*, for example, was *theta*. No one spoke of *love* in Scientology; they had *affinity*. The word *auditing* no longer referred to a task that accountants performed but instead meant "to listen and compute" in accordance with the *standard,* a word that seemed to denote the accepted application of Hubbard's technology. But commenting on the precise definition of *standard,* Walter said, "Who knows what that meant? It meant whatever he wanted it to mean," and this malleable use of words served as an effective instrument of control.

Before long, the accepted definitions for ordinary words had vanished, replaced with new meanings that separated Scientology from other subjects and Scientologists from other people. "It's very, very subtle stuff, changing words and giving them a whole different meaning — it creates an artificial reality," said Walter. "What happens is this new linguistic system undermines your ability to even monitor your own thoughts because nothing means what it used to mean. I couldn't believe that I could get taken over like that. I was the most independent-minded idiot that ever walked the planet. But that's what happened."

By the early 1960s, a close cadre of true believers surrounded L. Ron Hubbard. Most were young — Alan Walter was twenty-five — and convinced that Scientology would "unlock the truth and knowledge of our spiritual, mental, and human potential," as Walter put it.

But those who'd known Hubbard since the 1950s, and had once believed this as well, were no longer so sure. By the time he moved to Saint Hill, most of Hubbard's early acolytes had departed, disillusioned with Hubbard's leadership and also, in some cases, with the substance of Scientology itself. Helen O'Brien, for example, once among Hubbard's closest confidantes, had begun seeing the "holes appear in [the soap] bubble," as she phrased it, as far back as 1952. Scientology, though rooted in the same principles as Dianetics, was not like the previous movement. "The tremendous appeal of Dianetics came from Hubbard's apparent certainty that you could easily clear yourself in present time of the heritage of woe from past misadventures," she wrote in *Dianetics in Limbo*. But Hubbard no longer seemed interested in that. He was focused on spiritual awareness, constantly revising his theories on how better to attain it. He now spoke at length about imagination — something Hubbard had once tagged a "lie factory" for its inherent untrustworthiness. He introduced a technique called "creative processing," whereby he encouraged adherents to "mock up," or make up, scenarios and cast themselves in various roles. The switch from factual recall to imaginative invention struck O'Brien as almost a betrayal of the movement's core values. Before long, "the joy and frankness" that had imbued every Scientology lecture "shifted to pontification," she said. The therapies, which had once involved significant give-and-take between auditor and preclear, now seemed like "highly mechanistic verbal performances."

Then there was the matter of L. Ron Hubbard himself. Though he was charming in the presence of paying customers, a "weird foxiness" made him impossible to work for. "As soon as we became responsible for Hubbard's interests, a projection of hostility began, and he doubted and double-crossed us, and sniped at us without pause," O'Brien wrote. By October 1953, the work environment had become so toxic that she and her husband, John, resigned from the Hubbard Association of Scientologists and closed the Philadelphia operation.

Hubbard seemed to accept O'Brien's departure. He was far less charitable when it came to others. This was particularly true with regard to his son Nibs, Hubbard's eldest child. A distant father even with his most recent brood, Hubbard had almost completely absented himself from the lives of Nibs and his sister, Katherine. They had grown up with their mother and grandparents in Bremerton, Washington, with only a scant idea of what their father was doing. But when *Dianetics* was published, L. Ron Hubbard became a celebrity. And Nibs, a red-haired, husky young man who had long sought a relationship with his father, saw his chance. Upon turning eighteen, in 1952, he made his way to Phoenix, intent on becoming a Scientologist.

Hubbard welcomed this new association with his son. Within a few years, Nibs became an auditor — "one of the best auditors in the business," as Hubbard described him — and the executive director of the Church of Scientology in Washington, D.C. Then, in November 1959, Nibs abruptly left Scientology, claiming that he could no longer afford to support his family on his meager income. Viewing his son's defection as yet one more act of treachery, Hubbard immediately drafted a letter instructing his executives to ban Nibs from Scientology and withdraw his credentials if he tried to practice Scientology independently.

Hubbard stopped short of writing to the FBI about Nibs and his transgressions (something he might have done just a few years earlier). Instead, he made an example of Nibs, showing his flock the precise consequences of stepping out of line. Hubbard declared to his followers that Nibs had "unconfessed overts," or hidden crimes, which had caused him to leave. Hubbard would soon see all such departures from his movement as stemming from unspoken transgressions, an idea that became deeply entrenched in Scientology theory and philosophy. To this day, anyone who leaves Scientology is instantly viewed as guilty of a crime. But in 1959, this idea was new, and a telling indicator of the extent to which Hubbard's own psychology was driving his new movement.

To handle perceived traitors, Hubbard devised a new form of auditing called a "security check." This was interrogation by another name, with the E-meter serving as a helpful tool. Security checking gave tremendous power to auditors; Hubbard thought of them as "detectives" and charged them with uncovering unspoken thoughts, called "withholds" in his ever-evolving language. Under this examination, to which everyone in Hubbard's world — including household staff, students, and auditors — would eventually be subjected, a battery of questions probed both public and private aspects of personal history. Had the subject committed robbery or murder? What sexual proclivities and perversions* characterized his or her behavior? Had he or she ever been a member of the Communist Party, or been sent to the Church of Scientology as a saboteur? Had the person ever harbored a critical thought about L. Ron Hubbard?

The smallest misstep, such as a minor critique of the movement or

---

* Homosexuality was decreed one such "perversion."

a slight doubt as to its authority, was enough to warrant punishment, making the security check a particularly effective method of thought reform. "A Scientologist is heavily indoctrinated into the idea that if he finds himself being critical of Hubbard or the Church or its executives, then the very fact of his being critical is proof positive of the fact that he himself is harboring undisclosed dirty deeds," according to the former Scientologist Bent Corydon, who wrote *L. Ron Hubbard: Madman or Messiah?,* an intensely critical book about the founder of Scientology. "When somebody can look into your thoughts, giving you no option for privacy of consideration and opinion, some devastating things occur," Corydon stated. "This is especially so if you are (or consider that you are) dependent upon the approval of that somebody or group for your continued well-being and very survival as a spiritual being."

Numerous new philosophies were born and sold during the mid-twentieth century in the United States, many of them led by charismatic leaders who promised scientifically guaranteed remedies for everything from sickness to unemployment. With the exception of a few — Dr. Norman Vincent Peale, the Reverend Billy Graham — most of those prophets have long since been forgotten, along with their techniques. So why did L. Ron Hubbard's creed continue to exist, and to grow, well into the 1960s and beyond? Perhaps the easiest answer would be the singular force that was L. Ron Hubbard himself.

It would be wrong to cast Hubbard solely as a crank. One of Hubbard's acolytes, Cyril Vosper, later wrote of Hubbard's "incredible dynamism, a disarming, magnetic and overwhelming personality" that was apparent even in private moments. Wandering through Saint Hill on a Sunday morning, it wasn't unusual to run into the founder, who would unfailingly stop to chat. Though Hubbard was then in his fifties, "a breathtaking stream of ideas and new projects poured from him with youthful enthusiasm," wrote Vosper. "His brilliant red hair and broad smile, his benign authority, made it not difficult to believe that here was the new Messiah. The twentieth-century, science-orientated, super genius on whose broad shoulders and intellect the fate of the world rested. Yet not so far removed from the plain man as to be unable to stand and gossip while taking snapshots with his Leica."

It was this unique combination of majesty and accessibility that allowed Hubbard to thrive as a leader, inspiring both faith and fealty. As Russell Miller observed, "Scientology flourished in the post-war era of protest and uncertainty when young people were searching for a sense of belonging or meaning to their lives. Hubbard offered both, promised answers and nurtured an inner-group feeling of exclusiveness which separated Scientologists from the real world. Comforted by a sense of esoteric knowledge, of exaltation and self-absorption, they were ready to follow Ron through the very gates of Hell if need be." Miller's view is common among the numerous critical biographers, who tend to argue that it was the founder's personality, including his bouts of rage and paranoia, that elevated Scientology to something more than an obscure pseudo-scientific self-help program. That Hubbard was a forceful, brilliant, and charismatic presence is undeniable. But the ideas Hubbard put forth in his new spiritual technology should not be discounted, nor should the way in which he presented them.

Scientologists are taught to believe that every single word of their doctrine was written by and conceived of by the founder. In truth, most of Hubbard's ideas appear to have been taken or adapted from a wide variety of sources, ranging from Freud and Aleister Crowley to Lao Tzu and various Buddhist masters, and, quite possibly, to William Sargant, a British psychiatrist who wrote extensively about abreactive therapy and brainwashing in his 1957 book, *Battle for the Mind.* Where Hubbard did prove original, however, was in shrewdly boiling down those teachings, packaging them as both mental health technology and scientifically applied religious philosophy, and selling them to a society that was increasingly fixated on both.

As a product, Scientology embodied different things to different people. Like those of other churches, its ministers, most of whom were male, wore collars (in public, though not always within the orgs themselves) and adopted the sober mien thought to be typical of men of the cloth. The movement embraced standard ethical and moral themes. Like many fundamentalist Christian movements, Scientology opposed homosexuality and other forms of "sexual perversion." Like numerous mainline Christian sects, it was enthusiastically materialistic and staunchly anti-Communist. Idealists were drawn to Scientology because of its stated humanitarian goals. From the earliest days of Dianetics, Hubbard spoke of it as a direct response to the creation of weapons of mass destruction. "Man is now faced . . . with weapons so powerful that man himself might vanish from the earth," he wrote in *Dianetics*. "There is no problem in the control of these weapons . . . The problem is in the control of man."

Scientology simultaneously reflected the postwar era's optimism and its darkest and most profound anxieties. The same, perhaps, could be said for Hubbard himself, who often seemed to embody two distinct individuals: the kind and benevolent "Friend of Man," as Scientologists would later call him, and the paranoid and increasingly reclusive narcissist. He was amusing, kind, generous, and often brilliant, but also dismissive, punishing, and, at his worst, cruel.

By the mid-1960s, Hubbard had delivered thousands of lectures and written innumerable policy letters and bulletins that spelled out the essential code of Scientology. With the help of his many researchers, he had designed the vast majority of Scientology's auditing processes, which he tended to amend each year. Saint Hill, the hub of worldwide operations, was the buzzing factory of Scientology. Mail delivery trucks would arrive each day and deposit stacks of letters, most addressed to Hubbard himself. Hubbard referred to the daily-mail delivery bags as "the Santa Claus pack."

In 1964, Hubbard granted his first interview in several years to James Phelan, a reporter for the *Saturday Evening Post*. At the time, this magazine was considered second only to *Life* in terms of importance and pride of place on most American coffee tables. A man who "was always at pains to project the image of a benefactor to mankind," as one former Saint Hill associate recalled, Hubbard was flattered and hoped the story would help legitimize him, at long last, to mainstream Americans.

Phelan came to Saint Hill, toured the estate, and attended a few of Hubbard's lectures, where the founder strutted like a peacock. "He was excited, he was laughing, he was joking, he was huge," Alan Walter recalled. "Photographers were in the audience taking pictures of us. And he was as high as a kite on all of that."

In private talks with Phelan, Hubbard bragged that a new Scientology office opened "somewhere in the world . . . every three days" — though he would not produce an exact number of members because "it doubles every six months." He described himself as company man. "I control the operation as a general manager would control any operation of a company," he said. He insisted he did not profit from Scientology, drawing a "token salary" of $70 per week. In general, he maintained, Scientology was a "labor of love."

Phelan's article appeared in March. Contrary to the long-awaited acknowledgment of his accomplishments that Hubbard had hoped it would be, the story was a takedown of Scientology and its founder. Phelan made fun of Scientology's teachings and noted that Hubbard lacked credentials. "Records show that he enrolled [at George Washington University] in 1930 but never received a degree of any kind. Today, besides his 'Doctor of Scientology,' he appends a Ph.D. to his name. He got it, he says, from Sequoia University. This was a Los Angeles establishment, once housed in a residential dwelling, whose degrees are not recognized by any accredited college or university."

The only difference between Hubbard and an "old-time snake-oil peddler," Phelan wrote, was that "there is nothing old-time about L. Ron Hubbard." (The journalist marveled at the modern Telex machine — the high-speed fax of its day — on Hubbard's desk, and also noted that Hubbard appeared to be well versed in a wide range of scientific topics.) Cagey about church finances, yet obviously enjoying its plentiful fruits, he lived like a self-satisfied squire. At the end of a long day, "the master of Saint Hill Manor rings for his butler Shepheardson, who fetches his afternoon Coke on a tray. If he wishes a bit of air, his chauffeur will wheel out a new American car or the Jaguar, and as he gazes contentedly out over the broad acres of what was once a maharaja's estate, the profound truth of what he says becomes apparent. Lafayette Ronald Hubbard, 'Doctor' of Scientology, may indeed be a man who has this lifetime straightened out." The article meted out mockery of Hubbard in every sentence.

Hubbard was crushed. "That article was a disaster," said Alan Walter. "He'd waited for weeks, expecting all this recognition, and instead he was ridiculed in a major international magazine." And this disgrace only compounded Hubbard's woes. One year earlier, in

1963, the U.S. Food and Drug Administration had once again raided Scientology's headquarters in Washington, D.C., this time seizing its inventory of E-meters. The agency charged that the labels on this equipment made phony claims; they "represent, suggest and imply that the E-meter is adequate and effective for diagnosis, prevention, treatment, detection and elimination of the causes of all mental and nervous disorders and illnesses such as neuroses, psychoses . . . arthritis, cancer, stomach ulcers, and radiation burns from atomic bombs, poliomyelitis, the common cold, etc."

This, unlike the Dianazene raid, received significant press attention both in the United States and throughout the English-speaking world. In Victoria, Australia, the FDA's action added fuel to a debate that had been raging for some time over Scientology's physical and mental health benefits. As early as 1960, the Australian Medical Association and its Mental Health Authority had taken a keen interest in Scientology, and a formal board of inquiry would ultimately produce a scathing, 173-page report thoroughly denouncing Scientology and its founder. "If there should be detected in this report a note of unrelieved denunciation of Scientology, it is because the evidence has shown its theories to be fantastic and impossible, its principles perverted and ill-founded, and its techniques debased and harmful," the report concluded. "Scientology is a delusional belief system, based on fiction and fallacies and propagated by falsehood and deception . . . Its founder, with the merest smattering of knowledge in various sciences, has built upon the scintilla of his learning a crazy and dangerous edifice."

A careful reader of this report could detect not just ridicule, but fear. Scientology, as the sociologist Roy Wallis would later point out, had great success in the late 1950s and early 1960s, attracting ordinary people who willingly joined its ranks. Yet its ideas were anything but conventional. "For some," Wallis noted, "Scientology's conflict with conventional reality was a *moral* affront."

This view of Scientology — that it was not an innocuous therapy group, but rather a potentially dangerous and highly controlling global racket — in turn set the tone for the evolution of Scientology. It became what some members of the public feared it already was. For all of his life, L. Ron Hubbard, the showman and storyteller, had sought to connect with mainstream culture, only to be rejected and scorned. Certainly, the *Saturday Evening Post* had confirmed his doubts about the media; with one or two exceptions, he would never again allow a journalist to get close to him.

Now, in humiliation, he would withdraw from the world completely and seek revenge. Deeply depressed in the weeks after the story came out, Hubbard stopped socializing with his students, refrained from laughing and telling jokes, and retreated into an increasingly hostile zone from which many believe he never fully emerged. "He just crashed," said Walter. "And after that, he changed. I never saw him laugh after that day. He was just very angry from then on."

In February 1965, Hubbard wrote a seven-page manifesto titled "Keeping Scientology Working." This was his Sermon on the Mount, something Scientologists consider a sacred document, which in future years would serve as both an instruction manual and a rallying call to legions of idealistic believers. In it, Hubbard declared himself the sole creator, or "Source," of Scientology's technology, negating the work done by his many collaborators, and defined his movement as the salvation of the human race. His followers were charged with a divine mission to "hammer out of existence" any philosophy or technique that might compete with his own.

Recognizing a change in climate, a number of individuals left Saint Hill, and Scientology, shortly after reading this document. But those like Walter, who stayed in the church (he did so for another thirteen years), were forced to suppress their own ideas for fear of being denounced as "squirrels." "From that moment on," said Walter, "nobody but L. Ron Hubbard discovered anything."

The long period of experimentation and self-exploration was over, and with it, the entire concept of Scientology as an alternative to psychotherapy or even an innovative spiritual movement. Scientology was now more than that — it was, particularly for those willing to work alongside Hubbard or within his church, a highly regimented parallel universe. In this new world, where L. Ron Hubbard was king, there would be no criticism or snide remarks, no embarrassing revelations about his credentials or lack thereof. In fact there would be no critical thinking at all, for now there was only one form of thought, Hubbardian thought — with which one had affinity, or nothing.

To the uninitiated and the newly enamored, he would remain L. Ron Hubbard, quixotic troubadour, and Scientology a journey of psychological discovery. To his devoted and indoctrinated followers, he would be Source, the Founder, LRH — the inventor who'd used them, willingly, as test subjects. Only Scientology, Hubbard wrote in "Keeping Scientology Working," defined the route out of the labyrinth of human suffering and confusion. He would call that road "The Bridge to Total Freedom." And it would lead to a place few Scientologists could have imagined or suspected.

PART II

CHAPTER 4

The Bridge to Total Freedom

Do you know that absolutely Standard Tech — complete, utter, hairline, Standard Tech — used in organizations throughout the world, will at least triple the stats of each org within 90 days. Couldn't help it. And if it was really applied in a business-like fashion, and nobody messed it up in any way, shape, or form . . . we might even be able to take the planet within a year. It is hot! Scientology is so much hotter than anybody thinks it is . . . it is fantastic!

— L. RON HUBBARD, "WELCOME TO CLASS VII," 1968

JEFF HAWKINS WAS born in 1946, and grew up in the wealthy suburb of Arcadia near Pasadena, California, ten miles northeast of Los Angeles. The son of a prosperous advertising executive, he was a good student and a talented artist who, like many of his peers, was drawn into the social and political counterculture of the 1960s. At the University of Redlands, then a small conservative Baptist college near Riverside, California, where Jeff enrolled in 1965, he became part of a small circle of students who grew their hair long, smoked pot, and made regular sojourns to Los Angeles to take part in anti-war demonstrations. By the winter of 1967, feeling stifled by college, he transferred to the Chouinard Art Institute in Los Angeles (now known as Cal Arts), but stayed only a few months before he decided to drop out of school entirely and strike off on his own.

Finding a job designing posters and other promotional material for an organization in Los Angeles, Jeff moved to the Sierra Madre Canyon, an eclectic artists' refuge nestled in the foothills of the San Gabriel Mountains. Just a half-hour drive northeast from downtown L.A., the Canyon was home to hundreds of longhaired kids who'd migrated there during the mid-1960s — Jeff believed it to be one of the largest hippie outposts in the country after Haight-Ashbury. With its quirky bungalows and wooden footbridges, it was a rustic idyll and sanctuary for the drifters and dropouts of the greater Los Angeles area, and many more who'd come to party with their friends on the weekends.

But Jeff was bored. He was searching for something; he didn't know what. The Summer of Love had come and gone, along with its haze of promise. The war in Vietnam continued to kill thousands of young Americans. Many who made it back alive wore the dead-eyed stares of the walking wounded. Active in the anti-war movement, Jeff was haunted by the memory of one large demonstration outside the Los Angeles Convention Center, where he'd seen a twelve-year-old girl beaten up by the Los Angeles police. Drugs, Jeff knew, weren't the answer — a bad acid trip a few months earlier had cured him of that interest. He spent most of his spare time poring over books on meditation, yoga, cybernetics, hypnosis.

One Sunday afternoon in the fall of 1967, Jeff's roommate, Jerry Day, arrived home in a state of high fluster. "Wait until you hear about this," Jerry said, breathlessly.

Jeff yawned. "Hear about what?" he said.

"Scientology!" Jerry said.

"What's Scientology?"

Jerry took a deep breath and began to explain that he'd just met some guys, Scientologists from L.A., who'd been talking about a new "scientific form of spiritual enlightenment." They all seemed really into it — like *really*, Jerry said. They talked of Scientology as if it was a magical science that could help you — somehow — somehow — become a superman. Plus, there was some kind of past-life component that sounded really cool. "Don't you want to check it out?" Jerry asked.

Science, spiritual enlightenment, past lives — they all fit into Jeff's intellectual purview. "Sure, bring it on," he said. Later he would laugh at the memory. "We were all pretty crazy hippies back then," Jeff, now living in Portland, Oregon, told me not long ago. "We were pretty much up for anything."

The next night, Jeff and Jerry drove out of the Canyon and went down to Scientology's Los Angeles headquarters, the "Scientology

Place," as they called it, which was located in a rambling Spanish-style house on Ninth Street, near MacArthur Park. A crowd of maybe one hundred or more had gathered around a fountain on the front lawn; others were packed into the lobby. They were of different ages and, to Jeff's great surprise, they were *talking to one another* — graying, middle-aged parents standing side by side with longhaired hippies, laughing, discussing philosophy, trading jokes, as if the generation gap had been closed.

A few minutes later, everyone filed into a lecture hall. Jerry and Jeff found seats near the back. At the front, a handsome young man with dark hair walked up to the lectern. A hush fell over the room. The young man could have been a movie star; he was that good-looking, Jeff thought. He also had an intense, unwavering stare that seemed to penetrate right through a person. And he was an electrifying speaker, presenting Scientology as a lifesaving new philosophy that freed the mind and the spirit. Even war, he said, could be prevented with the correct application of Scientology's principles.

About halfway through the lecture, the young man stopped to show a film that featured an interview with Scientology's founder, L. Ron Hubbard. Here was the same smiling, fatherly-looking man whom Jeff had seen depicted on posters that were plastered everywhere in the building; a large portrait of Hubbard also hung in the lobby. He looked nearly sixty, but Jeff thought he had a puckish mien. He wore a jaunty ascot, and his presentation was irreverent, even wildly anti-establishment. He seemed to speak the language of youth, not that of his own dusty generation. And, Jeff noted, he was not a member of some austere academic or philosophical establishment; he didn't even have a degree!* Instead, his résumé listed his various exploits as an explorer, sailor, expedition leader, anthropologist, author, and all-around maverick. He was known as Ron.

After the film, the lecturer picked up where he had left off, explaining some core principles of Scientology. Society's reactive mind, he said, was to blame for all that was wrong in the world: the H-bomb, the Vietnam War, the plague of overpopulation and disease. When humans become free of the reactive mind and reach the state

---

* Hubbard had by then begun to downplay his degree from Sequoia University on his résumé.

of Clear, they become smarter, saner, more dynamic, more *alive*. Surely, Jeff thought, this young speaker possessed those traits himself. And indeed, he said, "I'm Clear," and fixed every member of the audience with his magnetic gaze. "You can be too."

"I was hooked," said Jeff.

And so Jeff Hawkins, a shy, somewhat awkward young man usually dressed in jeans, sandals, a blue work shirt, and tinted granny glasses, got into Scientology, as did his friend Jerry and thousands of other young people all across the United States. For those like Jeff, who were smart, curious, and searching, Scientology provided its own form of rebellion, which was perfectly timed, as it turned out.

Had the sixties never happened — which is to say, had a tremendous number of young people not become convinced of the moral and spiritual bankruptcy of their parents, the church, the Republican Party, and other people and institutions collectively known as the establishment — Scientology might have gone the way of other fringe movements and died a quiet death. Instead, repositioned as a mystical quest rather than an alternative mental health therapy or religious movement, Scientology rode the countercultural wave, and by the late 1960s, a whole new generation of spiritual seekers had caught on to the renegade vision of L. Ron Hubbard.

"Wherever you go," wrote the journalist George Malko in his 1970 book *Scientology: The Now Religion*, "the Scientology word is being shouted at you from Day-Glo posters showing an exultantly leaping man, his very vibrancy dividing his body into a discord of parallel striations." STEP INTO THE WORLD OF THE TOTALLY FREE, declared the posters, tacked to the walls of New York City subway stations. On campuses, Scientology was marketed as a movement for Flower Children. One church official in New York, Bob Thomas, described Scientology to Malko as a "drugless psychedelic" that offered young people a community and a new brand of hope.

"After drugs comes Scientology," said one series of church fliers posted in public urinals around the University of California, Berkeley. Other leaflets, handed out widely on street corners, urged young people to "be a member of Scientology. The world has waited thousands of years for a technology to change conditions for the better. Scientology is the answer."

In Kenmore Square or Washington Square, on Shattuck Avenue or Sunset Boulevard, in the Haight or Golden Gate Park, pretty young girls dressed in hot pants or mini-skirts, smiling radiantly as if they'd discovered a secret they were bursting to share, would approach young, mostly male college students or hippies and invite them to come with them. And, like lemmings, men would follow, said Nancy Many, who worked for the Scientology organization in Boston. It was unwritten policy that the church would deploy its most attractive staff to recruit people off the street. "No one had any idea where they were being taken," she said, chuckling, "but these girls were gorgeous and so the guys would go."

The girls would take the boys — or, alternately, though less frequently, a handsome young man might take a group of girls — to the local church of Scientology, which in those days was usually housed in a storefront or rundown office building, or, like the Los Angeles Org, in an old house. There, these potential recruits — "raw meat," as they were called — were delivered to someone like Many, who would seat them in a large auditorium with dozens, and at times hundreds, of other people, for an introductory lecture. By then, whoever had brought them in would have vanished back out onto the street to round up more prospects. Some of the new arrivals, detecting the bait and switch, would leave; others, intrigued, stayed.

The lectures could take various directions. Some, like the one Jeff and Jerry attended, were straightforward: an explanation of the reactive mind, a film, an invitation to become Clear. There was also the lecture-confessional. "I used to be a failure," the lecturer might begin. "I was a terrible father, a terrible husband, I was unhappy with my church, I had a dead-end job. And then I discovered Scientology."

"Beautiful," someone in the back of the room would murmur. Frequently it was another pretty girl. She was not, however, an audience member, but rather a Scientologist installed there to set the right tone. The lecturer would go on to describe how incredibly, magically mind-blowing the experience of auditing had been; how he'd discovered a "new reality" based on "affinity" and communication. "Reality is agreement," he might explain, adding that Scientology meant "the study of truth" and that a key principle was to know "what's true for you." He had found his truth, and he was so sure this *was* the truth that after just a short time in Scientology, he'd left his wife, quit his job, and was now working full-time at the church. And now he wanted everyone in the audience to immediately find a registrar (that is, a church salesperson) and do as he had: join the Church of Scientology and "step into the exciting world of the totally free."

"That was our job," Many, a perky, dark-haired woman in her fifties, told me. She left Scientology in 1997 and now lives with her husband, Chris, in the San Fernando Valley. She had been a girl of nineteen when she joined the church in Boston and was soon charged with delivering some of the lectures to an audience that frequently seemed confused. "There would be all these college kids in there, and they'd look around as if to say, 'Where'd that chick go who brought us here? Where's the chick?'" Many laughed. "She was out doing her job, bringing in tons of people. Our job was to get them interested enough to go to a registrar, who would then sell them. But if we weren't getting them to the registrar, we got in trouble. You had to sell them something — even if it was just a book."

Selling religion was by no means unique to Scientology. The Hare Krishnas sold copies of the Bhagavad Gita; the followers of the Reverend Sun Myung Moon and his Unification Church sold flowers at airports as a way of meeting naive and impressionable young people. More recently, the Kabbalah Centre, which promotes a self-help-inspired form of Jewish mysticism that became popular in the late 1990s, has made handsome profits selling candles and beaded bracelets at such high-end retail establishments as Barneys New York. But Scientology had a cooler, more mainstream appeal. "I never thought I was joining a religion," said Many, who was raised a Catholic. It was like yoga, in terms of its faddish popularity, but it was better than fuzzy Eastern philosophy: less "foreign," more fun. There was no dancing, chanting, or wearing of orange robes. No one was encouraged to abstain from sex, cigarettes, or alcohol, let alone shave their head. There was also no requirement to relinquish worldly possessions (nor to hand anything over to a guru).

Just as Mia Farrow and the Beatles embraced Transcendental

Meditation, Scientology gained its own celebrity following: in the 1960s, Leonard Cohen, Cass Elliot, William S. Burroughs, and even Jim Morrison ("*Jim?!?*" some kids asked, and this rumor, which remains just a rumor, always seemed a bit too good to be true) were said to have dabbled in Scientology. Of the church's processes, Burroughs, who'd made it all the way to Clear, once said, "Scientology can do more in ten hours than psychoanalysis can do in ten years."*

A few darker exemplars existed as well. Charles Manson, for one, studied Scientology in prison in the early 1960s, years before committing the Tate-LaBianca murders, and would later go on to use some of its techniques on his followers. But he was the exception. Scientology was geared not toward the dropouts and runaway youths who panhandled in the Haight or caught steamers to Morocco, but toward kids like Jeff Hawkins, who were idealistic and eager for social change, and who, as Jeff would say, were "looking for something that made sense."

And Scientology, it seemed to many young people, did. It was not a "cult" insofar as it did not require separation from mainstream society, nor from families — though it encouraged its acolytes to "disconnect" from those who were critical of Scientology. But it presented itself as a movement of people who were deeply engaged with the world. Parents were not necessarily the enemy; they were potential converts. The church encouraged its young members to connect with their families, devising special drills and other technology to help members repair fractured relationships and communicate their new beliefs. For those whose parents were hostile to Scientology, or to its costs — in 1968, as Jeff recalled, an introductory Scientology course package cost around $1,000; auditing, also sold in packages, began at roughly $175 for five hours — the church produced pamphlets and cassette tapes† to better explain Scientology's

---

* Burroughs would later denounce Scientology's organizational policies and Hubbard's "overtly fascist utterances" as suppressive of freedom of thought, though he maintained that some of Scientology's techniques were valid.

† In the late 1980s, Scientology produced a cassette tape titled "Can We Ever Be Friends?" to help members repair relationships with their families and "help you gain wide acceptance of Scientology in your area," as one promotion read. The forty-five-minute cassette presented Scientology as a tolerant, mainstream religion, not in any way a cult, as some families believed it was.

beliefs and practices and to present Scientology in a positive light.

Jeff had always been close to his mother, who approved of his interest in Scientology. When it came to the cost, he paid the fees; as a graphic designer, he had no problem affording them. Besides, as he saw it, the courses were educational. "These weren't someone's dusty old theories; they were 'technology,'" he said. "I thought what I was learning was science."

The first one Jeff took was called the Communications Course, which promised to help him become more comfortable in social situations. It consisted of a series of drills known as TRs, short for Training Routines, that students were told were used to train Scientology auditors. The drills were printed on white paper in red ink and bore the official-sounding title "Technical Bulletin." The first TR involved closing your eyes and sitting in a chair, sometimes for hours. The second drill involved sitting across from a partner for an hour or two and staring at the person, immobile. A third TR, known as "bull-bait," required students to tease, joke with, or otherwise try to distract their partner, who had to maintain a straight face. Jeff's partner was a pretty girl; to his surprise, he seemed to have no trouble talking to her after a few practice drills — he had even made her laugh.

But the most stunning result of the TRs was the sense of peace that washed over Jeff whenever he practiced them. It was meditative, and at times the feeling was so all-encompassing it seemed he had left his body. He told the course supervisor, who smiled. This was a common experience in Scientology, he said: it was called "exteriorization." As Jeff advanced and gained more awareness in Scientology, the supervisor said, he would be able to leave and return to his body at will.

"It all seemed so unreal — I was completely electrified," Jeff said. Back in the Sierra Madre Canyon, he began talking up Scientology to his girlfriend, Dixie. She was unimpressed. There was something weird about the people she met who were into Scientology, Dixie believed; they had an odd intensity, almost like religious fervor, but their god was neither a minister nor a guru, but a middle-aged science fiction writer. Though Scientology purported to promote total freedom, it was not free — virtually nothing, other than the introductory lecture, came without a price tag. And yet Jeff didn't even seem to see that part of it. "I think it's a cult," she told him.

"You don't know what you're talking about," he said. "It's about living up to your full potential."

It was also, he and many other sixties converts believed, on a mission to save the world. Not only did Scientology promise to get rid of war, but it had a written program to do so: "All we had to do was clear people of their reactive minds and they would become rational and ethical and sane, and see that war and violence were wrong," Jeff said. "To me, it sounded plausible. I couldn't just sit by and do nothing while the world went to hell."

If Dixie couldn't get behind that, then maybe the fault lay within her. One aspect of Scientology, which was not promoted until a person actually became a member, was the core belief that there were certain people in the world known as Suppressive Persons, or SPs. These were people who openly opposed Scientology—journalists, judges, politicians, tax collectors, psychiatrists—but they could also be hostile parents, or skeptical girlfriends. Maybe Dixie was one of *them*, several Scientologists suggested to Jeff; maybe she just didn't want him to get any better. Maybe she didn't want the *world* to get better. Maybe she was an SP.

Ultimately, Dixie gave Jeff an ultimatum: it was either her, she said in frustration, or Scientology. Jeff chose the latter. "It was just too important," he said.

By the early summer of 1968, many of the hippies in the Sierra Madre Canyon were into Scientology. Either that, or they were into hard drugs. It was a fractured, confusing, disheartening time: in April, Martin Luther King Jr. had been assassinated, followed two months later by Robert Kennedy. Riots had erupted in Watts, and then at the Chicago Democratic Convention. The anti-war protests, bloody and embattled, now seemed futile. Increasingly, many young searchers who'd drifted to the Canyon, particularly those just back from Vietnam, were using heroin. Shady characters followed them, hanging around on the fringes, dealing drugs. The scene in the Canyon became increasingly tense. After one young man was killed in a gunfight near his house, Jeff Hawkins decided it was time to move on.

But where should he go? The Vietnam War loomed. Jeff had already received a letter from his draft board, ordering him in for a pre-induction physical. He'd managed to get himself a psychiatric interview, and posing as "crazy" — something that only half-worked, he thought — was given a temporary deferment. But it was only temporary. He knew the army would eventually come for him.

To avoid this fate, one option was to become a Scientology minister and thus get a ministerial deferment. It was a bit of a ruse: being a Scientologist minister only meant that you *could* audit and perform Hubbard-approved birth and marriage ceremonies; actually doing ministerial duties was wholly voluntary. But the Scientology minister's course, which cost only around $15, was being sold to hundreds, if not thousands, of young men as a way to avoid the draft. Should he be ordained? Jeff considered it.

Then an even better option came along. Jeff was offered the chance to work for the Church of Scientology and leave the country entirely. The church published a number of magazines that Jeff thought were poorly designed. One day he approached a staff member at the Los Angeles Org and asked for a job. "I said something like 'Listen, I'm a graphic artist, do you need some help? Because I get your magazine and frankly it's a piece of shit.'"

The staffer, who seemed eager to have him join the team, took him into the back room and showed him a stack of amateurish-looking layouts. "These are all done at Saint Hill," he said. "We just fill in the information."

"I looked at them and thought, I could do better than this," Jeff said. But to do so, he'd have to move to England. "So I began to think about it." He'd decided to go ahead and get his minister's certificate — even if he left the country, it didn't mean he'd be able to escape the draft unless he became a minister. But no matter what, England would be a cool place to live for a while, he thought. To be at the center of Scientology, to join staff, which would elevate him above the level of a mere "public," or paying, church member; to use his artistic abilities to further the cause, and to be an ocean away from his draft board: who wouldn't want to go?

And so in June 1968, Jeff flew to England, excited to begin his new life at Scientology's worldwide headquarters at Saint Hill. Upon arriving, he was told that the church's promotions department had moved: the Publications Org, or Pubs, as it was called, was now located in Edinburgh, Scotland. Instead of settling into life at the manor, Jeff settled into a shabby, drafty, four-story building located "in an alley behind an alley." The place was filled with books, with a suite of editorial and design offices on the top floor. The hundred or so people on staff ranged in age from the early twenties to the midforties and had come to Edinburgh from America, England, Australia, and Scandinavia.

Scientology had taken off as a fad in the United States, and its popularity in the United Kingdom was nearly as high. At the close of 1967, the Church of Scientology in Great Britain reported it had made nearly $1 million that year — not as much as the Catholic Church, surely, but more than many new religious movements. At Saint Hill, where students now flocked from all over the world, the weekly income often averaged around $80,000. Working for Scientology, Jeff found out, was far different than simply doing Scientology. "We have a planet to clear," Jeff's supervisor told him on his first day on the job — a phrase he'd hear over and over again for many years to come. Staff members were paid £7 per week, which, amazingly, was enough for Jeff to rent a small flat with some friends, buy food and cigarettes, and still have a bit left over. He received most of his Scientology courses and auditing for free, but in return, he was expected to work every day and many nights, including weekends, with a day off only once every few weeks. "We don't keep a wog schedule here," the supervisor said.

Non-Scientologists were called wogs, a term thrown around liberally among church staff: "wog ideas," "wog justice," and "wog science." Hubbard began to use this offensive British slang term* in 1953 to denote any person who was not a Scientologist, in his estimation a "run-of-the-mill, garden-variety humanoid." For Jeff, who after the Kennedy assassinations and the conduct of the Vietnam War had, like many of his friends, bought into the idea of government conspiracies and other nefarious activities of "the establishment," *wog*

---

* The term, an acronym for Worthy Oriental Gentleman, is a holdover from British imperialism, once used to describe people of African or Asian descent.

was just another word for a member of mainstream society under the thumb of the Man.

The wog world, Jeff learned, was an "enturbulated" place. *Enturbulated* was a word that Hubbard made up and defined as "agitated and disturbed." There were many new words to learn in Scientology. Some were pure invention; and others were familiar but redefined by Hubbard. *Ethics*, for example, was a significant term in Scientology, perhaps the most significant. It was defined as "rationality toward the greatest good for the greatest number of dynamics." As one of the first lessons in Scientology, Jeff had learned that there were eight dynamics of existence, starting with your relationship with yourself, and then progressing to your relationship with your family, social group, society, plants, animals, the larger physical world, and ultimately, with the Supreme Being, however you chose to define that.

An ethical Scientologist, and an ethical person, in Hubbard's view, was someone who had successful relationships on all dynamics. But the most important relationship was with the group, or the third dynamic, which was understood to be the Church of Scientology. Upstanding members who made gains in Scientology, furthering the group's overall goals, were considered "in-ethics": in line with organizational principles. Those who misbehaved in some way were "out-ethics": impediments, or even enemies, of the group, malfunctioning cogs in the Scientology machine.

Among Hubbard's outpouring of new technology in the mid- and late 1960s was something he called "ethics tech," which would become one of the most crucial elements of Scientology. Hubbard designed quasi-scientific formulas to measure a person's ethical level, which he called the "Conditions of Existence," with the constant goal being to "improve conditions" for oneself and the group.*

Years earlier, Hubbard had divided the world into two eras: the dull past (Before Dianetics) and AD (After Dianetics), the glorious, Technicolor world of Now. In that now — AD 18, or 1968 — virtually anything that didn't directly relate to Scientology was considered suspect, if not overtly suppressive. It was crucial for the overall ethi-

---

* The twelve conditions, ranging from highest to lowest, are Power, Power Change, Affluence, Normal, Emergency, Danger, Non-Existence, Liability, Doubt, Enemy, Treason, and Confusion.

cal condition of the group, Jeff understood, that nothing seep into its world that was "counter-intentioned," or based on a goal against the interests of Scientology. A related concept, "other intentionedness," refers to ideas or philosophies that have nothing to do with Scientology. To be either counter-intentioned or other-intentioned was considered "open-minded," which in Scientology, Jeff learned, was a bad thing.

And yet these issues didn't much affect Jeff's daily life. He had made tremendous gains in Scientology: in just a year or two of auditing and courses, he'd lost his adolescent shyness and become far more confident and outgoing. He could talk to anyone, including the most beautiful women, and he felt better about his work too. Everyone he knew in Edinburgh was a Scientologist, and everyone believed the same thing: no questions, no doubts.

Like him, most of Jeff's co-workers were longhaired kids in their twenties, many onetime student radicals who shared not only beliefs, but a lifestyle. No one cared who you slept with or what you did. After a long day it was typical for everyone to troop off to a movie or to a restaurant, where they would take over a group of tables and order multiple bottles of wine. One of the Scottish Scientologists on staff took it upon himself to take the group on long pub crawls along Edinburgh's Rose Street, with the mission of drinking a pint of beer at every bar they passed (usually, Jeff said, they'd make it only halfway before, too drunk to continue, they staggered home). Overall, it was like college, he thought — except without the drugs, and with extremely long hours and intensely demanding work.

A few months after Jeff's arrival, an alert was sounded throughout the Publications Org: all staff members were required to report for an emergency briefing. Jeff put down his drafting pencils and ran downstairs to the conference room, where a woman in heavy makeup, wearing a naval dress uniform, sat behind a desk. She waited until the room was full. Then she introduced herself as Warrant Officer Doreen Casey, the new commanding officer of the Publications Org.

Casey was a special emissary of L. Ron Hubbard, the Founder, as he was now known, who smiled down at his followers from portraits and photographs throughout the orgs. Where Hubbard was living, exactly, was a bit of a mystery. He had resigned as the executive director of the Church of Scientology in the fall of 1966, announcing that he was going back to his first love: exploring. It was ridiculous, of course — everyone on the inside knew that the Old Man, as some staff members called him, retained control of Scientology; he continued to issue numerous policy letters and directives via Telex. But the trick, as he told his followers, was to stay below the radar so that *no one could see him.* He was "Fabian," as he called himself, a shape-shifter.

Rumors abounded within Scientology of Hubbard's whereabouts. He was in Africa, some said; others said he was sailing the high seas. In fact, both stories were true. Concerned for Scientology's security after the release of the Australian Board of Inquiry's "Anderson Report" in 1965 — a document whose negative findings provided fodder for investigations into Scientology's activities in several other countries, including Great Britain — Hubbard had journeyed to the southern African nation of Rhodesia in April 1966, hoping to find a base for Scientology in a more remote location.* He purchased a house in the capital city, Salisbury, and began to eye a resort hotel on Lake Kariba where — unbeknownst to the sellers — he hoped to start a new Scientology organization. To ingratiate himself with the Rhodesian prime minister, Ian Smith, Hubbard personally delivered two bottles of champagne to Smith's home, though as one former associate would recall, he was forced to leave the bottles with a butler when Smith wouldn't receive him.

The people of Rhodesia had no idea about Hubbard's plans. In several media interviews, he said he had come to Africa as a tour-

---

* According to a number of followers, Hubbard had become convinced during an auditing session that he was the reincarnation of Cecil Rhodes, the flamboyant adventurer and founder of the African country of Rhodesia. Acting on this belief, Hubbard had journeyed to southern Africa, hoping to "safe point," or establish, a safe haven in what is now Zimbabwe, to build a Scientology community. Some believed he planned to turn the realm of Cecil Rhodes into a country of Scientologists. "The entire objective," recalled one former follower, Hana Eltringham Whitfield, who would become a close aide to Hubbard, "was to find a place that Hubbard could eventually turn into his own kingdom, with his own government, his own passports, his own monetary system, in other words his own principality, of which he would be the benign dictator."

ist, claiming to have distanced himself from Scientology. But Hubbard's strategy fell apart when the Rhodesian government, apparently suspicious of his motives, refused to renew his visa. Returning to England, Hubbard began to consider the future. For Scientology to flourish, he knew, it needed a secure home away from government oversight. There weren't many places in the world where that could be found. Then it came to him: 75 percent of the earth's surface was free from the control of any government. It was ocean.

That fall, Hubbard purchased a small fleet of ships and set off for North Africa. The first ship, a fifty-foot Bermuda ketch called the *Enchanter*, sailed from England to the Canary Islands at the end of 1966, followed by a trawler, the *Avon River*, and later a larger, more impressive ship, the *Royal Scotsman*, the flagship of the fleet. For the better part of the next ten years, these ships plied the waters of the Mediterranean and the eastern Atlantic, finding temporary ports in Las Palmas, Tangier, Valencia, Corfu, Lisbon, Tenerife, Madeira, and many points in between. Hubbard was now commodore of this small fleet; Mary Sue was a captain, and his teenage daughter, Diana, a redhead like her father, was lieutenant commander. And those serving Hubbard and his family — a private navy, complete with uniforms — were called the Sea Organization.

These were Hubbard's closest disciples: longtime Scientologists who'd been with Hubbard since the 1950s, associates who had worked with him at Saint Hill, and increasingly, a cadre of younger and even more dedicated followers. Their work was highly confidential, and few other Scientologists knew anything about this shadowy team. Jeff's knowledge of the Sea Org was nil, except for the fact that Doreen was a member. And now she was running the show at Pubs.

"We are in the middle of a *war*, and this organization has been slack, slack, slack!" Casey screamed at the assembled Scientologists. "That's ending right now." Jeff almost laughed. Did she mean a literal war? Who was this woman? Then he looked around. The organization's leader, David Ziff, an heir to the Ziff-Davis publishing dynasty, was nowhere to be found. Casey announced that Ziff had been removed from his post and sent away for ethics handling. Scientology was on a campaign to get Hubbard's books into as many bookstores around the world as they could. But they were failing, said Casey, because Pubs failed to deliver the books. Now the Sea Org would be in control, and she had come to get this organization "back on the rails." From now on, everyone would report to her — and address her as "sir," she informed them. The "hippie atmosphere" would no longer be tolerated. Long hair was to be cut short, beards were to be shaved, and workers were to call *all* of their superiors "sir," even if the sir in question was a female.

Under this new military-style discipline, which would soon be reflected throughout Scientology, if a design wasn't finished on time or a production order not met, staffers would be ordered to sleep among the books on the cold cement floor of the stockroom. Those who still did not produce and ship books fast enough would be "offloaded": sent to a smaller, more remote organization as punishment. "Either you are one hundred percent with me or you are against me," Casey said, in a threatening way. "And you will be dealt with accordingly."

We are at war. This, in fact, was a proclamation coming from L. Ron Hubbard himself, though Jeff had always taken it to be a metaphor. Hubbard first hinted at this conflict in a taped message, titled "Ron's Journal '67," that began to make its way through Scientology organizations in early 1968. Speaking to his followers for the first time since his disappearance, the Founder said nothing about his whereabouts other than that he was on an island, with a view of "the wide blue sea with ships passing by, a few fleecy clouds overhead, and the bright sun shining down." Jeff, who had heard the tape months before Casey arrived, concluded that wherever Hubbard was, it sounded amazing. But far more astounding was what Hubbard had to say.

"I am giving you this short talk because you might have wondered what I was doing," Hubbard began. What he'd been doing, as it turned out, was discovering whole new levels of existence. He explained that he had been researching the most extraordinary realm of consciousness, a realm he had only just discovered, known as "Operating Thetan." An "OT," Hubbard said, was the most enlightened being in the universe, capable of operating "totally independent of his body, whether he had one or didn't have one." No one prior to the birth of Scientology had ever achieved this exalted state. Now, however, select Scientologists would be able to learn the techniques that made this possible, through a series of auditing processes known as the "OT levels."

Over the past year, Hubbard said, he'd been on a search for the deepest mysteries of the universe, a journey that took him through what he called the "Wall of Fire." The quest had been risky, and just that past winter, he said, he'd become very ill as a result of his efforts. And yet he managed to learn the truth and survived the experience, though barely. "The material involved . . . is so vicious that it is carefully arranged to kill anyone if he discovers the exact truth of it," he warned. "I am very sure that I was the first one that ever did live through any attempt to attain that material."

Hubbard didn't elaborate too much on the tape about what his adventures had entailed, nor what he had discovered. But he hinted that an incident of catastrophic proportions had occurred seventy-five million years ago, an event so traumatic that its residuals were still being felt on Earth to this day. His new OTs, represented initially by the Sea Org, would lead the charge to rehabilitate the planet against a small but powerful band of opponents.

"Our enemies are less than twelve men," he said via "Ron's Journal '67." "They are members of the Bank of England, and other higher financial circles. They own and control newspaper chains, and they are all, oddly enough, directors in all the mental health groups in the world." Most of the world's leading heads of state, including Britain's prime minister, Harold Wilson, were, according to Hubbard, under the control of these individuals.

The church now had private investigators in its employ, digging into the backgrounds of various bankers, journalists, and politicians. Scientologists would learn more about these activities, though only in vague references, as Hubbard issued many more directives pertaining to the battle ahead. "We are rolling up the heavy guns quietly and getting things exactly timed," he said in a letter to his staff on November 4, 1968. Several weeks later, Hubbard announced that he had isolated the enemy and was readying a counterattack.

Then, on November 29, 1968, Hubbard made his most dramatic declaration to date in a memo to all staff, titled "The War." Hubbard revealed that the twelve individuals he had formerly referred to were merely a front for a much larger, more dangerous enemy: the World

Federation of Mental Health. Hubbard often called it SMERSH, a reference to both the Stalin-era counterintelligence units of the Soviet army and the fictional nemesis of James Bond. This organization had been behind every attack on Dianetics and Scientology since 1950, Hubbard said. The Founder had begun to view psychiatrists as not simply suppressive but the ancient enemy of mankind, responsible for the enslavement of the human race. Psychiatry and the broader field of mental health, he explained, were chosen long ago as "a vehicle to undermine and destroy the West." But the Church of Scientology had stood in its way. Now, Hubbard said, Scientologists had "the goods" on SMERSH and intended to battle its forces worldwide, using every legal means at their disposal. "We don't stoop to murder and rough house. But man, the effectiveness of our means will become history," he wrote, though he never specified which tactics *would* be used. "It's a tough war. All wars are tough. It isn't over."

War. That was pretty much the opposite of what Jeff Hawkins, pacifist, ex-hippie, onetime anti-war protestor, stood for. One of the reasons he'd joined Scientology was because of its doctrine of world peace. But those thoughts would come much later — years later. At the time, Hubbard's directive, his "battle plan," as his missives were often called, seemed thrilling — a cause! Few staff members had time to wonder about all the evildoers. A wave of panic now washed over the organizations. The future of the world was at stake and they, the Scientologists, weren't doing enough. They *had* to do more. "In all the broad Universe," Hubbard said, "there is no other hope for Man than ourselves."

By the beginning of 1969, Scientologists around the world were dedicated to fighting Hubbard's war on psychiatry. In Britain, where L. Ron Hubbard had been declared an "undesirable alien" and his movement denounced in Parliament as a "pseudo-philosophical cult," Scientologists began to picket the London offices of national mental health organizations, carrying banners that said BUY YOUR MEAT FROM A PSYCHIATRIST and PSYCHIATRISTS MAIM AND KILL. In Edinburgh, Jeff and his Pubs colleagues conducted a late-night raid of what they were told was the local headquarters of the World Federation of Mental Health. "We rushed through the building, putting up lurid posters depicting psychiatrists as leering death's-head skulls, terrorizing innocent citizens," he said. "It seemed like a college prank."

But Hubbard's goals were deadly serious. As early as 1960, Hubbard had been considering how Scientology might take over society. "We are masters of IQ and ability," he wrote in a policy letter titled "The Special Zone Plan." "We have know-how. Any of us could select out a zone of life in which we are interested and then, entering it, bring order and victory to it." A housewife, for example, might take over her local garden club, and then, using Scientology's communications technology, could begin to present various Hubbardian ideas on marriage and child rearing. A junior executive might use the same techniques and "if only as 'an able person' he would rapidly expand a zone of control, to say nothing of his personal standing in the company." Hubbard also advised that the same techniques could be used in a more sophisticated sphere, such as government. "Don't bother to get elected," he instructed. "Get a job on the secretarial staff [of a politician] or [be] the bodyguard, use any talent one has to get a place close in." From that trusted post, he argued, Scientologists could wield tremendous power.

Hubbard also had instructed his troops how to do battle. "If attacked on some vulnerable point by anyone or anything or any organization, always find or manufacture enough threat against them to cause them to sue for peace," he instructed in one policy letter. "Don't ever defend, always attack. Don't ever do nothing. Unexpected attacks in the rear of the enemy's front ranks work best."

Now, in a memo to his wife written on December 2, 1969, Hubbard laid out the purpose of his war: "To take over absolutely the field of mental healing on this planet in all forms." That was not the original purpose of Scientology, he noted. "The original purpose was to clear Earth." But the various battles Scientology had engaged in over the years had led him to the inevitable conclusion that the enemy, psychiatry and its many front groups, would have to be eradicated.

Mary Sue Hubbard received in this missive her appointment as Chief Guardian and Controller of the Church of Scientology, reflecting her leadership of a special organ of the church known as the Guardian's Office. Created by Hubbard in 1966, its job was to enforce church policy and "safeguard Scientology orgs, Scientologists, and Scientology," as Hubbard put it. Guardians held the highest posts on Scientology's board of directors. They ran its legal apparatus, its finance office, and its public relations and social outreach bureaus, which targeted such areas of concern as drug and criminal rehabilitation, education reform, and "eradicating mental health abuse"; the latter was handled by the Citizens Commission on Human Rights, an advocacy group formed by the Guardian's Office in 1969. The Guardian's Office also ran a highly sophisticated intelligence operation that collected and maintained files on Scientology's growing list of enemies. Its guiding principle was attack. Under Mary Sue's leadership (though always, it was understood, with the approval of her husband), the Guardian's Office filed dozens of libel suits against media outlets that had run negative stories about Scientology; gathered intelligence on members of various state, local, and national governments; and launched myriad propaganda campaigns and attacks on psychiatrists and psychiatric organizations.

Hubbard directed his war through written proclamation; his operatives carried it out. On March 26, 1969, for example, the leader issued an order, titled "Zones of Action," instructing his followers to "invade the territory of Smersh" and "purify the mental health field." Several months later, the Guardian's Office, acting on Hubbard's orders, initiated a strategy to take over England's National Association of Mental Health. The plan was fairly simple: Scientologists, seeing that NAMH membership was open to the public, began joining the organization in large numbers — in October 1969, the NAMH, after receiving no more than 10 or 15 membership applications per month, suddenly saw the number jump to 227. By November, there were 302 new members. The organization's annual meeting, in which it elected new leaders, was scheduled for November 12, 1969; suddenly, there came a flurry of nominations from the new members, suggesting eight of their own for positions on the council.

As the British journalist C. H. Rolph pointed out in his 1973 book on the attempted takeover, *Believe What You Like*, the staff of the NAMH became suspicious when they noticed that all of the new membership applications had been mailed from either East Grinstead or a post office on Tottenham Court Road, the location of Scientology's London Org. Notifying the authorities, the group, just two days before the election, uncovered the scheme, which included a plan to elect the Scientologist David Gaiman, a member of the Guardian's Office, to the position of chairman. The Scientologists were subsequently asked to resign.*

Hubbard was careful to portray psychiatry not just as "barbaric," but also as barbarism endorsed by the state. It was the state that stuck with Jeff — Hubbard rarely attacked psychiatry without linking it in one way or another to Western governments or institutions. This wasn't outrageous; it was simply revolutionary, Jeff thought. But the voice of Scientology became increasingly strident. Psychiatrists were rapists, killers. They were fascists — indeed, psychiatrists were behind Hitler's death camps. The nefarious SMERSH, and its agents throughout the Wog World (including, Hubbard believed, *Time* magazine, whose purpose, he once wrote, was to "cause riots and disaffection"), needed to be destroyed. Only they, the Scientologists and L. Ron Hubbard, could do it.

It was within this increasingly combative mentality that Jeff found himself working for Warrant Officer Doreen Casey, who'd come to Pubs, it seemed to him, to reinforce the fact that Hubbard's war was literal. A new code of discipline, known as "lower conditions," was introduced and enforced. Based on Hubbard's Conditions of Existence, it prescribed punishment for any misstep or question that ran counter to the goal of clearing the planet and fighting the enemy, and it could be markedly humiliating.

A staff member who offended by, say, oversleeping was said to be in a condition of Liability, and made to wear blue overalls with a dirty gray rag tied around his arm. Someone who employed an unsuccess-

---

* Rolph also noted that in response, Scientologists filed an injunction against the NAMH, insisting they be reinstated, and Gaiman personally sent letters to members of the organization, and its chairman, urging them to adopt a policy of psychiatric reform. After many months of legal wrangling, the decision to eject the Scientologists from membership in the organization was upheld by a British high court. Gaiman went on to serve as public relations director for the Church of Scientology in Great Britain.

ful sales strategy might be labeled an Enemy and would also have to wear overalls, with a heavy chain linked around her waist. Some of the worst offenders, a staffer who misspent church funds, for instance, were assigned a condition of Treason. As Jeff recalled, "These people were ushered into the elevator and taken to a small space at the bottom of the elevator shaft where they were imprisoned until they had come to their senses." To get out of any of these conditions required a member to evaluate his or her own thoughts, actions, and goals based on those of the greater group.

"Basically, one rises up from the conditions by aligning oneself with group goals," Jeff said. "The inevitable conclusion is that one's friends are the group, one's own intentions and actions have been selfish and petty, and one has to 'get with the program.'" Then, to show renewed dedication, a member would be required to do a series of amends — scrubbing floors with a toothbrush was a common penance — which culminated with the humiliating act of petitioning each member of the group, individually, to be allowed to rejoin them.

To Jeff, this wasn't Scientology, at least not the Scientology he had signed up for. It was hazing, something with which he, and many others, were unfamiliar. And yet he was invested in Scientology, dedicated to its cause. Hubbard, whose rich but gentle voice had the power to lull him into an almost hypnotic state, was his leader.

So, unable to process the new discipline, Jeff dismissed it as an aberration: a punishment inflicted solely by Doreen Casey. In fact Casey represented a definitive new trend within the church. Though its members and low-ranking staffers like Jeff were ex-hippies and other free spirits, the Sea Organization operated on far more authoritarian principles. A failed war hero, Hubbard now commanded his own navy. And its staff, in turn, would soon command Scientology.

CHAPTER 5

Travels with the Commodore

THE SMALL PROPELLER plane sailed over the Straits of Gibraltar like a shuddering tin can. On board, Jeff Hawkins closed his eyes. He practiced a technique Scientologists often used to make things happen: he created an image in his mind, a "postulate," of the plane landing safely on the ground. A few minutes later, it made a bumpy landing in Tangier. Then the plane took off once again, and an hour later finally set down in Casablanca. Jeff breathed a happy sigh. He had no idea where he was going, but at least he was now on solid ground.

It was 1971 and Jeff, who had risen in the ranks of the Publications Org, had been summoned to attend a special training course for would-be Scientology executives aboard Hubbard's flagship, the *Royal Scotsman* — now renamed the *Apollo*. Exactly where the ship was sailing, Jeff didn't know. In Copenhagen, where Pubs had relocated to handle the dissemination of Scientology materials across Europe, Jeff had been given a plane ticket and told to fly to Madrid. There he was met by a Sea Org official working for a cover organization, the Operation and Transport Company, who put him on a plane bound for Casablanca. "When you land, get on a bus for a town called Safi," the official said.

Jeff waited for a bus on the crowded streets of Casablanca and finally found one headed for Safi, a seaport several hours away. After an uncomfortable journey, he arrived and made his way toward the docks. There he saw it: a gleaming white ship.

"Welcome aboard!" David Ziff, Jeff's old boss at Pubs, shouted from the gangplank. Jeff hadn't seen Ziff in three years. Back then he'd looked like a rumpled college professor. Now he was a spit-polished, stand-at-attention officer of the Sea Org, dressed in crisp military whites. "Welcome to Flag!" he said, referring to the ship, a three-story, 3,278-ton behemoth that, in a former life, had served as an Irish cattle ferry and then as a troop transport during World War II. Now it housed offices, dining facilities, cabins, and a Telex room. At the top were two large white stacks, each engraved with the letters LRH in elaborate gold script.

Jeff Hawkins may have hated Sea Org Warrant Officer Doreen Casey, but he had overwhelming respect for the Sea Organization as a whole. They were the "aristocracy of Scientology," as Hubbard described them, who'd signed contracts for one billion years of service, pledging their lives — current and future — to the Cause. Their motto, "We Come Back," signified eternal vigilance.

Originally called the Sea Project, the group was staffed with volunteers; most were recruited at Saint Hill. One of them, Neville Chamberlin, was a young British Scientologist who'd grown up around Hubbard — his mother had been one of earliest clients at Scientology's London Org, where Hubbard spent a great deal of time. Chamberlin had begun working at Saint Hill shortly after finishing high school, in the mid-1960s. One day in November 1966, a notice appeared on the Saint Hill bulletin board, asking for volunteers with naval or seagoing experience. Within the hour, the notice was taken down, and those who had seen it, including Chamberlin, were sworn to secrecy. "We began to notice certain staff members disappearing from their posts," recalled Chamberlin. "It was all very hush-hush." Finally, in April 1967, Chamberlin was recruited to join this "confidential project." He was told he'd need a valid passport and should pack a suitcase. Soon after, he and nineteen other Scientologists left Saint Hill for the northern seaport of Hull, where they set sail aboard a 414-foot trawler, the *Avon River*, for Las Palmas in the Canary Islands. Two other ships, the *Royal Scotsman* and the *Enchanter*, would follow.

Despite the call for volunteers with experience at sea, few in the Sea Project knew much about ships, which may explain why Hubbard hired professional seamen to sail the boat from England to the

Canary Islands. The *Avon River* had a particularly arduous journey—its skipper, Captain John Jones, would later recall the trip as the strangest excursion of his life. The sole navigational guide allowed on board was a sailing manual written by Hubbard, called the "Org Book," which banned the use of advanced navigational technology like radar and insisted the ships plot their course using radio frequencies. "My crew were sixteen men and four women Scientologists who wouldn't know a trawler from a tramcar. But they intended to sail this tub four thousand miles in accordance with the 'Org Book,'" Jones later told a reporter from the London *Sunday Mirror*. "We tried these methods. Getting out of Hull we bumped the dock. Then, using the 'Org Book' navigation system based on radio beams from the BBC and other stations, we [sailed only a few miles down the coast] before the navigator admitted he was lost. I stuck to my watch and sextant, so at least I knew where we were."

Chamberlin and the rest of the *Avon River*'s crew arrived in Las Palmas several weeks later. To conceal the fact that they were Scientologists, Hubbard had incorporated the Hubbard Explorational Company Ltd. before he left England, and now ordered his Sea Project to explain to anyone who asked that they were members of a team of archaeologists. With this as their cover, Chamberlin and the crew of the *Avon River* set to work giving the ship a major overhaul, converting cargo holds into bunks and offices, blasting away rust, and slapping on several coats of fresh white paint.

Hubbard occasionally stopped by, "dressed in his denim jeans and jacket and peaked cap," as Chamberlin recalled, but he spent most of his time in the hills, where he'd rented a hacienda overlooking the sea, known as the Villa Estrella. It was from the patio of the villa that Hubbard recorded "Ron's Journal '67" in September 1967, announcing his breakthrough discovery of the Wall of Fire, something so physically taxing, he told his followers, he'd broken his back, his knee, and his arm over the course of his research. Chamberlin didn't notice that Hubbard had any broken bones, but he did recall that he had a "pharmaceutical store of drugs" at the Villa Estrella. "Most of the stuff was codeine-type pills," he said. "But this wasn't just for migraine, it was a whole wall of stuff."

Chamberlin was one of a number of followers who believed Hubbard did most of his early OT research under the influence of drugs, as well as, perhaps, Jameson Irish whiskey, which Chamberlin recalled he'd drunk liberally at Saint Hill. In one oft-quoted 1967 letter to his wife, Hubbard admitted it: "I'm drinking lots of rum and popping pinks and greys."

In Las Palmas, Hubbard eventually sobered up. "I don't think that Hubbard did any drugs after 1967," said Chamberlin. Indeed, those who joined Hubbard in the late 1960s say they never saw Hubbard intoxicated at all. "When I was with LRH, only twice in eight years on the ship did I see him take a drink of alcohol, and it was whiskey to warm up after a storm," said one of Hubbard's former aides, Karen Gregory.* "I never saw LRH take drugs. And I had access to all of his drawers, his closets. I never saw anything."

By the end of 1967, Hubbard had recruited many more people to join the Sea Organization, as it was now called. They were a motley crew: of the fifty or so volunteers who'd sailed to Las Palmas on either the *Enchanter* or the *Avon River,* and the additional twenty Scientologists who left England several months later on the *Royal Scotsman,* almost no one could sail a ship. But that didn't seem to faze Hubbard. He convinced his devotees that they *had* sailed before — if not in this life, then in a previous one.

One young Scientologist, Hana Eltringham, a South African nurse who'd joined the Sea Organization as a "great adventure," later recalled her terror at being put in command of the *Avon River* in 1968. To remedy this fear, Hubbard put the twenty-two-year-old Eltringham on the E-meter and ordered her to recall the last time she'd been captain of a ship. "My first thought was, this is ridiculous," she said. "Then I started to get vague impressions of a time in some past life when I was a captain of a ship and there was a storm at sea . . . It was very real, not an imaginary thing at all." By the end of her session, she said, she felt calmer. "I went up on deck and felt the fear and terror in my stomach just disappear. I suddenly felt very able, very competent to tackle anything that came along."

While learning the ropes, Hubbard's Sea Organization (like mem-

---

* A pseudonym.

bers of the Pubs Org, as Jeff Hawkins recalled) became test subjects for Hubbard's ethics conditions. The whole series of awards and punishments was instituted, including the wearing of heavy chains or rags to signify a degraded state. Crew members who were punished for a particularly low ethics condition found themselves condemned to a few days, or even weeks, in a dark chain locker in the bowels of the ship.

By the latter part of 1968, the Sea Organization had arrived in Corfu, where Hubbard decided to give his ships heroic new names — the pedestrian-sounding *Avon River, Enchanter,* and *Royal Scotman* were rechristened the *Athena,* the *Diana,* and the *Apollo,* in honor of their Greek hosts. Of the three, the latter ship became Hubbard's flagship, also simply called "Flag." This ship became the setting for a particularly draconian punishment called overboarding, whereby errant Scientologists — be they Sea Org members or visitors who'd come to take a course aboard the *Apollo* and had somehow disappointed the Commodore (as Hubbard now was called) — were thrown into the Mediterranean. Hubbard or one of his immediate subordinates would initiate the ritual with a chant from the captain's deck: *"We commit your sins and errors to the deep and trust you will rise a better thetan."*

"There were degrees of being thrown overboard," says Chamberlin. "There was straight overboard, overboard with a blindfold, or with hands tied; overboard with a blindfold *and* with hands tied, and then blindfolded with both hands and feet tied." He was once thrown overboard, blindfolded, he says, for ordering secondhand tires without approval.

By the time Jeff Hawkins arrived on the *Apollo* in 1971, overboarding was no longer used* — or at least Jeff never saw it. The Sea Organization was now Scientology's senior management organization, and Hubbard's flagship, the only vessel of the original fleet to still be sailing Mediterranean waters,† was its headquarters.

---

* On land, some organizations continued the policy in a distinct way: forcing a staff member to stand against a wall while other Scientologists threw buckets of water at him or her.

† The *Diana* and the *Athena* were now anchored off the coasts of southern Cal-

Hubbard tended to remain out of view. He spent most of his time locked away in the Research Room, his private cabin above the main deck. No one was quite sure what he did in there, though it was assumed that he spent at least part of his time exploring new realms, such as the OT levels, by auditing himself. Once, Jeff almost ran headlong into the Commodore, who was standing at the foot of the stairs, talking with his aides. "H-h-hello, sir!" he stammered. The other Sea Org officers looked at Jeff as if he were a fish that had flopped onto the deck. But Hubbard smiled at him. "Well, hello there!" he boomed, and laughed.

That was the last time Jeff saw Hubbard on the *Apollo*. His days were taken up with the Executive Briefing Course, as the training was called. Much of it involved listening to taped lectures delivered by Hubbard, as well as studying, and in some cases memorizing, all of Hubbard's so-called policy letters, a voluminous collection of memos that outlined his concept of "management technology," a set of business principles Hubbard had come up with to streamline the administration of his organizations. His concept, Jeff learned, was the ne plus ultra of organizational theory, much better than anything one might learn at Harvard Business School. Every facet of Scientology — from sales figures and financial data, to membership, to the number of students being processed in auditing, to the employees themselves — was evaluated statistically. There was one guiding principle of this analysis: an organization or an individual should remain "upstat," or successful, at all times.

While the *Apollo* sailed up and down the Moroccan coast, Jeff sat in a hold of the ship that had been outfitted as a classroom, absorbing Hubbard's theories about promotion. As with all other topics, the Old Man had very specific ideas. "Don't explain. Penetrate," he wrote. Don't waste time describing Scientology to the public. Let the promotional literature do that for you. Even when asked point-blank what Scientology is, never tell anyone. Just encourage them to find out for themselves.

---

ifornia and Denmark, respectively, in close proximity to the Scientology Advanced Organizations in Los Angeles and Copenhagen. In addition, there were four other ships, including a small yacht called the *Neptune*, which one Sea Org recruitment brochure described as being part of the "Pacific flotilla."

But, Hubbard insisted, do it aggressively. He advocated the hard sell, a technique he'd picked up from studying the methods of car salesmen. An important tactic was to avoid giving potential customers an option: *telling* rather than asking them to buy. This method worked, said Hubbard, the old hypnotist, because most people lived "more or less in a hypnotic daze," due to their aberrant state, and thus tended to respond to direct commands. Early Scientology ads embodied this idea, featuring slogans cast in the imperative: "Buy This Book!" or "Get Auditing!"

Jeff wondered about this technique — wouldn't it be better to explain to people what Scientology was all about, rather than simply telling them to do something? But Hubbard was adamant. "We have learned the hard way that an individual from the public must never be asked to DECIDE or CHOOSE," he stated in one policy. Just tell them that Scientology could handle their problems, and then tell them to read a book or take a course. Then the Founder himself could explain Scientology to them.

Jeff spent close to six months on the *Apollo* in 1971, one of forty Scientologists selected for the Executive Briefing Course. At twenty-six, he was regarded as an up-and-comer in the movement, as he had recently taken over the largest division in the Publications Organization, the Production Division, where all of the books, recorded lectures, E-meters, and films were produced. He was successful, and aboard the *Apollo* he was treated like a VIP. He was impressed with the ship and with the highly enthusiastic men and women who ran it with military precision. Midway through his course, Jeff was invited to join them. "So what are your plans for the next billion years?" a Sea Org recruiter asked him.

Jeff looked at the woman. He had recently been doing a new, super-secret series of auditing procedures called the "L-Rundowns," which were meant to correct transgressions from billions of years past. Something about the process was exhilarating. Once you got the idea that you had lived countless lifetimes, had been all kinds of creatures — from space pirates to emperors to soldiers — your current life seemed fairly provincial, a mere blip on the screen. "Well, I guess I don't have any plans," he said.

The recruiter held out a contract. "How would you like to join the Sea Org and clear the planet?"

Jeff signed. And so did every other student on board who, one by one, had been pulled aside and asked the same question. In 1967, when Jeff joined the movement, there were twenty-one official churches of Scientology around the world. Four years later, that number had more than doubled, and smaller Scientology outposts, known as "missions," were springing up as well. Now Jeff and his colleagues were challenged to grow Scientology even further: to "boom" the movement planetwide.

Jeff was an artist, not a businessman. But he asked himself, Why can't I be an executive? The original Sea Org members, he was reminded, had been kids in their twenties, like him, with absolutely no technical experience. And yet they had learned to *sail ships*. It had been their duty to navigate the sea; now it was up to Jeff Hawkins and his colleagues to steer Scientology on land and make sure it kept growing, no matter what obstacles they faced. As Hubbard said, "The supreme test of a thetan is his ability to make things go right."

This cannot-fail posture instilled an intensely competitive attitude within Scientology. Ultimately, it helped feed the impression that Scientologists were highly materialistic. In one 1972 policy letter to his finance officers, Hubbard summed up his philosophy: "MAKE MONEY. MAKE MORE MONEY. MAKE OTHERS PRODUCE AS TO MAKE MONEY."

Despite this edict, Hubbard himself was not particularly concerned with money for himself. "He did not have extravagant needs or habits. His lifestyle was really quite modest," recalled his former steward, Ken Urqhart, who worked for Hubbard until 1974. "Neither he nor Mary Sue had huge wardrobes. Neither had noticeably expensive clothes" — although Hubbard did become attached, in the early 1970s, to "exotic naval uniforms," Urqhart added. Aside from his impressive camera collection and his beloved Jaguar sports car, said Urqhart, he didn't make a show of material possessions — quite in contrast to other gurus of the day, such as Indian mystic Bhagwan Shree Rajneesh, who owned ninety-three Rolls-Royces.

But profits were clearly important to Hubbard. He was, at the end of the day, a businessman, and he viewed success based on his prod-

uct and how well it sold.* To motivate his workers, Hubbard instituted corporate incentive policies. The sales statistics of all the organizations were handed in each Thursday at 2 P.M. and sent up the
chain of command, along with a portion of weekly proceeds. Successful orgs that raised their income statistic were rewarded with more
money, and their staff were given perks such as days off or dinners
out. Those orgs whose statistics fell, on the other hand, received less
funding; their staff members were punished with a harsh review and
"lower conditions" enforced by the ethics division. Individual Scientologists and organizations that brought in new clients or encouraged existing members to sign up for more advanced courses and auditing might also receive direct cash payments.

Most of the money made by Scientology organizations was plowed
back into the organizations themselves. But some was siphoned off
to pay the Founder, who by the 1970s held Swiss bank accounts as
well as secret accounts in Luxembourg and Lichtenstein.† Money was
transferred into these accounts from a Liberian shell corporation, the
Religious Research Foundation, which had been set up specifically to
build the Founder's coffers. In an interview with the *New York Times*,
a former Sea Org executive named Laurel Sullivan claimed that she
and other Scientologists "created fraudulent and retroactive billings"
to make it appear that Hubbard had earned this money legally. "It
was fraud," Sullivan said, "an out-and-out ripping off of funds that
were supposed to go to the church."

The pressure to keep raising more money was intense. Particularly in America, church staff struggled to stay productive, devising
ingenious measures to do so. Throughout the orgs, a take-no-pris-
oners approach resulted in a huge boom in both membership and
income. This had been accomplished by keeping staff up all night,
and in some cases, locking members into rooms until they wrote a
check for their next service. Those who couldn't afford it at the time
were encouraged to "postulate," or imagine, that they'd have the

---

* At one time, said Urqhart, Hubbard instituted a policy, later discarded, of raising Scientology prices by 10 percent every month in order to increase income.
† Hubbard also kept cash on hand — he was known to store $50,000 to
$100,000 in cash in shoeboxes, recalled one former follower, in increments of
$25,000 per box.

money in the near future, and then write what were called "postulate checks." According to this idea, the member would have the money to cover the check by the time it was deposited. In practice this didn't work — checks bounced all the time. But such voodoo accounting did at least temporarily raise the orgs' sales statistics.

To make sure the various organizations ran smoothly, Hubbard insisted that every member of the staff memorize a complex "org board," or management chart, listing every single post within a Scientology organization, from the executive division to the maintenance crew. In the 1970s, Scientologists recited the organizational chart at meetings. "All the staff would stand in front of that organizational board, and as a group they would chant every part of it," said Nancy Many, who worked at the Boston Org and held various senior executive posts at the international management level of Scientology. "There was a time when I could just rattle off that entire organizational board by heart."

Hubbard dubbed this method "Chinese School." In his writings, he described it as a joyous singsong affair that could be applied to anything one needed to learn — a foreign language, a mathematical or scientific theorem, or Hubbard's elaborate, eighty-point tone scale. It was also a form of social conditioning. "Chinese School was an effective means of robotically learning almost anything," said Many. "You knew who was responsible for what, and what everyone was supposed to do, and it was ingrained — you didn't even think about it. From a standard of efficiency, it was felt that the more each individual member of the organization understood about the functions in other departments and divisions, the stronger the group would be. That was the good part of Chinese School," she said. "The bad part, of course, is you got your mind to meld with LRH."

The Sea Org, of which Jeff Hawkins was now a member, enforced Scientology's codes, but only Scientology staff members were subjected to them. The paying public had no sense of the repressive environment at the orgs. They were being sold total freedom, even if the path to get there kept changing. Each year, new rundowns, or auditing procedures, were created to enhance members' understanding of themselves and their eternal nature. Tremendous emphasis was put on past lives — indeed, "Get 'em past life!" was one of L. Ron Hubbard's frequent proclamations, according to some former aides. If a Scientologist *didn't* have a past life experience, the argument went, something was wrong with his or her auditing.

In a similar vein, the original goal of Scientology and Dianetics — becoming Clear — was now only the beginning. Signs had been appearing at Scientology organizations around the world, declaring a new initiative: "Go OT." Operating Thetan was Scientology's new product line — there were eight OT levels, each one promising a higher level of personal power and spiritual enlightenment — and over time it came to define Scientology overall. Hubbard's OT discoveries were the most carefully guarded secret in Scientology, and this was particularly true with regard to its most exclusive product: OT 3.

Jeff Hawkins was primed for years for OT 3 by other Sea Org friends who'd done the level and hinted at something so fantastic, "it would blow my mind beyond anything I'd ever imagined." He waited more than five years to learn the secret. OT 3 wasn't something one simply purchased and then followed unreservedly, like other auditing processes. Scientologists had to be invited to pass through the Wall of Fire. Beforehand, they were put through a security check to verify that they were ready to receive this knowledge. They then signed a waiver promising never to reveal the secrets of OT 3, nor to hold the Church of Scientology responsible for any trauma or damage they might endure during this stage of auditing. Finally, they were given a manila folder, which they placed in a locked briefcase; they were instructed to read it in a private, guarded room. Inside was a single-page document, written in Hubbard's longhand script, which laid out what seemed, to some, to be Hubbard's book of Genesis.

It began like this: "The head of the Galactic Confederation (76 planets around larger stars visible from here — founded 95,000,000 yrs ago, very space opera) solved overpopulation (250 billion or so per planet — 178 billion average) by mass implanting." This leader, a tyrant named Xenu, set out to capture the trillions who opposed him and deposited them in volcanoes on the prison planet of Teegeeack, otherwise known as Earth. He then eradicated them and all life on the planet with hydrogen bombs, leaving only the thetans, or souls, of the captives — which were then brainwashed, or "implanted," to rid them of their original identities. Millions of years later, when life began again on Teegeeack, the traumatized thetans attached themselves to human bodies.

This was the crux of OT 3: that one's problems were not caused merely by the reactive mind, but by aberrant "body thetans," each one reliving the trauma of Xenu's ancient genocide. That trauma had set the course of human history, resulting in the social and political ills — war, famine, genocide, poverty, drugs, nuclear weapons, acts of terror — that had played out on the planet for generations. To truly clear oneself, a Scientologist had to audit each one of these body thetans through specific processes Hubbard had designed: unclustering them, clearing their engrams, and ultimately freeing them of their implants. This, Hubbard believed, would be each individual's salvation, and ultimately, it would be the salvation of mankind.

Jeff Hawkins believed every word of this new gospel. Nancy Many, the Scientology executive from Boston, took it with a grain of salt. But then, she'd also taken the idea that Christ walked on water with a grain of salt, she said. "I was raised as a Catholic to believe that Jesus turned water into wine and raised the dead. I mean, is that plausible? So, to me, the Xenu story was like a Bible story." More than a few Scientologists read the Xenu story as "a bizarre science fiction story," as one former member described it. But fearing they'd be denounced for doubting Hubbard's teachings — to do so would be a thought crime — they held their tongue.

Whatever OT 3 and the subsequent OT levels may have been, one thing is certain: they were perfectly timed. Mikael Rothstein, a professor of religion at the University of Copenhagen who specializes in new religious movements, has commented that a number of "UFO religions" emerged during the 1960s. "Hubbard's noting that human souls — thetans — are spiritual implants that originate in another world is . . . quite parallel to religious assumptions expressed by UFO religions," he said. Most of these groups were "very much concerned with the mind-body complex and the impact of extraterrestrials. Hubbard was not original in that respect."

But where Hubbard was original was in how he packaged this sci-fi mythology — just as he had been with Dianetics. Scientologists did not have to believe in OT 3. They had to do it. Then they would attain secret knowledge and wisdom unavailable to more pedestrian members. And the more they did it, the more enlightened — and invested — they became. This approach was so successful that within months of Hubbard's announcing OT 3, Scientologists from all over the world began beating a path to Valencia, Spain, to do the level aboard Hubbard's ship.

The stated purpose of becoming OT was to "help Ron clear the planet" — which included fighting psychiatry. But most public Scientologists had a far more selfish goal in becoming an Operating Thetan. "OT was talked about as the be all and end all," said Mike Henderson, who joined the Church of Scientology in the early 1970s. "You'd be completely powerful, would have total control of matter, energy, space, and time . . . you would be able to do anything." Though no one, to Henderson's knowledge, had ever achieved this level of consciousness (not even Jesus or Buddha had been OTs, but "just a shade above Clear," according to Hubbard), the fantasy was sold so effectively that "going OT" became for Scientologists the equivalent of reaching nirvana or finding the Holy Grail.*

By the late 1970s, thanks to massive promotion, nearly every Scientologist aspired to the OT levels. The headline of one ad summed up Scientology's new direction: "Clear, OT, and Total Freedom." And because Scientology was now a worldwide spiritual enterprise, it was easy to pursue that goal, provided one could afford it.† In addition to the ships and the Saint Hill Manor, there were now Advanced Scientology churches in cities such as Copenhagen and Los Angeles, enabling more people to go Clear and do the OT levels. To initiate them into the movement, large Scientology churches now functioned in most of the major cities in Europe and the United States; also,

---

* Hubbard himself apparently was of two minds. "If you think for a moment that it's the purpose of Scientology to produce something intensely spectacular like a ghost that can move cigarette paper or mountains, you have definitely gotten the wrong idea," he wrote in the Professional Auditor's Bulletin No. 2 (May 1953). "We are not trying to achieve the certainty of mysticism, necromancy, or, to be blunt, the Indian rope trick. We are trying to make sane, well beings."
† In the 1970s, the price for the complete package of OT levels was roughly $3,000.

dozens of franchised missions, some run by longtime Scientologists, were in operation, and many were far more successful than the formally established orgs.

Hubbard's role took on more and more characteristics of a messiah. As the "Source" of all of Scientology's teachings, Hubbard was decreed the creator of every bit of Scientology scripture, which was considered infallible. To guarantee that his word was followed exactly, an office was set up at every Scientology organization in the world — complete with a desk, chair, telephone, ashtray, and pack of Kools — and run by an official called the "LRH Communicator," whose job was, as Jeff Hawkins put it, "to make sure the org did exactly what Hubbard said to do." The standard tech became a fixed product, sold only at official Scientology organizations around the world.

Hubbard himself, at least the standardized version — maverick, adventurer, seaman; an ascot-wearing hero to whom members were encouraged to write letters, telling of their wins — was heavily marketed. By the early 1970s, a new addition appeared on the list of his personas. Hubbard had written a poem titled *The Hymn of Asia*, in which he presented himself as Metteya, the reincarnation of Buddha. The Scientology magazine *Advance* promoted this new image, presenting drawings of the Founder sporting a reddish topknot and dressed in Indian robes. Jeff Hawkins thought this was great marketing. Kids all over the world had been embracing Eastern philosophy. Why not cast L. Ron Hubbard as a modern Buddha?

If in doubt about a problem or decision, members were told to ask themselves, "What would Ron do?" Scientology events were punctuated by tributes to Ron. His followers, whipped into enthusiasm by passionately recounted success stories, stood to face Hubbard's portrait, clapped in unison, and saluted him with Scientology's official cheer: "Hip, hip hooray!"

As the Great Leader L. Ron Hubbard was becoming ever more iconic, the real L. Ron Hubbard was becoming increasingly isolated, locked into the fantasy world he'd created aboard the *Apollo*. To his followers, he was an aging Peter Pan who entertained them with talk of past lives. He'd been a racecar driver of the alien Marcab civilization. He'd sailed with the Carthaginian fleet and had served as a tax collector during the time of the Roman Empire. He was also convinced that he'd buried treasure during his previous incarnations and led his crew on expeditions to find it, following a course he said he'd charted two thousand years earlier and looking for hidden troves of gold and jewels in the Canary Islands and along the coasts of Italy, Spain, and North Africa.

But in the opinion of the parents of his young converts, particularly those in the United States (where in a pre-Internet era, news of Scientology's travails in England and Australia traveled slowly, if at all), the eccentric and volatile L. Ron Hubbard was no Peter Pan, but rather a Pied Piper, captivating their children with his idealistic vision of a cleared planet and then spiriting them away into a life of utter dedication to Ron and his mission. From the late 1960s onward, the FBI was flooded with mail from worried parents, urging the bureau to investigate the mysterious and, according to some, "sinister" and "subversive" church that seemed to have taken control of their children. ("I am literally petrified at this point that [my son] has been brainwashed by the 'processing' he has undergone in 'Scientology,'" one anguished father wrote to J. Edgar Hoover in the early 1970s. "I have seen my son's personality deteriorate and become progressively worse to the point where now there seems to be no sanity present.")

Aboard the *Apollo*, Hubbard urged his crew to write to their families — "If your parents or friends are the kind who worry about you, BE SURE AND WRITE THEM AN AIRMAIL LETTER regularly," he declared on May 2, 1969. "Otherwise they give us [problems] by asking the government to check up on you to see if you're all right."

But finding the Commodore and his crew would prove difficult. The *Apollo* had been ejected from Greece in 1969, after the Greek government received complaints about Scientologists proselytizing on Corfu. Hubbard and his Sea Org set out to find a new home. In 1971, the Sea Org set up a small land base outside Tangier, using what by now had become their new cover name: the Operation and Transport Corporation. If asked, they were to say that they were employees of an international business-management company.

Just a year later, Hubbard pulled up stakes again, after receiving word that the Church of Scientology in France was about to be indicted for fraud. Fearing he might be extradited from Morocco to Paris to testify, and worried about Morocco's worsening political situation, he decided to skip out of Europe altogether and spent most of the next year in New York City, hiding out from French authorities among its populace of eight million people.

It was Hubbard's first time in the United States since the mid-1960s and, accompanied by a bodyguard and a private nurse, he spent most of the year sequestered in an apartment in Forest Hills, Queens, watching TV. "He really wanted to see what was going on in the culture," said his former nurse, Jim Dinalci. "He wasn't very impressed, but he kept the TV on all the time because he wanted to understand the mindset, the buttons he'd have to push to get people into Scientology."

After ten months in New York, Hubbard flew back to Europe. He returned to the *Apollo,* now anchored off Lisbon, and set sail for the Canary Islands. In Tenerife, in early 1974, Hubbard suffered a motorcycle accident, breaking an arm and several ribs. Convalescing for several months, Hubbard spent most of the time in a red velvet chair, a throne of sorts, with various pillows and foot cushions, screaming at his aides. "The red chair to us became a symbol of the worst a human being can be," one young aide, Doreen Smith, later recalled. "All we wanted to do was chop it up in little pieces and throw it overboard."

In his isolation, Hubbard was coming to resemble the reclusive Howard Hughes. He'd insist that the ship, and any other place he ventured to, be given the white-glove treatment. He also became sensitive to smells and banned the use of perfume, and scented detergents and soaps. He was convinced that far more evil forces surrounded him than he'd ever let on. Now that he'd discovered body thetans, who knew what their intentions might be? He began to scrutinize the people around him, who, by Hubbard's own reckoning, were composed of scores of these individual entities. Did they mean him harm? Who — and what — among his own staff was friend, and who a secret foe?

Hubbard intensified his security checks, asking the Sea Org and even his own family if they had relationships with foreign governments, or if they'd ever had "unkind thoughts" about Hubbard. Those who fell victim to his wrath were subject to a particular disciplinary measure called the Rehabilitation Project Force (RPF). Members on the RPF were not allowed in normal crew areas of the *Apollo* and were banned from communicating with anyone outside their own group, said Glenn Samuels, a former Sea Org member who worked as an auditor aboard the *Apollo*. In 1974, Samuels, then twenty-five, was distracted by marital troubles, earning him a six-month stint on the RPF as punishment. "We lived in a dingy hold in the ship infested with roaches, and slept on pee-stained mattresses formerly designated to be thrown out. Study took place there as well." Members awoke at dawn and were sent off to clean toilets or duct shafts. If anyone made a mistake, he was made to do push-ups and run laps around the ship. Walking was prohibited; members had to run everywhere, and even in baking heat were required to wear black boiler suits.

"It was brutal," said Samuels. "But much worse than the menial labor was the extreme 'untouchable' aspect of the whole thing. You were considered 'evil' . . . especially if you had upset the Commodore, LRH." One boy who had committed such a sin was stowed in a chain locker for several days. "When he asked Hubbard if he could get out, LRH said, 'You got yourself in there; get yourself out,'" Samuels recalled. "Another young girl was so disoriented from working so hard that she fell into the hold, about twenty feet down. She was twelve years old."

As the 1970s wore on, Hubbard banished more people to the RPF. Virtually no one aboard the *Apollo* was safe. "It was scary because at his whim you could end up in the hellhole — for real or imagined errors," said Samuels. "And not just the Flag crew was sent; but executives, plus three of Hubbard's personal stewards, a cook or two, three of the ship's photographers."

When Hubbard finally recovered from his motorcycle accident, the *Apollo*, which had been sailing off the coast of Portugal, set course for Spain. But the Spanish authorities, like the Moroccans, wondered

about the strange, rust-streaked ship whose crew claimed to be affiliated with an international management group. The ship left Spanish
waters after the *Apollo* mistakenly tried to enter one of the country's
largest naval bases. Hubbard directed his captain to set a new course:
ejected from European and North African waters, the *Apollo* would
now cross the Sargasso Sea and ply the Caribbean.

A senior marketing executive at the Publications Org, Jeff Hawkins
now lived in Copenhagen with his wife, Tina, a fellow Sea Org member, and their seven-year-old daughter, Gwennie. In June 1975, he
was summoned back to the *Apollo* to become part of a new international dissemination unit. Thrilling to Jeff, Hubbard, impressed by
his work, had asked for him personally.

Much had changed aboard the *Apollo* in the four years Jeff had
been away. Gone was the spit-polished, crisply military style of its
crew. Now a bohemian atmosphere prevailed. Sea Org members
sported beards, long hair, shorts, T-shirts, and bikini tops. Theater
sets were strewn on the deck, along with musical equipment belonging to a band composed of Sea Org members, who called themselves the Apollo All-Stars. There also seemed to be a harem of young
girls at the center of things. They dressed provocatively in tiny white
shorts, white midriff-baring shirts, and chunky platform shoes.

These girls, the children of Scientologists, as it turned out, were
called the Commodore's Messengers. Many of them had grown up on
the *Apollo,* having been sent by their parents to serve in the Sea Organization. As the youngest people on the ship, they'd been deployed
at first as go-fers, running messages to and from L. Ron Hubbard and
other members of the crew, but over time, Hubbard began to rely on
the Messengers as his personal caretakers, and as his eyes and ears.

DeDe Reisdorf, one of Hubbard's favorite Messengers, was thirteen years old when she arrived on the *Apollo* in 1971, with her sixteen-year-old sister, Gale, and her parents, Charles and Pauline
Reisdorf, longtime Scientologists who'd joined the church in the
1950s. Most of the girls on the ship were also in their early or middle teens — the oldest, DeDe recalled, was perhaps seventeen. Many
were there without their parents (Charles and Pauline Reisdorf departed the *Apollo* in 1973, leaving their children behind). "I hated it

at first," recalled Gale, who served as a lookout on the ship and also as a steward to Mary Sue Hubbard and her daughter Diana. "I cried almost every night for two or three months. But then I just accepted it, and it became my life."

Messengers washed and ironed Hubbard's clothes, laid out his pajamas, prepared his bath, helped him dress, attended him while he ate, and took careful notes on every minute of his day. When Hubbard slept, two Messengers waited outside his door in case he happened to need anything (at which point he'd bellow, "Messenger!"). Messengers lit his cigarettes, and when he walked around on deck, two would accompany him at all times: one person carrying his ever-present pack of Kools, the other holding an ashtray to catch the droppings.

Messengers also parroted Hubbard's words, mimicked his tone of voice, and spoke for him. The job, as Gale explained, was to "pass on what he said, exactly, and then report back how the person responded — exactly." Jeff Hawkins recalled several occasions when, asleep in his bunk, he was awakened in the middle of the night by the small hand of a Messenger laid gently on his chest and the words "The Commodore wants to know . . ." He would then be expected to spring to attention and answer the question, after which, he said, "they'd say 'Thank you' and fade away into the night."

As "emissaries of the Commodore," Messengers were addressed as "sir." Eventually they would be given their own org, the Commodore's Messenger Organization, with their own hierarchy, and ultimately they held almost as much authority as the Commodore himself. Among the privileges allowed the Messengers were the right to enter any room (except Hubbard's) without permission, the right to view anyone's private case folders or personal auditing files (except Hubbard's), and the right to be disciplined or given orders only by a higher-ranking member of the Commodore's Messenger Organization or L. Ron Hubbard himself.

The Messengers, as Hubbard's envoys, were dispatched on assignments that ranged from finding out why a certain engine had failed aboard ship to discovering why a Scientology organization's statistics happened to be down. It was extremely demanding: even at thirteen or fourteen years of age, they were not allowed to return until they had solved the problem. While many referred to their service to the Commodore as fantastic training for jobs they'd hold later in life, they also admitted that they'd ceased being children the moment they entered his employ. The Messengers worked long hours, got time off only occasionally, and received hardly any education. "We had three hours a day of reading, writing, and arithmetic — nothing else," said Karen Gregory, a Messenger who came on board the *Apollo* when she was twelve. Their teachers were other Sea Org members — "no one in particular" — and often a person who lacked training as an educator. The students showed up if they wanted to; rarely would a Messenger be punished for not doing her homework, Gregory said. At the age of sixteen, they were allowed to stop school altogether. If they could type eighty words a minute, they could stop even earlier. "I spent hours trying to type eighty words a minute so I could be done," Gregory said.

Hubbard could be cruel to his Messengers, and his ever-shifting moods caused even the toughest to occasionally burst into tears. "He was a roller coaster," said DeDe Reisdorf. "His expectations were always the max and you wanted to please him and get a 'well done' from him. But sometimes he would be in such a crappy mood, you wanted to run and hide in the closet" — which several of the Messengers did, according to her.

But the mission motivated the Commodore's Messengers just as it had their parents. "Obviously we knew that other kids didn't live this way, but we didn't really think about it one way or another," said Gale. "Yes, the work was hard. I didn't go to school. A GED was not considered necessary or even thought about. But I never considered that I would be doing anything else, as I had given my life to this endeavor." She and everyone she knew "felt like we were doing the most important thing there was, which was to help people become happier and to help mankind get out of the mess we were in as a human race," she said. "It was a pretty noble cause."

It was also the great teen adventure of a lifetime. On his good days, L. Ron Hubbard was "charming and funny," as DeDe said, as well as generous. "He was never inappropriate," said Gale, but he doted on the Messengers: sending them flowers on their birthdays and often buying them expensive gold and sapphire rings or earrings as Christmas presents. He considered himself their surrogate father — many felt he was closer to them than he was to his own four children by Mary Sue, who were also on the *Apollo* — and he also considered himself their tutor. As Reisdorf recalled, he was particularly fond of teaching them tactics for use on covert missions. "Once, in Curaçao, he decided to teach us how to 'lose tail,' as he called it. So he gave us drills to do, like having one or two Messengers follow a third, and then see if she could lose them in town." The girls spent the entire afternoon practicing escaping from one another, she said.

Mary Sue Hubbard, the mother of four teenagers of her own, tried to take responsibility for the girls — sometimes at the behest of their parents — but it wasn't easy. "Some of the Messengers were pretty wild," Reisdorf said. "Our logbook always had notes as to where to find people. Like . . . 'If you're looking for Jill she is currently sleeping with Allen.'"

Eventually, Hubbard instituted a "no sex until marriage" rule (possibly at Mary Sue's insistence, DeDe thought) within the Sea Org. This toned things down a bit, though not much. The girls simply married their beaux. Hubbard did not oppose a teen marriage — indeed, he once informed his Messengers that anyone who got married would receive a promotion — but he insisted on approving the match. "He expected the guys we were dating to ask *him* for permission to marry us," said Reisdorf. Over the years at sea, there were numerous weddings on the ship, attended solely by the crew — even the Messengers' parents would not be allowed to attend, as the ship was always in a "secret" location. In 1974, one of Hubbard's favorite Messengers, Terry Gilham, was married to the Sea Org member Gerry Armstrong in a double wedding ceremony with friends and fellow shipmates Trudy Venter and Pat Broeker. Hubbard gave away the brides.

"It was a bizarre scene," said Jeff Hawkins, who spent the summer and early fall of 1975 aboard the *Apollo*, designing Scientology's new brochures. It was the first time Jeff had been admitted to Hubbard's rarefied circle, and he was both mystified by the goings-on around him and also determined not to let his perplexity show. What Hubbard said in meetings dealt largely with promotion — after his television-watching sojourn in Queens, Hubbard believed that Scientology needed to use more visual imagery to attract the younger generation. To accomplish this, he established a Photo Shoot Org to take pictures for Scientology publications, using the teenage Messengers as models.

For nine months, the crew of the *Apollo* sailed around the Caribbean, stopping at various ports to shoot photographs. As a public relations effort, the Apollo All-Stars held impromptu concerts on the docks. The group maintained its cover as the Operation and Transport Company. But the mysterious ship, its odd Commodore, young crew, and penchant for secrecy still raised suspicion at every island port in which it tried to dock. One Trinidadian newspaper, having heard a rumor that the *Apollo* was connected to the CIA, irresponsibly suggested that in addition to housing spies, the ship was also linked, in some nefarious way, to the gruesome Manson murders in Los Angeles.

Over the summer and into the fall, Jeff began to sense a subtle change in tone aboard the ship. "I could see executives rushing around and hurrying into meetings, but people were silent about what was going on." When Jeff asked, he was told it was confidential. By autumn, the *Apollo* had sailed to the Bahamas. From there, a cadre of Sea Org officers disembarked and flew to the United States.

The nearly decade-long voyage of the Commodore and his Sea Org was at an end. Flag had become too small to accommodate the number of Scientologists clamoring to do the OT levels and other exclusive courses. And the Sea Organization had grown — no longer based aboard ship only, it had offices all over the world. Scientology needed to return to terra firma and establish a land base. They would choose the sleepy Gulf Coast community of Clearwater, Florida, where at the end of 1975, the Scientologists quietly began to arrive.

Hubbard, Mary Sue, and a small retinue settled five miles north, in the town of Dunedin. As with everything about him, the Commodore's location was a closely guarded secret. Once or twice, however, Hubbard ventured out, appearing in Clearwater dressed in a beret and khaki safari uniform. Unaware of what Scientology would ultimately have in store for their town, few locals even recognized him.

CHAPTER 6

Over the Rainbow

O N THE EVENING of May 21, 1976, two covert operatives from the Guardian's Office, Gerald Wolfe and Michael Meisner, both using forged government IDs, entered the U.S. Courthouse in Washington, D.C., intent on breaking into the office of Nathan Dodell, an assistant U.S. attorney who was investigating Scientology. After informing the security guard that they were there to do legal research, the pair signed the log at the front desk, took the elevator to the law library, and then exited through a back door and walked down the hall to Dodell's office, where they entered with a stolen key. The men made copies of six inches of government files pertaining to the investigation, returned the originals, then left.

One week later, on the evening of May 28, Meisner and Wolfe returned to the same courthouse, and using the same tactic, removed and copied even more files from Dodell's office. On June 11, they attempted to do the same thing. But this time the night librarian, having noticed the men previously, had alerted authorities. Two FBI agents approached Meisner and Wolfe as they waited in the law library for a cleaning crew to vacate Dodell's office. Telling the agents that they were doing legal research, the men presented their identification and were allowed to leave. But Wolfe had mistakenly handed the FBI his actual identification card, resulting three weeks later in his arrest for use and possession of a forged government ID. By August, a grand jury investigation into the Wolfe case had turned up Meisner's name and connected him to the Church of Scientology.

At a hidden location in Los Angeles, Meisner, at the urging of Mary Sue Hubbard, among others, agreed to turn himself in. But he was kept waiting for eight months while the Guardian's Office sought to concoct an appropriate cover story. By the spring of 1977, a frustrated Meisner threatened to leave California and return to Washington if the situation was not resolved. Instead, he was put under watch by Scientology guards on orders from his Guardian's Office superiors. In June 1977, a full year after the courthouse incident, Meisner managed to escape his captors and placed a call to the U.S. Attorney's Office in Washington, D.C., which phoned the FBI. He was later taken to Washington, where he agreed to plead guilty to a conspiracy felony. Then he told all to the grand jury. Two weeks later, on the morning of July 8, 1977, FBI agents raided the Church of Scientology's headquarters in Los Angeles and Washington, D.C., and carted away close to fifty thousand incriminating documents. The government had uncovered Operation Snow White.

Hubbard's quiet small-town life in Florida didn't last long. Still paranoid, he'd fled Clearwater in February 1976, leaving the fledgling Flag Land Base behind when the Guardian's Office discovered that a local reporter was closing in on Hubbard's true identity. Mary Sue and a core group of Messengers joined him and found him a new refuge about two hours east of Los Angeles, in the desert community of La Quinta. They called this sprawling $1.3 million ranch their Winter Headquarters, which was immediately given a code name: "W." The large, hacienda-style main house, known as Olives, served as a dormitory, while another house, called Palms, became the dining hall. Hubbard's home, known as Rifle, was a bit removed from the main property, across several open fields. Aside from his Messengers, Hubbard's disciples were not told where he went. The Messengers simply said that he'd gone "over the rainbow."

Hubbard was now sixty-five, with thinning hair, an expanding belly, and a temperament that grew more bellicose by the day. But he had developed a new passion: the Commodore wanted to be a film director. At the ranch, Hubbard would eventually establish the Cine Org to produce instructional films for students learning to be auditors. He strolled the grounds dressed in a cowboy hat and boots, shouting orders at his young assistants, who quickly learned to operate camera and lighting equipment.

The Messengers had by now come to adopt Hubbard's mannerisms to a remarkable degree. "If Hubbard screamed at the Messenger when he issued his order, then the Messenger screamed at the person to whom the message was intended," one young Sea Org member, Sylvana Garritano, later recalled. "Some of the Messengers could duplicate Hubbard's voice almost perfectly." The longtime Scientologists who witnessed his behavior were appalled. "Hubbard had gotten to a point where he didn't have direct interactions or communications with anyone," said Alan Walter, who had watched the rise of the Messengers on board the *Apollo* between 1968 and 1975. "These kids became his voice."

But though the Messengers were closely involved with Hubbard, it was the Guardian's Office that had become the most powerful entity in the Church of Scientology, other than Hubbard himself. Based at Saint Hill, but with eleven hundred staff members all over the world, this extremely sophisticated branch stood outside the official chain of command, as a watchdog.

Scientologists hoping to join the Guardian's Office went through a rigorous screening process, not unlike what an applicant to work for the CIA might endure. A typical background check would include a review of the aspirant's activities and friendships as well as those of his or her parents, grandparents, and other relatives and friends. All of this material was then compiled in secret dossiers, which made the Guardians especially vulnerable. Though any Scientologist, staff or public, could be subject to internal investigation, these dossiers gave the church particularly sensitive material that could be used against any Guardian who stepped out of line; stringent loyalty was the only line of defense. If staff members rebelled, they might be followed, their phone might be tapped, or their family harassed with threatening phone calls. "It freaked you out," says one former official. "You had no idea what they were going to do, except that you knew that you would be hunted down."

This kind of harassment fell under a Scientology policy known as "Fair Game." Originally written by Hubbard in 1965, the "Fair Game Law," as Hubbard called it, instructed Scientologists on how to handle Suppressive Persons, both within and outside the church. "A truly Suppressive Person or Group has no rights of any kind, and actions taken against them are not punishable," Hubbard wrote. He later explained that such enemies "may be deprived of property or injured by any means by any Scientologist without any discipline of the Scientologist. May be tricked, sued or lied to or destroyed."

In 1968 Hubbard, concerned over the increasing international scrutiny of Scientology and its policies, issued an order to cancel Fair Game, stating that the phrase itself "causes bad public relations." But Hubbard did not ban the *practice* of Fair Game, which was implicit in his directions for how to treat journalists, judges, hostile lawyers, government agencies, psychiatrists, and myriad other forces that were, by Hubbard's definition, suppressive to Scientology.

To gather information on various targets, the Guardian's Office maintained a clandestine army of informants, both Scientologists and private investigators, all over the world. They were often "regular people you would never suspect, so they were never detected," recalled one former Guardian, and they often worked for free, performing tasks ranging from attending meetings of anti-Scientology groups to asking neighbors or friends about the person they were investigating. A special intelligence unit with the Guardian's Office Bureau of Information, known as Branch One, was charged with digging up sensitive material pertaining to the IRS, various psychiatric groups, and government agencies such as the FBI and the CIA. "If you wanted to apprentice in clandestine activities, that was the place to do it," recalled the former operative. "These guys were masters at deception."

Branch One was a self-contained cell that very few Scientologists, including other Guardian's Office officials, were aware of. It was headed by a longtime Scientology official named Jane Kember, a "fanatical Scientologist," as the writer Jon Atack described her, who served as the Deputy Guardian for Intelligence, working directly under Mary Sue Hubbard. Under Kember's direction, but with the blessing of Mary Sue (and, it is generally believed, that of L. Ron Hubbard), Branch One used illegal tactics to perpetrate what would later be revealed as the largest program of domestic espionage in U.S. history: Operation Snow White.

The scope of this operation, which was intended to "cleanse" Scientology of its negative image by purging any critical documents about the church or its founder, was enormous. Beginning in 1973, Branch One planted Scientology operatives inside the Internal Revenue Service, the FBI, the U.S. Justice Department, the Better Business Bureau, the American Medical Association, and many other local and federal agencies.* There they stole and copied tens of thousands of document files in hopes of gleaning information that could be used to threaten, or silence, opponents of the church. Guardian's Office operatives launched smear campaigns, bugged government offices, and engaged in breaking and entering. For these illegal acts, members received commendations, Scientology's equivalent of military medals. They penetrated anti-cult organizations and had even made moves to infiltrate U.S. military organizations, such as the Coast Guard. Though experienced agents of the Guardian's Office carried out the more sophisticated operations, many young Scientologists, believing they were protecting their religion from persecution, were pressed into service. "We were religious zealots, militants, in our viewpoint," recalls one former Guardian. "Our perspective was 'This is my religion, and I will do anything to help it survive, even kill for it.'"

"It was all very exciting, and also really confusing if you were a kid," recalled Nancy Many, who while a young staff member at the Boston Organization was trained in subterfuge by the Guardian's Office and then tasked with a number of "covert ops." Most involved getting herself hired for an administrative job at a government agency that collected information about Scientology. For example, Many worked for a year at the Boston Consumer Council, where, she said, her mission was steal and photocopy consumer complaints about the church, give them to her Guardian's Office handlers, and then replace the originals the following day. "I was nineteen or twenty, and though I knew what I was doing, I actually never thought it was illegal," she said. "I thought I was 'stealing Xerox paper,' as it had been explained to me. That's how naive I was."

---

* This practice, in fact, had been going on since 1969. According to Jon Atack (*A Piece of Blue Sky*, p. 253), the Guardian's Office had used "plants" to infiltrate a number of perceived "enemy" organizations, ranging from the Better Business Bureau to the American Medical Association.

Many was also asked to take part in the campaign against the journalist Paulette Cooper, the author of a highly critical book, *The Scandal of Scientology,* published in 1971. It painted a scathing portrait of Scientology's recruitment practices, its auditing processes, and its battles against government oversight in both the United States and abroad, causing the church to sue Cooper for libel; over the course of the decade it filed at least eighteen other lawsuits against her (all of which have been settled). Church operatives tapped her phones, broke into her apartment, posted her number on bathroom walls, and handed out fliers to her neighbors, alleging that she was a prostitute. They also stole Cooper's stationery; then they framed her. Using her stationery, they sent several bomb threats to the New York Church of Scientology in 1973. As a result, Cooper was arrested and indicted on three counts of felony; she faced fifteen years in prison if convicted.

"For months, my anxiety was so terrible I could taste it in my throat," Cooper later wrote. "I could barely write, and my bills, especially legal ones, kept mounting. I couldn't eat. I couldn't sleep. I smoked four packs of cigarettes a day, popped Valium like M&Ms, and drank too much vodka." Finally, in 1975, after Cooper took and passed a sodium amytal test (the "truth serum" test), the government decided not to pursue prosecution.

That same year, Nancy Many, working in the Boston Organization's covert intelligence office, was asked to break into the office of Dr. Stanley Cath, Cooper's psychiatrist during her student years at Brandeis University, in order to steal Cooper's psychiatric files. When Many refused — she clearly understood that breaking and entering was illegal, she said — another Scientologist in her office was tasked with the theft, which he committed with ease. About a week after this incident, Many said, the Boston Organization received a Telex from Hubbard, highly commending the Boston office for a job well done. "And that was the only thing we did," she said. "So anybody who says that LRH did not know what was going on — forget it. There was nothing else we had done to deserve a 'very well done' from Hubbard himself, except breaking and entering."

In 1976, Scientologists planned what they hoped would be their final offensive against Cooper, a five-point scheme known as Operation Freakout, intended to get the writer "incarcerated in a mental institution or jail," as the mission stated. Its central intent was to frame Cooper, who is Jewish, as the perpetrator of bomb threats against two Arab consulates as well as against Henry Kissinger and the president of the United States, Gerald Ford. Once again, Scientologists conspired to acquire a piece of paper with Cooper's fingerprints on it, similar to their tactic in using her stolen stationery. "One night, I was at this reporter's hangout in New York when someone came up to me and handed me a piece of paper, with a joke that wasn't funny," Cooper told me. "I couldn't figure out what that was all about and handed it back to him and continued joking with the other reporters. When I came home, I suddenly realized the guy who'd given me the paper had been wearing gloves indoors. And I just began shaking. The only reason he would have had to approach me like that with that piece of paper was to get my fingerprints again."

Fortunately for Cooper, Operation Freakout was never fully enacted, for by the summer of 1976, the Guardian's Office had become distracted by the apprehension of Meisner and Wolfe in Washington, D.C. By the following summer, the government had seized a huge cache of files from the church's headquarters in Los Angeles and Washington, D.C., which revealed the full extent of Operation Snow White. Hubbard's name was not found on any of the documents. This, his aides knew, did not mean he was not involved: Hubbard had not only ordered Snow White, but he had also quite probably been aware of every aspect of the operation. Mary Sue, the "Controller," had always been careful to brief her husband verbally so as to prevent any documentation of his connection to sensitive Guardian's Office operations. Nonetheless, Hubbard worried that the FBI might come looking for him.

One week after the government raid, Hubbard and three of his Messengers got into his Buick station wagon just after dusk, drove through the gates of "W," and sped off into the desert. At the wheel was Pat Broeker, age twenty-nine, who was at the time one of the few male Messengers at La Quinta. With him was DeDe Reisdorf and a third Messenger, Claire Rousseau. They arrived later the next day in the low-rent city of Sparks, Nevada, on the Truckee River. Here, they decided, was an out-of-the-way spot where no one would think to look for the flamboyant Commodore. Broeker was charged with finding Hubbard a suitable hideout. To make the hunt for lodging look legitimate, he and Rousseau posed as a married couple. Reisdorf was a cousin, and Hubbard an elderly uncle. Four days later, after spending a few nights at a motel under assumed names, the group moved into an anonymous little two-bedroom apartment.

Hubbard spent the next six months in Sparks, highly paranoid (at one point, Reisdorf recalled, Hubbard, believing FBI agents might be lurking in the bushes, wouldn't even walk in front of a window for fear of being spotted). But he quickly settled into a routine. He arose late in the morning, had a snack, and then did a solo auditing session. Then he began writing film scripts. In the evening, Reisdorf and her "uncle," often disguised in a hunter's cap, would walk to the grocery store or to a nearby K-Mart. "Along the way he would make up songs and sing to me. His big joke was to try to push me onto those tiny little carpeted areas in these stores in Nevada that have the slot machines. Then he would say rather loudly, 'Look, she isn't twenty-one!! Arrest her!'" (Reisdorf, who was only nineteen when they left La Quinta, turned twenty in Sparks.) Back at the apartment, the group would watch a late movie. Then Hubbard would turn in for the night. In his bedroom, Reisdorf gave him a backrub while the other two Messengers sat on the floor with Hubbard's ashtray and a glass of water or juice as he told stories or chatted to them about his latest writing project.

Only Broeker maintained contact with the rest of the Church of Scientology. When Hubbard ran out of money, or needed to pass on important orders, Broeker would notify the ranch, then meet another Messenger in Los Angeles. Broeker, who'd joined Scientology in the late 1960s after graduating from high school in Buffalo, New York, was an adventurous young man who had previously worked as a finance courier for L. Ron Hubbard, traveling back and forth from the *Apollo* to Luxembourg with a suitcase of cash. A passionate reader of spy novels, he was nicknamed "007." Having studied up on all things espionage related, he took Hubbard's pronouncements about maintaining security very seriously. To avoid detection en route to and from California, he'd switch planes, dye his hair, change his clothes, or even, recalled Reisdorf, stuff cotton balls in his cheeks to alter his appearance. The La Quinta–based Messengers, in the meantime, would alert Broeker of the meeting place by putting an advertisement in the *Los Angeles Times* classified section, indicating the location: the Los Angeles International Airport, a movie theater, or someplace else.

By the late autumn, Hubbard was getting tired of being on the lam. He yearned to go home, though he realized it would entail significant risk. The church had taken the government to court, arguing that the FBI had violated Scientology's Fourth Amendment rights in the raid. It was a complaint that would go all the way to the Supreme Court, which, early in 1978, would refuse to hear the case. Meanwhile, word from La Quinta was that the FBI had Mary Sue and the ranch under constant surveillance. Hubbard's wife had stood by him and loyally refused to implicate him in any of the misdeeds of the Guardian's Office. Hubbard, nonetheless, worried she might still betray him. In Sparks, he tried to distance himself from her. "LRH would say over and over: 'I didn't know about what the GO was doing, right?'" said DeDe Reisdorf. "Pat and Claire and I would look at each other later and wonder if he was trying to convince us or himself. We all knew that Mary Sue ran pretty much everything by him . . . maybe not the details of each mission, but up until then, he was very much in the loop on the Guardian's Office stuff."

In December, Hubbard caught a cold that turned into pneumonia. Now he felt an even greater urgency to return to the warmth of southern California. But for Hubbard to arrive, Mary Sue and her staff would have to leave. This was upsetting to many of the Messengers, including Gale Reisdorf. "Mary Sue was a wonderful sweet delicate lady, very much of a *lady*," Gale noted. Having helped to raise many of the Messengers from childhood, she tended to treat them as if they were her children. She made sure they ate and slept, and had days off — something that was unheard of with Hubbard, who often demanded that his Messengers stay up all night.

On January 2, 1978, Hubbard returned to La Quinta. Prior to his arrival, Mary Sue Hubbard had left the ranch in her BMW, moving into a house in the Hollywood Hills, secured for her by the church. After nearly twenty-six years of marriage, she would never live with L. Ron Hubbard again.

For now, Hubbard was in the clear, but elaborate plans were made to protect him in La Quinta. "W" was now a secret hideout. Security guards patrolled the property day and night, scouting for FBI agents, journalists, or other curious parties. Scientology books, tapes, and paraphernalia were kept strictly out of view, so as to maintain the cover story that the ranch was simply a movie studio. His young Messengers, staff, and crew were instructed to adopt "civilian" clothes — most wore jeans, T-shirts, and shorts — and when applying for driver's licenses or other identification, doctored their social security numbers and used "safe addresses," which had been arranged for them by the Guardian's Office so as not to reveal their actual residence. They were also designated aliases, which they were instructed to use even among themselves.

"My name was Steve something or other, and I had an ID saying I was from La Jolla," said Sinar Parman, a Los Angeles–based Scientologist who joined the Sea Org in 1977. A chef by training, he was sent to Rifle in June 1978 to work as Hubbard's cook. Though it was only two and a half hours from Los Angeles, getting to La Quinta took almost two days, he recalled. "First, I was dropped off at a motel on Sunset Boulevard. The next day, someone picked me up and took me to a shopping center in the Valley. There, this other guy met me and drove me out to the desert." The driver took the longest and most circuitous way possible, he recalled, so as to shake anyone who might be following them. Finally they arrived at the gates of "W," where a teenage girl dressed in hot pants came out to greet Parman. "Welcome aboard," she said. "The Commodore welcomes you." Then she took him to the kitchen.

Hubbard by now had grown tremendously finicky and at times believed his cooks were trying to poison him. Suffering from ulcers and high blood pressure, among other ailments, he ate only bland food, banning onions, leeks, and garlic from his table. Some cooks prepared several meals at once for "The Boss." Frequently, he rejected a dish immediately upon tasting it. "Things changed," said Parman, who ultimately learned to adopt a Zen-like attitude in the face of Hubbard's many eccentricities. "One day he'd love what you made him, the next day he'd throw it across the room."

A team of Messengers washed Hubbard's clothes, always by hand, using filtered water and then rinsing the clothes in buckets, sometimes more than a dozen times. "We'd go through this about ten times for every single piece of clothing," said Maureen Bolstad, a Messenger who was charged with cleaning Hubbard's shirts. "Then we'd have to hang them up and hand-press them and dry them with fans. And then the clothes would get sniffed to make sure they didn't smell of anything."

Bolstad, who'd joined Scientology in 1979 as a thirteen-year-old, had been recruited for the Sea Organization with the promise of help in finishing her high school education and paying for college. Instead, she'd been given a Scientology education, which consisted solely of learning how to serve L. Ron Hubbard. "I learned how to hold an ashtray and follow him around. Then I learned how to hold the ashtray and also hold a tape recorder at the same time. " Messengers recorded his every word and then transcribed it later. "I was trained to carry his bag filled with sunscreen and stuff, to look after his every need."

In addition to La Quinta, the church maintained a summer headquarters for Hubbard, known as "S." This was located on the site of a dilapidated resort in Gilman Hot Springs, an outpost thirty-six miles from Palm Springs. Purchased for $2.7 million in cash, the Gilman complex was set on over five hundred acres and featured a faded golf course, a worn motel, and several other ramshackle buildings. No one in the local San Jacinto area knew that L. Ron Hubbard was anywhere in the vicinity, nor that Scientologists had bought the resort. The new owners referred to themselves, variously, as the Scottish Highland Quietude Club, and the Western States Scientific Communications Association. Richard Hoag, a Los Angeles attorney affiliated with the church, claimed to have purchased the resort for a condominium project.

An even more secret hideout, known only as "X," was also purchased in 1978. In March of that year, the La Quinta property was permanently closed down, and Hubbard moved with his staff to "X," a faceless apartment complex fourteen miles from "S," in the tiny town of Hemet. A sleepy agricultural town once surrounded by orange groves but now vanishing under layers of dust, Hemet was as far off the beaten track as Sparks, Nevada. The apartment complex couldn't have been more pedestrian: it was located behind an acupuncture clinic and next to a Pick 'n Save supermarket.

The Commodore's Messengers shuttled back and forth between "X" and "S" in weekly shifts. They typically took a circuitous route and traveled in the middle of the night. "It was real CIA stuff," said Parman, then twenty-five, who found it thrilling: switching locations every week; driving, four people to a car, through the desert to arrive at a secret hideaway known only by an initial; using aliases; and relaying information covertly, by pay phone or by meeting in person to exchange information in supermarkets — a practice known as "cookie drops."

Some Messengers dreaded their weeks in Hemet because Hubbard was often in a black mood. The female Messengers suspected he missed his wife. "Mary Sue was always a calming influence on LRH and when she was around him, he was not as moody," recalled Messenger Julie Holloway.* "However, with her gone to L.A. he had major mood changes." He railed at his staff, exploding into tirades and then sinking into a sulky silence.

Hoping to one day live at "S," Hubbard ordered that a new house be built for him at the Gilman resort, perched on high. He specified that it be "dust-free, defensible," and surrounded by high walls with "openings for gun emplacements," according to one account. On most days, Hubbard went to Gilman to work on his movies and to oversee progress at the house, a rambling Tudor-style home named Bonnie View, with a sweeping view of the San Jacinto Valley.

In Los Angeles, Mary Sue Hubbard was trying to stay out of jail. On August 15, 1978, she and ten other Scientologists, including Jane Kember, who remained in England, had been indicted by a federal

_____
* A pseudonym.

grand jury on twenty-eight counts of theft, burglary, conspiracy, and obstruction of justice for their roles in Operation Snow White. If convicted, Mary Sue faced a fine of $40,000 and up to 175 years in prison. She and eight other defendants pleaded not guilty to the charges, and for the next year, a score of Scientology lawyers fought tirelessly to prevent the case from coming to trial. Finally, on October 8, 1979, Mary Sue Hubbard and six other Guardian's Office executives reached an agreement with the government to plead guilty to one count of conspiracy,* signing their names to a 282-page document detailing their various misdeeds, in lieu of a trial. Federal prosecutors petitioned the court, insisting the defendants be shown no mercy. "The crime committed by these defendants is of a breadth and scope previously unheard of," it stated. "No building, office, desk, or file was safe from their snooping and prying. No individual or organization was free from their despicable conspiratorial minds."

On October 26, 1979, the defendants, minus Kember and another church official, who were still fighting extradition,† stood before U.S. District Judge Charles R. Richey and formally pleaded guilty to conspiracy in Operation Snow White. Mary Sue Hubbard and three other Guardian's Office executives each received a five-year prison sentence and a $10,000 fine. The others received lesser sentences and fines, but all nine appealed on the grounds that the evidence against them had been acquired illegally. In April 1982, Mary Sue Hubbard lost her final appeal, and in January 1983, she was sent to a federal prison in Lexington, Kentucky. By then suffering from health problems, she served one year and was released. L. Ron Hubbard was named an "unindicted co-conspirator" in Operation Snow White. None of the seized Guardian's Office files linked him directly to the crimes, and the federal prosecutors failed to make a persuasive case for his involvement.

Though Hubbard remained free, he grew increasingly worried

---

* Two more Scientology officials also pleaded guilty, one to a similar charge, and a second to a misdemeanor.
† In November 1980, Kember and her deputy, Mo Budlong, lost their extradition battle and were convicted on nine counts of aiding and abetting the burglary of government offices. In December 1980, they were sentenced to two to six years in prison.

that he might be subpoenaed, or harassed by the FBI, the IRS, or attorneys for several disaffected Scientologists who were suing him for fraud. Since the late 1970s, several top aides had left Scientology, including Hubbard's longtime nurse, Kima Douglass. The Operation Snow White documents had been unsealed, meaning that the scope of Scientology's covert operations was now open to scrutiny by the press. Not even his top-secret new home seemed secure enough. On Valentine's Day, 1980, Hubbard fled Hemet with his trusted aide Pat Broeker and Broeker's wife, Annie. For the next six years, the press, federal investigators, and even his own children searched for him. He was never seen publicly again.

CHAPTER 7

DM

URING HIS FINAL years in exile, L. Ron Hubbard's only conduit of communication with the world of Scientology, aside from Pat and Annie Broeker, was another young Messenger named David Miscavige. Over time, Miscavige would become Broeker's most crucial aide and, as Hubbard would later call him, "a trusted associate, and a good friend to me." It was odd, many longtime Sea Org members would note: Hubbard had neither known Miscavige particularly well, nor did he ever see him personally while he was in hiding. But Miscavige, it would become eminently clear, was a uniquely determined young man. In due course, he would make himself Hubbard's inheritor through sheer force of will.

Miscavige was born in Philadelphia in 1960 and grew up in a modest suburban home in Willingboro, New Jersey. His parents, Ronald Sr. and Loretta, a professional trumpet player and a nurse, were Catholics who raised their four children — Ronnie Jr., the oldest, followed by the twins David and Denise, and the younger sister, Laurie — to believe in Jesus and attend Mass at least somewhat regularly. Despite his Catholic faith, Ronald Sr. was drawn to Scientology, which he'd heard about from a business contact, and began to read some of Hubbard's books, hoping it might help his younger son. A pint-sized, headstrong little boy, David was sickly, suffering from severe asthma and allergies. Though he yearned to play football — his father once reportedly filled his son's pockets with metal plates so that David would meet the sixty-pound weight requirement for a Pop Warner team — his health problems often kept him on the sidelines. When David was around eight or nine, he was wheezing through an asthma attack when his father, rather than take him to a doctor, took him to a Scientologist for auditing. As the Miscavige father and son later told the story, the attack went away after a single forty-five-minute session.

"It was the reactive mind," David Miscavige later explained during an interview with the *St. Petersburg Times.* "From that moment I knew, this is it," he said. "That is the point in my life where I said . . . 'I have the answer.'"

Ronald Sr. was also convinced that Scientology offered answers, and before long he'd enrolled his entire family in Scientology courses at the local mission in Cherry Hill, New Jersey. In 1971, he took his children out of school and moved the family to England, where they began advanced training at Scientology's world headquarters at Saint Hill. For the sheltered boy from the Philadelphia suburbs, moving to Sussex was a drastic change and would mark the end of his childhood.

There were many kids at Saint Hill in the early 1970s, many of them the children of Scientologists. Hubbard, who encouraged parents to look at their children as men and women whose bodies simply hadn't attained full growth — "big thetans in little bodies," as some parents said — had never established rules about when a child could or couldn't be audited, go to work, or audit others. A precocious overachiever, David Miscavige learned to audit when he was twelve. By thirteen, he was counseling people two or three times his age and, some recalled, giving security checks to senior Scientology executives. There was nothing for kids to do at Saint Hill other than work or study, but even so, David seemed unusually driven, recalled Neville Chamberlin, the onetime crewman on Hubbard's *Apollo.* Chamberlin, who left Scientology in 1982 and later became an outspoken critic, had returned to England in 1979, and he met the Miscaviges soon after they arrived at Saint Hill.

They struck him as a dysfunctional family, particularly Ronald Sr., a notorious flirt who was reputed to have a violent streak. But David, still severely asthmatic, "was completely motivated to make something of himself," said Chamberlin. "I remember seeing him outside the auditing rooms one day, leaning, back against the wall, just desperately trying to catch his breath. He was on the way to give someone a session, and he was just standing there, holding his client's folder, trying to get it together before he went into the room. He was thirteen or fourteen."

By the time he was fifteen, David Miscavige had returned to the United States with his family. Now a sophomore in high school, he was, like many children raised in Scientology, enamored with the idea of helping L. Ron Hubbard clear the planet. It was a goal that didn't necessarily jibe with his new life as a tenth-grader, and Miscavige would later tell friends in Scientology that he hated school and couldn't wait to leave. He was shocked by the level of drug use among his peers and was quite sure of what he wanted to do with his life. Anything he still needed to learn, he reasoned, he could discover by working for the Church of Scientology as a member of the Sea Organization.

On his sixteenth birthday, April 30, 1976, Miscavige dropped out of high school, and with his parents' blessing signed a billion-year Sea Org contract. Shortly afterward, he was dispatched to Scientology's new land base in Clearwater, Florida, where he was trained as a Commodore's Messenger. Ten months later, he went to join Hubbard and his group in La Quinta.

Miscavige was one of the many young disciples who formed a protective shield around Hubbard at his desert hideaway, "W." Assigned first as a "traffic Messenger," managing the flow of communications to and from Hubbard, he showed an interest in cinematography and ultimately became a member of the camera crew, working with the Commodore on his technical films. Though he was barely seventeen, Miscavige struck numerous people as remarkably self-assured; he seemed to believe that he could do anything, including challenge the word of the Founder of Scientology himself. One day, the Scientologist Dan Koon recalled, while Hubbard was directing a film, Miscavige, on the camera, missed a shot. Hubbard furiously ordered the teenager to step aside and give the camera to someone else. To the surprise of everyone on the crew, Miscavige refused. "He looked right at LRH and said, 'No, sir. This is my job and I'm going to do it,'" said Koon. "They had this big confrontation right on the set, and LRH finally said, 'Okay, do it, but you better do it right.' And he did. That was the only time I'd seen someone stand up to LRH."

Miscavige, however, didn't work with Hubbard often. He was a junior Messenger whose access to Hubbard was limited. Unlike senior Messengers like Julie Holloway, Pat Broeker, or the Reisdorf sisters, Miscavige was never given the privilege of waiting on the Founder personally, and only occasionally stood watch outside his door. He seemed to hate the weekly watches, said Julie Holloway, and when Hubbard moved from La Quinta to "X," his Hemet apartment, Miscavige avoided going there almost entirely. "Not many Messengers enjoyed going to 'X,'" she admitted. "LRH was in a very bad mood a lot of the time." Hubbard was at his most volatile during the period when David Miscavige knew him. "Unfortunately, David got the worst of LRH," said Holloway. "But I would never say that he knew how Hubbard operated or managed the organizations. I think his cumulative history with LRH didn't even add up to a year."

And yet Miscavige, despite having only a tenth-grade education, was a quick study with a shrewd understanding of power and where it lay. Miscavige was extremely deferential to Pat Broeker, for example, recalled Sinar Parman; of all the male Messengers, Broeker was closest to Hubbard. Miscavige also became friendly with Gale Reisdorf, who served as a member of a senior body of Messengers known as the Watchdog Committee, which oversaw the church. In 1979, the Watchdog Committee and the Commodore's Messengers took full control of Scientology's international management, shifting the power base from Saint Hill Manor to Los Angeles. Miscavige, by then nineteen, was given a new task: in addition to his camera duties, he was asked to run missions to other organizations.

The assignments varied: sometimes he'd investigate reports that Scientology executives were not doing their jobs; at other times, he might simply go to pick up some camera equipment. He enthusiastically threw himself into his duties, one of which entailed recruiting Sea Org members to renovate the church's new base, a former hospital complex on Sunset Boulevard known as the Cedars of Lebanon complex. Through these efforts, DM, as Miscavige was called, soon become a rising star in the Commodore's Messenger Organization.

There were seven important things to understand about power, L. Ron Hubbard wrote in a 1967 policy letter entitled "The Responsibilities of Leaders." The most crucial point was to "push power in the direction of anyone on whose power you depend." It could take the form of sending the leader more money, handling the leader's tedious business concerns, offering a "snarling defense" of the leader to his critics, "or even," as Hubbard said, "the dull thud of one of his enemies in the dark or the glorious blaze of the whole enemy camp as a birthday surprise." But the bottom line was that if one succeeded, he too would become powerful. "Don't ever feel weaker because you work for somebody stronger," said the Founder.

It was a bit of advice David Miscavige would take very much to heart.

At the time of Hubbard's disappearance, in 1980, a key priority for the Church of Scientology was protecting their Founder from legal action. The Operation Snow White documents had given the public its first glimpse into the secretive world of Scientology and the mindset of its followers. Now a New York grand jury was investigating the church's longtime harassment of the writer Paulette Cooper and the role L. Ron Hubbard may have played in it. The IRS, meanwhile, had begun a criminal investigation of Hubbard; the government suspected he was still in charge of the church and profiting from it handsomely, wherever he was.

In Los Angeles, David Miscavige, who'd impressed his superiors with his gung-ho attitude and problem-solving skills, became part of a special team within the Commodore's Messenger Organization called the "All Clear Unit." Its mission was to meet with church attorneys to find ways to get around the myriad legal issues that had driven Hubbard into exile. One way to do that, they decided, was to design a new corporate architecture for the church, an undertaking that, with Hubbard's blessing, became known within Scientology as the "Corporate Sort-out." The overall idea, said Larry Brennan, then the senior executive in the Scientology legal department who oversaw the project, was to create a legally defensible structure that would give Hubbard and the Commodore's Messenger Organization full legal control over Scientology while at the same time "insulat[ing] both Hubbard and the CMO from any legal liability for running the organizations of Scientology by lying about the level of control they really had." This reorganization seemed like fraud, said Brennan, but the structure was so complex that deciphering the fraud was almost impossible.

The new structure would also establish a new hierarchy, giving unprecedented power to the Commodore's Messengers, who would soon maneuver their way into control of every facet of the organized church. "The new corporate structure made top management think they could do just about anything without legal worry," said Brennan. "In other words, Miscavige could now do just about anything he wanted and there was no one to stop him, unless Hubbard did."

Brennan, who'd served as the legal director of the Guardian's Office, became the overseer of Scientology's legal bureau once the Commodore's Messengers took control of the church. He met Miscavige in 1981. Now the self-appointed head of the All Clear Unit, Miscavige was twenty-one years old and, a highly aggressive and frequently belligerent young man, had come into his own. Though he could be supportive of those upon whose approval he depended, Miscavige was mistrustful of many others, with an "almost pathological" certainty, according to one former colleague, that he, of all the Messengers, was right. To some he seemed like a reflection of L. Ron Hubbard on his very worst days, cursing and barking orders at other Sea Org members, including some staffers much older than he, or screaming at those who disagreed with him. He chewed tobacco and in meetings would frequently make a show of spitting the juice into a cup. Brennan was appalled. "As I saw him, DM was like a highly impressionable spoiled child."

DM idolized L. Ron Hubbard, the only boss he'd ever known; but unlike many seasoned Sea Org members who knew the Founder's propensity for changing his mind, Miscavige also took everything that Hubbard said literally. And what Hubbard was saying from his secret location was, by his second year in hiding, increasingly extreme. The Founder had returned to his original love, writing fiction, in seclusion, and was at work on the book that would become his opus: *Battlefield Earth.** But he was also convinced that Suppressives

---

* *Battlefield Earth,* published in October 1982, became an instant bestseller, reportedly due to a dedicated effort by Scientologists to buy out the books, thus artificially inflating sales (*San Diego Union-Tribune,* April 15, 1990; *Los Angeles Times,* June 28, 1990).

had infiltrated the movement, particularly the Guardian's Office, and in missives signed only with an asterisk (in an effort to distance himself from Scientology management, Hubbard had adopted the asterisk as his "signature" on church documents) issued directives for his aides to spit on other staff members, strike those who seemed to oppose his wishes, or even send people to jail. While it would have been an act of sacrilege to disobey L. Ron Hubbard, "some of us would still not do the most awful things Hubbard talked about as they violated our sense of right and wrong just too much," said Brennan. "DM, on the other hand, would blindly, and violently, follow such orders."

Among the first of Hubbard's orders had been to clean up the Guardian's Office, which the Founder had determined was infested with "criminals." Miscavige and his All Clear Unit attacked this task with gusto, soon altogether dismantling the Guardian's Office — whose power had exceeded the Messengers' own. The first maneuver in this offensive was to remove the person Hubbard now saw as wholly responsible for the debacle: his wife, Mary Sue. Out on bail and appealing her conviction, she still held the lifetime position of Controller.

In May 1981, Miscavige visited Mary Sue in her Los Angeles office and told her that, as a convicted criminal, she could no longer be officially connected to the Church of Scientology. It would be "for the good of the church," as well as for the good of her husband, if she resigned, he said. Furious, Mary Sue refused and, in one often-told account, became so enraged that she threw an ashtray at Miscavige's head. But the twenty-one-year-old was intractable.

Numerous Scientology officials, particularly those loyal to David Miscavige, applauded his initiative. It was felt that Mary Sue Hubbard had blackened the name of the church; now it was only right that she be ostracized. But some members of the Sea Organization, particularly those who'd known the Hubbards aboard the *Apollo*, believed that Mary Sue had been treated too harshly. Among them was DeDe Reisdorf, by then married and known as DeDe Voegeding.

Voegeding was the Commanding Officer of the Commodore's Messenger Organization. L. Ron Hubbard had appointed her to this post in the spring of 1981, and it was a daunting responsibility for the twenty-three-year-old. Her job involved not only parroting Hubbard's demands but also making executive decisions and giving orders to longtime Sea Org officials. It also required Voegeding to serve as the main communication line between the Church of Scientology at large and L. Ron Hubbard, via Pat Broeker.

Broeker had devised a strategy by which an aide needing to meet with him went to a remote pay phone to call him, let it ring twice, and then hang up, signaling for Broeker to call back. Then the aide drove to an appointed spot between Gilman Hot Springs and Los Angeles. Because these meetings generally took place at night, Voegeding wanted a male Messenger to accompany her. David Miscavige often volunteered.

Broeker was always happy to see Miscavige, who'd been his roommate for a period in La Quinta. "I think Pat was dying for someone to talk to," said Voegeding. "He was holed up with LRH." Unfortunately, Voegeding never had the time for small talk — running the church was more than a full-time job. But Miscavige and Broeker would spend an hour or two joking and smoking cigarettes. After a while, they'd developed such a rapport that they would walk off together to speak privately, leaving Voegeding waiting by the car.

Not long after Miscavige began accompanying her to these meetings, in August 1981, L. Ron Hubbard abruptly removed DeDe Voegeding from her post as head of the Commodore's Messenger Organization. The reason, she was told, was that Hubbard had found out that she'd ordered Scientology's prices reduced without his permission, a grave sin; even worse, she was accused of breaching security by hinting at Hubbard's true whereabouts to the British writer Omar Garrison, who'd been commissioned by the church to write a biography of the Founder.

Hubbard had signed the order for her removal. Nonetheless, Voegeding felt sure that the Founder had been fed false information. "I had been with him enough times in hiding, so knew how it worked, and how it worked was that all communication to him was vetted," she said. "I'd never told anywhere where he was — I had no idea where he was. And the other things I was 'guilty' of were basic management decisions I would do again, like lowering prices to bring in more customers. I still feel that LRH would have agreed, if

I'd been given the chance to explain. But there was no opportunity for an explanation."

Within weeks, more Scientology officials had been removed, including Hubbard's longtime public relations adviser, Laurel Sullivan, who was accused of "spying" on the Commodore's Messenger Organization for the Guardian's Office. Both Sullivan and Voegeding had been close to Mary Sue, whom Miscavige and Pat Broeker had mutually declared a "criminal."

Now, with the Controller out of the way and some of her key supporters sidelined, David Miscavige and his allies in the All Clear Unit embarked on a brutal purge of most the Guardian's Office, stripping hundreds of people of their positions with no warning. Also removed were many other Sea Org executives who'd had nothing to do with intelligence activities but who, like Sullivan and Voegeding, had simply been close to L. Ron Hubbard or his wife. Over the next year, Miscavige, on orders from Hubbard, accused hundreds of Scientology officials of crimes ranging from stealing church funds, to disobeying Hubbard's instructions, to being on the payroll of "external influences" such as the CIA.

The "crims," as Miscavige and his associates called these officials, were summoned to Gilman Hot Springs, where the Messengers, led by Miscavige, ordered them to scrub floors, eat table scraps out of buckets, and sleep on the floor, watched over by armed guards. They were also made to endure hours of interrogation, sometimes performed by up to six Messengers at once. These were known as "gang bang" security checks.

Here is how Homer Schomer, once a chief financial officer for the Church of Scientology, described one of several gang-bang security checks he was given in the early 1980s: "It lasted from about ten o'clock in the evening to eight o'clock in the morning . . . During this time I was just bombarded with these questions asking who I was working for. Was I working for the CIA? Was I a plant? Was I working for the FBI? Where was all the money I stole? Where were all the jewels I stole?"

Those officials who didn't answer the Messengers' questions were slapped, shoved, punched, and sometimes locked in a room for hours.

Often, the person being grilled would answer, the reply would be belittled, and the abuse would continue. "It was horrible what went on," recalled Larry Brennan, who was asked to participate in a gang-bang "sec check" and refused. "They wanted me to scream at some poor guy they said owed money to Hubbard. I said no and walked out. I always refused to do the abuses, but I saw it happen. They knew that if they screamed in your face loud enough and intimidated you enough, you would come out with some crime. I'd never heard of anything like that [in Scientology] before."

Many Scientology executives, broken by this treatment, admitted to a wide range of criminal acts, if only to make the interrogation stop. A good number were then assigned to do menial labor while awaiting judgment before a Scientology tribunal called a Committee of Evidence, which was often assembled by Miscavige. A Commodore's Messenger named Mark Fisher, then the head of Miscavige's household unit and his administrative chief, was chosen as a juror on several of these tribunals, in which the E-meter, now serving as a true "lie detector," proved to be a remarkably efficient, if biased, judge. Almost everyone who went in front of one of these tribunals, said Fisher, was found guilty and denounced as a traitor.

"It was completely surreal and just appalling," said Fisher, a heavyset, good-tempered man. Just a single negative thought — about L. Ron Hubbard, David Miscavige, or anything else that might be viewed as critical of Scientology — would be discovered by the E-meter and "boom, you were denounced and out of there." (Fisher, who'd joined the Sea Org in Clearwater the same year as Miscavige, was loyal to the Sea Org mission and remained in Scientology, working for Miscavige, for nine more years.)

In the end, the officials departed Gilman, having had what Miscavige described as a "severe reality adjustment," affirming their obedience, and agreeing to become church janitors or groundskeepers, or, far more frequently, to simply leave the Church of Scientology altogether. Upon doing so, many signed confidentiality agreements pledging they would never sue or speak publicly about what had happened to them.

• • •

Gale Reisdorf, who had also married and was going by her married name, Gale Irwin, had been given her sister's job as Commanding Officer of the Commodore's Messenger Organization.* Long before the major purging had even begun, Irwin had become concerned about David Miscavige. He seemed to take pleasure in others' misery, an irony, given that Miscavige was often miserable himself, still suffering from chronic asthma. Irwin would recall one instance in the summer of 1980 when Miscavige had a severe asthma attack and was rushed to the emergency room. He survived the attack and upon returning from the hospital said he'd had an amazing revelation. "Power," he said, "is assumed." Irwin had no idea what he meant.

But toward the end of 1981, Irwin began to think more about that statement as she considered how far Miscavige had risen in such a short time. He had taken over the All Clear Unit, sidelined Mary Sue and several others, and witnessed the removal of her sister as his boss — or had he simply commandeered her removal himself? Irwin wasn't sure. In the same letter from Hubbard that demoted DeDe and promoted Gale, Miscavige had also been given a new job: Special Project Ops, a post that stood outside the standard chain of command, making Miscavige answerable to no one other than Broeker and Hubbard.

Irwin had no idea if Hubbard had created this post for Miscavige or if he and Broeker had come up with it themselves. But Miscavige's friendship with Broeker bothered her. Miscavige, not Irwin, seemed to have the main line of communication to L. Ron Hubbard. And Irwin realized that this might be her fault: she had once or twice allowed Miscavige to meet with Broeker alone when she'd been too busy to accompany him.

As the messages coming from L. Ron Hubbard became increasingly paranoid, Irwin and others started to wonder exactly what Hubbard was being told. Scientology was now under scrutiny by both the FBI and the Internal Revenue Service. This would have elevated

---

* Irwin never knew why she had been promoted while her sister had been purged, other than that she had been next in line for the position. "I can't say why DM thought I would be able to be manipulated, or if he even had such a plan," she said. "In any case, it didn't last long."

the Founder's already profound suspiciousness to astronomical levels. In response, Hubbard began sending increasingly strident missives railing against a wide number of phantom enemies — "external influences" — whom he blamed for keeping him in exile. "You could feel his fear coming at you left, right, and center," said Julie Holloway. "He was mad about everything. No matter what we sent him, we'd get nothing good back, it was all this 'external influences' stuff." At one point, Hubbard's paranoia appeared to be at such a high point that Pat Broeker went so far as to buy armored cars for the Founder. "I mean, why?" said Holloway. "I thought that was ridiculous — who was going to be shooting at him?"

Before long, long-serving Messengers like Holloway came to see that Hubbard had stopped trusting the aides who'd served him faithfully for years. Instead, he seemed to trust David Miscavige and his group, who portrayed themselves as Hubbard's representatives, anointed to not only carry out his wishes but also rescue Scientology from all but certain doom.

Alarmed by this unregulated hubris, David Mayo, L. Ron Hubbard's personal auditor, pulled Miscavige aside in December 1981 and ordered him to get a security check. Miscavige balked. Outraged by his insubordination, Gale Irwin confronted Miscavige. His response, she recalled, was to physically tackle her, sending her flying through an open door.

Now genuinely afraid of Miscavige, Irwin slipped off the base at Gilman Hot Springs to call Pat Broeker, using his special callback system. Waiting at a gas-station pay phone for Broeker to return her call, Irwin suddenly saw Miscavige roll up with a number of his aides in a black van. As she'd later recall, he got out, walked to the back of the van, took out a tire iron, and as she watched, proceeded to smash the pay phone so it wouldn't work. Then he grabbed a terrified Irwin, ordered her into the van, and accused her of mutiny. Upon her arrival back at Gilman Hot Springs, she was stripped of her position as the head of the Commodore's Messenger Organization by Miscavige, and soon replaced with one of his own protégés, a nineteen-year-old Messenger named Marc Yeager.

Soon after, Irwin was sent to Scientology's base in Clearwater, Florida, along with her brother and sister and their spouses, where the entire family was made to do heavy physical labor. But that wasn't punishment enough. She and her sister, DeDe, were then sent to the sprawling new Scientology compound on Sunset Boulevard. There, they were put in a shower room and told they would live there, under twenty-four-hour guard. This was not the RPF. "We were beneath the RPF," Irwin said.

Fed up, Irwin said she wanted to leave the Sea Org. In response, she underwent the gang-bang interrogation, asked whether she was working for the CIA or plotting to overthrow Scientology. "Every once in a while, DM and one of his crew would call us over to their offices and they would scream at us," she recalled. After weeks of this treatment, Irwin felt as if she'd gone insane.

Finally, in the spring of 1982, Gale and DeDe were awakened in the middle of the night and informed that they'd been declared Suppressive Persons. After more than ten years at the highest levels of Scientology, they left that night, disgraced. Within the next few years, virtually all of the original Commodore's Messengers who had sailed with L. Ron Hubbard aboard the *Apollo* were treated in much the same fashion by Miscavige and his allies and ultimately left the church.

This revolution within Scientology was at first not felt beyond the confines of Gilman Hot Springs and the international management. Many ordinary Scientologists, particularly those affiliated with its missions, were unaware of what was going on at the top. Like the McDonald's corporation, whose methods church executives reportedly had studied, Scientology was rigorously expansion-oriented and during its first twenty years had opened missions around the globe. These franchises were of limited scope, offering lower-level Scientology services, but they were run by some of the most experienced Scientology executives; Alan Walter, for example, opened Scientology missions in New York City, Boston, St. Louis, Dallas, New Orleans, Kansas City, and Beverly Hills, among other cities. Most were extremely profitable, and by the late 1970s, the Scientology "mission network" was booming: some individual franchises grossed up to $100,000 a week.

Organized churches of Scientology, which offered a much wider range of spiritual counseling and training, made less money despite, or perhaps because of, being more tightly controlled by the larger church. As a result, many Scientology organizations struggled to pay both their bills and their staff, while Scientology franchise holders, who were allowed to keep most of their profits, could make a six-figure salary by selling some of the same Scientology services in a smaller and frequently more relaxed environment.

On October 17, 1982, roughly four hundred Scientology mission holders from across the United States were called to a meeting with church management on the fourth floor of the San Francisco Hilton Hotel. Inside a large conference room, twenty-two-year-old David Miscavige, his deputy Norman Starkey, and members of a militant unit of the Sea Organization known as the International Finance Police declared a new world order. The independence of the missions was abolished: from now on, the larger Church of Scientology would run the franchises like a diocese, with missions reduced to little more than local parishes.

The audience members were stunned. The franchises could still offer basic Scientology counseling and courses, Miscavige and his cohorts announced, but they would be required to send a much higher quota of their clientele to the nearest Scientology org, thus dramatically limiting both the missions' power and earning potential. To make sure the mission holders followed the rules, they were required to sign an agreement giving total control to a new and powerful church entity, the Religious Technology Center, or RTC. Those who didn't sign would lose their missions entirely and be subjected to heavy fines, or even, the new regime threatened, time in jail.

Those franchise owners who objected to the new mandate were declared "mutinous" and immediately shuffled into private rooms where, behind locked doors, they were interrogated on the E-meter to uncover their crimes. Others were ordered to Gilman Hot Springs for security checking and, in some cases, were subjected to a new punishment known as the "Running Program," in which the victims were forced to run around a pole in the high desert for up to nine or ten hours a day. Still others, like Alan Walter, were declared a Suppressive Person on the spot and expelled. The mission holders who survived were expected to turn over whatever money was demanded of them to the International Finance Police. Those who refused were swiftly excommunicated.

One of the main enforcers of this policy was Don Larson, who served for a time as head of the International Finance Police. As the official hatchet man, Larson estimated he personally sent three hundred Scientologists to the RPF. He also collected money. "If you could force someone to be scared enough of the church, they would cough up the money that you wanted," Larson told the BBC in 1987. "It was my job to scare people." Once, he recalled, he and fourteen other Sea Org executives, including David Miscavige, drove to a San Francisco mission to confront its commanding officer. It was a "beat-'em-up kind of meeting . . . this has nothing to do with religion anymore, right? This is, 'Where's the money, Jack — I want the money! Where did you put the money?'" When the man insisted he didn't have any money, in Larson's words, "David Miscavige comes up, grabs him by the tie, and starts bashing him into the filing cabinet."

Larson, who was purged from Scientology in 1983 after a little more than a year as enforcer, described Miscavige as "a very, very macho 1950s tough guy." He liked to shoot with bow and arrow, practiced karate, and collected guns; an avid trap and skeet shooter, he was said to own at least a dozen rifles and perhaps a dozen pistols. He surrounded himself with young men like himself, many who had grown up in Scientology, as he had. Their motto, recalled Larson, was "We're tough, we're ruthless" — Miscavige most of all.

Miscavige's coup was now nearly complete. He had dubbed himself Captain of the Sea Organization and created two powerful new entities: the aforementioned RTC, which controlled and licensed L. Ron Hubbard's works, and Author Services, Inc. (ASI), which handled the proceeds. ASI had been created as L. Ron Hubbard's personal literary agency, managing the sales of his books and the income he made from his non-Scientology-related works. But in fact, ASI was the clearinghouse through which Hubbard issued his orders to lower organizations and the secret funnel through which he received his money from all areas of the church — up to $1 million per week, according to the former finance officer Homer Schomer, who was an executive at ASI between April and November 1982. David Miscavige ran ASI. It was a singularly powerful position, putting him in direct control of not only Hubbard's communiqués, but also the Church of Scientology's finances.

Scientologists were told that all of these changes, including the appointment of David Miscavige to the helm of Author Services, had not only been approved but in fact ordered by L. Ron Hubbard. Most believed this unquestioningly; a few, however, had doubts. Hubbard's long-estranged son, Nibs, for one, was suspicious of Miscavige, and though he had been detached from Scientology since 1959, he was worried about the consolidated control the Messengers now seemed to have over the movement. In November 1982, Nibs went to Superior Court in Riverside, California; asserting his belief that his father was dead or was possibly being held prisoner against his will, he sued for control of Hubbard's assets.

In response, the Founder submitted a lengthy signed affidavit, asserting that Nibs's suit had been "brought maliciously, in bad faith," and, he indicated, for personal reasons having nothing to do with protecting Hubbard's estate. "I am not a missing person," he said. "I am in seclusion of my own choosing. As Thoreau secluded himself by Walden Pond, so I have chosen to do so in my own fashion."*

Hubbard made a special point of stating his "unequivocal confidence in David Miscavige," whom Nibs had accused of "stealing" from Hubbard, and from Scientology, by mismanaging the Founder's money. "Any activities which he may have engaged in at any time concerning my personal or business affairs have been done with my knowledge and authorization and for my benefit," Hubbard said. He refuted the charge that Miscavige was organizing the theft of his assets as "completely false," noting that Miscavige was a "long time devoted Scientologist." And Scientologists, he explained, "are my most trusted associates and would never do anything to harm me, much less . . . steal from me."

In June 1983, a California Superior Court judge, convinced by Hubbard's declaration, dismissed Nibs's case.

Now Miscavige had no rival other than Pat Broeker, who was still the sole conduit to Hubbard and, it was widely believed, Miscavige's co-

---

* Having published *Battlefield Earth* while in hiding, Hubbard was now at work on his next novel, *Mission Earth*.

conspirator. The two men met regularly and secretly at a truck stop off the 10 Freeway, near Barstow. From there, they drove in unmarked rented cars to a safe house in the nearby town of Newberry Springs, where they exchanged boxes: Broeker giving Miscavige Hubbard's communiqués, Miscavige giving Broeker reports from various organizations and officials and also cash. "Hundreds of thousands of dollars in cash would show up for LRH in that banking box," said Mark Fisher, who then served as corporate liaison between Miscavige, ASI, and the rest of Scientology.

Virtually everything that went on in Scientology was filtered through Broeker and Miscavige, who returned to Gilman Hot Springs with increasingly angry missives from Hubbard, who continued to be convinced that Scientology was falling prey to external influences. Sea Org officials hardly knew what they were guilty of, but there was no defense, said Fisher, because while legally the corporations of Scientology were supposed to be separate, in reality they all depended entirely on Miscavige's goodwill. "Only people who worked in the Commodore's Messenger Organization or on other parts of the base were aware of this — it was not something known to the average Scientologist. But all of the executives understood that if they didn't do what Miscavige ordered, he could report them to Hubbard and they'd be removed."

Before presenting anything meant for Hubbard, Miscavige screened all of the written communiqués and reports. "If he didn't like anything in them, he kicked them back [to whoever wrote them]" — or just threw them out, said Fisher. "Whoever controlled that communication line had the power, and Miscavige controlled it entirely. Hubbard just got this box, and whatever was in there is what he believed."

In January 1984, Hubbard delivered an unusual taped message to his flock titled "Today and Tomorrow: The Proof." As Jon Atack noted in *A Piece of Blue Sky*, it was not the typical Hubbard talk in that it was scripted, with frequent interruptions where the Founder "was asked questions, given answers, even corrected on some slight underestimation of a statistic." At the crux were a bitter indictment of what he saw as the corruption of the former management of Scientology and an elevation of individuals he called "a small hardcore group of founding members, devoted on-Policy, in-Tech Scientologists who suddenly understood what was happening . . . and just as it looked like the churches were finished and about to fall into hostile hands, they suddenly isolated the infiltrators and threw them out."

It was an undisputable homage to Miscavige and his posse. But whether Hubbard was ever fully aware of the extent of Miscavige's changes was, and remains, unclear. In five years, the young Messenger and his allies had demoted or otherwise dispensed with nearly every person who'd served Hubbard aboard the *Apollo*, eased out long-serving executives, and dismantled the independent franchises, a network the Founder had established and relied upon as a feeder for his movement. The overhaul did away with most of the institutional memory, technical expertise, and earning power of the church.

On January 27, 1986, Captain David Miscavige, light brown hair cut short, his blue Sea Org uniform pressed and starched, epaulets sitting smartly on his shoulders, stood before a crowd of eighteen hundred fellow Scientologists at the Hollywood Palladium, in Los Angeles. "Fellow Sea Org members, Org staff, and Scientology public, I am here before you today to announce that Ron has moved forward to his next level of research," he said. A hush fell over the audience. "It is a level reaching beyond the imagination," Miscavige continued, "and in a state exterior to the body. Thus at 2000 hours, on Friday, the 24th of January, 1986, L. Ron Hubbard discarded the body he had used in this lifetime for seventy-four years, ten months, and eleven days."

L. Ron Hubbard died in a luxury forty-foot Bluebird motor home on his property in Creston, California, a 160-acre spread called the Whispering Winds Ranch. There, overlooking a vista of rolling green hills and sprawling meadows studded with wildflowers, Hubbard had been living in seclusion with the Broekers since 1983.

For a man who'd sought both notoriety and refuge his entire life, Creston, population 270, was an obscurely apropos place for L. Ron Hubbard to end up. The ranch was down a dirt road, not obvious from any approach. The neighbors rarely saw him. Those who did would later recall an old man, noticeably overweight, usually dressed in baggy trousers and a straw hat. His name, they were told, was Jack.

The three-story, ten-room ranch house had been gutted, remodeled, and then (upon Hubbard's orders) remodeled again, making it uninhabitable while the renovations were going on. One group of painters would later tell a patron of a local tavern that the old man was so demanding he'd insisted they paint the white walls over and over again because, as he told them, they "weren't white enough."

While the house was being worked on, "Jack" lived in the Bluebird trailer, which was parked just behind the stables. He could occasionally be seen driving a Subaru Brat around the property, or padding around the stables in his robe and slippers. Once in a while, he'd stop to chat with the Scientologist caretaker, Steve Pfauth, who was the only other full-time custodian at the ranch, aside from the Broekers. The group was generally unfriendly to outsiders, although "Jack" could surprise people. The ranch's former fencing contractor, Jim Froelicher, later told the *Los Angeles Times* that he'd once asked the old man for advice on buying a camera. A few days later, Hubbard gave the contractor a 35-mm camera as a gift.

During his exile Hubbard was attended by his Scientologist physician, Dr. Eugene Denk, who was one of only a few people, other than Pat and Annie Broeker and Pfauth, who saw the Founder in his final years. Obsessed with Hubbard's security, Pat Broeker ordered that Denk be kept in the dark about the ranch's exact location, sometimes blindfolding the doctor during the drive there. In early 1985, Denk moved onto the property and into his own trailer, the Country Aire, where he would live for the rest of the year as he tended the Founder, who would frequently yell at the doctor to leave him alone. "LRH was not a good patient," Pfauth recalled.

Denk, setting aside all talk of "dropping the body," later stated that Hubbard had died of a stroke. His health had been failing for several years. A month before his death, said Denk, Hubbard had suffered a brain hemorrhage, which had made it impossible for him to speak and had left him bedridden. The San Luis Obispo County coroner, who briefly took possession of Hubbard's body, accepted the diagnosis of a stroke, and a blood test revealed the presence of anti-stroke medication in Hubbard's system. It also revealed a quantity of hydroxyzine, sold under the brand name Vistaril, an anti-anxiety medication often used to treat psychosis. This suggested that Hubbard, who'd preached against the use of "psych" drugs for decades, had been taking them himself.

This bit of information would never be imparted to the faithful, however. Nor would it be known that Hubbard had been left without medical attention for several days while gravely ill. Roughly a week prior to Hubbard's death, Broeker, Miscavige, and several other Commodore's Messengers took Dr. Denk on a gambling trip to Reno. While they were gone, Hubbard summoned Ray Mithoff, Scientology's top auditor, to administer a "death assist," a form of auditing that is comparable to last rites. Whether Hubbard had ordered his aides to dispense with Denk, or whether the Messengers had taken it upon themselves to whisk him away, would never be firmly established — some former Messengers would later say that Hubbard would not have wanted his doctor nearby, as Scientology forbids a person to have any medication in the system within twenty-four hours of auditing. "Gene was the kind of guy who believed in keeping his patients alive. So if LRH wanted to leave his body, Gene wouldn't have wanted to be a part of that," said Julie Holloway. By the time Denk returned, Hubbard was prepared. He died a few days later.

By 11 P.M., January 24, Pat Broeker had notified a small group of Scientology officials that the Founder was dead. They gathered at the ranch to await the mortician and discuss the future. The flock, of course, would have to be told that Hubbard was gone. But Scientology had to go on. And so a story was concocted.

"The being we knew as L. Ron Hubbard still exists, and is still with us," Miscavige continued, days later, from the podium. "He has simply moved on to his next step on the Bridge." This was the central theme of the official story. Hubbard, Miscavige explained to the audience, had found that his physical body had "ceased to be useful, and in fact had become an impediment to the work he now must do outside its confines." He reminded the audience that they should not feel sorrow, for Hubbard had used his life to "accomplish what no man has ever accomplished. He unlocked the mysteries of life and gave us the tools so we could free ourselves and our fellow men."

Then Pat Broeker, a tall, thin, dark-haired man who, like his boss, had not been seen publicly for six years, took the stage. "I want to reiterate that it was absolutely Ron's causative decision to discard his body," Broeker said. Indeed, as far back as 1984, he pointed out, Hubbard had known that he'd have to "move on from where he was, through phenomena that required him to be free from encumbrances." Just a few days earlier, said Broeker, Hubbard had completed his earthly research, declared "this was it," and then "handled in [an auditing] session all things that were necessary so that he could completely sever all ties."

Broeker also announced that the balance of Hubbard's estate, "which is substantial," would go to the church. "It is Ron's wish and postulate that we Clear this planet now, and he has given us this gift in order to get the job done." As for who might lead the charge, neither Broeker nor Miscavige, nor any of the other representatives of Scientology's senior management, all of whom stood onstage, said a word. "There is only one Source," said Broeker. "Source does not pass to Management. Source is Ron, the only one! The Power of Source is the Route to Total Freedom."

The crowd rose to their feet and cheered.

CHAPTER 8

Power Is Assumed

Power in my estimation is if people will listen to you.

—DAVID MISCAVIGE

THERE WAS NO PUBLIC outpouring of grief among Scientologists when L. Ron Hubbard died. To mourn excessively would have been to deny one of the fundamental tenets of Hubbard's teachings: that one life is a mere blip on the screen of a thetan's eternal existence. And yet, despite this assurance, Scientologists were stunned by Hubbard's demise, most notably the dedicated Sea Org members who'd spent years hoping and preparing for their leader's return. Among them, Mark Fisher, for example, had worked diligently at Gilman Hot Springs, helping to build Hubbard's mansion, Bonnie View. On the evening of January 27, 1986, Fisher and his wife drove to Los Angeles, attended the memorial at the Hollywood Palladium, and drove back to Hemet in silence. "My biggest dream at the time was to work for LRH directly, and now that goal and dream were shattered for me," said Fisher. "We were shocked, to say the least. We were wondering what would happen now."

Whether Hubbard had intended to will most of his estate to Scientology has been an enduring question. Just one day before he died, the Founder's will — the third* will he'd drawn up since 1979 — was

---

* Hubbard's will has been a sore point for Scientology's critics. The original will, dated December 15, 1979, left all of Hubbard's personal effects to Mary Sue and established a trust to handle the remainder of his estate. A second will was drawn up on May 10, 1982, which omitted any mention of Mary Sue's inheriting Hubbard's personal items and ceded most of his estate to the new Author's Family Trust. A codicil to that will was added on November 14, 1983, which con-

revised, leaving most of his fortune to a trust, appointing as trustee Norman Starkey, a close ally of Miscavige's and executor of the will. In previous wills, Hubbard's personal attorney and then Pat Broeker had been named the executor. Given reports that the Founder was seriously ill for some time before he died, some conspiracy theorists have maintained, and will no doubt continue to maintain, that Hubbard's will was illegitimate. But considering the manner in which Hubbard had always regarded his family, there is little doubt that he intended to leave the majority of his estate to the Church of Scientology. To ensure that there would be no challenge from the family, however improbable that it might succeed, Miscavige made a side agreement with Mary Sue Hubbard, whereby she agreed to a settlement of $100,000 in exchange for giving up her share of a claim to Hubbard's estate — a fortune worth approximately $400 million. Each of Hubbard's children by Mary Sue received settlements of $50,000. Hubbard's children by his previous marriages, L. Ron Hubbard Jr., Katherine, and Alexis, were also paid settlements; Nibs received his after threatening litigation.

But aside from bequeathing his material wealth, Hubbard had never appointed a successor, nor had he provided his followers with a clear road map for the future. Who among them had the vision and strength of purpose to ensure that Scientology would continue to grow and prosper?

Many in the Commodore's Messenger Organization already viewed Miscavige as that leader. Just twenty-five, he had been slavishly devoted to Hubbard, and though he spent most of his time at Scientology's Los Angeles headquarters, where Author Services was based, he made weekly trips to Gilman Hot Springs to meet with executives in the Commodore's Messenger Organization and other branches of the Sea Org. His wife, Michele "Shelly" Barnett,* a cool and pretty young

---

firmed Hubbard's intention to disinherit L. Ron Hubbard Jr. and his issue; it also inserted a paragraph to express Hubbard's desire to have his body cremated and the ashes buried at sea, as well as this statement: "Under no circumstances shall my body lie in state or be subjected to an autopsy." The codicil didn't replace that second will, which remained in force, with the codicil amendments, until the third will, executed on January 23, 1986, in Creston, California, which made the church primary beneficiary.

* Shelly was one of the few original "ship Messengers" who'd served L. Ron Hub-

woman with long strawberry-blonde hair, usually accompanied him on these trips as his assistant.

Miscavige was generally well received at the base, said the Scientologist Dan Koon. He embodied toughness, a value L. Ron Hubbard had promoted strongly within the Sea Org. If he took it to extremes, the staff at Gilman believed it had to be necessary. He had incredible "confront," or the ability to face situations head-on, one of the highest compliments a Scientologist could receive, explained Koon. "He was certainly tough, but he was extremely capable and determined to get things done." And many things did seem to be improving. Scientology's membership and income were on the upswing, said Koon; *Dianetics* had made it onto the *New York Times* bestseller list* for the first time since 1950. Though Miscavige had nothing to do with this — the success of *Dianetics* was due to the work of Jeff Hawkins and his strategic marketing unit — he threw himself into projects with the unwavering passion of a young L. Ron Hubbard, inspiring his staff to work harder, and longer, than they ever imagined they could. Koon was impressed. "You met Miscavige and you knew he was an extraordinary personality," he said. "The guy had personal power not to be believed."

If the volatile and driven Miscavige resembled one side of L. Ron Hubbard, Pat Broeker reflected another. Broeker was ten years older than Miscavige and was arguably even more devoted to the Founder, having spent the better part of the past decade in hiding with him. A handsome man with dark hair and brown eyes, Broeker was personable, well read, and charming; he was also independent. "Pat was extremely charismatic, but he didn't like rules," said Julie Holloway. "He liked to do things his own way, and he wouldn't ask permission; he'd just do it." Holloway recalled that Broeker once posed as a veterinarian at an animal hospital in order to buy vaccines for a litter of new puppies — simply waiting as a customer, he'd told her, would have wasted too much time. "He assumed no one was going to ques-

---

bard aboard the *Apollo*. She and Miscavige were married in 1981.

* One possible reason for this was that Scientologists were frequently urged to buy books to boost sales. Jeff Hawkins insists this was not the case with *Dianetics*, though it was reportedly true with subsequent books.

tion him and he was just going to fake it the whole way, and he did. And that's how he was about everything."

Unbeknownst to many people in the Sea Organization, Broeker had not spent much time at Creston during the last year of Hubbard's life. He'd decided to turn both the Creston property and a secondary ranch in Newberry Springs into showcases for American quarter horses — posing as a gentleman rancher would be a good cover for L. Ron Hubbard, Broeker thought. He spent most of 1985 traveling around the West on horse-buying trips.

Broeker's wife, Annie, on the other hand, had spent the years in exile catering to Hubbard's every need. Like several of the other messengers, Annie had served L. Ron Hubbard on the *Apollo*, starting at the age of twelve. A quiet, pretty young woman with wavy blonde hair, she was twenty-four when he went into hiding. During the last year of Hubbard's life in particular, she served as the link between the Founder and her husband.

As a reward, Hubbard appointed Annie Inspector General of the Religious Technology Center, at that time the highest position in the church bureaucracy. It was a job for which Annie Broeker was ill-suited, as she was painfully shy, with few friends other than those she'd grown up with on the ship. "She hadn't been part of any sort of group or social circle from 1980 to 1986 — the only people she associated with during that time were LRH, Pat, Gene Denk, Sarge" (a nickname for Steve Pfauth, the caretaker), "a horse trainer or two, and a ranch hand," said Julie Holloway. "I remember the first time she took the stage, which was at an event in March 1986 for Hubbard's birthday. She was a nervous wreck."

Since 1980, Broeker had rarely been seen around Gilman Hot Springs, now the home of Scientology's film studio, Golden Era Productions, and frequently referred to as Gold Base, or International Base, or simply Int, for its distinction as the home of Scientology's international management. When he did make an appearance, he did so in his trademark highly covert fashion. "Pat had a silver cargo van with no windows," recalled Mark Fisher. "When you saw the silver van you knew he was around, but you never saw him. He would only come out at night." Once, Fisher recalled, he did spot Broeker on the base during the day but hardly recognized him: he was wearing a long full beard as a disguise and had jumped out of his van holding an Uzi submachine gun.

Broeker could have argued that Hubbard had intended for him to become the leader of Scientology, based on a message Hubbard had written to the church management shortly before dying, titled "The Sea Org and the Future." In this, his one gesture toward giving the church a direction to move in after his passing, Hubbard promoted himself to the role of Admiral and then bid farewell to the Sea Organization, naming Pat and Annie Broeker his "Loyal Officers,"* an appointment that suggested the baton had been passed to them. But Broeker did not argue for this interpretation of Hubbard's intentions — rather than return to Gold Base after closing down the ranch in Creston, he moved with his wife and several others to the Newberry Springs ranch, near Barstow. He seemed intent on continuing with the horse business. "DM thought it was crazy," said Mark Fisher. "The only reason for having the horses in the first place was to provide a cover story for LRH. But even after LRH was dead, Pat wanted to continue to spend thousands of dollars of LRH's money on the horse ranches."

At Newberry Springs, Broeker had a small staff of aides who came and went. Annie Broeker had a retinue as well, including the Sea Org officials Vicki Aznaran and Jesse Prince, her deputies at the RTC. With Pat Broeker issuing orders from this remote location, and Annie declining to say much of anything, David Miscavige, notably unmentioned in the "Sea Org and the Future," faced little competition for center stage.

Hubbard's daughters Diana and Suzette, once looked upon as Scientology royalty, were given low-ranking jobs at Int: Diana became a film editor, and Suzette served as a laundress, assigned to wash David Miscavige's shirts. Anyone at Int or at Scientology's base in Los Angeles who seemed sympathetic to Pat Broeker was also demoted, while those who remained loyal to Miscavige were elevated within Author

* In Hubbard's OT 3 doctrine, the Loyal Officers were the trusted men of the realm, soldiers of light who ultimately defeated Xenu, the personification of evil.

Services. One who fell into the latter camp was ASI's legal executive, Mark "Marty" Rathbun.

A tall, reserved, steely-eyed man, Rathbun was known within the Sea Org as Miscavige's "enforcer." He'd joined Scientology as a twenty-year-old, in 1977, having become interested in Hubbard's ideas, he'd later say, out of concern for his brother, who was at the time a psychiatric patient at Dammasch State Hospital in Wilsonville, Oregon, suffering from schizophrenia. "I was kind of afraid he was going to wind up living the rest of his life in the back ward, so I was seeking some tools and some answers on how I might be able to [help] him," Rathbun told the *St. Petersburg Times* in 2009. A Scientology recruiter he'd met on the street recommended he read *Dianetics*, and Rathbun signed up to take Scientology's basic communication course. By January 1978, he had signed a billion-year Sea Org contract, and by the end of that year he was dispatched to the Winter Headquarters ranch at La Quinta.

Hubbard was just leaving the ranch for his apartment in Hemet when Rathbun arrived; the two were never personally acquainted. But Rathbun soon got to know David Miscavige. Though he was quieter and more intellectual than the hotheaded "Action Chief," Rathbun, who'd played a few years of college basketball, bonded with the younger man over sports. In January 1981, the two drove from Los Angeles to New Orleans to see Miscavige's beloved Philadelphia Eagles play in the Super Bowl. The Eagles lost, but Rathbun and Miscavige, then twenty-four and twenty-one, formed a lasting friendship.

A talented strategist, Rathbun soon became a key member of Miscavige's All Clear Unit. In 1983 he'd helped dismantle the Guardian's Office, replacing it with a new legal and investigative body known as the Office of Special Affairs. Mike Rinder, another Commodore's Messenger, would ultimately become head of OSA, but Rathbun, who also had a gift for subversive tactics, would direct legal and investigative strategy as Miscavige's point man and, crucially, became the executive to whom Miscavige turned when he wanted an enemy investigated or an associate "de-powered," as some Scientology executives referred to it.

It had already dawned on Miscavige that Pat Broeker was anointed in name only. As the emissary to L. Ron Hubbard, he had never been a part of Scientology's official management structure and remained off its organizational chart. He had been removed from the day-to-day operations of Scientology for seven years. Half of the staff at Int and at the base in Los Angeles had never met him or heard of him.

Now Miscavige's loyalists launched a whisper campaign that asserted that Broeker, far from a "loyal officer," was actually a thief and an alcoholic, unfit to command. And indeed, life at both ranches was notably laid back, compared to the regimented attitude on the base. To ingratiate himself with the ranch hands and other workers, Broeker had stocked beer, frozen pizza, and other snack food in the refrigerators at both Creston and Newberry Springs. His staff were permitted to watch satellite TV, sleep a full eight hours per night, and even attend concerts in nearby Paso Robles. Perhaps the worst offense was that Broeker had reportedly purchased racehorses with church funds while other Sea Org members slaved away serving Scientology. He had even invested in a new hobby — flying ultralight aircraft — and now stored one such plane, also reportedly bought with church funds, at the Paso Robles airport.

But Broeker still maintained control of Hubbard's handwritten auditing notes, including his research for the as-yet-unreleased OT levels 9–15. This was Hubbard's final legacy: original material that was both lofty in purpose and, church officials well knew, potentially lucrative. Scientology made most of its money off auditing fees; many Scientologist OTs had been waiting for the vaunted "upper levels" for years. Whoever controlled this sacred doctrine, Miscavige understood, controlled the church. The younger Messenger now set out to get it.

Toward the end of 1987, Miscavige gathered a team led by Rathbun, and together they drove to see Broeker to demand that he relinquish the documents. Rathbun later said that Miscavige confronted Broeker but that it was Annie who "finally broke under the pressure" and, when her husband wasn't in the room, told Miscavige where Broeker was hiding the materials: in several filing cabinets in his storage space at Newberry Springs.

Not long after this confrontation, Miscavige and Broeker were in

Washington, D.C., to meet with church lawyers. Taking advantage
of Broeker's absence, Rathbun, in California, assembled a team of
roughly twenty men to drive to Newberry Springs. When they got
there, Rathbun called the ranch's caretaker with an alarming bit of
news. He had just received a tip, Rathbun said, that the FBI was preparing to raid the property. They'd be there in two hours, and they
would surely cart away every bit of paper in the place. It was essential
that he be let in to safeguard Hubbard's papers — there was no time
to waste. The story, which Rathbun said he'd cooked up with Miscavige days before, "worked like a charm." Within an hour, the men had
entered the ranch and, with the caretaker's permission, took possession of the filing cabinets.*

Just after midnight that evening, Mark Fisher, one of Miscavige's
senior aides, was awakened by a call. It was Miscavige, still in Washington. In a few hours, Miscavige said, Rathbun and Norman Starkey,
another ASI executive, would be arriving at the Int Base in a truck.
Fisher was to let them into the "LRH safe room," a private chamber
located next to his office. Miscavige didn't elaborate on what the men
were going to put in the safe, but Fisher knew it was important because Miscavige told him to change the security codes to the room
once they left. "Don't let anyone in — and especially not Pat Broeker,"
Miscavige said.

Fisher then got a call from Starkey. "We're here," he said. Fisher
got dressed and rode his Honda 110 up the hill to his office, on the
other side of the property. Rathbun and Starkey were waiting, with
several other men and a set of large filing cabinets.

The safe room, which looked like a study, had bookshelves con-
cealing false walls. Behind these walls were safes for Hubbard's personal valuables, including jewelry, and some filing cabinets, the contents of which Fisher never knew. "There was room for these new

---

* According to Marty Rathbun, there are no OT 9 and 10, let alone anything
higher. "The idea of OT 9 and 10 was a creation of Pat Broeker, dreamt up on the
heels of the death of LRH to keep the masses from open revolt" — and to keep
Miscavige from deposing Broeker immediately. Rathbun made these claims on
his blog. He also said that neither OT 9 nor 10 was contained in Hubbard's
auditing files. "When Broeker's bluffs were all called, he resorted to claiming
he was channeling LRH and LRH was pissed about Broeker's being reined in,"
Rathbun said.

filing cabinets to be added, and so they just wheeled them in. Marty and Norman didn't say anything to me about it at all, but I could tell what this stuff was," Fisher said. "LRH had been dead for over a year at that point and I assumed that his research materials were in Pat's care. So when these papers showed up in filing cabinets in the middle of the night, and I was told that I wasn't to let Pat near them — well, it was pretty obvious what they were."

David Miscavige now held all the cards, and Pat Broeker knew it. Soon after Miscavige acquired the documents, Broeker left the Sea Organization and the Church of Scientology. He headed east, settling first in Colorado and later in Wyoming. For several years after, Marty Rathbun, on Miscavige's orders, had Broeker watched by private investigators. He was never seen in church circles again.

Broeker's wife, Annie, stayed behind. Still loyal to Scientology, she was allowed to remain in the Sea Organization, but she was forced out of her position at the RTC by Miscavige and sentenced to a period of "rehabilitation" on the RPF, along with most of the couple's staff. The Broekers' possessions, including a new Ford Bronco, the horses, and a car that Hubbard had bought for Annie, were seized and sold by the Church of Scientology.

With his last rival out of the way, Miscavige decided to remove himself as head of ASI, which was no longer the seat of power after Hubbard's death. The RTC, which held the rights to Scientology's trademarks and copyrights, was now the central policing and enforcement body of the church, and to gain control over it, Miscavige purged its top officials, including the Broeker loyalists Vicki Aznaran and Jesse Prince, both of whom had signed undated resignation letters when they began their jobs (something still required of all Scientology executives). Miscavige put himself at the helm of the RTC, creating a new title for himself: Chairman of the Board. Rathbun was appointed Inspector General of the RTC, one of the highest positions in the Church of Scientology.

Only one task remained for Miscavige: to assert that Hubbard had never intended for the Broekers to lead Scientology in the first place. In 1988, he issued a proclamation declaring the "Sea Org and the Future" document a fake — though Miscavige notably did not cancel the rank of Admiral that Hubbard had bestowed upon himself in this document. "Of course, DM never provided anything [to prove that Hubbard hadn't written it] and no one was willing to ask and risk being sent to the RPF," wrote the church's onetime spokesman, Robert Vaughn Young, several years later. Miscavige claimed the Broekers had fabricated the document and had also altered other writings of Hubbard's creation, made during his exile. And since there were no handwritten notes or tape recordings of Hubbard's to contradict this account, most Scientologists, including the Sea Org members at Gilman Hot Springs, accepted Miscavige's allegation as truth. "DM had thoroughly discredited Pat by then, and the only information we had was what DM told us," said Dan Koon.

"In the end, we were told that Pat was an estates manager for Hubbard and that's all he really was," said Tom De Vocht, another Sea Org member at the base. "Now that's odd because 'Big P,' which was Pat, was carbon-copied on every piece of written advice. But Dave said no, he was an estates manager. And Annie was the laundry person. And that was accepted because Pat and Annie were people no one knew. You saw them at the LRH death event and they were like gods, but then they were gone again. And Dave's in charge."

"For the rest of my stay in [Scientology], Pat Brocker was never mentioned," wrote Young, a Brocker loyalist who was removed from his job as head of worldwide public relations for the church and sent to the RPF in 1989. Pat "became what in Orwell's *1984* is a non-person. He had been written out of history, with anyone who cared (such as me) being sent to the RPF or interrogated . . . until they got the point, which meant . . . that everyone else got the point."

Two years after being sent to the RPF, in December 1989, Annie Broeker returned to Int Base. Upon her release, she and her friend Julie Holloway went Christmas shopping. She had almost no money, Holloway recalled, since the church had seized Broeker's valuables. But she was nonetheless determined to spend what little she had on a gift for David Miscavige. "She told me she wanted to buy something special for DM since he had helped her so much," Holloway said. "I couldn't believe it, after everything he'd done to her." Holloway, who left Scientology in 1990, had come to hate Miscavige. But Annie, who remains at Int to this day, never expressed anything but love for him, Holloway said. "She was totally broken."

Outside of the closed circle of Sea Org executives, no one in Scientology knew of this hostile takeover. Most Scientologists simply saw David Miscavige as the anointed leader and the right man for the job. Among Hubbard's apostles, he was viewed as the truest of true believers: a purist who embraced even the most dogmatic of the Founder's scriptures, perhaps more stringently, some suggested, than Hubbard had himself.

But Miscavige was also a notably sheltered young man who grew up within the bubble-like world of the Sea Organization. He knew virtually nothing of the needs of everyday people, nor was he particularly curious. "Miscavige is very, very cloistered," said Jeff Hawkins. "He never worked in a business. He never went to college. He never even ran a Scientology church or mission. The only example he had of a 'leader' was Hubbard, who, by the time Miscavige worked for him, was already on his way over the edge of sanity."

In his prime, L. Ron Hubbard was a tall, robust, larger-than-life character: a Pied Piper who drew followers through the force of his own charisma. Miscavige was short, boyish-looking, and abrasive. Hubbard was a dreamer with great persuasive skill; Miscavige was a tactician who accomplished many of his goals through pure intimidation. "To call David pugnacious would be one of the nicest things anyone has ever said about him," said one former associate. "You will never be as intimidated in your life as you are when you are confronted by David Miscavige."

Hubbard seemed to crave approval; Miscavige kept his own counsel — he was not interested in Scientologists' love, but in their dedication and obedience. His role would not be the visionary but rather the steward who would consolidate Hubbard's movement, cleanse and repackage its image, sell it aggressively, and guide it into a new age. Ten years after his ascension, in a one-time-only interview with the *St. Petersburg Times*, Miscavige was asked about his rise to power. "Nobody gives you power," he replied. "I'll tell you what power is. Power in my estimation is if people will listen to you. That's it."

At the time of L. Ron Hubbard's death, in 1986, the Church of Scientology, having weathered nearly a decade of scandal, was now the citadel of rules and codes its Founder had once imagined. In Los Angeles, Scientology's sprawling headquarters on Sunset Boulevard was a fortress, staffed by eager young Sea Org members in crisp naval-style uniforms and patrolled around the clock by security guards. Sophisticated locks, whose combinations "continuously changed," as one story in the *LA Weekly* noted, protected the church's offices and course rooms. But perhaps most striking, particularly for a movement promoting "total freedom," were the wanted posters that hung on the walls of the Los Angeles base, offering a $500 reward for information on different church "enemies."

Miscavige's revolution had intensified Scientology's us-versus-them atmosphere. It had also created defectors, including some of Scientology's highest-ranking executives, who charged, among other things, that over the past several decades the Church of Scientology had defrauded and in some cases brainwashed them, subjected them to abuse through its punitive ethics policies, and then, after they left the church, continued to harass them.

Though Miscavige and his allies denied these allegations, the defections proved to be a public relations disaster for the church. By the mid-1980s, juries across the United States were hearing cases brought against Scientology by its dissidents, occasionally returning judgments in the tens of millions of dollars. At the same time, a splinter network of Scientologists, known as the "Free Zone," was posing a challenge to the organized church by forming independent Scientology groups.

The most prominent leader of the Free Zone was David Mayo, once the highest-ranking technical officer in Scientology and the creator of some of the church's most sophisticated auditing techniques. A Scientologist since the late 1950s, Mayo had been trained by Hubbard personally and later supervised the Founder's auditing; he also audited Hubbard himself. In April 1982, Mayo received a letter from L. Ron Hubbard appointing him the guardian of Scientology's doctrine in the event of Hubbard's death. Shortly after, the Commodore's Messengers, who'd received copies of the letter, circumvented Hubbard's orders by accusing Mayo, with a group of sixteen other senior executives, of trying to take over the Commodore's Messenger Organization. Mayo was quickly removed from his post in the purges overseen by Miscavige.

But where many other executives in his position had abandoned Scientology, Mayo set up an independent auditing practice in Santa Barbara, called the Advanced Ability Center. Then he sent out a letter to the many Scientologists he knew, explaining the circumstances of his removal, and announced that he was open for business. Gale Irwin and DeDe Voegeding were among many Scientologists who flocked to the center in Santa Barbara. "It was wonderful," said Irwin. "There was none of the BS but all of the goodness of what we'd known Scientology to be."

Before long, Mayo's operation was grossing $20,000 to $30,000 per week, using the same techniques and materials that Hubbard had created for Scientology. This, to the church, constituted "squirreling," which made Mayo a target for Fair Game. As Jesse Prince, then a senior executive in RTC, recalled, "DM became infuriated and ordered Mayo's new group to be destroyed using all means possible." The RTC began a newsletter campaign, denouncing Mayo as a squirrel and accusing him of a broad range of crimes ranging from falsifying records and "altering" Hubbard's teachings to "sexually perverted conduct."

The RTC also organized groups of Scientologists who called themselves the Minutemen to hold noisy protests in front of Mayo's Advanced Ability Center. The church also hired private investigators to rent office space above Mayo's center and electronically bug his offices. One of these investigators, Eugene Ingram, was a former sergeant of the Los Angeles Police Department who'd been fired by the department in 1981. Enlisting the help of other ex-cops, Ingram began a campaign of harassment, informing local business owners that they were investigating Mayo for white-collar crime and linking him, falsely, to international drug smuggling. The church also filed a RICO suit against Mayo's group, arguing that they were conspiring with other Free Zone dissidents to use some advanced auditing materials that the church claimed had been stolen from a European Scientology organization. In 1985, the church succeeded in getting a federal injunction preventing Mayo from selling Scientology services; by 1986, the Advanced Ability Center, bankrupt after several years of harassment and litigation, shut down.

But by then, thousands of Scientologists in Europe and the United States had dropped out of the organized church, disillusioned by Miscavige's destruction of the mission network, which many people saw as Scientology's life blood. By 1986, though Scientology officially claimed two million adherents, Sea Org members put the numbers at far lower: perhaps 500,000. Anecdotal accounts during the early and mid-1980s reported an exodus of hundreds from individual Scientology missions across the United States and thousands, perhaps even as many as thirty-five thousand, by Alan Walter's estimate, leaving the Church of Scientology.

But the tens of thousands of Scientologists who didn't abandon the movement readily accepted their leaders' assertions that Scientology was the victim of religious persecution and that the defectors were "heretics." The church responded according to the Hubbard playbook — with an adamant defense of Scientology. This campaign, known as the "Religious Freedom Crusade," peaked in 1985 and 1986 and involved thousands of Scientologists around the world. Its high point was the so-called Battle of Portland, in which thousands of Scientologists — a huge gathering of Minutemen — descended upon Portland, Oregon, in May and June 1985 to protest a $39 million judgment awarded to Julie Christofferson Titchbourne, a twenty-seven-year-old former Scientologist who had sued the church for fraud. When the judge in the Christofferson Titchbourne case threw out the jury's decision on a technicality and declared a mistrial, the Scientologists in the courtroom that day erupted in whoops and applause.

The Christofferson Titchbourne reversal was a pivotal moment for David Miscavige. He not only needed to defend Scientology and establish his leadership, but he also knew the future depended on recasting Scientology as a mainstream church. Just as Hubbard had before him, Miscavige understood the power religion had in the culture and its effectiveness at bringing in cash. The 1980s were not unlike the 1950s in their conservatism and materialism, and churches that embraced those values flourished in this era. With the patronage of Ronald Reagan, and later George H. W. Bush, the Reverend Jerry Falwell became the most prominent religious leader in America, and his group, the Moral Majority, became a national political movement in which faith — fundamentalist Christian faith — was linked with upstanding social, economic, and religious values for the first time in decades.

In a campaign spearheaded by Jeff Hawkins and his marketing group, Scientology now began to promote itself aggressively as a "major religion" — just like "Protestantism, Buddhism, Judaism, Catholicism" — in glossy newspaper supplements. To forge bonds with mainstream Christian groups, the church urged members to attend local Sunday church services, mingle with the congregation, and introduce themselves to the minister and his wife. A key goal was to get local ministers to sign notarized affidavits affirming that Scientology was a "bona fide religion," according to one tip sheet published by the church. To butter them up, the document urged, Scientologists might tell the minister his sermon was "brilliant" and ask if he'd be willing to speak at their church. "He'll have a hard time refusing that one!" it noted.

To further reinforce Scientology's legitimacy, the Religious Freedom Crusade began to sponsor ecumenical conferences in Los Angeles, reaching out to religious leaders of other faiths by impressing upon them that any legal action brought against the Church of Scientology was a threat to all religions. By December 1985, such mainstream organizations as the National Council of Churches and the Coalition for Religious Freedom had voiced support for Scientology and its "right to compete for converts without interference from the courts."

But the cases against Scientology continued. In 1986, a jury in Los Angeles awarded $30 million to the former Scientologist Larry Wollersheim, who'd waged a six-year lawsuit against the church, which he charged had driven him to the point of suicide. In response to the verdict, the Religious Freedom Crusade descended on the Los Angeles County Courthouse much as it had the year before in Portland. This time it was the Reverend Ken Hoden, president of the Church of Scientology of Los Angeles, who spearheaded the campaign, at one point addressing a rally of over a thousand Scientologists; in his speech he compared them to the foot soldiers of the American Revolution. "If you want your rights guaranteed, you have to fight for them," he said. "Larry Wollersheim will never get one thin dime from the Church of Scientology!" "Not one thin dime for Wollersheim" became a refrain for the next twenty-two years, as the church fought consistently against awarding Wollersheim any damages.*

With Miscavige's full assumption of power in 1988, Scientology began to settle many of the lawsuits filed against it, often by offering litigants and their attorneys cash payouts to stop their assault on Scientology. Along with a coalition of other religious groups, the church also pushed a bill through the California state legislature protecting churches and members of the clergy from being assessed large punitive damages in lawsuits brought against them.

But Scientology faced one last formidable adversary: the Internal Revenue Service. Scientology's conflict with the IRS originated in 1967, when the agency, which had previously granted tax exemption to Scientology, revoked its tax-exempt status after finding that Scientology, and Hubbard in particular, seemed to be profiting from the operation. The Church of Scientology appealed this decision and refused to pay taxes — a stance it would maintain for the next twenty-six years.

This reaction prompted the IRS to embark on a deeper examination of Scientology as a "dissident group." Between 1969 and 1975, the Church of Scientology and its activities were monitored by three different agencies within the IRS. Scientology, in turn, monitored the IRS as part of Operation Snow White.

Even after Operation Snow White was uncovered, Scientology's war with the IRS only intensified. In September 1984, the U.S. Tax Court denied the church's appeal of the IRS's original 1967 ruling, concluding, as others had done before, that Scientology "made a business out of selling religion." The judge went into great detail about Scientology's many acts of obstruction, noting how Hubbard had once ordered his staff to mix up some two million pages of tax-related documents to make it difficult for IRS agents to sort through them. The court noted that "criminal manipulation of the

---

* In 2002, the Church of Scientology finally agreed to pay Larry Wollersheim $8.6 million, most of which Wollersheim said went to cover his legal fees.

IRS to maintain its tax exemption (and the exemption of affiliated churches) was a crucial and purposeful element of [Scientology's] financial planning."

Meanwhile, the IRS's criminal investigation into Hubbard's finances had moved on to examine the activities of the RTC and Author Services, as well as their key officials. For several years, Miscavige would later maintain, he and several other officials were the target of investigation by the IRS's Criminal Investigations Division. The IRS didn't comment on the investigation, and the case was dropped with Hubbard's death in 1986. But Miscavige never forgot. To Scientology's new leader, as to its Founder, the IRS represented far more than a powerful government agency determined to "suck the blood from the whole country," as Miscavige once put it; it was the vanguard of a global campaign, launched by psychiatrists, to crush the church.

"A tax-exempt organization is not subject to the myriad complexities of the Internal Revenue Code which can be used to harass and destroy organizations the IRS does not like," Miscavige told his flock. "But most importantly, because all bona-fide religions and churches in the United States do have tax exemption . . . if the IRS refused to grant such to Scientology that fact alone could be used to [discredit] the church internationally." Without tax exemption, he argued, Scientology would never be seen as a religion. Nothing, in Miscavige's mind, could damage Scientology more.

In 1988, Marty Rathbun received his next assignment from Miscavige: launch a campaign to win tax exemption from the IRS. The plan, according to Rathbun, was to follow L. Ron Hubbard's edicts in the most strategic way possible in order to overwhelm the agency and wear it down. To prosecute this war, Rathbun would rely upon the Office of Special Affairs, which he had helped establish five years earlier. Since then, OSA had carried out numerous assignments, ranging from litigating against Scientology enemies to far stealthier black operations, just as the Guardian's Office had always done.

Staffed by some of Miscavige's closest associates, OSA also employed numerous former Guardian's Office officials who, having survived the purges of the early 1980s, had been offered a second chance. "The measuring stick in the Church of Scientology has never been whether you were participating in illegal activities — it's whether you were caught," Jesse Prince, who took part in several intelligence operations in his capacity as an RTC executive, told me. "Those who weren't caught and punished were still used."

Like the old Guardian's Office, OSA handled public-facing activities: legal affairs, public relations, and Scientology's various social betterment programs. It also handled its most secret undertakings and continued to use Scientologists as informants and operatives, as well as employing a cadre of private investigators. It had been OSA that had ruined David Mayo and destroyed his independent Scientology network, using private investigators like Eugene Ingram, who served OSA for many years. The Office of Special Affairs had also created Scientology's Crusade for Religious Freedom as a public relations strategy.

But whereas the Guardian's Office had been an impregnable entity so covert as to not even appear by name on the church's organizational chart, OSA was listed in Scientology's incorporation papers. "Where OSA differs from the Guardian's Office," explained one former Scientologist who was an operative for both intelligence bureaus, "is that OSA wants to seem above board and approachable. That makes Scientology seem more approachable, which, they hope, will help the church operate as a religion freely, without harassment." In service to this goal, OSA made more of an effort to create a legal wall between the church and any covert activities, relying much more on private investigators, and paying a legion of outside attorneys.*

They kept busy. Throughout the late 1980s and into the early 1990s, the Church of Scientology filed some two hundred lawsuits against the IRS, while more than twenty-three hundred individual Scientologists sued the agency over its refusal to allow them to claim their Scientology contributions as tax deductible. These "cookie-cutter suits," as Rathbun described them, soon became cases that cost Scientology tens of millions of dollars in legal fees — with presumably similar cost to the IRS.

---

* Scientology's attorneys were not always wholly independent. One Los Angeles–based lawyer for the church, cited as "outside counsel," was Kendrick Moxon, a Scientologist and former Guardian's Office legal officer who, like L. Ron Hubbard, was named an unindicted co-conspirator in Operation Snow White.

At the same time, the church, long an expert on using the Freedom of Information Act, filed hundreds of requests for internal IRS documents. Some of their findings were published in *Freedom,* a magazine created by the Office of Special Affairs to shed light on various government agencies and their abuses. In Washington, D.C., OSA deployed Scientology operatives to flock Capitol Hill, attend congressional hearings, and network with Hill staffers. One former OSA official explained that for more than a year, she'd fed congressional aides information on the IRS's handling of groups as divergent as the Amish and owners of small businesses, to shed light on its often prejudicial auditing and investigative practices. "They all knew we were from the church. It was a public relations thing," she said. "We were trying to get people to come forward and show that there were attacks on other members of the public, not just on Scientology."

To further this effort, OSA created, and financed, a grassroots lobbying organization known as the National Coalition of IRS Whistleblowers to support IRS employees who wanted to expose corruption. The coalition was planned through *Freedom* magazine and hired as its president a former IRS agent named Paul DesFosses. Stacy Young, then the managing editor of *Freedom,* later told the *New York Times* that "the whole idea was to create a coalition that was at arm's length from Scientology so that it had more credibility."

By the summer of 1989, these efforts were beginning to pay off. The National Coalition of IRS Whistleblowers helped spark congressional hearings on IRS abuses, based on leaked documents and other records that showed, among other things, that several Los Angeles IRS agents had shielded a California apparel manufacturer from a tax investigation after the agents bought property from the manufacturer. The *New York Times,* in an op-ed published on July 24, 1989, predicted that the proceedings might be the "most startling Congressional hearings since Watergate."

The hearings did expose significant abuse within the agency. The Church of Scientology, emboldened, began to press for further IRS reform. On April 16, 1990, David Miscavige wrote an editorial in *USA Today* calling for the abolition of the IRS and the creation of a new "value added" tax on goods and services. In October 1990, bands of whistle-blowing Scientologists with the National Coalition of IRS Whistleblowers protested in front of the IRS offices in Washington, D.C., offering a $10,000 reward to any agent willing to expose IRS abuses.

The church also spent roughly $6 million on a series of full-page advertisements that ran in *USA Today* and the *Wall Street Journal.* One advertisement, with the heading "Don't You Kill My Daddy!" addressed an incident in which "a band of armed IRS agents" supposedly tried to choke an Idaho man who hadn't paid his taxes. Several of the ads also featured photographs of individual agents, including the IRS chief, Fred Goldberg Jr.

Scientology did not confine its war to the IRS as an organization. Following the well-worn path that L. Ron Hubbard had laid out, the church hired private investigators to dig into the lives of IRS employees. One of these investigators, Michael L. Shomers, later told the *New York Times* that in 1990 and 1991, he was retained by the Church of Scientology to perform a variety of services, including "looking for [the] vulnerabilities" of various IRS agents. Posing as an IRS employee, Shomers said he attended IRS conferences, where he took notes on those agents who seemed to have a drinking problem or were being unfaithful to a spouse. He then provided the church with the names, and in some cases the phone numbers, of agents he thought it might be easy to blackmail.*

In August 1991, the church filed a $120 million federal lawsuit

---

* According to Marty Rathbun, anyone suspected of blocking Miscavige's quest for tax exemption was perceived as an enemy, including the onetime church executive Terri Gamboa, a former Messenger to L. Ron Hubbard aboard the *Apollo,* who'd left Scientology with her husband in 1989. Gamboa had been the executive director of Author Services when it was the main financial organ of the church, and thus knew a great deal about financial irregularities concerning Hubbard, Miscavige, and the Church of Scientology overall. That she left was "a seven-alert fire," said Rathbun, which Miscavige dealt with by dispatching a team of officials, including Rathbun, to confront Gamboa while she was on a trip with her husband and simultaneously break into a briefcase kept in her car, which Miscavige feared contained documents pertaining to L. Ron Hubbard's estate. "As it turns out the briefcase had nothing of use in it and it was returned to Terri's car," said Rathbun. Gamboa never uttered a word publicly about church finances.

against seventeen individual IRS officials, accusing them of various illegal acts, including infiltrating the church using paid informants, conspiring to plant phony documents in Scientology's files, and in one case, attempting to rewrite the IRS definition of *church* to enable the agency to deny the Church of Scientology its exemption.

The agency, overwhelmed, began to feel the cumulative effect of the church's pressure campaign. "It was blatant harassment," opined one formerly high-ranking IRS official. He'd been harassed by Scientologists, he noted, since the 1970s. "They have a nasty habit of finding your unlisted telephone number and calling you at two A.M., just to let you know they're there." One assistant commissioner repeatedly found his garden hose mysteriously turned on in the middle of the night. Other agents reported that their dogs and cats had disappeared.

In the fall of 1991, Miscavige proposed meeting with the IRS commissioner Fred Goldberg, personally, to work out a deal. He floated the idea, said Rathbun, during a meeting with the church's lawyers based in Washington, D.C. The attorneys balked. But Miscavige insisted, and Goldberg agreed to see them later that week.

As Rathbun later recalled, Miscavige opened the meeting with a twenty-minute speech that included a passionate defense of Scientology as a legitimate religion. He acknowledged the Church of Scientology's history of harassment and lawsuits, but claimed that the church had never had much choice. "We're just trying to defend ourselves," he said.

Then he made a peace offering. "Look, we can just turn this off," he told Goldberg, in reference to the lawsuits — provided that the Church of Scientology could get "what we feel we are actually entitled to," which was full exemption. Goldberg had been with the IRS since 1982, and was, by all accounts, eager to make the messy Scientology battles go away. During a break Goldberg came up to Rathbun and asked if Miscavige was serious. "We can really turn it off?"

Rathbun looked at the commissioner. "Like a faucet."

For the next two years, Rathbun and Miscavige made weekly trips to Washington, D.C., to meet with a five-man working group of IRS officials that had been put together by Commissioner Goldberg, outside normal channels. The group was highly irregular; it bypassed the IRS's Exempt Organizations Division, which would have normally handled the review of the Church of Scientology's status. When asked about this, Rathbun suggested that Goldberg had tried to eliminate the "Scientology haters" from the review process, which required creating his own side group to review the claims.

Every week, Rathbun and Miscavige returned to Los Angeles with questions from the tax authorities; their aides would work diligently to prepare answers for the officials' next trip. "There was a huge number of people putting together all of this information: binders and pictures, charts," recalled Tanja Castle, who was one of David Miscavige's secretaries at the time. "The whole religion of Scientology was basically explained to the IRS: the Grade Chart, the ethics conditions . . . [Dave and Marty] were trying to show these guys how Scientology *is* a religion, how it actually did conform to the basic tenets of a religion, how it wasn't for profit — we gave them all the finance records from all the treasuries, all the way down to the lowest org. The entirety of Scientology had to get their financial records straight" — a difficult task, as most of the organizations kept few if any records.

Indeed, said one church finance officer, the church's finances were such a mess, it had to reconstruct its books wholesale. "There really were no books," she said. "Had anyone from the IRS come in and looked at our finances, they would have never given us any kind of exemption. Some of these orgs hadn't recorded their income, yet their members were claiming on their tax forms that they'd donated tens of thousands of dollars to Scientology, and no one could prove it. They had no records that actually gave you any idea of what a church had, or what it spent — and I'm talking about all the organizations all over the country."

To fix this problem, David Miscavige had created an "audit task force" in 1987 to do forensic accounting. In Los Angeles, Scientology's Pacific Area Command Base became the site of a frenzied audit involving 120 Scientologists who worked nearly round the clock to make sense of the church's finances. In New York, a task force of around 50 people set up shop on a floor of the New York Org in midtown Manhattan and did the same thing. Over the next several years, as the church's lawsuits and investigations of the IRS ballooned, these Scientologists pieced together the books of every Scientology organization, mission, and church-affiliated entity in the United States.

Finally, in the fall of 1993 the two sides reach a settlement, the details of which would not be fully known until the end of 1997. In a highly unusual move, the IRS had declared the agreement secret, not subject to release through the Freedom of Information Act or its own code of regulations.* It was a sharp departure from how other religious organizations had been treated. As the *New York Times* later noted, both the Jimmy Swaggart Ministries and an affiliate of the Reverend Jerry Falwell's had been "required by the I.R.S. to disclose that they had paid back taxes in settling disputes in recent years."

The excuse given within the agency was that the Scientology fight had been tying up IRS resources for too long. But it was puzzling, the official noted, because the IRS staff involved in the agreement had also been fairly confident they'd ultimately win the war.

For twenty-five years, the IRS had steadfastly insisted that Scientology was a business, and it had prevailed in all of the substantive suits brought by the church. As late as June 1992, the U.S. Claims Court had upheld the IRS's denial of tax-exempt status to the Church of Scientology. The ruling strongly supported the agency's position that the church was a commercial organization, and again the judge reproved it for deliberately deceptive practices — this time in designing its financial structure. "The decision [to settle] came as an enormous shock to all of us," the official said.

In an editorial, the *St. Petersburg Times* wrote that the IRS had "surrendered" to the Scientologists. "Instead of tough tax law enforcement, taxpayers are seeing a Scientology sellout." Privately, many people within the IRS agreed. Several agents who'd been assigned to process the church's formal application after the agreement was reached later confessed that they had been instructed to ignore substantive issues while processing the application. "If you ask me, Gold-

---

* In 1998, the agency was ordered by a district court to release internal documents relating to the negotiations. At about the same time, the settlement document was leaked to the press.

berg couldn't put up with the harassment like the rest of us did," said the former high-ranking IRS official, whose tenure with the agency dated back to the 1970s and Operation Snow White.

On the evening of October 8, 1993, more than ten thousand Scientologists, the largest meeting of Scientologists in history, gathered at the Los Angeles Sports Arena. The stage at one end of the arena was draped in blue banners, with gilded romanesque columns and torches. Miscavige stood at the podium in a black tuxedo, beaming.

"There will be no billion dollar tax bill [to the IRS] which we can't pay," Miscavige announced. "There will be no more discrimination. There will be no more twenty-five hundred cases against parishioners across the United States. The pipeline of IRS false reports [about Scientology's activities] won't keep flowing across the planet. There will be no more nothing — because" — Miscavige paused for dramatic effect — "the war is over!" The band launched into triumphant music and the audience rose to their feet, screaming and cheering as the words "THE WAR IS OVER!" flashed on giant screens behind Miscavige's head.

Marty Rathbun has always insisted that the Church of Scientology won its exemption legitimately, through lawsuits and other aboveboard forms of pressure. Aside from the testimony of Michael Shomers, there has never been any evidence to prove that Scientologists brought into play some of the more underhanded tactics they had used, for example, in the prior assault on the IRS, Operation Snow White. But the sheer magnitude of the church's exemption was astounding. The deal granted tax exemption to all of Scientology's 150 U.S. entities, including Miscavige's RTC; the seat of its international management, the Church of Scientology International; the Flag Service Organization in Clearwater, Scientology's largest and most successful "church"; and its advanced organizations in Los Angeles. It also gave exemption to the church's various social betterment programs. These included Narconon, a franchised network of drug treatment and rehabilitation centers, whose directors often claim to have no direct association with the Church of Scientology; Applied Scholastics, an organization that licenses a special, Hubbard-endorsed educational method called "study technology" to Scientology-run schools as well as to secular public schools and tutoring programs;

and the Citizens Commission for Human Rights, a lobbying organization that promotes Scientology's anti-psychiatry agenda in Washington and elsewhere. Also exempt were the two publishing houses that were the exclusive publishers of Hubbard's books, both the Scientology-related texts and his wholly secular, and profit-generating, fictional works.

Though it owed roughly $1 billion in back taxes, Scientology had been fined just $12.5 million. The IRS also canceled payroll taxes and penalties against seven top Scientology officials, including Miscavige, and dropped audits of thirteen Scientology organizations, including the Church of Scientology International. In exchange for all of this, Scientology agreed to drop the thousands of lawsuits it had brought against the IRS and its officials.

And not only that, Miscavige announced triumphantly, but all future Scientology churches would never have to go through the exhaustive paperwork the IRS requires to prove tax-exempt status: all they would have to do would be to meet specific qualifications laid out and enforced by Scientology's Mother Church, which would grant these new organizations exemption themselves and then pass along the pertinent data to the IRS for its records.

Every audit or tax action currently pending against Scientologists was canceled. "There are no more tax court cases, there are no more disallowed deductions," Miscavige said. The IRS had even agreed to send, at U.S. taxpayers' expense, a special church-written fact sheet, "Description of the Scientology Religion," to many foreign governments, with a letter explaining that after thorough review, the U.S. tax authorities found Scientology to be "organized and operated exclusively for religious or charitable purposes." It would be a significant step, church leaders hoped, in resolving some of Scientology's conflicts abroad — and, like everything else about the agreement, this was an unusual step.

While many other religious groups in America have been given sweeping exemptions, no organization with the contentious history of the Church of Scientology has ever been exempted in such an overarching manner. In 1994, one year after Scientology's tax exemption was announced, an Orthodox Jewish couple from Los Angeles, Michael and Marla Sklar, tested the fairness of this agreement by su-

ing the IRS for the right to deduct their children's religious education from their taxes just as Scientologists were allowed to deduct
the price of auditing.* The Sklars lost and appealed, and ultimately
took their case all the way to the Supreme Court. In October 2009,
the justices refused to hear the case, without comment.†

"The power of our group is greater than you can imagine," Miscavige, in his victory speech, told his flock, who had met his announcement with almost ten minutes of uninterrupted applause. Scientology was now a religion, protected by the laws of the U.S. government.
Those Scientologists who'd ever doubted the mission, or Miscavige,
had long since departed. Those who remained were the truest of believers, and David Miscavige, the young disciple of L. Ron Hubbard,
was unequivocally their leader. Scientologists would follow him anywhere, unquestioningly, from now on.

"What exactly does this [exemption] mean?" Miscavige said. "My
answer is: everything. The magnitude of this is greater than you may
imagine . . . The future is ours."

Not a soul in the audience had reason to doubt him.

---

* Scientologists are allowed to deduct only 80 percent of the cost of auditing as
charitable contributions.
† Equating a religious education like that received at a yeshiva with Scientology
auditing is in some ways a bad analogy. Far better would be to equate the education Scientologist children receive at Applied Scholastics–sponsored schools,
which reinforce Hubbard's principles. These schools were given tax exemption
under the 1993 agreement, and parents may deduct the cost of these schools
from their income taxes — as well as deduct any donations they might make directly to ABLE, the Association for Better Living, a nonprofit organization set
up by the Church of Scientology to administer its social betterment programs,
including the Applied Scholastics program.

PART III

CHAPTER 9

Lisa

TRY TO DEFINE Scientology, and even those who understand its basic concepts will inevitably come up with a multiplicity of descriptions: alternative to psychotherapy, social movement, transnational corporation, cult, religion. One of its essential characteristics is its aggressive response to challenges, whether they arise from within the movement or outside it. Some journalists have referred to Scientology as a hydra for this uncanny ability to restore itself despite numerous blows to the head. This power to reinvent itself lies at the heart of the church's business plan.

Scientology means different things to different people; simultaneously its essential qualities remain hidden from public view. This combination of flexibility and mystery has allowed church leaders to turn Scientology into whatever they want it to be, depending on time period and need. In the sixty-plus years since it was founded, Scientology has changed its image over and over through a savvy marketing strategy that has presented the church as forever new and improved and, in some cases, as transformed altogether. At no time was this more obvious, or necessary, than during the late 1970s and early 1980s when, fresh from the ignominy of Operation Snow White, Scientology needed to rebrand itself almost entirely.

The Scientology name had been tarnished by scandal. And the product, which had been continuously refreshed by Hubbard during his twenty-five years at the helm, was beginning to stagnate, thanks to the Founder's increasing isolation. But the packaging, church officials realized, could still be vibrant. Which is how it came to be that Scientology was suddenly reimagined as a self-help movement.

The 1970s, as the conservative journalist David Frum points out, have often been overlooked in favor of the far more colorful, and seemingly more influential, 1960s. But as he notes in his book *How We Got Here,* an engrossing analysis of the 1970s, it was those "strange feverish years" following the sixties, the years when the bottom seemed to drop out of America, and indeed, out of many parts of the world, that transformed U.S. society into the branded, self-obsessed, confessional, technologically efficient, widely overconfident yet deeply vulnerable place it is today. "They were a time of unease and despair, punctuated by disaster," according to Frum.

This was the culture the Church of Scientology found itself in after L. Ron Hubbard went into hiding and David Miscavige, having never experienced the "wog world" in any substantive way, began his ascent to power. Jeff Hawkins, who'd joined Scientology at the peak of its hippy-dippy era, was now charged, as head of strategic marketing, with selling the church to a new generation. With the approval of L. Ron Hubbard, and with the help of outside consultants, including a former creative executive from the ad agency Chiat/Day, Hawkins set about devising a strategy that would remove the word *Scientology* altogether from many promotions and replace it with what he and others saw as a safer substitute: *Dianetics.* This term, having died a quiet death in the 1950s, was unfamiliar to the population at large, making it the perfect name for a product that could be shaped to fit the current cultural moment and, Hawkins hoped, signify a new beginning for the movement.

To sell this new Dianetics, which was still Scientology, but with different packaging, Hawkins and his marketing team conducted national surveys. They discovered that what had worked in the 1960s and early 1970s — promoting Hubbard's ideas as a form of spiritual enlightenment, or alternatively, as rebellion against the status quo — would not work in the go-go 1980s. What might capture potential converts, they found, was promoting the philosophy as a form of self-improvement and, for those in need of it, "recovery" from the various indulgences of the past. This fit neatly with the entire premise of Dianetics, which had always been marketed as a set of techniques to increase physical and psychological health, self-confidence, and success.

The pitch Hawkins came up with, a promotion that would ultimately put the book *Dianetics* on the New York Times Best-Seller List, was "Invest in Yourself." The campaign kicked off in 1982. Over the next five or six years, as leaders were purged and longtime members departed Scientology in disillusionment, tens of thousands of new people were drawn into it through books on Dianetics, self-improvement seminars, and one-on-one evangelism. One of these new converts was a smart, assertive, impressionable young woman named Lisa McPherson.

Lisa was the younger of two children raised by Jim McPherson, an insurance salesman, and his wife, Fannie, a homemaker. Born in Dallas, Texas, she grew up in a middle-class neighborhood on the northeastern side of the city, where she was a popular, diligent student and a member of the drill team. Lisa was also pretty, with wavy light brown hair, a curvaceous figure, and a vivacity that typically made her the center of attention. Acquaintances recalled her as "fearless" when it came to making friends, a person who could start a conversation with anybody.

Lisa's outward joie de vivre masked a host of insecurities, however. As the daughter of alcoholics, she had endured a rocky childhood. Her mother often took her first drink at ten in the morning and continued imbibing throughout the day: more than once, Lisa would come home from school to find her mother passed out, sometimes wearing only her underwear. "I hated her for always being a drunk," Lisa later wrote.* But she rarely confronted her mother for fear of what she might do. Fannie was prone to drunken rages. "She let loose on me, not spanking but hitting," Lisa wrote.

This abuse also traumatized Lisa's older brother, Steve, who committed suicide when he was sixteen. Lisa, then fourteen, was devastated, and turned to sex and drugs to mask her anguish. Over the next several years, Lisa led an accomplished double life: maintaining a good-girl exterior while drinking, smoking pot, and, by her own admission, sleeping with virtually anyone who asked, including the husband in a family that employed her as a babysitter.

---

* This comment, like many remarks Lisa made about her early life, were later recorded in various church-ordered confessionals, including the "life history" that Lisa was required to write as part of her indoctrination into Scientology.

After high school, Lisa, who'd decided to skip college, went to work as a customer service representative at the Southwestern Bell phone company, where her natural effervescence made her a hit with both clients and co-workers. But she was still troubled and soon became involved with Don Boss, the owner of a Dallas sheet metal shop. They'd met in 1979, when Lisa was nineteen and Boss thirty-five. One month after they met, the couple eloped.

Boss was violent and a heavy drinker, and Lisa soon realized she'd made a mistake. "They had a real rocky time," recalled her childhood friend Carol Hawk. "He was very abusive and I think at one point he tried to kill her and that's when she decided to divorce him." Nine weeks after marrying, Lisa divorced Don, but he remained in her life. She found it impossible to completely break away from him, and in the spring of 1982, Lisa agreed to marry him again.

It was around that time that one of Lisa's co-workers began to talk to her about Dianetics, describing it as a "tool to improve your life" and urging Lisa to try it. Lisa latched onto the proposal. "I don't know why," she wrote later. "I just knew something about Scientology could save me from the mess I was in."

Lisa paid a visit to the Scientology organization in Dallas, then known as the Mission of the Southwest and also called the Center for Personal Enhancement. It was small, with just a few hundred members, but they were a young and enthusiastic bunch. Melanie Stokes, who ran the mission through 1981, had created a positive environment; she described the membership as "a big life-coaching group." Every night brought new prospects: friends of current members and random young people who'd found out about Scientology or Dianetics from a street recruiter.

During the late 1970s and early 1980s in Dallas, Scientologist "volunteer ministers," as proselytizers were called, handed out Dianetics leaflets and free personality tests at clubs, on college campuses, and in hospitals. Steve Hall, a Dallas Scientologist who would later work at the church's International Base, first found out about Scientology from a flier handed to him at a Rolling Stones concert. Hall wound up joining and was a regular at the mission in the early 1980s. Unlike the more regimented atmosphere at the Scientology orgs, the mission fostered a spirit of fun and experimentation. Nights and weekends were its busiest hours; free lectures and auditing demonstrations occurred frequently as did larger events like the annual Halloween party, which featured dancing, live music, and "plenty of beer," according to Hall. Among those who joined the mission were several members of a local rock band, some businesspeople, a scientist, students from Southern Methodist University and other local colleges, and many other kids in their twenties who, as Hall recalled, "just came to hang out. It was a happening place."

Lisa McPherson fit right in. "She was a ball of fun," said Greg Barnes, who was Lisa's registrar in Dallas. "She was funny, she was exuberant, she was excited, she was humble — she was a great person." But Lisa was also unaware of what Scientology would require of her, he said. "Was she naive? No. But did she know what she was getting herself into? No way. None of us did."

The path from neophyte to committed new member of the Church of Scientology is standard, beginning with the personality test, called the Oxford Capacity Analysis; its serious-sounding name has led some members to assert, mistakenly, that it was developed at Oxford University. Next comes an introductory lecture and auditing package to explain the basic principles behind Dianetics and Scientology. After that, prospective members with a drug history are required to undergo the Purification Rundown, the holistic detoxification program Hubbard created in 1979 to cleanse the body of impurities, leaving a person in a "clean" state that makes him or her more receptive to auditing.*

In August 1982, Lisa, having passed through these preliminaries, arrived at the first stage of the so-called Bridge to Total Freedom: Life Repair, which is tailored to address whatever crucial difficul-

---

* Doctors have questioned the effectiveness of the Purification Rundown, which has never been scientifically proven as effective and might in fact be dangerous. Its central component, niacin, is administered in extremely high doses. The recommended daily allowance of niacin is fifteen milligrams; the Purification Rundown calls for it to be administered in cocktails containing one hundred to five thousand milligrams, gradually increasing in potency over time. Such high doses produce a flush on the skin, which Hubbard interpreted as a sign that the body was expelling impurities. Dosages of this size can also cause liver damage. Nonetheless, the Purification Rundown is required of every new member with a history of drug use, which Lisa McPherson had.

ties a candidate for membership is having in life. Lisa's major difficulty — her "ruin" — was her relationship with her husband, which she hoped to improve. Lisa's church counselors saw things differently: they believed her best course would be to leave Don, who was skeptical of Scientology and suspicious of its costs.

Barnes and other staff members laid out their case. What was best for Lisa, they said, was for her to stay in the church and handle the situation with her husband, who was quite clearly a Suppressive Person. To make sure that Lisa understood just what that term meant, Barnes sat her down with Scientology's *Technical Dictionary* to look up its definition, directing her to Hubbard's statement that a Suppressive Person would "automatically and immediately . . . curve any betterment activity into something evil or bad." The implication was that Don Boss fell into this category, and what was truly dangerous, Lisa was told, was that being connected to such a person made her a Potential Trouble Source, or PTS, which was someone susceptible to all kinds of physical and psychological illnesses. To lead a happier life, Lisa would have to free herself from Boss's suppression — and any other suppressive forces in her life — by either changing his mind about Scientology or disconnecting from him altogether.

Over the next several months, Lisa underwent a PTS Handling, a program Hubbard designed for members who are "roller coasting," or experiencing ups and downs or simply having doubts of one sort or another. She searched deep within herself to find her own flaws, and during the spring of 1982, she wrote extensive confessions — known as "overt/withhold write-ups." In these reports, she noted every sexual dalliance, flirtation, or "perverted" thought or act she'd ever committed, and with whom: pool boys, neighbors, friends of her brother's, a cousin of her husband's.

Prompted by Greg Barnes, Lisa also wrote an affidavit attesting to Boss's criminal history. "I was never informed as to exactly what was said [to him]," Lisa later recalled. "[But] the next time he phoned [the mission], one of his crimes was read off to him and he never contacted the mission again." After a year of this work, Lisa disconnected from Don, and the couple divorced. "Lisa was in an abusive relationship and we basically helped her end it," said Barnes.

Now liberated, Lisa was determined to follow the path toward self-improvement. Her first step was to enroll in a course whose purpose was to teach students how to study; according to her Scientologist friends, it would enable her to learn anything with ease. Lisa had always done well in school, but L. Ron Hubbard wrote that even the best students often didn't fully grasp what they were studying. They might find they'd read an entire page, or even an entire book chapter, without remembering it. They might suffer headaches or feel tired. While many people attributed this to boredom or distraction, Hubbard explained that all of these symptoms, and many others, were caused by three distinct blocks: the "lack of mass," or absence of physical examples to illustrate the subject being studied; "too steep a gradient," or moving to the next phase of study before the previous stage had been mastered, which could result in the feeling of being overwhelmed; and "the misunderstood word."

Originally conceived of in the 1960s by Charles and Ava Berner, Scientologists and teachers in California, "study technology" was co-opted and launched by Hubbard as his own during a series of lectures he delivered at Saint Hill in 1964. Over the years, it would become Scientology's main form of indoctrination and a central facet of the church's ongoing strategy to use what, in a mainstream context, might seem valuable, or even progressive,* to draw people deeper into Scientology's alternative universe. It was based on three principles: students learn at their own pace, use physical examples — pictures, marbles, or clay models — to help work out complex concepts, and need to focus intensely on vocabulary, never skipping an unfamiliar word without looking it up in the dictionary. Anyone who wanted to move up the Bridge was required to master study technology, which was defined to Scientologists as a method of "learning how to learn."

At the Dallas mission, students busied themselves with studying what seemed to be ordinary concepts like affinity or communication, and then with modeling them in clay, a process known as a "clay demo." To make sure they understood every word and concept they read, they were instructed in a process known as "word clearing,"

---

* Though not in vogue when Hubbard first adopted it, the concept of "learning styles," meaning that different approaches to presenting material — visual, auditory, kinesthetic, and so on — suit different students, is now accepted and informs educational practice in many U.S. schools.

which entails relearning the definitions of even basic words, such as *a* or *on*. There are nine distinct types of word clearing, some done with an E-meter, some without; the most rigorous is called "Method 9," or M9. This required students to work with a partner, reading aloud from a book or, more often, from Hubbard's policies, in alternating paragraphs. Each time one partner blinked, twitched, yawned, or simply mispronounced a word, the other was required to stop, yell "Flunk!," and instruct the person to go back and find the word he or she didn't fully grasp, look it up, and then use it in sentences until the partner felt the confusion had been "cleared." Then the partners would resume reading aloud.

Some critics of Scientology maintain that study tech, particularly its word-clearing and clay-demo processes, is harmful, as it essentially breaks down the entire semantic and thought structure of the individual, reducing a person to an almost childlike state. Lisa, however, loved her Scientology studies. She felt smarter, more competent. To her friends, she expressed a sense of being in control for the very first time in her life. Scientology was an adventure, and the people she met through the church were bright, friendly, easy to talk to, and united in the sense of being on a mission of self-discovery. "Nobody else that [Lisa] knew of with the exception of the woman that she worked with was involved in Scientology," said Carol Hawk. "Her family was not aware of what Scientology was . . . and to be honest, I'm not sure Lisa was either. At that point, she was very young, and she was very excited about the process of learning about it, and feeling like she was doing something for herself."

Lisa began spending long hours at the mission, forgoing personal pastimes like country-western dancing, once her favorite activity. She stopped drinking and smoking pot; she also left off attending parties and family functions. Her vocabulary changed. People were "terminals." Cars, houses, clothes, jewelry, and other physical or material goods were "MEST" — matter, energy, space, and time. A person with a positive attitude was "uptone." Someone who worked hard and did well was "upstat." She was a "thetan," and her life was not singular — she had lived many lifetimes, she informed her old friends.

Lisa's odd behavior worried Hawk. "I would say, 'Who are these people, these auditors? They're not psychologists, they're not doctors

. . . what happens if you're in this auditing session and this person who has no formal training gets you to a place that you can't handle?"

But Lisa was sanguine. "Oh, they know how to handle any kind of situation. They know exactly the right questions to ask."

"It got to the point where we weren't really communicating because you are just kind of looking at her thinking, 'What are you talking about?'" Hawk recalled. One by one, friends drifted away. By 1984, virtually everyone left in Lisa McPherson's life was a Scientologist.

Fannie McPherson, widowed in 1985, worried deeply about her daughter's growing involvement with Scientology. A lifelong Baptist, Fannie, who'd stopped drinking and had joined Alcoholics Anonymous in the late 1970s, had initially been thrilled when Lisa came home in 1982 and announced that she'd joined a church. But as she watched Lisa spend less and less time with her friends and family and more and more money on Scientology, her anxiety grew.

Lisa, Fannie knew, fervently believed that L. Ron Hubbard was a savior. She wrote letters to the Founder. She referenced Hubbard's sayings on issues ranging from stress at work to more abstract notions such as "truth." Lisa tolerated no dissenting opinions, no criticism. She refused to read the newspapers or watch the news. When, in December 1985, CBS aired an episode of *60 Minutes* that presented an investigative report on Scientology, featuring interviews with recent defectors from the church, Lisa said it was "entheta," or harmful to her spiritual well-being, and she declined to watch.

The defectors featured on this broadcast, and in other stories like it, were for the most part people who'd joined Scientology in the 1960s as part of a spiritual quest, as Jeff Hawkins had. Lisa McPherson had come to Scientology out of desperation — she later said she'd joined the church to help her "get loose from the criminal psychotic I was connected to," Don Boss. "I think Lisa saw Scientology as her strength," said Carol Hawk. "She had done well there, she felt better. Whether there were any larger concepts of doing wonderful things for the world, I don't know . . . but I know that she felt very strongly that it was what was going to make her whole."

And, by all appearances, it had. Lisa found a community at the

Dallas mission, where she began working part-time in 1983, helping administer personality tests and volunteering at church phone drives and fundraising events. In the goal-oriented environment of the organization, Lisa's energy and sales talents were appreciated, and she made scores of new friends, including Bennetta Slaughter, one of the most prominent Scientologists in Dallas.

Slaughter, a tall, handsome woman with a cascade of wavy dark brown hair, had an unmistakable air of power — or what Scientologists call "purpose." She and her husband, a Scientologist and successful businessman named David Slaughter, were partners in a brokerage firm called the Atlantic Financial Mortgage Corporation. Dallas, the center of high-tech industry in Texas, was in the midst of a real estate boom, and the Slaughters by every account made a killing during the mid-1980s. They bought a house in suburban Plano, one of the wealthiest communities in the United States, and became prominent on church boards and committees. Scientology has always moved prominent donors up the spiritual ladder more quickly; the high-status Slaughters rocketed to the top of the Scientology food chain. Before long, they were Operating Thetans.

In 1985, Lisa, eager to "expand and make more money to go up the Bridge," as she put it, quit her job at the phone company and went to work for the Slaughters as a loan officer at Atlantic Financial. There is a certain type of personality that flourishes in sales, and Lisa, charming and well mannered, "aggressive without being obnoxious," as one co-worker put it, possessed it in spades. Soon she was making roughly $70,000 per year.

Lisa had remarried; her husband, Gene Skonetski, was a Scientologist she'd met at the mission. Now they began to acquire the trappings of wealth: a new condo, new furniture, new clothes, a diamond necklace, a new Porsche, a $700 vacuum cleaner. Virtually everything was bought with Lisa's salary, as Gene worked full-time at the Mission of the Southwest as a registrar. "You make almost nothing" in such a job, said Greg Barnes.

By 1986, this arrangement was beginning to cause problems. Gene appeared disinclined to earn a living, yet he was in charge of the couple's finances. Then, at the end of 1987, the Dallas real estate market collapsed because of the savings and loan crisis, and the Slaughters, looking for new opportunity, decided to relocate to the San Francisco Bay area, where real estate values had skyrocketed. Left without a job when the Slaughters departed, Lisa was also $40,000 in debt, having "squandered a lot of my earnings," as she confessed in a church report, while borrowing substantial amounts of money to pay for her auditing.

Usually registrars would pitch a new product to people almost immediately after they'd finished a course or an auditing process; at this point they were usually in a state of euphoria and eager to do more. The registrar's next task was to help them figure out how to pay for it. If a Scientologist didn't have enough in her checking account or available credit on a credit card, the registrar might offer to help the member secure a loan from a fellow Scientologist. Or the member might be encouraged to borrow money from friends or family, or to borrow against a home or other property. Sandra Mercer,* a former Scientologist who worked as a registrar for many years, often rationalized this pressure by explaining to her clients — and to herself — that they would become more empowered in the end. As she explained it, "When you sit somebody down and you convince them to give over their entire life savings for the cause, you look at it this way: sometimes you have to go into debt to make money."

But some people simply couldn't handle the financial pressure. For them, there was another option, which was joining the church staff. Even though it meant one less paying client, Scientology encouraged its members to work at the orgs, since they were so often understaffed. Virtually everyone that Mercer knew in Scientology who became a staff member had signed up at least in part for financial reasons. Lisa McPherson was no different. In February 1988, Lisa told Gene her "life's purpose" was to work for the org full-time (the Mission of the Southwest had by this time been absorbed into the official Church of Scientology and was now called the Dallas Celebrity Centre, an org focused on the upscale and more prominent Scientologists in the area), if only to force him to take more responsibility for their bills.

But by this point, their debt to the church was so high that the

---

* A pseudonym.

church would not allow Lisa to be employed there full-time without paying at least some of it off. So Lisa agreed to work for a local dentist, also a member of the Dallas Scientology community. After finishing that job each day, she went straight to the org and labored until midnight. Lisa's job entailed handling communications, interacting with members, and helping keep tabs on the number of paying Scientologists currently taking courses or being audited — "bodies in the shop," as they were known. She also reached out to "recover" those who, for one reason or another, may have stopped attending the church.

No one could have been more determined, said Greg Barnes. Hers was among the loudest voices at daily musters, or roll calls, which always ended with a salute to the portrait of L. Ron Hubbard and a group cheer of "Hip, hip hooray!" She was so enthusiastic that she convinced many lapsed members to resume auditing. "Lisa was a seductress," said Barnes. "She had a very pleasant smile, she could engage people in conversation, she was no dummy. And she was also very attractive — and she used that. I remember people at the org talking about her, saying, 'God, what a fox.'"

But working for the org meant abiding by a disciplinary system not wholly unlike that of the Sea Organization. When Lisa did well, she was given commendations for her diligence and enthusiasm. When there were errors — if she showed up late for a study session or had to miss a few evenings at the org because she had to work late at the dentist's office — she was reported. Though Scientologists are not supposed to evaluate one another's thoughts or motivations, something that they believe would invalidate each individual's "truth," they are encouraged to take responsibility for one another's moral failings. Every Scientologist, whether public or staff member, is expected to report any "out-ethics" or "off-policy" behavior in others as a security measure; "to show up bad apples," as Steve Hall put it. All Scientology entities, from the smallest mission to the most advanced of the organizations, keep "ethics files" on every member, which includes every "chit," or rules violation, that he or she has ever committed.

At the Dallas church, as at all Scientology churches, staff members were reported for any drop-off or action that got in the way of an "up" statistic — a decrease in the number of people enrolled in Scientology courses or in the number of books sold. During Lisa's tenure at the Dallas org, she was given chits for lateness, or "job endangerment"; for mistakes that resulted in more work for her colleagues, such as using the wrong-size envelope or folder, or failing to get a FedEx package out on time; for missing her targets by not placing enough radio and newspaper ads for the ongoing Dianetics campaign and failing to write follow-up letters to members — the latter being matters of "non-compliance," a Scientology crime. She was also the subject of several lengthy "Knowledge Reports" about her shaky finances and the tensions in her marriage. On one occasion, she was reported for having left a hot plate on overnight — a "Thing That Shouldn't Be."

By the summer of 1988, overworked between the demands of her day job and her long shifts at the org, Lisa was exhausted. She suffered another blow when Gene, having repeatedly ignored his wife's entreaties to help out financially, left Dallas in October and flew to Los Angeles, where he signed a billion-year contract and was absorbed into Scientology's inner sanctum, the Sea Organization. Lisa, who was not consulted about Gene's decision, was now saddled with the couple's entire debt. Furious, she resolved to join the Sea Org too. But once in California, Lisa found the regimentation and strict discipline overwhelming and, desperately homesick for Dallas, soon returned home.

Leaving the Sea Organization, or any staff position, is called "blowing." It came with its own cost, an onerous one: "blown" staff members receive a "freeloader's bill," charging them the full price for all the courses or auditing services they had taken, for free, while in the church's employ. Therefore when Lisa returned to Dallas in the spring of 1989, she found herself $45,000 in debt, and, in accordance with church policy, she was barred from receiving any Scientology services until the money was repaid and she had gone through the appropriate "amends" process to show that she could once again be trusted.

It was a dark time, said Carol Hawk, who reconnected with Lisa during this period. Excluded from auditing, she divorced Gene and declared bankruptcy. Then, over the next six months, Lisa struggled to make reparations, working three jobs, including one at a Domino's pizza shop. Isolated and removed from the structure of the org, she relapsed into long-discarded habits, dancing up a storm at country-western bars and even dating wogs.

But though Lisa was cut off from the services the church provided, she was not cut off from Scientology entirely. She shared an apartment with Brenda Hubert, an active member of the Dallas org, and remained in contact with several other friends and former colleagues from the church. Mixing praise with pressure, they reminded her that she was "loved" within Scientology and urged her to straighten out her finances, "get back in session," and move up the Bridge. "I am looking forward to getting your regular flows"—communications—"and seeing you have your debt fully paid off," the director of registration, Annie Morlin, wrote Lisa in June 1990. "I'll send you a few BREs [business reply envelopes] to make it even easier."

In the summer of 1990, David and Bennetta Slaughter returned to Dallas. Looking for a new venture, they joined forces with their friend and fellow Scientologist Jeffrey Schaffner, hammering out a deal for a three-way partnership in Schaffner's company, AMC Publishing, which would publish advertising packets and sell leads to the insurance industry.

As is typical with many Scientologist-owned companies, AMC used the management and administrative principles of L. Ron Hubbard, licensed to it by the World Institute of Scientology Enterprises (WISE), the organization through which the Church of Scientology has, for more than thirty years, reached out directly to the high-earning professionals who fund most of its work. The stated purpose of WISE is to introduce Hubbard management theory into the non-Scientology world, though WISE often acts more as an intermediary between the church and the Scientology business community, licensing Hubbard's "admin tech" to secular, Scientologist-owned companies for a fee—usually 10 or 15 percent of the gross revenue or money made from courses and consulting. These companies are then charged with instilling their work with key Scientology principles: using an "org board" to delegate responsibilities, managing employees by statistical analyses of their individual productivity, and, crucially, assigning them various "conditions of existence" to improve output.

All of this is standard Scientology fare, promoted at every church and mission of Scientology in the world — and indeed, there is almost no practical difference between the technology licensed to WISE for business and that which is licensed to individual churches of Scientology to promote religion. It would be unthinkable for a Scientologist to *not* use Hubbard's technology in business, just as it would be unthinkable for WISE businesses to not employ fellow Scientologists, for a key function of any WISE company is to make money: for itself and also, through donations, for the church.

With that in mind, Schaffner and the Slaughters set out to hire fellow Scientologists. Lisa McPherson, whom everyone knew to be a particularly dedicated and talented telemarketer, was an obvious and early choice. Every morning, Lisa arrived at work at 8 A.M., her hair in a ponytail, and immediately started making phone calls. Salespeople endure tremendous rejection — hang-ups, insults, even threats — but Lisa took everything in stride. She never used a script but instead chatted extemporaneously with her prospects, talking about the weather, cracking jokes, often for nearly an hour. She was astonishingly good at her job — so good, her former sales supervisor, Shirley Cage, would later reflect, that she soon began setting increasingly high targets for herself, trying to best her own quotas, which would ultimately average up to $20,000 per week.

Within a year, Lisa had righted her finances and repaid her debts to the church. Now that she was eligible to receive auditing, encouraging letters from the Dallas Org once again began to flow her way. "VWD [Very well done] on getting that debt paid off!" one staffer enthused. "Now, get into session, gal!" And Lisa did, donating $12,000 to the Dallas Organization in 1991 and then, redoubling her efforts, giving close to $22,000 to Scientology in 1992 and $27,000 in 1993.

Still, she would have had little choice in the matter. She was now one of more than a dozen Scientologist employees at AMC, where staffers cited Hubbard's thinking on business practices such as interoffice communication and upheld his ethics code by writing up employees' "overts" and "withholds," usually at the request of a company ethics officer. Working for a WISE company can be a singularly insular experience, due to the daily indoctrination of Scientology principles; this sense of isolation is intensified by the presence of church salespeople. "When you work for one of these companies, there is constant pressure to forward Scientology's agenda," said Sandra Mercer, who was once employed by WISE and also worked for a number of WISE-affiliated businesses. In many Scientologist companies it is not unusual to find registrars from the local organization making weekly visits to sell Scientology services to workers. Business owners see this practice as "totally acceptable," said Mercer; it provides evidence of commitment to the faith.* And it is even more "acceptable" for both business owners and their employees to become field staff members (FSMs): off-site recruiters who select services for employees, colleagues, clients, or friends, earning a commission of 10 or 15 percent. In the fractured, franchise-like structure of Scientology, the FSM is a crucial component of any operation; it is the conduit by which many new members are brought into the church and the vehicle by which existing members are kept "on course" and "in session."

Sandi Sampson, who worked with Lisa at the Southwestern Bell phone company, was acting as an FSM when she first "selected" and then "disseminated" to Lisa in 1982. For years after, Sampson was paid a commission on every course or auditing procedure she'd suggested to Lisa. By the early 1990s, Bennetta Slaughter was serving as Lisa's FSM as well as her boss. Slaughter was also, by both women's account, Lisa's best friend. If this posed any conflict of interest, Lisa never let on. "I know that she felt like these people were her family," said Hawk.

By 1993, AMC Publishing had become a highly profitable company, employing more than twenty people. Almost all of them were Scientologists who had come up together in the Dallas church. They were ambitious, expansion-oriented, and eager to advance on the Bridge. That spring, Bennetta and David Slaughter floated the idea

---

* The pressure to sign up for these services can be intense. Owners of a small business in Florida, Mercer and her husband routinely found Scientology salespeople sitting outside their house. "They would call you maybe the day before to feel you out and see how much cash was available. Then the pressure would begin to build until they'd come sit at your doorstep. I had registrars circling my house, waiting for us to get home, and they would sit all around the house, knocking on the doors and windows to get money out of us."

of relocating AMC from Dallas to Clearwater, Florida, Scientology's spiritual mecca. The Tampa Bay area was booming. And "Flag," as Scientology's operation in Clearwater was called, offered the most sophisticated spiritual counseling on earth.

With the Slaughters leading the way, AMC closed the operation in Dallas just before Christmas of 1993 and moved, with all twenty employees, to Florida. Tremendous fanfare accompanied their arrival. Bennetta and David Slaughter were known within the international Scientology world as important and rich OTs. At the Fort Harrison Hotel, Scientology's central base of operations in Clearwater, a steak dinner was prepared for the Slaughters and their staff at the elegant Hibiscus restaurant. The group was photographed for *Source*, the magazine of the Flag Land Base. "This ends the most exciting month I can ever recall," Lisa McPherson wrote to her friend Robin Rhyne, a Dallas Scientologist, on January 31, 1994. "I glow constantly."

Thousands of Scientologists came to Clearwater each year, lured by the church's depiction of Flag as the "Mecca of Technical Perfection." AMC was one of dozens of Scientologist-owned companies in Clearwater. There were Scientologist-run schools, nail salons, and cafés. Scientologists frequented the same restaurants and shops. They patronized one another's businesses, most of which were listed in a local guide, "The Word of Mouth Directory of Honest & Reliable Businesses," which listed every Scientology-friendly business in town: plumbers, realtors, doctors, dentists, chiropractors, auto mechanics, locksmiths, and health food stores. Walking down Cleveland Street, a key downtown thoroughfare that was dominated by Scientology-owned businesses, Lisa could pick up copies of church newspapers and glance through classified ads written in Scientology's lingo. "I don't know how I could truly convey what it's like living here," Lisa wrote to one friend in Dallas. "It's like Utopia."

CHAPTER 10

Flag

I T WAS NO ACCIDENT that Scientology picked Clearwater for its mecca. A balmy outpost on a crystalline bay, it struck the church hierarchy as "a city that could be owned," according to Larry Brennan, who helped scout the Gulf Coast for locations in 1975 when Hubbard, still sailing on the *Apollo*, declared his intent to move back on land.

Clearwater in the mid-1970s was a conservative, largely elderly community, deeply resistant to change. One of the city's most illustrious landmarks, the fifty-year-old Fort Harrison Hotel, looked like a moldy, forlorn relic of times past. In 1975, the hotel's owners put the Fort Harrison up for sale, and that October, a company named the Southern Land Development and Leasing Corporation offered just under $3 million in cash to buy both the hotel and the similarly rundown Bank of Clearwater building, across the street.

The new owner of the buildings, it was announced, was an ecumenical group called the United Churches of Florida. Local reporters, curious as to how a church could have access to that much cash, made inquiries but could find no records about United Churches or Southern Land Sales and Development. If that wasn't odd enough, security guards soon began to appear on the streets, lending the United Churches a rather military mien. Clearwater's mayor, Gabriel Cazares, began asking questions but found few answers. "I am discomfited by the increasing visibility of security personnel, armed with billy clubs and mace, employed by the United Churches of Florida," he said in a speech made shortly after the group arrived. "I am unable to understand why this degree of security is required by a religious organization."

Reporters from two of the local newspapers, the *Clearwater Sun* and the *St. Petersburg Times,* were equally puzzled and spent the next several months digging for information about the suspicious new church. Finally, in January 1976, a *St. Petersburg Times* reporter named Bette Orsini began to close in on the truth: the United Churches of Florida was really a front for the controversial and wealthy Church of Scientology.* Before Orsini could break the story, church leaders, having been tipped off, decided to make the announcement themselves; they sent a representative to reassure the community that the church meant no harm and that its members, who by now were streaming into Clearwater, were law-abiding citizens who simply wanted to practice their religion in peace.

But the people of Clearwater did not take kindly to this intrusion. Most resented the clandestine way that Scientologists had arrived and wondered about the church's true motives. These suspicions did not go away, particularly once the Church of Scientology filed lawsuits against both Cazares and the *Clearwater Sun* (and threatened to sue the *St. Petersburg Times*), accusing them of libel and, in the case of Cazares, violation of the church's civil rights. But what alienated the people of Clearwater most was the Scientologists' insularity: the strange shirt-and-tie formality of their clothes; the secretiveness with which they went about their business; the strange penchant they had for suing anyone who spoke negatively of them or even asked a simple question about them or their practices.

Everything the Scientologists did seemed to put them at odds with the local community. The church purchased property from local sellers but refused to pay taxes. They closed off the Fort Harrison to the public. In March 1976, a couple who had run a gift shop inside the Fort Harrison sued for loss of business after the church abruptly shut down their air conditioning, telephone, and alarm system and refused to restore the services.

---

* Indeed, as the *St. Petersburg Times* later reported (in its issue of March 25, 1976), on December 1, 1975, the day the sale was finalized, the United Churches sold the Fort Harrison to the Church of Scientology for $10.

Then, in the fall of 1978, word began to leak out of Washington, D.C., that Scientology had far broader plans for Clearwater than simply buying property. During the FBI raid that uncovered Operation Snow White, the feds discovered documents that detailed the Church of Scientology's plans to "take over" the sleepy Florida city, a project code-named Operation Goldmine. As the *St. Petersburg Times* reported it, "Church functionaries were directed 'to fully investigate the Clearwater city and county area so we can distinguish our friends from our enemies and handle as needed.'"

Church officials were directed to identify key media and political leaders and either win their allegiance or, if that failed, discredit them through a variety of covert tactics. Reporters at the *St. Petersburg Times* and the *Clearwater Sun* who had investigated Scientology were put on an "enemies list." This list also included the legendary publisher of the *Times*, Nelson Poynter, and the paper's editor, Eugene Patterson; Mayor Cazares and the Clearwater chief of police were also cited, among others. Scientology's "covert agents" had taken jobs at local newspapers, law firms, community agencies, and even the Greater Clearwater Chamber of Commerce. When Clearwater citizens became aware of this plot, they took it as a declaration of war. "People were in a frenzy against Scientology when those documents started coming out," recalled the *Washington Post* writer and editor Richard Leiby, who was then a reporter for the *Clearwater Sun*. "They thought they had a crazy cult in their midst."

This was no small thing in 1978, the year of the Jonestown massacre in Guyana. The story of the group's mass suicide was horrifying: a paranoid cult leader, Jim Jones, urging his followers to drink vats of Kool-Aid laced with cyanide, leaving more than nine hundred people dead, their bodies bloated by exposure to the sun. It was one of the most heavily covered stories of the 1970s, leading the news for months after the November 1978 incident. "Cult of Death" was the label that both *Time* and *Newsweek* gave to Jonestown. In Clearwater, people looked at the Scientologists and wondered what was next.

In the wake of the "Clearwater Conspiracy," as the CBS news program *60 Minutes* dubbed the plot, thousands of Clearwater residents took to the streets in protest, demanding that the Church of Scientology leave town. Mayor Cazares, who'd resigned in 1978 and learned through the Snow White documents that Scientologists intent on ruining his political career had once tried to frame him as the driver in a hit-and-run accident in Washington, D.C., called upon the federal government to be wary, warning that the Church of Scientology was a "politically fascist organization." Richard Tenney, one of the Clearwater city commissioners, spearheaded a concerned citizens group, Save Sparkling Clearwater, that held anti-Scientology rallies in public stadiums and parks. (In one particularly heated exchange, local Scientologists, infuriated by the vociferous criticism of editorialists at the *Clearwater Sun,* marched on the paper's downtown headquarters dressed as Nazi storm troopers, an alarming sight for the city's elderly Jewish population.)

But Scientology's acquisition of properties in Clearwater continued. "We knew that no one, government or individual, could beat us legally and make us leave town," said Larry Brennan, who, arguing that Scientology's services were religious in nature, had helped persuade the state of Florida to grant the Scientology organization a "consumer's certificate of exemption," which recognized it as a religious institution and exempted it from paying, or charging, sales tax on its courses or auditing processes. "After that, we knew we could buy whatever buildings we wanted using whatever corporate shell games we wanted as we were now out of the closet and legally safeguarded," Brennan said.

By 1980, the church owned four hotels and three office complexes, assessed at $8.9 million, brokering the deals in cash. About fifteen hundred Scientologists now lived in the area full-time, it was estimated, while another five hundred or so well-off Scientologists streamed into Flag annually from all over the world, spending weeks, and sometimes months, luxuriating at the Fort Harrison, with its newly renovated rooms, its lobby decked with crystal chandeliers, and its swimming pool. Church officials, hoping to combat the negative publicity caused by the Snow White revelations, reversed previous policy and threw open the doors of the Fort Harrison. With great fanfare, the church announced a downtown revitalization project and also began donating heavily to local charities. By the fall of 1980, the *Clearwater Sun* had to conclude that "Scientology is going to be part of Clearwater for a very long time."

Over the next decade, Scientologists continued to face significant opposition. In May 1982, the city's new mayor, Charles LeCher, held public hearings to probe Scientology's activities in Clearwater, which revealed shocking tales: break-ins and infiltration of government offices, local charities, and community organizations, as well as incidents of child neglect, maggot-infested food fed to staff, and an unreported hepatitis outbreak at the Fort Harrison. "I'm not here to complain about what the church has done to me," said a former church executive named Scott Mayer. "I'm here to really impress upon you what you're actually dealing with, the magnitude of what you're dealing with."

Scientology, nonetheless, continued its public relations campaign. The church hosted more open houses at the Fort Harrison, as well as free courses and Sunday worship services. Scientology officials took out newspaper ads and began to make regular appearances on local cable and radio talk shows, presenting the typical Scientologist as "the person you work with, your friend, or the person next door." By the early 1990s, the Church of Scientology's promotional materials openly boasted of Clearwater as a spiritual mecca, inviting members to come to "the largest community of Scientologists and OTs in the world." And thousands did. It was no surprise that Bennetta Slaughter would want to move her company there.

It was also not surprising that David Miscavige would have looked to Clearwater for inspiration when plotting the next phase of Scientology's advancement. Fresh from his victory over the IRS, Miscavige had taken on a new, and in some ways even more ambitious, scheme: modernizing L. Ron Hubbard's teachings, specifically those pertaining to auditor training, a project he called the Golden Age of Tech, or GAT.

This was a venture the Founder, having recognized that not all auditing was performed with the same level of care or efficiency, had initiated in the late 1970s, said the Scientologist Dan Koon, who helped design part of the Golden Age of Tech. But Miscavige, said Koon and others, seized upon the idea in the 1990s as, among other things, a money-making scheme: GAT would enforce new, rote methods that every auditor, no matter how experienced, would have to learn at his or her own expense, and then follow exactly. Ultimately, everyone in Scientology would be initiated into Miscavige's GAT approach, a massive retraining project that, over the coming years, would make millions of dollars for the church while overhauling Scientology's auditing procedures. Flag, already the church's cash cow, would be the testing ground for this new system.

Bennetta Slaughter wasted no time in Clearwater. Within a few months of her arrival, she'd ingratiated herself with the Clearwater Chamber of Commerce and begun to network with local politicians. "We called her the Queen of Clearwater," said Sandra Mercer, who'd moved to Florida from Los Angeles in 1990. "She put herself on all the political communication lines, on all the business communication lines . . . on every communication line that she needed to get on. Had she not done that," Mercer added, "I don't know that the church would have done that well in Clearwater."

David Miscavige knew Bennetta Slaughter as a prominent donor who attended yearly Scientology events in England and on the church's exclusive cruise ship, *Freewinds*. Now the leader of Scientology began to hear that she was making inroads into Clearwater society. Miscavige became concerned. For all its efforts, the official Church of Scientology had very little relationship with the mayor's office or the city commission, and it had an openly antagonistic relationship with the police. Miscavige ordered Tom De Vocht, a senior official at Flag, to find out what Slaughter was doing. "Make sure that she's forwarding our purposes," he said.

"So I got her in to find out what she was doing, and to explain what we wanted her to be doing," said De Vocht, who now lives not far from Clearwater, in Tarpon Springs. "She was an important public figure and we wanted her to be an ambassador, to introduce us to people." Slaughter, said De Vocht, agreed to act as an emissary.

Largely spurred by Slaughter's efforts, Scientologists became increasingly civic-minded: stringing the downtown streets with Christmas lights, funding blood drives, painting murals, organizing local cleanup projects. A group Slaughter founded, the Tampa Bay Organization of Women, sponsored a carnival, dubbed Winter Wonder-land, to benefit poor children, and for a few weeks each December transformed a local park into an Alpine village, complete with artificial snow, a fifty-foot Christmas tree, and Santa Claus.

This softened some of the skeptics in town. Sandra Mercer described their reaction: "'Oh, they celebrate Christmas? We didn't know that — they're just like us!' Of course we didn't really celebrate Christmas, but that was part of the overall 'safe pointing' strategy."

"Safe pointing" is a specific Scientology policy about how to create allies. L. Ron Hubbard frequently urged his followers to present themselves as "stable, reliable, expert [and] productive," which would then allow them to disseminate Scientology more effectively. Slaughter prosecuted this strategy with gusto.

Lisa McPherson was a vastly different sort of person. "She was just a sweetheart," Mercer recalled with affection. She'd met Lisa for the first time at a Scientology event in early 1994. "She was not at *all* the intense person that Bennetta was." But Lisa was the top producer at AMC, after Slaughter herself. It was Lisa's steady productivity that allowed Slaughter to busy herself in town. "In Scientology, Lisa was what we'd call a 'working installation,'" Mercer explained. "She was a workhorse. And Bennetta worked her and used her."

For ten years since she'd become a Scientologist, Lisa McPherson's goal had been to go Clear. But a variety of obstacles, including her previous lack of financial resources, always stood in the way. Now, with a newly tax exempt church encouraging members to "move up the Bridge even faster" by claiming their Scientology courses and auditing as tax-exempt donations, Lisa began climbing the Bridge in earnest. In 1993, she earned more than $136,000 at AMC and donated $57,000 to the church, claiming a $17,000 refund on her taxes for "charitable deductions" — more than four times the average for taxpayers in her income bracket, the *St. Petersburg Times* would later note. Lisa also received a bill of $75,000 for auditing fees.* Though

---

* The first service Lisa did at Flag was an expensive auditing process called the L-11 Rundown, which is offered only in Clearwater. In 1995, the Flag Service Organization listed the price of the L-11 rundown as $10,000 per intensive. A

the money she spent on Scientology still claimed most of her earnings, Lisa never spoke of it as a financial sacrifice.

Scientology sells itself as a self-betterment program — a route to eternal happiness. But its processes target a member's weaknesses. And, as Mercer explained, there is always a weakness that can be exploited. "You might think you've solved your big problem, but wait — your boyfriend broke up with you, or your boss is giving you a hard time, or something else. There is always *something* that is ruining your life and needs fixing." It is this cycle of problem–realization–cure–new problem that ultimately melds a person with Scientology's collective mindset. "It's an ongoing process," Mercer said. "After a while, your self-esteem is so low, you think everything is a problem."

For Lisa, the problem was often men. She had suffered a string of failed romances, and in the spring of 1995 had broken up with a man named Kurt Paine, whom she'd once planned to marry. Between her sadness and work pressures, she began to appear "downstat." Her sales plummeted, and her commissions, once averaging between $4,000 and $6,000 every two weeks, now sank to just $600 or $700. With her statistics in the tank, Lisa was given an ethics handling at work and was also being audited at church. She told her auditor that it was "bullshit" and also resented the increasing pressure to put in more volunteer hours on projects like Winter Wonderland. Tensions with Bennetta Slaughter began to boil over. In his notes, her auditor wrote that Lisa was "fixated on Bennetta."

"Bennetta was totally focused on getting Lisa to do what she wanted, all the time," said Michael Pattinson, a Scientologist who was working in Clearwater that spring, overseeing the design of the Slaughters' new house. "She was the boss, the money-maker, the FSM, and now she was the ethics officer as well — she had a vested interest in getting Lisa to make more money for the company and for Scientology, and for her." At one point, Pattinson recalled, "she said, 'I'd much rather go back to Dallas and just pursue my own life and my own career, and just be myself.' So I said, 'Listen: you should follow your own purposes in life and not someone else's purposes.'"

minimum of two intensives, or twenty-five hours of auditing, are required to complete this process, raising the cost to at least $20,000.

But Lisa had lost track of her own purposes. In her auditing sessions, she complained that she was unable to "find" herself. She was despondent, racked with guilt, and confused — Scientology, in which Lisa had so fervently believed, had stopped working. "God damn it I feel so *desperate*," she told her auditor. "[I] don't want to do this anymore."

As the former Scientology official Jesse Prince, who examined Lisa's auditing records in 1998, points out, telling your auditor you don't want auditing or that it is not working is a crime in Scientology. Once a person makes these assertions, the director of processing, who manages all auditing for the church, "retrieves" the person from his or her usual auditor and places the person in an "auditing repair program." This program, says Prince, "is designed to repair past auditing mistakes. Lisa McPherson had several of these programs, yet they did not work."

Instead, the new program drove Lisa deeper into despair. Over and over, she spoke of leaving Scientology — "blowing," in the group's parlance; she also told her auditor that she'd been contemplating suicide. Scientologists believe very strongly that a person is fully responsible for their own condition in life, good or bad. Lisa repeatedly searched for reasons she had failed to get better. She saw herself as a "potential trouble source" to Bennetta, unhappy at work, wanting to leave. But she felt incapable of walking away. Her anger turned to despondency and finally to helplessness. "Nothing matters anymore," she told her auditor. "I just want to be left alone."

Depressed and exhausted, Lisa took a leave of absence from AMC and in late June 1995 checked into the Fort Harrison to begin an intensive auditing program known as the Introspection Rundown, which Hubbard designed to help members who were having emotional difficulties. If done correctly, the person should ultimately readjust his or her mentality and "extrovert," or focus attention less on the self and more on others, and the goals of the larger group. "The rundown is *very* simple and its results are magical in effectiveness," Hubbard had maintained.

At the hotel, Lisa was assigned a roommate named Susan Schnurrenberger, a Sea Org member who worked in the base's medical of-

fice. Schnurrenberger, who had a nursing background, was charged
with watching over Lisa to make sure she ate, slept, and was "sessionable" — able to receive auditing. Schnurrenberger was also supposed
to prevent Lisa from hurting herself, as she had repeatedly threatened suicide. During the first few weeks, Lisa's moods roller-coast-
ered from upbeat and "gleaming bright," as one staff member wrote
in a memo, to dark and depressive. She felt as if she had an "enemy"
inside of her. "Susan," she told Schnurrenberger one night, "I think
I'm going crazy."

Late that summer, however, she seemed to emerge from her confusion. The past few months had been a "blank," she wrote to Robin
Rhyne on September 2, 1995, adding that she was finally out of the
woods and feeling more hopeful. She was still at the Fort Harrison
and being audited every day. "You will never believe the level of care
and service I've received at Flag. I'm ready to go on tour and tell the
world how anything CAN BE HANDLED!" she wrote.

Finally, on September 7, 1995, Lisa achieved her longtime goal and
went Clear. The struggle, as she later described it, had been like "a go-
pher being pulled through a garden hose," but she attributed her success to the support of her friends "and of course LRH." "It has been
. . . worth every single thing I've had to go through . . . I am so full
of life I am overwhelmed at the joy of it all!" she wrote. "Now, I understand!" she added, underlining the word *understand* five times.
"WOW!"

That evening, Lisa stood in front of an audience of fellow Scientologists at the Fort Harrison, where, framed certificate in hand, she announced her achievement. She looked thin; her short-sleeved black-
and-white-striped dress hung loose on her frame. Her face, now
framed by a short haircut, looked drawn. Yet her voice was strong.
"Being Clear," she said, "is more exciting than anything I've ever experienced."

But Lisa's glow wore off quickly. She returned to AMC but found it
hard to regain her momentum, and by October, her statistics had begun to dip once again. She worked harder, putting in long hours and
pushing herself, even taking on the role of chief fundraiser for Winter Wonderland; yet sometimes she failed to raise money, a situation,

she decided, that put her in a condition of "treason" to AMC. She now endured even more rigorous ethics handlings, writing painstaking confessions in which she blamed herself for her "case" — her psychological issues.

The confessions were exhausting. And yet, in letters to her friend Robin, she tried to be upbeat about the process, talking about her "cognitions" and "gains." Lisa expressed the same enthusiasm during a phone call she made to her friend Carol Hawk. "The conversation was a little different than our usual talks," Hawk recalled. "Lisa and I [generally] talked about things that were going on in our lives. She usually talked about Scientology only in terms of how she might respond to a particular situation or person and rarely pushed regarding the 'technology' of Scientology." But during this conversation, Hawk said, "she made a little speech about how 'great the tech was' and how every day she woke up 'wonderfully happy and ready to play.' She 'had never experienced anything like it,' and 'couldn't say enough good about the tech' . . . I remember thinking she was a commercial for Scientology."

That was the last time Hawk talked to Lisa. Not long after, Lisa called another childhood friend, Kellie Davis, and apologized for having been out of touch for so many years. Davis had the impression that Lisa was going to leave Scientology. "She said she couldn't get into it over the phone but she said she had a lot to talk about," Davis later told the *Tampa Tribune*. "She said she would explain when she got here." Lisa told Davis that she was hoping to return to Dallas for Thanksgiving, but one way or another, she would be home, possibly for good, by Christmas. "She had made the decision to get out and come back here and she seemed happy," Davis said.

But on the phone with her mother a few weeks before Thanksgiving, Lisa sounded ragged. She was having trouble at work, she told Fannie, and cried. "Mother, I've let my group down," she said. "And that was the last time I talked to her," said Fannie.

The ethics handling that Lisa was receiving during this time was the very same method that had driven her to a breakdown just a few months before. "It was therefore extremely foreseeable," as Ken Dandar, an attorney for the McPherson family, later asserted, "that given Lisa McPherson's prior experience of being psychotic in June of 1995, coupled with her troubles in taking Scientology instruction, she would very likely experience another psychotic episode."

And she did. On November 15, 1995, Lisa was sent to a trade show in Orlando with several AMC colleagues. She packed numerous books by Hubbard that she hoped would help her with her job. But even before they left, Brenda Hubert, who was managing AMC's role in the trade show, found Lisa to be unusually disorganized. "She was very frantic," Hubert wrote in a subsequent memo to church officials. "She talked constantly and couldn't recall what she had just said." When they got to the convention, she began "disseminating" to total strangers, accosting a waiter at a local café and then another one later that night at the hotel restaurant, demanding that they read *Dianetics* — right that minute.

By the second day of the conference, Lisa had become more desperate. That night, Hubert awoke at 3 A.M. to find Lisa pinned on top of her. She was sobbing hysterically. "Get up!" Lisa said. "There's something going on on this planet that you don't know!"

Hubert tried to calm her, but it was useless. Lisa seemed disoriented. She was ranting, saying, "I'm afraid I'm going to flip out again like I did before." The next day, Lisa was sent back to Clearwater under Brenda Hubert's care.

At Bennetta Slaughter's request, Hubert wrote a lengthy memo detailing what had happened during the trade show. In this letter, Hubert noted that Lisa's ethics officer, Katie Chamberlain, had instructed her to rigorously supervise Lisa. "I was told that she was just pretending to be incapable and need directions and orders and that I should not grant that any life or credence." Her own observations, Hubert said, "did not align with what I was told."

And yet, Hubert said she "did what I was told to do. I did try to impinge upon her by yelling at her a few times; I did tell her with force to knock it off; I did tell her that she was at risk of losing her job if she didn't straighten up . . . I am afraid that I might have made this whole thing worse or further upset her and that was not what I wanted to have happen." Then she provided her phone numbers as a contact. "I love Lisa and want to see this get handled," she said. "Please do everything you can for her."

Hubert's concern was genuine. Despite her worry, however, she didn't alert a doctor or take Lisa to the hospital. Instead, she simply typed the letter and delivered it to the church, where she instructed an administrative aide to put the document in Lisa's preclear folder. Whether anyone read her note, Hubert never knew.

The next morning, back in Clearwater, Lisa seemed better. She spent the morning painting sets for Winter Wonderland with her ethics officer Katie Chamberlain, Bennetta Slaughter, and other volunteers at a downtown warehouse. But soon she began to appear "mentally tired [and] stressed," said Chamberlain, and by lunchtime she'd gone home to take a nap. Just before dusk, Lisa got back into her red Jeep Cherokee and headed toward the center of Clearwater. It was rush hour, and the line of cars was moving slower than usual, the result of a motorcycle accident at the corner of South Fort Harrison and Bellevue Boulevards, which had forced traffic into a single lane. As she approached the intersection, Lisa, perhaps distracted by the accident, rear-ended a boat that was fastened to the back of a pickup truck, which had stopped in front of her. "It was just a bump. It was nothing serious," recalled a paramedic named Bonnie Portolano.

Portolano, who had been on the scene of a motorcycle crash, saw the accident and approached the Jeep; in the driver's seat, a pretty young woman, dressed in a loose-fitting white shirt, looked up at her. "I'm . . . I'm sorry," Lisa said.

"Are you okay?"

"I'm fine," she replied, her voice shaking.

The paramedic checked her for scrapes and bruises. "You're sure you didn't hurt yourself?"

"No," Lisa said. "I did not."

There was something off about the woman, Portolano thought. She seemed dazed and her voice was strangely formal, almost programmed. When she was asked a question, she answered with short yes and no answers and, most unnervingly, stared fixedly at Portolano and her partner while doing so. "Can you tell me where you live?" Portolano asked. Lisa couldn't recall. "I could take you there," she offered, "but I don't know what [my address] is."

Portolano didn't know what to do. "I attributed all of this to maybe shock," she said. It was not unusual for victims of even minor collisions to be disoriented immediately afterward. Physically, Lisa didn't have a scratch and assured the paramedics that she didn't need medical treatment. Portolano gave Lisa a release form to sign, then she and her partner, Mark Fabyanic, walked back to their ambulance. They were just about to leave the scene when Fabyanic, the driver, looked in his side-view mirror. "Bonnie, she's taking off her clothes," he said.

"No, she's not."

"I'm not lying."

Lisa walked down the middle of the street, past the ambulance, naked. Portolano jumped out. "Lisa, what are you doing? Why did you take off your clothes?"

Lisa turned. "Well, you see, nobody knows this but I'm an OT," she said. "I don't need a body."

Portolano didn't know what Lisa was talking about. Grabbing her arm, she managed to escort Lisa to the ambulance, where she laid her on a stretcher and covered her with a blanket. "Why did you take off your clothes?" Portolano asked again.

Lisa gave the paramedic a searing look. "I wanted people to think I was crazy because I need help," she said. "I just need someone to talk to." Then she closed her eyes. "I'm so tired," Lisa said in a dull monotone. "I need help."

The paramedics took Lisa to the nearby Morton Plant Hospital emergency room. There, she struck the staff as lucid but resistant to questions, opening her eyes only on command. "She was being very robotic," recalled Kimberly Brennan, one of the nurses on call. Brennan called Dr. Flynn Lovett, the emergency physician on call, who felt strongly that Lisa should be admitted for a psychiatric evaluation and phoned the hospital's mental health unit.

It was just around then, Brennan recalled, that an official from the Church of Scientology showed up. It was perplexing because to Brennan's knowledge, Lisa hadn't called anyone, nor had anyone else phoned the church. Moments later, another church official walked into the emergency room, and then a third. With great agitation they explained to the hospital staff that any form of psychiatry was against the Scientology religion and that Lisa would be better off in the church's care. "They were very upset that we were going to have an evaluation done," Brennan later told the police. "And basically, they did not leave her bedside."

Joe Price, a psychiatric nurse who'd been called to examine Lisa, didn't know what to make of this. "I've never had someone . . . just straight out tell you that they don't believe in psychiatry and that they really don't want your help or need your help," he said. One Church of Scientology official, a well-dressed man in a silk tie and tailored suit, handed Price a brochure. "The basis of the brochure," Price recalled, was that "all psychiatrists will either rape or sexually intimidate or molest their female patients."

Price assured the officials that he wasn't a psychiatrist or psychologist, but a nurse who simply wanted to ask Lisa some questions. The Scientologists allowed this, though they remained in the room. He introduced himself to Lisa and then asked if she wanted the Scientologists to leave. "I remember her saying that she didn't mind if they stayed at her side," he said. "And so they did and I completed my assessment."

Lisa was slow to answer Price's questions and exhibited other odd behavior, such as crossing her eyes, which she told him helped her to concentrate. She spoke calmly, but Price had a "gut feeling" that she wasn't speaking freely. The Scientologists "did not interrupt me while I was questioning her [but] I did notice and I felt that she was intimidated by their presence. So after I initially interviewed her, I went and spoke to Dr. Lovett and we asked them [if they would] mind if I talked to her alone."

The officials hesitated but ultimately agreed and walked a few feet away, around a corner. Price recalled, "I said, 'Lisa, do you need help? Do you want our help?' She said no . . . She denied to me that anything was wrong." Price asked her if she was being held captive, or if she was being intimidated by anyone from the church. Again, Lisa said no.

The Florida Mental Health Act, also known as the "Baker Act," stipulates that patients can be involuntarily committed to a hospital only if they pose a danger to themselves or others, or in other ways exhibit obvious signs of mental illness. Lisa McPherson, Price said, did not meet these criteria. "She was alert and oriented times three. She was able to think abstractly . . . She wasn't suicidal . . . she wasn't homicidal. Was there any psychosis going on at the time — by that I mean, was she out of touch with reality? I don't think so." Granted, her behavior was strange, but he could find no reason to commit her. The Scientologists assured Price that Lisa wouldn't harm herself. "I want to go home with my friends from the congregation," Lisa said, in a passive voice.

Reluctantly the hospital agreed. At 8:40 that evening, less than two hours after being admitted, Lisa McPherson checked herself out of Morton Plant Hospital "against medical advice," and left with six Scientology officials, three at each arm. Standing by the door to the emergency room, Nurse Price watched them go. "My impression was . . . 'My God, this lady's a prisoner,'" he said.

CHAPTER 11

Seventeen Days

I NSANITY," WROTE L. Ron Hubbard in 1970, "is the overt or covert but always complex and continuous determination to harm or destroy. Possibly the only frightening thing about it," he added, "is the cleverness with which it can be hidden." This condition, Hubbard believed, afflicted 15 to 20 percent of the human race, though he maintained that the vast majority of the insane had no "reality" on how irrational they might be, nor did anyone else.

The last, and most obvious, stage of insanity, the "psychotic break," according to Hubbard, was present only in someone who has become what Hubbard called a "PTS Type III," or simply Type Three.* This would be an individual who "sometimes has ghosts about him or demons," a person whom even the Founder believed was most often found in mental institutions. That such a person might be found in Scientology was, by the church's own doctrine, taboo. The purpose of Scientology, as Hubbard wrote, was to "make the able more able," not to treat the mentally ill. He did not consider psychosis to be a field of practice in Scientology, he wrote, "and Scientology was not researched or designed as a cure for psychosis or 'substitute for psychiatry.'"

---

* According to L. Ron Hubbard, "Level IV Search and Discovery," HCO Bulletin, November 24, 1965, all PTS classifications connect to the doctrine of suppression. An SP (Suppressive Person) is actually present in the life of a Type One individual; a Type Two believes himself or herself to be presently connected to an SP, when in fact, the "actual" SP can be traced back well into the past; a Type Three has become suppressive himself or herself, and thus is "entirely psychotic."

And yet, from as far back as 1950, when Dr. Joseph Winter first noticed that clients at the Elizabeth Foundation were suffering breakdowns as a result of their auditing, the phenomenon of Scientologists "going Type Three" was far from uncommon. So much was this the case, in fact, that in June 1971, Hubbard wrote a confidential memo to his senior officials advising them how to handle the prospect of a member becoming emotionally unstable. "Policy is that we assign any case or upset in Scientology to past damage and interference with the person by medicine or psychiatry," he wrote. "They were sent to us after medicine or psychiatry had already destroyed them. We cannot be blamed for psychiatric or medical failures."

Three years later, the church unveiled the Introspection Rundown, which Hubbard, with typical brio, announced as a "cure" for what he called the last "unsolvable" mental condition, the psychotic break. "I have made a technical breakthrough which possibly ranks with the major discoveries of the Twentieth Century," he proclaimed in a bulletin dated November 24, 1973. "THIS MEANS THE LAST REASON TO HAVE PSYCHIATRY AROUND IS GONE."

The Introspection Rundown began with providing a patient with a regimen of peace and quiet. This, Hubbard was clear to point out, was not a cure itself, but a temporary measure aimed at calming an individual to a point where he or she could receive the rundown — which, Hubbard believed, would then deliver the cure. To this end, he instructed his followers to "isolate the person wholly with all attendants *completely* muzzled (no speech)," which would, he said, "destimulate and . . . protect them and others from possible damage." Vitamins and minerals, such as B complex and calcium magnesium compound (known as "Cal Mag"), were to be administered "to build the person up." If needed, medical care "of a very unbrutal nature," such as intravenous feedings or tranquilizers, might also be administered. Then, once the initial upset had subsided, a person could begin auditing in short sessions, though between the sessions the muzzling would still be in effect. The Founder was very proud of his creation. "You have in your hands the tool to take over mental therapy in full," he said. "Do it flawlessly and we all win."

Over the next twenty years, numerous Scientologists suffered psychotic breaks and were handled in accordance with Hubbard's policies. "I'd heard about people going Type Three for years," recalled Jeff Hawkins, who said that in the Sea Org, these people were usually sent away, "presumably to family," though not always. "I remember there was one lady who was sent to a ranch Scientology owned near Santa Clarita, and spent probably a year in isolation with one or two other people. Other people who went crazy were sent to a ranch near the Int Base." Hawkins didn't know what happened to these people. "All you knew was they flipped out somehow."

Scientologists knew better than to ask what happened to a member who went Type Three, which was not to say that church insiders were unaware of how psychotic breaks were handled. "Without question, most seasoned Sea Org members are aware of what is done to a person when someone is declared PTS Type Three," said Nancy Many, who was based in Clearwater in the late 1970s and early 1980s. Though she never took part in an Introspection Rundown, she was well aware when they were occurring, as she often saw guards posted outside various hotel rooms at the Fort Harrison. "I'd ask them why they were there and they'd tell me that a member had just gone Type Three and needed to be watched," she said. As a church official in charge of external relations, "I'd see Telexes come in from other organizations all the time, reporting that someone had gone Type Three and needed to be 'fixed.'"

What that meant, she understood, was very specific, not only for the person suffering the breakdown but also for the organization. "The worst thing that could happen would be that someone would lose it and cause a lot of work for staffers, which would cause the organization to lose money," she said. "You wanted to get these people isolated and away from the org and its income lines as fast as you could."

In October 1989, one Scientologist, thirty-one-year-old Marianne Coenan, suffered a breakdown and was confined in a ranch house in a well-do-to section of Pomona, California, by her husband and family, who were all church members. Two months later, the police received a tip and went to the house, where they found Coenan locked in a sparsely furnished room, behind a bolted door "into which a small, square opening was cut and steel bars had been inserted" as an observation grate, according to one report in the *Los Angeles Times*. Authorities described her as "incoherent," with "bruises and scratches on her legs, wrists, and neck." Scientology material was found in the house, including information about the Introspection Rundown. A church spokesman insisted that Coenan's treatment "was not a church matter . . . nor did the church take any stand with relationship to her treatment."

With Lisa McPherson it would be different. That a newly minted Clear, someone "in control of their own mind" by Scientology's own definition, could suffer what by all appearances seemed like a total mental breakdown on a public street in Clearwater, the heart of Scientology's spiritual empire, was not only a situation that needed "fixing" but also a potential public relations nightmare for the church, and particularly for the Flag Land Base, the highest-grossing organization in Scientology. "This is not what the members pay $100,000 or more to get," said Many. "There are many, many Scientologists who have moved to Clearwater to advance on the Bridge and are regularly paying big money to Flag. You would never want them knowing that one of these high-ranking people just went crazy."

But there was also another reason McPherson's breakdown caused such a fuss: according to several former church officials, it had been Scientology's leader, David Miscavige, who'd declared Lisa McPherson Clear to begin with.

For the better part of 1995, Miscavige was in Clearwater, where he was working on his project to "remake the face of Flag," as one former official put it, through the Golden Age of Tech. To do this, he involved himself in every facet of the base's daily operations, issuing streams of orders that staff were expected to follow exactly, and right away. "In the Sea Org, if you get an order from Dave Miscavige, everything else in your entire life stops until that order is complied with and he accepts it as done," Marc Headley, a former Sea Org member, told me in an interview. Headley was based at Scientology's Golden Era Productions studio on the Int Base but was sent to Flag in 1995 to oversee the installation of new audiovisual systems. As he recalled, Miscavige put "relentless pressure on the Florida staff to crank as many people through Flag as possible." The ultimate result was that the Clearwater organization grossed more than $1 million per week.

By the summer and fall of 1995, when Lisa McPherson was struggling most profoundly, Miscavige, though not a highly trained auditor (by all accounts, the leader's experience with auditing others stopped after his teenage forays at Saint Hill in the early 1970s), began to take control of the auditing delivered at the base. One summer evening, Headley was in the Flag auditorium when Miscavige held a briefing. In attendance were all of Flag's top auditors, men and women who were revered throughout the church for their years of expertise in counseling and understanding the intricacies of Hubbard's processes.* The leader was infuriated, as Headley recalled, by the slowness and, as he viewed it, the arbitrariness of auditing at Flag: some clients advanced very quickly, while others floundered for years. As an example, Miscavige cited the case of Lisa McPherson, who, he told his staff, had paid for a large number of services and should be treated with the best of care.

The leader began to leaf through Lisa's auditing folder, pointing out things that had been done wrong concerning her case. As Headley recalled it, "He told the staff that he was going to review her folders and make sure that she was being handled correctly."

Whether Miscavige took an interest in Lisa's case purely by chance, or because of his budding friendship with Bennetta Slaughter — several ex-officials suggest the latter not long after this meeting, Tom De Vocht, who headed the Commodore's Messenger Organization at Flag, recalled Miscavige personally supervising several of Lisa McPherson's auditing sessions.

---

* Scientology's Bridge is divided into two tracks: the auditing track, by which members advance through the various levels of enlightenment, and the training track, by which members learn to audit others. Hubbard envisioned Scientologists progressing on both tracks, often simultaneously, and all Scientologists are required to learn how to audit in order to advance to the upper levels. Only a select group of Scientologists, however, become true technical experts in the subject of auditing, and these "professional auditors," as they are known, are responsible for most of Scientology's counseling. The most elite of these professionals, who are also Sea Org members, work at Flag and are held in particularly high esteem by other church members.

Standing in a control room, with video feeds from several different counseling rooms, Miscavige could see everything that went on during Lisa's counseling. As De Vocht recalled, "He's watching live with the video cameras every session that she's in and [supervising], saying 'Do this next, do that next' and so forth." He watched Miscavige make notations on Lisa's auditing folder, which De Vocht also saw being taken in and out of Miscavige's office in Clearwater, which was next to his own.

Another former top Flag official, Don Jason, said he witnessed Miscavige watching one of Lisa's sessions; Miscavige then took off his headphones and announced that she had achieved the state of Clear. According to Jason, Miscavige wrote a note to Lisa's auditor, declaring her new status. "He wrote out a very lengthy four-page communication to her . . . by hand, I watched him do it," Jason told me. "Then it was typed up and she went into session and was told she was Clear." It was notable, he said, because Scientology staffers are required to take a special course to help them identify a person who's become Clear. He wasn't aware that Miscavige had completed that course.

Marty Rathbun was also at the Fort Harrison on the day that Lisa became Clear. He'd been walking down a corridor of the closed-off floor where auditing sessions were held, when a door to one of the auditing rooms suddenly kicked open and a woman's voice could be heard whooping with joy. Rathbun was shocked — noise of any sort is strictly prohibited near auditing rooms — but there was something more than that, a strange quality to Lisa's voice. When he returned to the RTC office later that day, he mentioned Lisa to Angie Trent, the RTC official in charge of supervising Flag's technical training. "You've got somebody up [at the Fort Harrison] who just attested to Clear who looks to me to be on the verge of psychosis," Rathbun said.

Trent told him to mind his own business. "That's Lisa McPherson. David Miscavige is programming her case," she said. In other words, as Rathbun interpreted it, he ought to "buzz off."

Six weeks later, Rathbun and other top-level staff were informed that Lisa McPherson had suffered a psychotic break and that Miscavige, who was now in Los Angeles, would be directing the staff on how to treat her. De Vocht and Jason said they were aware of this as well. "People at Flag knew that DM had case-supervised her, but no one said anything," De Vocht told me. "You're talking about the pope of Scientology."

Though it has long been policy that when a member suffers a breakdown, the church's international management, specifically the RTC, must be informed,* says De Vocht, "for Miscavige to be personally handling Lisa's Type Three situation was astounding." And it was because of Miscavige's personal investment, he and others believe, that officials who intervened at the hospital on Lisa's behalf did not make arrangements to have her brought to her apartment or to stay with friends or family. Instead, Lisa was driven to the Fort Harrison Hotel, where she would to undergo the Introspection Rundown for the second time, under the supervision of Scientology's international management.

Assuming command of Lisa's welfare was Flag's senior case supervisor, Alain Kartuzinski. Though he lacked medical training, Kartuzinski, the "minister" in charge of the spiritual welfare of the entire congregation, served as the point person for Lisa's treatment. Kartuzinski was a Class 12 auditor, an elite counselor in Scientology whose rank in the spiritual hierarchy is comparable to a church bishop's. It was he who had been in charge during the summer of 1995 when Lisa had suffered her first breakdown, recovered, and attested to Clear. Now Kartuzinski would review Lisa's confessional folders, direct the base's medical officers, and supervise her isolation. Behind the scenes, according to Rathbun and De Vocht, RTC officials in Clearwater, and ultimately David Miscavige in Los Angeles, were kept informed of Lisa's condition and had the final say over the details of her care.

Understanding how a woman suffering psychosis would be taken to the equivalent of corporate headquarters is crucial to understanding what happened to Lisa and why. Many said, "I have asked many,

---

* In her exhaustive "overt/withhold write-up" of Halloween 1995, Lisa specifically noted that during her breakdown in the summer of 1995, Scientology's international management had become involved "to sort me out," which, she noted guiltily, "took time away from their expansion or helping someone who wasn't as able as I was."

many former Sea Org members whether they would call 911 if they saw someone fall from a balcony at the church. The answer is always no, never. And that's because on that org board you've been chanting, chanting, chanting, as demanded by Hubbard's 'Chinese School,' only the security guard can call 911. So you would run to the security guard and tell him to do it."

It is this doctrinal principle — the principle of the org board — that determined the treatment of Lisa McPherson; its tragic outcome was determined by another precept, which reduced individual Scientologists to mere cogs by making autonomous thought, or speech, a crime. "There is a policy letter in Scientology that says that you are your job title," said Many. "I could not send a Telex or a report without citing L. Ron Hubbard. And it did not come from me; it came from 'LRH Staff Aide for Division Six,' which was my job title."

All of this, as Many pointed out, sprung from the mind of L. Ron Hubbard. But starting in the 1990s, these policies were meted out by David Miscavige, who, in his typical style, enforced them to an extreme. According to former Scientology officials, for David Miscavige, "keeping Scientology working" meant doing whatever it took to consistently generate profit, particularly at Flag.

A multitude of reasons — the dogmatism of Hubbard's technology, the exacting nature of Scientology ethics, the church doctrine governing public relations and self-preservation — explain why the next two weeks unfolded as they did. Above all was the fundamental tragedy that from the moment she left Morton Plant Hospital on November 18, 1995, Lisa McPherson put herself in the hands of the Sea Org rather than family or friends. By doing this, she ceded control to a group who, in their inexorable commitment to Hubbard's doctrine, believed they were doing the right thing. Instead, this commitment would lead to her death.

That night, Lisa arrived at the Fort Harrison from the hospital just before midnight. By all accounts she was calm, quiet, and physically healthy. According to Emma Schammerhorn, a Flag medical liaison officer who accompanied her, she had even told Kartuzinski that she was glad he'd come to retrieve her. She was given a room at the back of the hotel, next to the housekeeping office and far from most hotel guests.

To manage Lisa's physical care, Kartuzinski pulled Dr. Janice Johnson, a senior medical officer at Flag, from her regular duties. Susan Schnurrenberger, the medical officer who had cared for Lisa over the summer, initially supervised Lisa's day-to-day management. An aide named Gabriella Sanchez was tasked by Kartuzinski to staff the watch around the clock. About twenty women were ultimately assembled, generally low-level or interim employees with little or no medical experience, nor much background with the Introspection Rundown or isolation watches. "This wasn't supposed to go on very long," said Sanchez. "The whole purpose of it . . . was just so that she starts to calm down, she can get some rest, start to eat and start to . . . chill out."

The instructions for the watch were simple. The caretakers were to provide Lisa with water and whatever food was available from the cafeteria, plus daily doses of Cal Mag and various other vitamin and mineral supplements. The caretakers were to keep a log of Lisa's food and fluid intake and also note her behavior. If she needed to talk, they should let her, but, per Hubbard's guidelines, they could communicate with her only by writing notes. Every day they were to submit their log to the senior case supervisor, who would determine when Lisa was well enough to be audited. "This is what I was told," said Heather Petzold, then a seventeen-year-old who was one of the caretakers. "We need to get her enough food and enough sleep so we can get her in session."

By mid-afternoon on Sunday, November 19, her first day in room 174, Lisa McPherson was talking incessantly. By the second day of isolation, Lisa was refusing to eat, had barely slept, and was restlessly jumping in and out of bed. Her caretakers found it impossible to get her to drink any fluids.

Lisa's friend Susanne Reich, who'd help watch her that Sunday night, was horrified. "I would not stay with Lisa alone for one second," she later told the police. "The way she was, in my eyes, I thought she would kill me." That afternoon Reich wrote a report, marked the word *rush* on the document, and sent it to Kartuzinski. She never returned to Lisa's room. Not long after, Susan Schnurrenberger followed suit.

One member of the Flag medical staff who *did* want to look after Lisa was Judy Goldsberry-Weber. She had been one of the officials who'd gone to the hospital after Lisa's accident and had helped convince the doctors at Morton Plant to allow Lisa to be released into her care. They had not been easily won over, she recalled later. "I'm holding you personally responsible," an angry Dr. Flynn Lovett at the hospital had told Goldsberry-Weber before agreeing to the discharge. "And if anything happens, I'm gonna nail you."

Goldsberry-Weber promised Lovett that she'd personally take responsibility for Lisa. But no sooner had she made this promise than one of the OSA officials informed her that she should return to her job as the staff medical officer. "I was angry about that," said Goldsberry-Weber. "If I promise somebody I'm going to do something, I take that promise very, very seriously. And it upset me greatly that my promise was being trashed."

Nonetheless, Goldsberry-Weber returned to her post. She assumed that Lisa was being well taken care of at her apartment, under the watchful eye of Schnurrenberger, until she was asked to drive to a drugstore and pick up what she was told were "sedatives" for Lisa McPherson. She thought it was strange that the drugstore was located in Largo, almost half an hour away, rather than the usual Eckerd's pharmacy Flag used in Clearwater. Upon her return to the Fort Harrison, Goldsberry-Weber was told to give the prescription to a Flag security officer. Now realizing that Lisa was staying at the Fort Harrison, she once again offered to care for Lisa; again she was rebuffed.

Goldsberry-Weber was a nurse with experience in Hubbard's techniques, including the Introspection Rundown. But from what she could piece together, Hubbard's policies weren't being followed. There were no set caretakers, to begin with. Instead, Janis Johnson and others were apparently scouring the base to find people to take part. Goldsberry-Weber had even heard that some of the caretakers didn't speak English.

She was right: there were multiple caretakers looking after Lisa, including some who didn't speak English, and none of them stayed for very long. One of them, Lesley Woodcraft, the British-born personnel manager at Flag, was pulled onto the watch on November 22 and almost immediately passed the responsibility to her roommate, Alice Vangrondelle, the Flag librarian.

Vangrondelle complained that it wasn't her job but grudgingly got out of bed. She found Lisa talking gibberish, freezing cold, with blotches on her face that looked like those caused by measles. She'd run around the room in a frenzied manner; later, exhausted, she'd collapse on the bed. At one point she rested her head on the librarian's shoulder. "E.T., go home," Lisa cried. "E.T., go home."

When Vangrondelle returned to her room later that day, she wrote a "Knowledge Report" on Woodcraft, whom she felt had improperly posted her to the watch. The report contained a lengthy description of Lisa's mania and noted that Lisa's breath was "foul." This is a sign of a toxic condition called uremia, caused by poor function of the kidneys. She also wrote that Lisa looked feverish.

This report, dated November 22, 1995, is the last one detailing Lisa's condition for several days. There are no logs for November 23–25, a period that was marked by an upsurge of violent behavior, as Lisa's caretakers later testified. Lisa, they said, pulled things off shelves, destroyed furniture, broke lights, threw a ficus plant at one of her watchers, screamed, and banged her head on the wall, floor, and bed. One minder recalled her gouging at her own face with her fingernails. Another stated that she drenched the floor with water, stripped naked, and lashed out with her fists. Security personnel removed everything breakable or dangerous, including the lamps, leaving Lisa in total darkness.

At three in the morning on November 24, Sam Ghiora, a Flag security staffer, was seated on a small bench outside of Lisa's room when he heard the doorknob rattle. Slowly, the door to room 174 opened, and Lisa stood at the threshold, fully dressed.

"Hey," she said calmly, walking a few steps toward him. "You're not CMO."

"You're right," Ghiora said. He was not a member of the Commodore's Messenger Organization but a new Flag security trainee.

"You can't tell me what to do," Lisa said.

"You're right," Ghiora said again. He knew he'd broken protocol by speaking to her, but he was momentarily shocked: How had she just walked out of the room? Where were her minders? Ghiora gently put his hand on Lisa's shoulder and steered her back toward her room. She stopped at the threshold. "I just don't know what's happening," she said.

Ghiora said nothing.

"Could you help me?"

Nothing.

"I need help," she said, and slowly entering her room, shut the door.

On November 29, about a week after she'd taken her turn on the watch, Alice Vangrondelle went to see Judy Goldsberry-Weber in the medical liaison's office. "I want to know how a person would act if they didn't get enough to eat or drink," she said. "What are the symptoms of dehydration?"

Goldsberry-Weber took out some medical books and gave Vangrondelle a list of symptoms, which include dry skin, loss of appetite, flushed complexion, dry mouth, weakness, chills, and in more serious cases, fever, increased heart rate and respiration, confusion, chest pain, and unconsciousness. "Have you ever taken care of anyone like that?" Vangrondelle asked. "How would they behave?"

Goldsberry-Weber told her that it would not be uncommon for a patient in this condition to behave "irrationally" for a short period, but given enough fluids, the condition could be turned around in a matter of hours. "If you have concerns, you need to let it be known what your concerns are to the proper people," she said. "And sooner, rather than later."

Vangrondelle told Goldsberry-Weber that she'd written a report. (No log from Vangrondelle was ever found, or included, in the official record.) Other caretakers also grew concerned. Lisa, several noted, had "lost a lot of weight," "looked thin," and her skin had become jaundiced and bruised.*

---

* One possible reason for Lisa's bruising was the numerous times she had been restrained by her caretakers and security guards so that the Flag dentist, Dr. David Houghton, could administer a concoction of Benadryl, aspirin, and or-

By the end of November, one caretaker, seventeen-year-old Heather Petzold, was "frantic," as she'd later say. Lisa had by now regressed to an infantile state. She was urinating and defecating on her bed. "I wouldn't say there was any day that she ate sufficiently," she noted; by the first of December, Lisa's caretakers were spoon-feeding her bites of mashed banana, sometimes forcibly opening her mouth.

Petzold had never spoken to any of the other caretakers about her concerns — remarkably, none of Lisa's minders spoke to one another about their experience, despite the fact that several felt so distraught, they cried in Lisa's room. Instead, Petzold sat down and wrote a letter to Alain Kartuzinski, explaining that Lisa was neither eating nor sleeping. "I said, hey, we need to change something," she recalled. Petzold herself didn't know how to handle the situation. "I was there, I was doing the watch [sixteen hours at a time], and I had eight hours to go home, sleep, and come back in. It wasn't like I had an extra hour to figure out what else could be done."

Petzold delivered her report to Kartuzinski's office, as she had been instructed to do. She never received a reply. Later she'd regret that she hadn't said enough. "If I had gone to higher terminals . . . if I would have walked to the senior-most terminal there and said, 'Listen.'" But despite misgivings, neither Petzold nor any of the other caretakers took it upon themselves to call a doctor or go to a hospital — as several would later admit, taking that kind of initiative wasn't their job and would have broken with Sea Org protocol. "She had been seen by a doctor in the hospital," Rita Boykin, another minder, later said. "She signed herself out, and she didn't want to be there. She *wanted* to come back to the church."

In the early hours of Saturday, December 2, Boykin wrote in her log that she had given Lisa four valerian-root capsules, four other herbal sleeping tablets, and approximately six ounces of Cal Mag. At 3 A.M., Lisa was "still awake and talking," she wrote. "She has

---

ange juice, which he and other officials believed might help calm her. Houghton, who, like Janis Johnson, was not licensed to practice medicine in the state of Florida, administered this potion with a turkey baster–like syringe on several occasions between November 25 and November 28, 1995, each time with others holding Lisa down. When Judy Goldsberry-Weber found out about this, she was incensed. Johnson, as Goldsberry-Weber later said, told her to "butt out."

scratches and abrasions all over her body & on elbows & knees has pressure sores."

By late that night, Boykin wrote, Lisa, who'd tried to stand several times without success, was no longer moving herself, but being "moved" by her caretakers. She also accused her caretakers of being "psychs" — psychiatrists — "or other enemies who wanted to kill her," Boykin said. This psychosis extended into Sunday, December 3.

Boykin made another entry: "4:30 She had about 2½ hours of sound sleep — interspersed with restlessness. At one point it seemed she wanted a sweater on. I put it on her & she thanked me."

This is where the log ends. There are no other records for the remainder of December 3 or for December 4 or 5. However, the caretakers later testified that during those days, Lisa's condition declined dramatically. By the morning of December 5, she was lying in bed and barely moving. "There was one time when she rolled over . . . and she fell on the floor," Petzold said. "So I picked her back up and put her back on the bed, of course."

Lisa also wasn't talking much, which Petzold immediately noticed. "Prior [to this] it was like a broken record, just all of the time." Now Lisa was mumbling. "That's when I got pretty worried," Petzold said.

That afternoon, Petzold and Laura Arrunada, the other caretaker, decided to give Lisa a bath. She was too weak to walk to the tub, so the women carried her. As they were putting her in the tub, Lisa's sphincter muscle relaxed. "She shit herself," Laura Arrunada later said.

A relaxed anus is a sign that the body has begun to deteriorate. Petzold, a teenager with no medical experience, didn't know this. Arrunada, who had graduated from medical school in Mexico City but was not a licensed physician, might have been familiar with this warning sign. But as she told the police, Lisa "was not looking like she was [going] to die."

Arrunada was nonetheless concerned, and at six o'clock that evening, she called Johnson and told her that Lisa needed medical attention.

At approximately 7 P.M., Dr. David Minkoff received yet another call from Johnson about Lisa McPherson. The girl for whom he had written the prescription, she said, was suffering from acute diarrhea, had lost an extreme amount of weight, and also complained of a sore throat. Johnson thought Lisa had strep and requested penicillin. This time, Minkoff refused to call in a prescription.

"If she's sick enough to need an injection, then she needs to be seen by a doctor," he said. And if she were seriously ill, they shouldn't bring Lisa to him, but to a closer hospital like Morton Plant.

"No, she's not that sick," Johnson assured him. She told Minkoff they'd be there within the hour.

Soon after, Paul Greenwood, a Flag security officer, was dispatched to room 174. With Janis Johnson and Laura Arrunada assisting, Greenwood put Lisa in a van. Johnson got behind the wheel and drove north, past Morton Plant Hospital, where she and the others dared not stop, fearing the doctors might call the psychiatrists. They drove past several other hospitals as well, bound for Minkoff's facility, the Columbia HCA Hospital in New Port Richey, about forty-five minutes away. No one spoke. "When someone is sick or injured you don't talk around them because it puts impressions in the mind which create things . . . later on," said Greenwood.

Johnson later said she heard Lisa's breath become labored, then grow faint. Sitting with her in the back of the van, Greenwood monitored Lisa's pulse. It slowly dwindled. Then Greenwood couldn't feel it anymore.

At approximately 9:30 that evening, Dr. David Minkoff was just finishing his shift when he heard the doors to the Columbia New Port Richey Hospital's emergency room swing open and an orderly cry out for help. A disheveled-looking woman, draped awkwardly over a wheelchair, was wheeled into the trauma room. She was drastically, almost skeletally thin; her skin was papery, had a grayish pallor, and was marked with small dark brown lesions. One emergency room nurse, shocked by the woman's emaciated state, concluded that she must have AIDS; another, noting the multiple bruises and lesions on her body, wondered if she might have an infectious disease such as Ebola. To Minkoff, it looked like a classic picture of "meningococcemia," a devastating bacterial infection that can cause inflammation of blood vessels, organ failure, and meningitis.

Lisa McPherson, the robust, five foot nine woman described as "voluptuous" by the paramedic Bonnie Portolano, was dead. Her arms and legs were covered with bruises, she had scrapes on her face, and her weight had dwindled to an emaciated 108 pounds. She was also dirty — a nurse later said she wondered if Lisa had been abused. "I was appalled," Minkoff later told police. After trying to revive Lisa to no avail, Minkoff confronted Janis Johnson in the waiting area. "What did you bring me?" he said. "What did you do?"

At least one other person at the Columbia HCA Hospital wondered the same thing. That night, the head ER nurse at the Columbia Hospital, Barbara Schmid, alarmed by the condition of Lisa's body, called the local authorities. By the next morning, a "suspicious death" investigation would be officially launched by the Clearwater Police Department on the matter of Lisa McPherson.

CHAPTER 12

The Greatest Good

G ET THE FUCK over here." Tom De Vocht, commanding officer of the Commodore's Messenger Organization in Clearwater, barked into the phone at his twenty-year-old aide, Jason Knapmeyer. It was late in the evening of December 5, 1995, and De Vocht was calling from his office in the West Coast Building, on Fort Harrison Avenue. With him was Marty Rathbun, the senior RTC official and deputy to Scientology's leader, David Miscavige. There was very little time, the men told Knapmeyer when he arrived, breathless, a few minutes later. "Something had happened" to a parishioner named Lisa McPherson, they said — neither Rathbun nor De Vocht went into details — and, bottom line, the police might be by, asking questions. Before that happened, the office of the medical liaison, Janis Johnson, had to be totally cleared out, cleansed of any sign that Johnson, an unlicensed physician in the state of Florida, had been practicing medicine. "We've got to get all of this shit packed up," De Vocht said. "Any medicines, any needles, anything medical or medicine-related — just get it the fuck out of here."

Knapmeyer did as he was told. At the same time, another group of Messengers whom Knapmeyer knew were cleaning out Lisa McPherson's room. Knapmeyer combed every inch of Johnson's office for incriminating evidence, dumping everything he found in a large trash bag. Finally, he gave the bag to another Commodore's Messenger, who put it in the back of a blue Honda Civic and drove away. By morning, the police would arrive at the Fort Harrison.

• • •

Brian Anderson, the head of the Office of Special Affairs at Flag, was in a panic from the moment he received the call from Janis Johnson, still at the hospital in New Port Richey. The woman who'd been isolated in room 174 was dead, she informed him.

Johnson admitted the truth. "She seemed a lot worse when I saw her earlier tonight, and so we took her to the hospital and . . . I'm not really sure what happened."

"What do you mean, you're not sure?" Anderson was livid. He'd known that Lisa McPherson was being treated at the Fort Harrison and asked Paul Kellerhals, the chief of security, for frequent updates on her condition. Recently, his deputies had reported that Lisa seemed to be getting better.

By midnight, all of the base's top executives had gathered in Anderson's office on the second floor of the West Coast Building, including the representative from the RTC. Many of the people gathered in Anderson's office were aware of David Miscavige's personal involvement in Lisa's auditing progress during the fall of 1995. Some aides maintained that, though Miscavige had returned to California by the time Lisa was brought to the Fort Harrison, he continued to monitor her situation through his RTC surrogates in Clearwater, who sent him regular reports. "You have to understand how controlling Dave Miscavige is, and how big a deal this was," said Tom De Vocht. How had Lisa broken down after going Clear? Though Alain Kartuzinski was ostensibly in charge of Lisa's care, De Vocht described him as "Miscavige's fall guy. All the direction came from RTC, and I can guarantee you the attitude was, 'we're handling this, not you.' The people who were on the ground were freaked out by the idea of Dave Miscavige getting upset, and they mishandled the situation. But they were under the threat of God from Dave."

Over the next several hours, Marcus Quirino, Flag's deputy chief officer, and Paul Kellerhals rounded up the caretakers and interviewed them. From these debriefing sessions and individual reports the caretakers were asked to write up, Quirino constructed a detailed memo summarizing the last seventeen days of Lisa's life. He gave it to Anderson, along with the caretakers' handwritten recollections.*

---

* Anderson later admitted he'd put the handwritten notes in his shred basket. "To me [the notes were] a duplication of what was in this summary," he said.

While this was going on, Flag's highest-ranking official, Debbie Cook, phoned Bennetta Slaughter, often listed as Lisa's "next of kin" on official papers, and broke the news that Lisa was dead.

Slaughter had known that Lisa was in the Fort Harrison since the day of her accident. In an interview with police, Slaughter later admitted that she'd found out about the accident when she drove by in her car and saw Lisa's Jeep parked by the side of the road. When Slaughter asked where Lisa was, a police officer told her that she'd been taken to the hospital. Slaughter decided not to go. "I was covered in paint from head to foot because I'd been working on the props for [Winter Wonderland]," she said. "I looked awful . . . and frankly, hospitals are not my thing."

Instead, Slaughter phoned Lisa's chiropractor, Dr. Jeannie DeCuypere, and asked her to check up on Lisa. She also asked her husband, David, to drive over to Morton Plant, where he joined the other Scientologists in the waiting room. But after Lisa was taken to the Fort Harrison, the Slaughters had lost track of her, other than being informed by church officials that she was getting "rest, quiet, and relaxation," as Slaughter said.

"[Bennetta] cried a lot," said Cook. "I tried to comfort her some . . . We were all a little freaked out."

The next day, the Clearwater police paid a visit to the Hacienda Gardens apartment complex, the church-owned property in Clearwater where Janis Johnson and other Scientology staffers lived, to question Johnson. Several other cops went to the Fort Harrison, where they questioned Alain Kartuzinski, Paul Greenwood, and Laura Arrunada. All four Scientologists maintained that Lisa had been a regular hotel guest who'd checked in for "rest and relaxation" and had suddenly taken ill.

Marty Rathbun, meanwhile, sought out Lisa's caretakers. Most of them were quarantined in an apartment at the Hacienda Gardens, where they'd been sent until it could be determined whether or not Lisa had died of an infectious disease.* Interviewing them was like walking into a disaster area, Rathbun recalled. "They all looked dev-

---

* Dr. Minkoff, prior to getting the results of Lisa's blood tests, theorized that she might have contracted, and died of, meningitis.

astated, they lacked sleep, some of them had scratches and bruises from getting hit by Lisa, [and] all of them were extremely emotionally distraught, because each one of them put it on her shoulders that she had done something wrong."

Rathbun then interviewed Alain Kartuzinski and Janis Johnson, both of whom pointed the finger at each other for botching Lisa's care. Johnson, in particular, worried Rathbun. Having practiced medicine in Tucson for six years, Johnson had come under suspicion by the Arizona Board of Medical Examiners for abusing painkillers and other drugs, and had voluntarily agreed to withdraw from medical practice. In 1994, her Arizona medical license lapsed, and Johnson had never renewed it. How had she been posted to the medical liaison's office in the first place? And why in the world did Kartuzinski put her in charge of Lisa's health care? "It was the worst possible perfect storm of incompetence and irresponsibility," Rathbun later said.

Worse still was that Miscavige's handwriting was allegedly all over Lisa's auditing files. While Rathbun was interviewing the caretakers, another RTC official, he said, was charged with "getting rid of any evidence of Miscavige's handling of the deal."* Once that was accomplished, a night or so after Lisa's death, Rathbun and Tom De Vocht once again called Jason Knapmeyer to the West Coast building. Looking grave, Rathbun handed Knapmeyer a set of sealed folders with the name "Lisa McPherson" written on them. They were Lisa's preclear, or auditing, folders. "These need to go to Int," Rathbun said. Knapmeyer took the folders, got in his car, drove to the Tampa airport, and boarded a flight to Los Angeles. An OSA representative met him at LAX and took possession of the folders. Then he told Knapmeyer to go home. "Don't tell anyone about this trip," he said. The Messenger agreed and flew back to Florida on the next plane.

$$\bullet \quad \bullet \quad \bullet$$

---

* Miscavige, to this day, has denied having anything to do with Lisa McPherson's auditing or her isolation treatment, and church officials insist that Rathbun, De Vocht, and Don Jason, all of whom have left Scientology, are lying when they claim that Miscavige was involved. In 1997, when the police subpoenaed Lisa's auditing folders, the contents, which were incomplete, contained no indication that Miscavige had anything to do with Lisa McPherson or her counseling.

It was just after two o'clock on the afternoon of December 6, 1995, when Fannie McPherson's telephone rang in Dallas. "Fannie," a woman said, "it's Bennetta Slaughter."

"Bennetta?" Fannie had a bad feeling. "Is Lisa all right?"

There was a pause. "Fannie, Lisa's dead."

"She's *what*?" Fannie began to cry. "What in the world happened?"

Slaughter still had no idea; from what she'd been told, Lisa may have died of meningitis. But she did know that Lisa had died while in the Church of Scientology's care. Right or wrong, Scientology had to be protected from scandal; more than any other Scientologist in Clearwater, Slaughter, who'd spent the better part of two years networking tirelessly with local politicos and community leaders in hopes of improving Scientology's image, understood the potential ramifications.

So she told what L. Ron Hubbard called an "acceptable truth." Lisa had fallen sick at work, Slaughter explained to Fannie. She'd begun feeling ill around noon and then "just kept getting sicker and sicker" until they finally took her to a hospital. By then, said Slaughter, it was too late. The doctor concluded she'd had "fast-acting meningitis."

"I just fell to pieces," Fannie later told police.

Slaughter also told Fannie that Lisa had wanted to be cremated. In her shock and grief Lisa's mother agreed, though she later "regretted it a million times," said Fannie's sister, Ann Carlson. "Bennetta had said it was her last wish. Well, I don't know why a thirty-six-year-old girl would be discussing cremation and her death, you know? Why would she be?"

At Lisa's memorial service on December 11, 1995, Dallas's Restland Memorial Funeral Home was "filled with Scientology people that we'd never seen before," said Carlson. Some had come from Clearwater, and arrived in a white limousine. They hovered over the family "like vultures," another one of Fannie's sisters, Dell Liebreich, later told the police. "They didn't talk too much, [but] every time we would try to talk to each other or anybody, they were just . . . listening." The Scientologists even followed them into the restroom, she said.

Fannie's sister Ann, who was seventy-six years old, had always felt there was something strange about these Scientologists. Now she was sure of it. The way they lingered was unnerving, but there was more to it than just that, Carlson believed. Lisa had died on the evening of December 5, 1995; Fannie wasn't told until the middle of the next afternoon. Why had Bennetta Slaughter waited so long to call her? And had Lisa really been at her office when she got sick? Slaughter said yes. But when Carlson asked Brenda Hubert, she said that Lisa had been at a seminar in Orlando. A third Scientologist friend later told Carlson that Lisa had gotten sick at her apartment. Who had taken Lisa to the hospital? "An acquaintance," the family was told. Which acquaintance? No one would say.

On December 16, 1995, ten days after Lisa's death, Fannie McPherson and her sisters Ann and Dell flew to Tampa and arrived, unannounced, in Clearwater. As they pulled up to Lisa's apartment on Osceola Avenue, Lisa's roommate, Gloria Cruz, rushed out to greet them. "Hi, Fannie!" she said.

"How she knew us I'll never know," said Carlson. Neither Fannie nor her sisters had ever met Cruz, who did not go to the memorial service in Texas. The women had taken pains not to tell Bennetta Slaughter or anyone else in Clearwater that they were coming. Yet Cruz seemed to be waiting for them.

Cruz and several friends were carting out boxes from the apartment. She was moving, Cruz told the women from Texas. And she, or someone, the women thought, seemed to have taken whatever they wanted.* Lisa's stereo was gone, as were her television, answering machine, telephone, and plants. Fannie looked in vain for Lisa's jewelry, but that was missing too. "I had given her a little diamond ring that she treasured very much; I didn't get that. Her daddy's wedding band she wore on her right hand, I didn't get." The expensive clothes that Lisa wore — silk pajamas, designer jeans, dresses from Neiman Marcus — all gone. "We saw one roll of toilet tissue, a newspaper laying on the floor, and a roll of paper towels on the sink," said Carlson.

Lisa's bank statements and laptop computer were also missing.

---

* Gloria Cruz later told the Florida state attorney that Lisa's furniture had been in the apartment when the women showed up and added that she had "no idea" where any of her personal effects, such as her jewelry, went.

But one box, tucked inside a hall closet, had been overlooked. Inside, Carlson found Lisa's diaries, her 1994 tax return, and the police report from the accident on November 18.* This was the first the women knew of Lisa's accident. On the report was the phone number of the driver of the vehicle that Lisa had rear-ended, a local mechanic named Joe McDonald. Carlson called him.

McDonald told the women a variation of the story that the paramedic Bonnie Portolano later told police. Fannie was beside herself. "I didn't know she'd had the wreck and I didn't know she'd cracked up," she later told police. "They hadn't contacted me . . . or told me she was sick or anything."

Hoping to learn more, the family went to the Clearwater police station. They were told that an investigation was in process — a "matter of routine," the police explained — and that the medical examiner was still awaiting the results from certain tests. The women were shown a copy of the preliminary autopsy report. There was no mention of meningitis. Rather, the cause of death was listed as a pulmonary embolism — an arterial blood clot.

For days, the McPherson family searched for answers. Few were forthcoming. Most of Lisa's friends from Scientology seemed as much in the dark as they were. Those who may have known more were not talking. "She *asked* to go there," Bennetta Slaughter said about the Fort Harrison, where she'd finally admitted Lisa had been taken after "bumping her leg on a desk" at work. "She just loved it there." As to what had occurred during those two weeks, Slaughter claimed she had no idea.

Convinced that something sinister had happened to Lisa, the women returned to the Clearwater Police Department and met with Detective Ron Sudler, who was investigating the case. Sudler, a burly cop in his late twenties, looked uneasy. "Look, I want to tell you something," he said. "You can't bring Lisa back, so why don't you just take what you can and get out of town."

"But we think something bad has happened to her," said Carlson.

---

* How the police report found its way into the box was one of many questions the police never answered conclusively, though it is assumed that either Slaughter or Cruz took the report from Lisa's car and put it in the box.

Sudler had been called in to this case just a week or so earlier. He had, however, lived in Clearwater a long time. "We're going to do our best," he promised. "But if I were you, I'd go home."

In his quiet suburban home in Dunedin, near Clearwater, Special Agent Allan "Lee" Strope put down his morning newspaper. It was December 1996, and Strope, a taciturn detective with the Florida Department of Law Enforcement, had just read a story about Lisa McPherson on the front page of the *Tampa Tribune* with the headline "Mystery Surrounds Scientologist's Death." The story fascinated him. A healthy young woman got into a minor car accident, stripped naked, asked for help, and went to the hospital. A few hours later, she checked out of the hospital against medical advice and left with members of the Church of Scientology, who brought her to the Fort Harrison Hotel for "rest and relaxation." Seventeen days later, she was dead.

Though the woman had died over a year ago, Strope realized, there had been no obituary in the local papers and no public police report on Lisa's death. Neither the McPherson family nor the Clearwater police seemed to have any idea of what had happened to her. The police had been so stymied in their investigation, in fact, that in the fall of 1996, nearly twelve months after Lisa's death, they'd finally posted a note on the Internet looking for help in finding three Scientologists, including the medical officers Laura Arrunada and Susanne Schnurrenberger, who they believed had contact with Lisa during her stay at the Fort Harrison.

Strope had lived in Clearwater for more than ten years, but he knew very little about the Church of Scientology. Like most local residents, he'd taken note of the church's uniformed staffers, who milled around downtown. Out of curiosity, he'd even purchased a copy of *Dianetics* but found the book dense and concluded it was "gibberish." By his reading, Scientologists were a clannish bunch, not very friendly to outsiders. Now he began to wonder if there was something more ominous about the group.

The condition of Lisa's body was particularly disturbing to Strope. So was that fact that she'd been taken to a hospital in Pasco County, more than twenty miles away, when Pinellas County had several closer hospitals, including two right in Clearwater.

The detective considered the matter while he drank his coffee. Then he showered, dressed, got into his government-issued Chevy Monte Carlo, and drove to the Clearwater field office of the Florida Department of Law Enforcement, or FDLE, where he suggested the state agency help the local police with the Lisa McPherson investigation.

The FDLE is a small but powerful investigative body whose members often work in tandem with local police forces on major criminal cases. Lee Strope, forty-nine years old, was one of its best agents. Like many investigators, he'd come up from the streets, walking a beat in his native Detroit in the 1970s, then working as an undercover narcotics agent and later as a homicide investigator. He joined the FDLE in 1988, after moving to Florida, and two years later distinguished himself as the lead agent in one of Florida's most notorious and high-profile cases: the August 1990 serial murder and mutilation of five Gainesville college students by an itinerant criminal named Danny Rolling, often known as the "Gainesville Ripper" case. Strope frequently consulted with the Clearwater Police Department, which late in 1996 had assigned one of his golfing buddies, Sergeant Wayne Andrews, to be the lead detective on the McPherson case.

If Strope was new to Scientology, the same was not true for the Clearwater cops. At their headquarters, just around the corner from the Fort Harrison Hotel, the police had amassed nearly a roomful of investigative files on the Church of Scientology, dating back to the late 1970s. Some of the key complaints in those files came from former members, many with a personal ax to grind, though their claims — fraud, intimidation, harsh punishment, even some unreported deaths — made them hard to overlook.

Lisa McPherson was not the first Scientologist to die in Clearwater, nor was she the first to die in the Fort Harrison, as police knew. There had been at least eight cases since the 1980s, including one fifty-one-year-old woman who had gone off her lithium, upon the insistence of church officials, and then drowned after walking, fully clothed, into Clearwater Bay, and a man who'd died of a seizure after replacing his anti-seizure medications with a Scientology-endorsed regimen of vitamins and minerals. But in all of these cases, there had never been sufficient proof of wrongdoing to warrant an arrest, let alone an indictment.

The same had held true with regard to Lisa McPherson. There had been no crime scene. When the police first arrived at the Fort Harrison after Lisa's death, they found room 174 thoroughly cleaned and decorated, with a king-sized bed, a pitcher of water, and a fruit basket in place. "There did not appear to be any clothing, any medications, or other indications that the room had previously been occupied," Detective Ron Sudler had written in his report.

There was also no body — cremation had left the few tissue and fluid samples taken during the autopsy as the only physical evidence — nor were there material witnesses to offer firsthand knowledge of her condition. Lisa's co-workers, roommate, boss, and even Lisa's ex-boyfriend, Kurt Paine, had no idea what had happened to her at the Fort Harrison. Dr. David Minkoff claimed he'd never had anything to do with Lisa's treatment prior to the night she died. Janis Johnson and Alain Kartuzinski had at first told the police they'd barely known Lisa. When they were re-interviewed in the spring of 1996, Johnson admitted she'd seen Lisa but insisted that Lisa had simply been "upset" and was in no way mentally incapable. Kartuzinski said she'd simply been a "regular hotel guest" and he had almost nothing to do with her. The two other witnesses the police had identified, Arrunada and Schnurrenberger, had vanished: the church had told the police they'd left the country, and Scientology, and church officials had no idea how to contact them.*

As a result, Strope and Andrews were left with a small and largely inconclusive investigative file and numerous statements from church officials that Lisa was a hotel guest who "suddenly took ill." But the postmortem photographs of Lisa suggested a much different story.

---

* The church did ultimately make Arrunada available; in March 1996, she'd returned to her native Mexico but went back to Florida in 1997 to be interviewed by Strope, Andrews, and the assistant state attorney. Schnurrenberger, whom Strope managed to find in Switzerland, refused to be interviewed.

They were gruesome, showing Lisa's starved-looking, hollow face, cracked lips, and arms and legs scarred by abrasions and what looked to the coroner to be cockroach bites. Her neck, shoulders, and upper back were red and blotchy, as if she'd been hit or struck. She had several large bruises on her leg. "There's not a jury in the world who won't look at this and say someone is guilty of something," Strope thought.

The Pinellas-Pasco County medical examiner, Dr. Joan Wood, felt similarly. Due to the typical slow pace of a metropolitan area coroner's office, Lisa's autopsy had taken several months to complete. Most of it had been conducted by Dr. Robert Davis, the associate medical examiner for Pinellas-Pasco County, though Wood had weighed in early, and also toward the end, concluding that Lisa's embolism had been caused by "bed rest and severe dehydration." On January 14, 1996, a week or so after the FDLE formally joined the investigation, Wood, a longtime friend of Strope's, asked him to come down to her office. Having served as the county medical examiner for twenty-two years, the fifty-year-old Wood was bothered by what she saw as a Scientology-orchestrated "campaign of misinformation" about McPherson. In numerous media accounts, the church maintained that Lisa died from a fast-moving staph infection and had been fully conscious, even talking, when the decision was made to take her to the hospital. Seeing Dr. Minkoff in New Port Richey was her idea, church officials explained. "Lisa at first didn't want to see a doctor, but we talked her into seeing a doctor," the Scientology spokesman Brian Anderson told the media. "She knew Dr. Minkoff and he is an expert in infectious diseases, so that's why she was taken there."

That was simply impossible, said Wood. Lisa's autopsy results showed that she been so dehydrated, she may have been without fluids for five to ten days. She was almost certainly comatose for a day or two before her death, the coroner said. This was not a sudden death, but rather a chronic decline — for a week, said Wood, it would have been obvious that Lisa needed help. That no one had called 911 was negligent to such an extreme that Wood thought Lisa's death a homicide.

Going public with these concerns would certainly kick the investigation into higher gear; it would also no doubt anger the Pinellas-Pasco state attorney, Bernie McCabe, by putting pressure on him to bring charges against the Church of Scientology. McCabe's office had agreed to assist the police and the FDLE in their investigation, but Strope and Wood knew there wasn't a prosecutor in Pinellas County eager to take on the church in court. Wood, described by the local press as a "plainspoken" medical examiner, had never been shy about voicing her opinions.

"I'm thinking of issuing a press release," Wood told Strope. "I'm not sure if that's the right thing to do."

Strope told Wood to trust her instincts.

On January 21, 1997, Wood appeared on *Inside Edition* and later spoke to several newspapers, maintaining that Lisa McPherson had not died a natural death. "This is the most severe case of dehydration I've ever seen," she said.

In most homicide cases, compiling a list of witnesses poses more challenges to police than getting those witnesses to talk. In the Lisa McPherson case, Strope and Andrews quickly assembled a full list of Lisa's friends and co-workers, as well as the church staffers and officials who'd seen her in the last weeks of her life. But getting access to these people was daunting.

No one they sought to speak with at the Fort Harrison was "available," the detectives were told. The same was true at the Hacienda Gardens apartment complex, where Strope and Andrews, hoping to talk with Janis Johnson and other residents, knocked on several doors, receiving no reply. A few days later, they returned to the Hacienda to find eight-foot-tall wrought iron gates behind the manicured hedges. The fencing had gone up in less than a week. There were also security guards posted at the entrance to the complex. "That's when we realized this wasn't going to be easy," said Strope.

Then the detectives began hearing from lawyers. The first was Morris "Sandy" Weinberg, an ex-federal prosecutor now representing the church, who paid a special visit to police headquarters to inform the detectives that the Church of Scientology was a "new church" run by "new people" and was perfectly willing to assist with the investigation. But Weinberg refused to hand over many of the files, notably Lisa's auditing folders, which police requested. Scientology was a religion, he explained; anything that Lisa said or did in the church, including records of her financial donations, were private religious documents, protected by "priest-penitent privilege." Would they ask a Catholic priest to reveal the confessions of one of his parishioners?

A devout Catholic himself, Strope took deep offense at the comparison between his church and the Church of Scientology. "This is about Lisa, not about the Church of Scientology," he said.

"We'll go all the way to the Supreme Court before we turn over any of those files voluntarily," said Weinberg. "If you want them, file a subpoena."

So the detectives filed subpoenas. The documents arrived with pages missing; some of the most crucial data, the caretaker logs from the last fifty-three hours of Lisa's life, never materialized at all. "We have given the police everything we have," Weinberg told a Tampa Bay news channel in July 1997. The missing files, he said, had simply vanished.*

The church was no more cooperative when it came to turning over witnesses. Virtually every person the police sought was represented by counsel, many of them former prosecutors like Weinberg, who refused to allow the detectives access to their clients without a subpoena. Ultimately, twenty-six individual attorneys, hired by Morris Weinberg and the Church of Scientology, represented some fifty to sixty witnesses, ranging from church janitors to Lisa's caretakers to Bennetta Slaughter and her employees at AMC.

In exchange for their sworn testimony, close to forty of these witnesses were given immunity. "We really argued against that," said Strope, "but if we didn't give it to them, the lawyers and their clients would get up and walk right out of the room."

In addition to this obfuscation, the church attempted to block and intimidate the police in other ways. Detective Andrews noticed unmarked cars parked across the street from his house, and had once or twice found a man rifling through his trash. His sixteen-year-old

---

* Jason Knapmeyer was transferred to a new job at the Int Base soon after McPherson's death and was never called to testify.

daughter told him that a man she'd never seen before had followed her to school.

Strope too found a man sorting through his trash. Then his son, a fifth-grader, began receiving Scientology literature addressed to him at his private Catholic school. Unmarked cars began to follow Strope as he drove around the city. The hardened cop began to wear his gun more prominently, check his rearview mirror, and take alternate routes home at night. "Let me tell you something," Strope says. "I know the streets, I've worked organized crime cases, biker gangs — but I worried less about them than I did about the Scientologists."

But the police were undeterred. At the end of November 1997, Strope and Andrews concluded their investigation. The Church of Scientology, they found, had been the sole caregiver to Lisa McPherson, and Alain Kartuzinski and, notably, the two doctors, Johnson and Arrunada — who "did little more than merely observe as Lisa's health deteriorated during her watch" — were, through their failure to act, culpable in her death.

On December 5, 1997, two years to the day from Lisa's death, the Clearwater police and the Florida Department of Law Enforcement submitted their findings to the state prosecutor. They recommended that Janis Johnson and Laura Arrunada be charged with practicing medicine without a license, and all three primary caregivers, including Alain Kartuzinski, be charged with manslaughter.

Shortly after the FDLE launched their investigation in early 1997, Marty Rathbun met with Church of Scientology staffers at the Office of Special Affairs headquarters on Sunset Boulevard. There they reviewed the caretakers' logs of Lisa's seventeen days at the Fort Harrison. The logs painted a devastating portrait — particularly those written during Lisa's final two days. One log contained a caretaker's recommendation that Lisa be taken to a doctor. It was a recommendation that Rathbun knew had been ignored until the very last minutes of her life.

"If it isn't written, it isn't true," L. Ron Hubbard had always told his followers.

Rathbun gathered the three or four most incriminating logs. "Lose 'em," he said to an aide. Then he walked out of the room.*

From the day after the *Tampa Tribune* ran its first December 1996 story on the case, the Church of Scientology went on the attack, using every technique in Hubbard's arsenal. Its officials accused the Clearwater police of harassment and religious discrimination and insisted that the rigorous coverage of the case in the *St. Petersburg Times* was meant to "forward an agenda of hate." They also accused Dr. Joan Wood of "lying" on Lisa's autopsy report and then sued for her medical records. After a Pinellas County circuit judge allowed the church to see five pages of Wood's records, Scientology hired its own forensics experts to review her findings.

Agents Strope and Andrews, in the meantime, continued to assist the state attorney as he debated whether to bring criminal charges. The investigators and attorneys knew that the Church of Scientology would view that as a declaration of war. It might also prove difficult to refute the church's experts, which soon included such luminaries as Dr. Michael Baden, the former chief medical examiner for New York City and a former member of the O. J. Simpson defense team. With a seemingly bottomless war chest, the church apparently had no problem paying Baden, who'd testified during the Simpson trial that he customarily worked for $2,000 to $3,000 per day.†

These were the challenges facing the state. Complicating matters for the church was a civil suit filed in February 1997 by Lisa McPherson's family, charging the Church of Scientology with wrongful death. The church's Los Angeles–based lawyer, Elliot Abelson, called the suit "an extortion attempt" and maintained that Lisa would be outraged by the actions being taken in her name. "Lisa McPherson loved the church, and the church loved Lisa," he said.

---

* Rathbun admitted to ordering the destruction of evidence during a 2009 interview with the *St. Petersburg Times*, several years after breaking with the church and aware that he'd committed a crime. However, there is a three-year statute of limitations for destruction of evidence. The state prosecutor, Bernie McCabe, has said he would not pursue other charges against Rathbun.

† Baden nonetheless said that due to Simpson's dwindling financial resources, he'd accepted a fee of $1,500 a day. He never commented on what the Church of Scientology paid him.

But the McPhersons' trial lawyer, Kennan Dandar, sued for access to church documents, and soon Scientology's sanitized version of events — Abelson long argued that Lisa had luxuriated in four-star comfort during her stay at the Fort Harrison — began to wear thin. In July 1997, a Florida court ordered the church to release the caretaker logs, which, save the few that Rathbun had ordered destroyed, were intact, amounting to thirty-three pages. Their exposure sent church attorneys scrambling to revise their version of events. Yes, Lisa had been "psychotic," the church admitted; but the Scientologists had done the best they could for her. "What the documents demonstrate are very caring women who went to extraordinary lengths to care for a person who was deeply mentally ill," said the attorney Morris Weinberg. "They knew they could not take her to a psychiatrist because of their religious beliefs . . . People weren't trying to hurt her; they were trying to help her."

At Scientology's International Base at Gilman Hot Springs, in the vast California scrubland near Hemet, David Miscavige, by all accounts, was obsessed by the Lisa McPherson case. A man known to "react really insanely to bad media," as Rathbun said, the leader of Scientology was now reading about the death of this one Florida parishioner every day. Each new development, whether in the criminal investigation or the civil suit, was covered relentlessly by the Tampa Bay media. McPherson's death had also been reported by national publications such as *Newsweek,* the *Washington Post,* and the *New York Times,* and it was getting significant play abroad, particularly in Germany, where Scientology was considered a potentially dangerous cult.

Critics of Scientology discussed the case in Internet chat rooms and set up anti-Scientology websites in Lisa McPherson's name. Former Scientologists from as far away as Greece and Australia contacted the Clearwater police, offering tips or insight into the church and its precepts. By the summer of 1997, anti-Scientology protestors, many carrying signs plastered with Lisa's photo, had once again begun to appear in downtown Clearwater, disturbing what for fifteen years had been a fragile peace between the church and the community.

This, Miscavige knew, could be catastrophic, for Scientology had big plans for Clearwater. A religious training center was slated to be built across from the Fort Harrison Hotel. This, a 300,000-square-foot structure, referred to as the Mecca Building, was intended to be Scientology's biggest church in the world.

More important, within the intricately worded IRS agreement of 1993 was a requirement that Scientology guarantee, each year, that neither the church nor any of its employees had committed a crime that could jeopardize its status as a tax-exempt religious organization. Though the decision would always be up to the IRS, Scientologists that feared any criminal conviction could put their exemption at risk.

Deciding to take matters into his own hands, Miscavige gathered a sizable entourage, including his wife, Shelly, several female assistants, his private chef, his personal trainer, and several bodyguards — and left California for Clearwater in early 1998. He spent the better part of the next two years there.

The first item on Miscavige's agenda was to ingratiate himself with civic leaders, specifically Clearwater's new city manager, Michael Roberto, who was a champion of downtown development. Bennetta Slaughter had laid the groundwork the previous fall, hosting a cocktail party for Roberto at her home. About fifty of the most elite local members of the Church of Scientology attended the catered event: wealthy investors, artists, business owners, lawyers, and dentists, as well as a number of church executives. Sandra Mercer and her husband were there, and Sandra Mercer recalled that though it was a warm night, Roberto arrived wearing an overcoat. He seemed visibly uncomfortable and standoffish.

Then the jazz musician Chick Corea, a longtime Scientologist, arrived. Roberto, church officials knew, idolized Corea. "It was the most amazing thing I'd ever seen," Mercer said. "Roberto just turned into putty in front of all of us. It was like he was talking to God. All of a sudden, everybody's wonderful. He spent the rest of the night listening to Chick tell him all about Scientology, and by the end, it was as if there was a red carpet rolled out, where before there had been a locked door. His attitude was 'come into my office anytime.'"

Over the next few months, David Miscavige met several times

with Roberto, who became the first Clearwater official to meet with Scientologists in a nonconfrontational setting.

In May 1998, the Church of Scientology was given the go-ahead for a sweeping new development plan, which included a seven-story auditorium and the Mecca Building. To some residents this suggested that the city, seeking investment dollars, had sold out. But Scientologists rejoiced. In a rare move, David Miscavige even agreed to sit for an interview with the church's archenemy, the *St. Petersburg Times,* and described himself as a conciliator. "I take a great deal of pride in creating peace," he said.

But the Lisa McPherson case refused to go away. When asked when he was made aware of the parishioner's death, Miscavige's ever-present certainty seemed to fade. "I would have heard about it sometime around the time period that she died," he said.

"That night?" the paper's interviewer asked.

"No. No . . . That doesn't come to me," he replied. "At the time I don't think it was really thought to be that significant an issue. She died. People die."

On November 13, 1998, the state of Florida charged the Church of Scientology's Flag Service Organization with two felony counts in the death of Lisa McPherson, first, for "knowingly, willfully, or by culpable negligence abus[ing] and/or neglect[ing] a disabled adult," a second-degree felony, and second, for practicing medicine without a license, a third-degree felony. Combined, the charges carried a maximum fine of $15,000.

Agent Lee Strope, who'd waited close to a year for the state to reach a decision, felt "blindsided" by the charges. What had happened to charging the Flag officials with manslaughter?

The state attorney, McCabe, was blunt. "The evidence isn't there," he said.

What the state had, McCabe believed, was simply not enough to prove that any single individual was responsible for Lisa's death. Instead, they found a pattern of neglect and concluded it was more appropriate to charge the Clearwater church, as an organization. "I truly think Bernie didn't want to be the first prosecutor to charge the Church of Scientology with manslaughter," admitted a Clearwater law enforcement official. "So he went with what he felt was a safe charge — negligence."

Publicly, the church met these charges with "surprising calm," as one newspaper report noted. A week after the indictments were filed, the Church of Scientology broke ground on its Mecca Building. The "Hollywood-style ceremony," as the *St. Petersburg Times* described the event, "featured green lasers, colored spotlights, fireworks, and shooting flames, all choreographed with pulsating song." City Manager Roberto and other officials were in attendance, as were some six thousand Scientologists, seated in a grandstand erected for the occasion. Miscavige, tanned and smiling, served as the master of ceremonies and described Scientology's commitment to Clearwater as "now, tomorrow, and forever." The Scientologists in the crowd roared their approval.

This was the public face Miscavige showed to Clearwater. Privately, Miscavige approached the prosecutor McCabe and offered him a deal: dismiss the charges, and the Church of Scientology would do everything it could to ensure that what had happened to Lisa would never happen again. It would hire a full-time, non-Scientologist medical doctor to serve at church facilities and would refer any serious injuries or illness to a local hospital. The church would donate half a million dollars to the county's emergency medical services "as a sign of its commitment to using available services whenever necessary." It would also pay the full cost of the state's criminal investigation, an estimated $180,000.

But if the state refused, Miscavige added, a "holy war" of litigation would rain down on the state attorney's office, tying up precious resources for years. Those who understood the tactics of the Church of Scientology, including many people in the prosecutor's office, did not see this as an empty threat. "We knew what to expect," said Assistant State Attorney Doug Crow, whom McCabe assigned to handle the case. Crow, regarded in legal circles as McCabe's best prosecutor, had worked in the state attorney's office since the late 1970s, back when Scientologists infiltrated the office as part of Operation Goldmine. "I knew they'd hire experts and pursue this defense with everything they had," he said.

Indeed, harassment by lawsuit was not simply a matter of practice; it was a matter of doctrine. The purpose of a lawsuit, L. Ron Hubbard wrote in 1955, was "to harass and discourage rather than to win," and defending oneself against legal charges was "untenable," he added. "The only way to defend anything is to ATTACK, and if you ever forget that, then you will lose every battle you are ever engaged in, whether it is in terms of personal conversation, public debate, or a court of law."

McCabe had settled for lesser charges; he was not going to be bullied into dropping them entirely. The state attorney rejected Miscavige's proposal. On December 1, 1998, the Church of Scientology's Flag Service Organization pleaded innocent to the felony charges. In a letter to the court, the church's lawyer, Lee Fugate, promised a long legal battle. Fugate even went so far as to suggest the case be assigned a special docket to handle the "complex" and "voluminous" motions Scientology attorneys planned to file, which, he vowed, would require "a significant number of hearings and significant hearing time."

With these threats purveyed, on January 22, 1999, David Miscavige once again approached McCabe with an offer to "bring a peaceful resolution to the charges your office has brought against my religion."

McCabe again rejected Miscavige's plea. If the Church of Scientology was seriously interested in reforms, he noted, then why had it not instituted any in the three years since Lisa's death?

The state of Florida's case against the Church of Scientology continued for the next year. During that period, recalled Tom De Vocht, Miscavige "worked day and night" to defeat the prosecution, meeting with church attorneys week after week to debate or redirect strategy. A trial was set for March 2000.

Meanwhile, the civil suit ground on at a steady pace. Compounding Miscavige's woes was the fact that the McPherson family sought to involve Miscavige personally in litigation. In December 1999, the family's lawyer, Ken Dandar, succeeded in adding Miscavige's name to the list of defendants and accused him of personally directing the Flag staff on how to treat Lisa McPherson, including having her "imprisoned" at the Fort Harrison for seventeen days.

The Church of Scientology had already spent millions of dollars fighting the Lisa McPherson case. While the attorneys filed motions and debated the case on constitutional grounds, David Miscavige pored over medical books and journals, trying to figure out how to counter the coroner's evidence. "That's when Dave learned how to use the Internet," joked the former Sea Org member Marc Headley, who was also at Flag during this period. "They had hundreds and hundreds of files, and medical books, and he was reading everything he could find."

With its long list of medical experts expanding by the day, the church produced thousands of pages of documentation refuting the coroner's evidence. Reports were produced questioning the quality of the coroner's lab equipment, stating that some of the tests on Lisa's body had been botched and that evidence had ultimately been contaminated. As their coup de grâce, church lawyers produced the sworn testimony of Dr. Robert Davis, the assistant coroner who had done the original autopsy on McPherson. He had since left his job at the Pinellas-Pasco County Medical Examiner's Office after falling out with Dr. Wood, and, after being contacted by the Church of Scientology and one of its investigators, now said that he "strongly disagreed" with virtually all of Wood's findings.*

Finally, the matter came down to a specific protein, known as ketone, which is usually found in someone who is severely malnourished and dehydrated. Wood's autopsy report found no evidence of ketones in Lisa's body, and Scientology's experts seized upon this as indicative that Lisa may not have been as "severely dehydrated" as Wood maintained. In February 2000, with Scientology's own toxicologist, Dr. Frederic Rieders, another former member of the O. J. Simpson defense team, standing by, Wood retested Lisa's bodily fluids and found ketones, once again, to be absent.

Shaken, Wood e-mailed a colleague, Dr. Jay Whitworth, begging for help. "URGENT!!!!!!!" she wrote in the subject line. "Life and career at stake!" She wrote, "Please don't let me down . . . I will do what-

---

* Davis, who, according to Crow's report, had suffered from psychological problems, may have been under significant duress from the church. However, he refused to implicate Scientology as the reason for his abrupt change of heart. (Letter from Douglas Crow to Bernie McCabe re Review of Evidence in *State v. Church of Scientology Flag Service Organization, Inc.*, June 9, 2000.)

ever is right, but if we are vulnerable because [we] cannot explain absence of ketones, I will have to back down."

Wood had dug herself into a serious predicament by insisting that Lisa had been comatose prior to her death. Other medical experts hired by the prosecution posited a slightly less extreme theory: that Lisa had been unresponsive, though not truly comatose, thus leaving open the possibility that she might have received some form of nutrition, which would have explained why the ketone protein was missing. But with this one forensic declaration, Wood was cornered, and she knew it. And it would prove to be her undoing.

On February 23, 2000, Dr. Joan Wood, emotionally exhausted after being deluged with what some associates recalled as more than six thousand pages of contravening evidence provided by the Church of Scientology's experts, amended Lisa McPherson's death certificate. She continued to assert that Lisa had died of a blood clot in the lung. But her death, Wood now maintained, had been "accidental" — there was no mention of bed rest and severe dehydration as causes. Instead, Wood suggested, just as Scientology's experts had asserted, that the clot had originated from a bruise on Lisa's left leg. She listed "psychosis" and "history of a car accident" as factors in her death.

Scientology quickly moved to have the charges dismissed. "If that death certificate, as it exists now, had been issued originally, there wouldn't even have been an investigation, let alone charges," the church spokesman Mike Rinder stated. "Nobody investigates a pulmonary embolism that comes about as a result of an accident."

Over the next several months, McCabe's deputy, the prosecutor Doug Crow, reviewed all of the evidence supporting the criminal charges. He also questioned Dr. Wood as to why she had altered her findings. Wood, said Crow, offered no plausible explanation. She had been a close friend of his for twenty-five years; Crow stated that her "inability to coherently explain her decision even under benign questioning by me is completely perplexing."

Wood's equivocation, and what Crow called the "very real possibility" that the cause of death originally listed by the medical examiner was incorrect, led the assistant state's attorney to conclude that her testimony could not be presented at trial. Without it, all the state had to go on was the testimony and notes of Lisa's caretakers. And the notes were incomplete. "The likelihood that these witnesses would still be available to us was something we couldn't control," Crow said. These and other "existing problems with the case" led Crow to an inevitable conclusion that the state could no longer pursue the prosecution.

On June 12, 2000, the state of Florida, unable "to prove critical forensic and causation issues beyond and to the exclusion of reasonable doubt," dropped all criminal charges against the Church of Scientology. As for Dr. Joan Wood, the case had "taken a toll far greater than anything else in my life," she told the press. On June 30, 2000, Wood resigned. She was later checked into Morton Plant Hospital after suffering a nervous breakdown. To this day she has never commented about the McPherson case or the rationale behind her amended decision.

Almost a year after the criminal charges were dropped, in April 2001, a Scientologist from Chicago named Greg Bashaw wrote a strongly worded letter to Flag's Captain Debbie Cook, complaining of treatment he'd received at Flag the previous fall. A Scientologist for more than twenty years, and an OT 7, Bashaw, a former vice president of the Leo Burnett advertising agency, had suffered a psychotic break during a "review session" with a Scientology auditor on October 31, 2000. Bashaw told his auditor and his case supervisor, expecting help; to his shock, he was told to pack his bags and was promptly sent home.

Initially, Bashaw blamed himself for his instability, just as Lisa McPherson had: the technology was fine, he believed; he just hadn't been in the right state to receive it. But he also considered the facts: he had gone to Flag for what he believed would be a routine "refresher" but had been kept there for two months; upon his return to Chicago, he'd lost his job. Now, having spent even his retirement funds to pay for Scientology services, he was facing bankruptcy. The church offered no assistance* other than to suggest he visit a doctor to find a

---

* In an article about Bashaw that appeared in the *Chicago Reader* in August 2002, church officials denied they'd had anything to do with Bashaw's decline.

physical cause for his problems — to his horror, his case supervisor had recommended Bashaw try "pep drinks" to restore his lost vitality. Finally, upon his family's urging, Bashaw had sought help in exactly the place Scientology warned against: the psychiatric ward of his local hospital. But that too had proved ineffective. What had been "broken" at Flag, Bashaw was convinced, could only be fixed there, so he was doomed: the organization had kicked him out.

"I understand the need for the organization to protect itself," Bashaw wrote to Cook. "If someone falls into psychosis during his services, Flag is worried about lawsuits, about its responsibilities, about more situations like the one with Lisa McPherson . . . But I was completely abandoned in my time of most urgent need. I did not come to Flag in psychosis . . . I got *into* the psychosis at Flag." As a result, he said, "I am now the worst state I have been in my entire life."

Two months later, in June 2001, Greg Bashaw committed suicide.

When Nancy Many heard the news, she was devastated. She herself had left Scientology in 1996 after suffering a psychotic break; for twenty-five years she had served the church with dedication. Like Bashaw, Many had felt her "mind break" during an intensive period of security checking in Los Angeles; later, on a Burbank street, she experienced a full-blown mental breakdown for which she was briefly hospitalized and then sent home to undergo a modified "baby watch" under the care of her husband, Chris. During that period, the church had offered no practical assistance other than a recommendation that Many take vitamins and chloral hydrate, a medication that Lisa McPherson had also been given.

Many recalled the day that Bashaw phoned her after being given her name by a mutual friend. He was looking for support. "It was tremendously cathartic, I think, for both of us to talk about this," Many told me. "We spoke a lot about the similarities in what had happened to us, and how it felt to be dumped by Scientology after all these

---

"[He] left the church to go sort out his life," said one spokeswoman, Mary Anne Ahmad, who knew Bashaw. Ahmad blamed "family troubles" for Bashaw's problems and said that he'd declined "help" when it had been offered by the church, opting to go with psychiatry, upon his family's advice. "Frankly," she said, "no Scientologist would ever seek psychiatry as a solution to problems."

years. We had both given our lives to Scientology: we'd volunteered for them, had never given them any trouble, and then, the one time we both needed help, they were nowhere, just nowhere."

Many recalled that a month or so after her breakdown, which church officials referred to as her "period of stress," an OSA representative visited her at home to present her with some documents to sign, absolving Scientology of responsibility in her condition and affirming that Scientology "worked" and made people better. Laura Bashaw, Greg's widow, received a similar visit, and similar papers, after her husband died, Many said. "What they learned from Lisa McPherson, if anything, was to cover their asses."

Today, at Flag, Scientologists hoping to receive auditing are asked to sign several new waivers. One gives the church full legal control over the subject's auditing and other personal files, regardless of whether the person is alive or dead. Another form confirms the adherent's desire that in the "unlikely" instance that he or she is judged by others to be in need of psychiatric treatment, they be "helped exclusively through religious, spiritual means and not through any form of psychiatric treatment . . . regardless of what any psychiatrist, medical person, designated member of the state, or family member may assert supposedly on my behalf."

One particularly notable passage in this latter form, often referred to by church critics as the "Lisa Clause," states this spiritual assistance might include the Introspection Rundown, "an intensive, rigorous Religious Service that includes being isolated from all sources of potential spiritual upset, including but not limited to family members, friends or others with whom I might normally interact." In addition the adherent agrees to "accept and assume all known and unknown risks . . . and specifically absolve all persons and entities from all liabilities of any kind, without limitation, associated with my participation or their participation in my Introspection Rundown."

With that, the church protects itself from legal liability. But the church has never backed away from promoting Scientology as a cure for mental illness — indeed, even after Bashaw's suicide in 2001, as the McPherson family continued to press on with their civil lawsuit, a Scientology promotion bragged that "a Flag Ship Class XII [auditor] could turn a severe mental case from raving lunacy to not only sane but bright and normal in about 8 or 9 hours."

Many has since opened her home to Scientologists needing a place to recover from psychotic breaks, and in 2009, she self-published a memoir, *My Billion Year Contract*, in which she detailed her own collapse. In the previous year or two, she said, she has received hundreds of e-mails from former members detailing their emotional breakdowns. One was from a woman who'd spent thirty-six years in Scientology and millions of dollars in donations, and had reached OT 8, the highest place on the Bridge. She arrived at the Manys' door last year, suicidal.

"I could brush off my cognitive dissonance with the other Type Threes I had known of in the past, as they were all very low in Scientology. But here was someone at the top, the end of the Bridge, on my doorstep, wanting to kill herself," said Many.

As a young Sea Org member in Boston, Many helped spread the church's anti-psychiatry agenda by putting up fliers that encouraged people to report malpractice by local psychiatrists and mental hospitals. "I thought I was doing something to help mankind. I never asked myself what Scientology had to put in its place — nothing," she says.

PART IV

CHAPTER 13

The Celebrity Strategy

MORE THAN FIFTEEN years since the death of Lisa McPherson and over seventeen since Scientology won tax exemption, the church's embattled legal history seems, at least on the surface, a thing of the past. Most people today do not think of scandal when they think of Scientology; they think of celebrities, and this is the fruit of a carefully plotted marketing and PR strategy. Compared with all the other tactics the church has tried (many of them eventually abandoned), this one has reaped lasting, even unparalleled success.

Recruiting the famous has long been a central strategy of the Church of Scientology, dating back more than half a century to a program known as Project Celebrity, which Hubbard launched in 1955 with the specific aim of converting luminaries in the arts, sports, management, and government — people he dubbed "Opinion Leaders" — in hopes that they'd become disseminators of church doctrine. As he stated in Scientology's *Ability* magazine, "There are many to whom America and the world listens. It is obvious what would happen to Scientology if prime communicators benefiting from it were to mention it now and then."

Hubbard drew up a list of high-profile targets, urging Scientologists to choose one of them as their "quarry." They included Ernest Hemingway, Edward R. Murrow, Marlene Dietrich, Howard Hughes, Pablo Picasso, Greta Garbo, Jackie Gleason, Cecil B. De Mille, and the publisher of *Time* magazine, Henry Luce, among others. Hubbard issued precise instructions: "Having been awarded one of these celebrities, it will be up to you to learn what you can about your quarry and then put yourself at every hand across his or her path." And he implied that it wouldn't be easy, since the celebrities were "well guarded, well barricaded, over-worked, aloof quarry." But if Scientologists succeeded in bringing one in for an auditing session, Hubbard promised, they would be rewarded with a small plaque.

No one on Hubbard's original list ever became a Scientologist. But his hopes of drawing in high-profile members never waned. By the late 1960s, with Scientology controversial in both the United States and abroad, Hubbard began to refine Scientology's appeal to the elite by opening special churches, known as Celebrity Centres, to cater to artists and other prominent individuals, as well as their friends, family, and any other members of their entourage. In 1969, Yvonne Gilham, one of Hubbard's top Sea Org lieutenants, came to Los Angeles to open the first Celebrity Centre in a former appliance store on West Eighth Street, near MacArthur Park. The small organization hosted cocktail parties, open mike nights, and poetry readings, and though it was located in a seedy part of town, it soon became a fashionable hangout for artsy Scientologists and their friends. "It was as close to a bohemian Scientology center as you could imagine," said Nancy Many's husband, Chris, a former Scientology executive who began working at Celebrity Centre in 1970. "None of the staff wore uniforms; everyone had long hair. It had that hippie vibe that people responded to at the time."

It helped that Hubbard made a direct appeal to artists, whom he described as "a cut above" ordinary people; an artist was "a higher being who builds new worlds," as he wrote in his book *The Science of Survival*. They were "rebels against the status quo" who could, with the right enhancement, accomplish "peaceful revolution." Before long, said Chris Many, Celebrity Centre became the most successful org in Los Angeles, with hundreds of staff and several thousand people enrolled in courses and auditing.

Gilham, an Australian with irrepressible charm, had a unique talent for hooking new members by way of a method some former Scientologists called "admiration bombing": she showered church initiates with such overwhelming praise and attention that they couldn't help but come back for more. This fawning worked particularly well with the two celebrity groups that L. Ron Hubbard wished to target:

first, up-and-coming young actors and other artists who were bat-
tling insecurity as they attempted to make a career in Hollywood,
and second, established, if somewhat faded, stars who were hoping
to rejuvenate their reputation. Both groups could in turn reach out
to their friends in the entertainment business, helping to brand Scientology not only as the "Now Religion," the image the church cultivated in the late 1960s, but also as a ticket into the rarefied world of
Hollywood.

One struggling young actor drawn into Scientology in the late
1960s was Bobby Lipton, the brother of Peggy Lipton, an actor who
was then starring in the hit TV series *The Mod Squad.* Though he was
not a celebrity, Lipton, as he later told *Premiere* magazine, basked in
a certain "reflected glory" at Celebrity Centre because he had a famous sibling. Meanwhile, he struggled to afford the price of Scientology's services. To help defray the cost, Lipton agreed to proselytize
among other actors, including his sister, whom he ultimately brought
into the fold.

Peggy Lipton tried to interest her boyfriend, Elvis Presley, in Scientology, according to one of Presley's associates, Lamar Fike. "One
day, in L.A., we got into the limousine and went down to the Scientology center on Sunset, and Elvis went in and talked to them," Fike
later recalled. "Apparently they started doing all these charts and
crap for him. Elvis came out and said, 'Fuck those people! There's no
way I'll ever get involved with that son-of-a-bitchin' group. All they
want is my money.'" Though Lipton stayed in the group for a number
of years, Presley, said Fike, "stayed away from Scientology like it was
a cobra."

But many others in Hollywood were curious. Scientology, a funda-
mentally narcissistic philosophy that demonizes doubt and insecurity as products of the "reactive mind," is a belief system tailor-made
for actors. The Training Routines that are part of early Scientology
indoctrination have been compared to acting exercises: students are
taught to "duplicate," or mirror, a partner's actions; project their "intention," or thoughts, onto inanimate objects; experiment with vocal
tones, the most dominant being a commanding bark known as "tone
40"; and deepen their ability to "be in their bodies" without reacting
to outside stimuli. In auditing, Scientologists re-create scenes from

past lives. Some processes focus directly on members "mocking up," or visualizing themselves, in different scenarios.

Scores of famous, once-famous, and soon-to-be famous people drifted through Scientology in the late 1960s and 1970s, among them Candice Bergen, Rock Hudson, Leonard Cohen, writer William S. Burroughs, the screenwriter Ernest Lehman, Van Morrison, and Carly Simon, as well as the future *Top Gun* producer Don Simpson and the still-undiscovered Oliver Stone. "That's the sign," the church noted in an issue of *The Auditor* magazine. "Remember twenty years ago when artists were taking up psychoanalysis? It's always the beginning of the big win when celebrities — song-writers, actors, artists, writers, begin to take something up."

Most artists dabbled only briefly in Scientology: Rock Hudson reportedly had a single unsuccessful auditing session. Others spent a significant amount of money on courses and auditing before opting out. Don Simpson, for example, said in a 1993 interview that he'd invested $25,000 in Scientology in the 1970s before he realized that, though nearly Clear, he'd seen very little improvement in his life. "At that point, I realized it was a con," he said.

Yet there were others who embraced Scientology. The jazz musician Chick Corea, who joined the Church of Scientology in the late 1960s, referred to L. Ron Hubbard as an "inspiration" and claimed that Scientology was a major influence on his music. Karen Black, an Academy Award–nominated actress who starred in such films as *Easy Rider* and *Five Easy Pieces,* maintained that Scientology helped her portray characters more authentically.

But Scientology's biggest catch of the 1970s was John Travolta, who was just twenty-one when he joined the church in 1974. Newly arrived in Los Angeles, he was in many ways the ideal quarry: sensitive, naive (a mediocre student, Travolta left high school after tenth grade), and prone to frequent bouts of depression. He'd been given a copy of *Dianetics* while shooting his first movie, *The Devil's Rain.* Soon after, he paid a visit to Celebrity Centre.

There, like many initiates before him, Travolta found a ready-made community. He also found guidance, in the form of officials like Chris Many, who counseled the actor during the early stages of his career. "We'd talk about film and TV and what he wanted to do next, and how Scientology could help him achieve his goals," Many recalled. Travolta would later credit Hubbard's techniques with helping him overcome his crippling fear of rejection. "My career immediately took off," the actor wrote in a personal "success story" published in the book *What Is Scientology?*

But Travolta was cautious when it came to promoting Scientology in the broad way that L. Ron Hubbard had envisioned. "I talk about it when it's appropriate," the actor told the writer Cameron Crowe in a 1977 interview, adding that he realized that many people got "upset" by the idea of Scientology. "Only if [people] ask me, do I talk about it."

And it wasn't just Travolta who was reticent. "There was a lot of skittishness among the celebrities to talk about Scientology," said Many, who became the captain, or executive director, of Celebrity Centre in the mid-1970s. "That was really the great irony in all of this. Hubbard's whole idea was to help artists become more successful and influential so they'd disseminate Scientology on a wide scale. But since Scientology was looked at as a cult at this time, there was a lot of concern, particularly among actors, that being vocal about Scientology might have a negative impact on their careers."

Celebrities did prove willing to promote Scientology's social agenda, however, which could often be done without ever mentioning the church. The use of social reform groups to spread L. Ron Hubbard's ideas had long been an integral part of Scientology, and was in fact one of the original objectives of the Guardian's Office. Since the late 1960s, the church has disseminated its philosophy through a number of organizations with hidden ties to Scientology, notably Narconon, a program that treats drug addiction and promotes Hubbard's holistic detoxification regimen, the Purification Rundown.

Created in 1966 by William C. Benitez, a former inmate at Arizona State Prison, Narconon was intended to help people break addictions without the use of alternative drugs like methadone. Benitez had reached out to Hubbard after reading his book *The Fundamentals of Thought,* and in 1970 the founder of Scientology helped incorporate Narconon as an organization that would use his purification program in the secular world. Over time, it would also assimilate core elements of Scientology teaching, including study technology, the TRs (Training Routines), and Hubbardian "ethics."

By the late 1970s, the Narconon program was being implemented in prisons across the United States, and a number of drug treatment centers had opened in the United States and abroad to administer it. Narconon was headquartered in Los Angeles, where it won the support of celebrity Scientologists, notably the former professional tennis player Cathy Lee Crosby, best known as the blonde co-host of a popular TV stunt show, *That's Incredible!*

In the fall of 1980, Crosby, an adamant anti-drug crusader, appeared before the House Select Committee on Narcotics Abuse and Control to decry Americans' increasing reliance on chemical substances of all sorts. Without mentioning their Scientology connection, she extolled the virtues of Narconon and the Purification Rundown. "I did the program myself," she boasted, admitting that she'd once been a "dabbler" in drugs but had quit, with the help of the Purification Rundown. "It was so fantastic, I wanted to get it out into the world."

A few weeks after she delivered this testimony, Crosby's friend Robert Evans, the former head of Paramount Pictures, pleaded guilty in a New York federal court for cocaine possession. In lieu of prison, Judge Vincent Broderick sentenced Evans, the producer of films like *Chinatown* and *The Godfather,* to one year's probation and added a provision whereby his criminal record would be expunged if Evans used his "unique talents" to create a sixty-second TV spot, to be aired within a year, that would discourage young people from using drugs.

Crosby suggested a campaign called "Get High on Yourself," which would enlist a diverse group of celebrities to appear in various ads as so-called drug-free heroes. This concept was a public relations cornerstone of Narconon, which Crosby and her manager, a former Celebrity Centre employee named Kathy Wasserman, had made their pet project.

Evans latched onto Crosby's idea and set about planning the spots, which would feature prominent people talking "about the pleasure, and glamour, of life on a natural high," as *Time* magazine later described the ads. Among the dozens of celebrities recruited to sing the "Get High on Yourself" jingle — in pop, rock, country, and gospel versions — were Paul Newman, Bob Hope, Cheryl Tiegs, Bruce Jenner, Carol Burnett, Magic Johnson, Ted Nugent, Burt Reynolds, Muhammad Ali, and John Travolta. Only a few, like Crosby and Travolta, were Scientologists. But Scientologists were integral to the spots, which were taped in one six-hour session, serving as go-fers and assistants to the stars who took part in the campaign.

This strategy had always been part of the plan, said Nancy Many, who was then president of Celebrity Centre, working in tandem with her husband. One of her functions was to help identify and meet high-profile targets and strategize ways to bring them into the church, often with the help of fellow members. "The lower-level celebs, people like Cathy Lee Crosby, always knew the higher-level celebs, which is why people who were not big stars in real life became very important to Scientology," Many said.

Once a target had been identified, staffers would research the person to pinpoint his or her "ruin," then, based on this knowledge, they customized an approach. They might also drill the Scientologist friend or family member on how best to make the pitch to the star. The goal, said Many, was not always to convert the A-list star, but simply to "safe-point" him or her, which would be helpful as Scientology was so often a target of criticism or ridicule. Quite a bit could be accomplished simply by having a Scientologist work for a celebrity, she said, noting that the powerful talent agent Sue Mengers once had a Scientologist working on her staff, as did several other agents and managers in Hollywood.

This was the subtle approach that Scientologists used at the taping session for "Get High on Yourself," where "every single celebrity was assigned a Scientologist," said Many, who was in attendance. "They didn't know we were Scientologists, and I don't think Bob Evans ever knew we were Scientologists. They were told we were volunteers who came in to help out and make sure the celebrities had what they needed." No one bothered to ask where the volunteers came from. "This was like a meet-and-greet for mega A-listers. They were so busy talking to one another, they didn't even notice."

Many's designated celebrity was the actor Henry Winkler, a star of TV's *Happy Days*. Over the course of the day, she served as his stand-in, fetched him coffee, and chatted him up. The idea was *not* to disseminate (the Scientology term for *proselytize*), she said, but simply to get to know the celebrity. This covert approach didn't yield much — Winkler had brought his son to the taping, and the two spent most of their time hunting down sports stars to get autographs.

Nonetheless, she felt confident that if she ever met Winkler at a party — a "chance meeting" she would set up beforehand, through the efforts of an acquaintance of Winkler's — the actor would remember her. "From there, you could start a conversation. It might take a few meetings, but the goal was to gradually get the celebrity to talk with you and then feel safe enough to really start opening up to you," she said. "At that point you'd be able to find the person's ruin and make the case that Scientology could help."

Evans' sixty-second commercial led to what he described as "the largest anti-drug media blitz in television history." Airing in September 1981 on NBC, the spots became part of a network-sponsored "Get High on Yourself Week," during which the television commercials were broadcast every hour during prime time.

Having used the stars to get the message out, Crosby and her manager, Wasserman, created the Get High on Yourself Foundation to raise money for the prevention of drug abuse. Over the next year, the foundation reportedly raised $6 million through various fundraising events, though where the money went was never made clear. Narconon was a distinct possibility, however, as by 1982, some of the same "drug-free heroes" who'd promoted "Get High on Yourself," including Henry Winkler, were now unwittingly promoting Narconon through participation in celebrity softball games and other events that Crosby and Wasserman helped organize, sponsored by a Beverly Hills group called Friends of Narconon.*

---

* According to one report, Crosby also sent a list of Narconon's celebrity sponsors to the House Select Committee on Narcotics Abuse and Control to illustrate how many celebrities were opposed to drugs. When the Scientology scheme was exposed — by the *National Enquirer*, in a report that was never refuted — stars like Rob Reiner and Henry Winkler, feeling duped, demanded that their names

Robert Evans did no more promotion but later described "Get High on Yourself" as one of the singular accomplishments of his career. "To this day," said Nancy Many, "I don't think anyone knows that Scientology had anything to do with that campaign."

The unsuspecting recruitment of the non-Scientologist Robert Evans by the Scientologist Cathy Lee Crosby in order to promote a keystone of Scientology's agenda was a perfect example of L. Ron Hubbard's strategy in practice. David Miscavige would also embrace this approach, and celebrities like Tom Cruise would later have a profound effect on non-Scientologists like Will Smith and Jada Pinkett-Smith, who started a private school in Los Angeles that employed Hubbard's study technology.

But Miscavige had far grander plans for his celebrity members, whom he saw less as high-value trophies than as weapons to be deployed when needed to shore up Scientology's image and draw attention away from any negative church story or scandal. "Dave didn't like to keep them in the closet," said one former church senior executive. "His view was that celebrities should be out there, proselytizing. And if you didn't talk, you were betraying the cause."

Miscavige himself was a relentless promoter, cooler and less eccentric than L. Ron Hubbard; not as managerially gifted, he was far more adept at generating buzz. Under his leadership, Scientology's brand would become flashier, if in some ways less substantive, abandoning long-term advertising and PR strategies like the television ads (which Miscavige deemed too expensive) for the book *Dianetics* in favor of more elaborate schemes: the church tried to promote Hubbard's book by sponsoring a Formula One racecar, for example, a venture that caused a minor scandal when the car's driver, Mario Andretti, said he was upset with the Scientologists for plastering his car with the Dianetics logo without his permission. The church also became a sponsor of Ted Turner's Goodwill Games in Seattle, joining such mega corporations as Sony and Pepsi. Scientologists also turned some twenty books by L. Ron Hubbard into bestsellers between 1985

---

be taken off the list. See David McCrindell, "Bizarre Brainwashing Cult Cons Top Stars into Backing Its Drug Program," *National Enquirer*, April 21, 1981.

and 1990, reportedly showing up en masse at major booksellers like B. Dalton and leaving with armloads of purchases.

But no branding strategy worked as well as having celebrity sponsors, and to nurture these valuable assets, Miscavige elevated them to a position far above any other members of the church. This didn't sit well with many Sea Org members, like the Manys, who left Celebrity Centre, and later the Sea Org, around 1982 to become public Scientologists.

"When Hubbard was still running the church, celebrities were parishioners and the Sea Org members were the elite," explained Nancy Many. Now it was the celebrities who were put on a pedestal and given top-flight auditors and other perks previously unheard of in the church. Travolta's auditors, for example, were on call to fly to the set of any movie he was shooting. If he or another well-known celebrity was sick, auditors trained in a special healing technique called a "touch assist" would be summoned to his or her home. In later years, celebrities needing a driver, or a nanny, could find one through Celebrity Centre, which, upon request, acted as an unofficial human resources department, placing upstanding Scientologists from Los Angeles in the employment of high-profile members who requested such assistance. Celebrities were afforded a special entrance into Celebrity Centre, a private VIP lounge, and special auditing and course rooms far away from the rank and file. "We gave them Scientology on a silver platter, and in exchange, we wanted their undying loyalty and love, and only glowing words when they talked about Scientology," said Karen Pressley, who replaced Chris Many as commanding officer of Celebrity Centre. "They were absolutely expected to get out in the media and say something positive, particularly if there was bad press around Scientology."

But this approach evolved over time. In the beginning, Miscavige was more concerned with simply retaining Scientology's high-profile members. Put off by the scandals and lawsuits, not to mention the purges of the early 1980s, artists, as well as ordinary members, had begun to drift away. One them was John Travolta, who in an August 1983 interview with *Rolling Stone* admitted that although he continued to find Hubbard's teachings "pretty brilliant," he had not had any auditing in over a year. "I don't agree with the way the organization is being run," he said, pointedly taking aim at Scientology's new leaders.

For the ascendant David Miscavige, John Travolta, if not quite heretical for his unscripted comments, was dramatically "off-Source" — the most severe judgment the hierarchy could make against an individual, just short of declaring a person suppressive. And yet, losing Travolta would have been profoundly embarrassing for Scientology, particularly since the church had used the actor as part of its internal promotion machine (sometimes without Travolta's full cooperation) for years: reproducing his photograph on posters and quoting from his "success stories" in various pamphlets and other publications.

So he and others were approached, in a widespread effort called the Celebrity Recovery Project, by selected church officials and offered free auditing and other perks, all in hopes of bringing them back into the fold. "What people began to realize was that having a famous person as a member was a double-edged sword," explained the former Sea Org executive Bruce Hines, who audited Travolta and several other celebrities. "They could be great promotion but, if they went sour on Scientology or did something bad, they could be horrendously bad publicity."

To stave off this potential problem, the church had Travolta and other lapsed stars like Edgar Winter and Van Morrison go through the False Purpose Rundown, a targeted form of counseling that addressed a person's failures or weaknesses — their "evil purposes." Promoted as clarifying — somewhat akin to making oneself "right with God" — the process, said Hines, gave a person a new sense of power and control, as well as a conviction that Scientology, which had helped him or her achieve this state, "worked." At which point, the star "would not only feel born again, but also feel a pressing need to make up for the damage" he or she had caused. Travolta, by Hines's recollection, was given the False Purpose Rundown several times during the 1980s, during which time he began to show renewed commitment, most publicly by testifying from the audience during the Larry Wollersheim case in Los Angeles. "It is very important for me to express my satisfaction with the results of being involved with Scientology these last eleven years," Travolta later told the press gathered in front of the Los Angeles Criminal Courts building. "It works one hundred percent for me."

"When you look at that statement, it is very telling," noted Karen Pressley. "He offered a defense of the church, and of the tech, which 'worked' for him" — not coincidentally, at around the same time Celebrity Centre began issuing to members bright yellow T-shirts with bold black lettering on the front, stating SCIENTOLOGY WORKS, as a form of advertising. "Travolta linking Scientology to his success steered the subject away from Scientology being all about spirituality or mental health and toward the idea of its being something that could deliver measurable career results," she said. "That was the way he and other celebrities recruited other actors into the group."*

Pressley, who'd written the pop song "On the Wings of Love" with her husband, the composer Peter Schless, was considered a "celebrity Scientologist" when she joined the Sea Organization in 1986. Her mission was to bring more celebrities into the church, and the pressure to do so, she said, became increasingly intense after Miscavige assumed leadership of the RTC in 1988. A special org board was set up in Celebrity Centre with the names of individual targets and where they stood in the recruitment process. As church officials were compiling these lists, David Miscavige was refining a much larger strategy: to establish the Church of Scientology as the alternative religion of the stars. Central to this plan was Celebrity Centre itself, which had long ago moved from its low-rent quarters in downtown L.A. to a far more elegant address at 5930 Franklin Avenue, in the shadow of the Hollywood Hills.

Celebrity Centre's new home was an ornate, cream-colored Norman revival castle with fanciful turrets and balustrades; built in 1929, it was known as the Chateau Elysee. Its original owner, Eleanor Ince, the widow of the silent film producer Thomas Ince, had built the place as a luxury residence for her friends, many of them

---

* Travolta, according to several former officials, proved to be an effective recruiter, introducing stars like Priscilla Presley, Mikhail Baryshnikov, Patrick Swayze, Tom Berenger, and Forest Whitaker to Scientology. None but Presley, who remains a Scientologist, stayed for long.

retired movie stars. By the 1970s, however, the Chateau had fallen on hard times and was scheduled for demolition when the Church of Scientology bought it, and the surrounding three-acre property, in 1973, for $1 million in cash. Over the next twenty years, the church poured millions from its own reserves into renovating the Chateau, newly landscaping the formal gardens, and transforming the entire property into a kitschy Versailles.

Inside the manor, crystal chandeliers sparkled against a rococo tableau heavy on the gold leaf, trompe l'oeil paintings, and ceiling frescoes. In the lobby, decorated in Louis XIV style, a bronze bust of L. Ron Hubbard stood opposite a white piano that would have made Liberace feel at home. In addition to these ornate finishes, Celebrity Centre boasted thirty-nine hotel rooms, several theaters and perfor-mance spaces, a screening room, an upscale French restaurant, a ca-sual bistro and coffee bar, tennis courts, and an exercise room and spa done in elegant black and white tiles. On the roof of the Chateau, an enormous neon sign, visible from the Hollywood Freeway, pro-claimed SCIENTOLOGY in large gold lettering.

Into this gaudy palace, a structure was put in place to lure, acquire, service, and ultimately profit off not only the A-list stars, whose faces and endorsements graced the posters in the lobby, but also the many young hopefuls aspiring to stardom. To attract the up-and-coming, ads were placed in *Variety, Backstage,* and the *Hollywood Reporter,* promoting Scientology as a form of professional development. "Want to Make It in the Industry?" one asked. "Learn Human Communica-tions Secrets in the Success Through Communications Course." An-other ad pitched a seminar package whose topics included how to get an agent, how to write a screenplay, and how to break into soap operas. All seminars, the ad was careful to say, included booklets by L. Ron Hubbard on "Targets and Goals, Public Relations and more," and would feature talks by "special guest celebrity speakers."

Students who showed up to take the seminar found it to be a vari-ation on a self-improvement course. Getting an agent was only a pe-ripheral topic. "The guy who teaches the course on getting an agent never even had an agent," said Art Cohan, an actor and acting coach who studied at Celebrity Centre for several years. "It was a good promise, though — everyone comes to Hollywood hoping to get an agent. Celebrity Centre would get you in there with these ads, they'd sit you in a seminar and give you a few basic truths, and the students would walk away thinking, Wow, maybe they have the key!"

Cohan, who left Scientology in 1998, now runs the Beverly Hills Playhouse, one of the premiere acting schools in Los Angeles. Founded by the late acting coach Milton Katselas, a longtime Scientologist, the Playhouse had provided a home in the 1970s and 1980s for the young George Clooney, Michelle Pfeiffer, and Alec Baldwin, among many others. It was also an unofficial feeder to Celebrity Centre, particularly during the 1990s and early 2000s, when roughly one-fifth of the school's approximately five hundred students were studying Scientology. Among them were the actress Anne Archer and her husband, the producer Terry Jastrow; Priscilla Presley; Nancy Cartwright, the voice of *The Simpsons'* Bart Simpson; Kelly Preston, who later married John Travolta; and Jenna Elfman and her husband, Bodhi, who, like Giovanni Ribisi, another student of Katselas's, had grown up in the church.

When Cohan arrived at the Playhouse, in 1992, nearly everyone on the staff was a member of the Church of Scientology, and some met regularly with Celebrity Centre staff to discuss which students might be targeted that particular week. If a student had problems or showed insecurity about an aspect of his or her career, Playhouse staff members, in exchange for credits toward free auditing or courses, would suggest the person read one of Hubbard's books, or, even better, take a course at Celebrity Centre to stay "on purpose." Cohan himself was introduced to Scientology this way and admits that he later used the same technique on others. "The indoctrination is if you pay for this auditing and get rid of this negativity, then you can *really think clearly*," he chuckled. "Actors are really vulnerable in Los Angeles. Anything they will think will work, they will try."

One of the actors who joined Scientology through the Beverly Hills Playhouse was Jason Beghe. A handsome thirty-four-year-old who'd grown up in Manhattan and attended the elite Collegiate School, Beghe began studying with Katselas in 1993. By then, Katselas's advanced classes, of which Beghe was a part, were filled with students who were Scientologists. Some received partial scholarships for serving as class "ethics officers," taking notes on which students were late, who seemed tired, who might be having a problem. The great Katselas himself, whom students revered as a god, kept a photograph of L. Ron Hubbard on his desk.

Curious about the church, Beghe asked his friend Bodhi Elfman to give him a few books about Scientology. Elfman obliged and gave Beghe the primer *What Is Scientology?* Beghe found the book's description of the Purification Rundown intriguing. "And that Clear thing sounded good too," he said. The next day he approached Elfman. "Take me to that castle," he said, referring to Celebrity Centre.

At the Chateau Elysee, a cadre of eager Sea Org members greeted Beghe; they seemed to be waiting just for him. And in fact, this may have been the case, for unlike many newcomers, Beghe, whose visit had been arranged by Elfman, was a valuable target: a working actor with a recurring role on the nighttime soap *Melrose Place*. He spent most of that day at Celebrity Centre, touring the grounds, talking to the staff, and otherwise being "admiration bombed," which, he confessed, worked. "Even the most successful artists are extremely insecure about their career," he said. "Everybody is your best friend over there; they just love you to death."

Within a few days, Beghe had invested $50,000 in Scientology, paying up front for the Bridge all the way to Clear. "I figured I could do this in five or six months," he said. Soon Beghe was skipping auditions to take Scientology courses. Within a year or two, he had ascended farther up the Bridge than John Travolta. "I was as gung-ho as you can get," he said. "David Miscavige called me the poster boy for Scientology."

But as Beghe, who reached OT 5, became more involved in Scientology, he was also expected to promote it. Internally, that meant providing the voiceover for a Sea Org recruiting film, which was shot at Golden Era Studios, the Scientology-owned production facility on the International Base. He also made about half a dozen ads for the various "career development" workshops at Celebrity Centre and led one of those seminars himself. Though he recognized the seminars as good PR, Beghe was reluctant to say some of the things he was pressured to say, which included attributing all of his success — by 1997, Beghe had landed a role on *Chicago Hope* and costarred with Demi

Moore in the film *GI Jane* — to Scientology. "You sell a little piece of your soul when you tell that lie," said Beghe, who left Scientology in 2007. "You tell yourself it's for a good cause . . . but a part of you knows you're full of shit."

Nonetheless, Beghe did as he was told, and he was not the only one speaking the party line. By the late 1990s, celebrity Scientologists had begun promoting Scientology's social agenda like never before. John Travolta, for instance, became a key booster of Applied Scholastics, an organization created in the early 1970s to help introduce Hubbard's study technology to the general public. The actor's claim: that Hubbard's study technology had allowed him to realize a lifelong dream of becoming a jet pilot.

Kirstie Alley, who'd struggled with a cocaine problem before joining Scientology in the late 1970s, championed Narconon. In several interviews in the 1990s, she confessed to having checked into a Narconon detox center not long after arriving in Los Angeles in 1979 and credited the program with "saving her life" by helping her get off drugs* (something Alley's auditors from the late 1970s and early 1980s strenuously deny — indeed, they say, she never enrolled in the Narconon program).

A long roster of Scientologist celebrities took up the charge against psychiatry. The screenwriter-director Paul Haggis, for example, who'd joined Scientology in 1975, was one of a number of bold-face names on the membership rolls of the Citizens Commission on Human Rights (CCHR), which was founded in 1969 by the Guardian's Office to combat "mental health abuse." By the 1990s, it had become a powerful anti-psychiatry lobbying force, taking on such pharmaceutical giants as Eli Lilly, and, with help from its celebrity sponsors, bringing Scientology into the national conversation over the effectiveness, and possible misuse, of psychiatric drugs, particularly with regard to children diagnosed with ADD or ADHD — conditions CCHR, and Scientology, maintained were fraudulent.

Beghe also joined the CCHR board of commissioners. And he was

---

* When I interviewed Alley in 2005, she made no mention of Narconon in relation to her own prior history of drug use but told me that she'd kicked a cocaine habit thanks to a single Scientology auditing session. "It was *highly dramatic*," she said. "I did one Scientology session and I never wanted to do drugs again."

expected to attend the annual Celebrity Centre gala each August, an invitation-only event, closed to the general Scientology membership. The highlight of the evening was Miscavige's speech, which stroked the celebrities for their importance to society and also urged them to move up the Bridge. This was not a hard-sell speech promoting a product, such as a new series of books, but rather a call to action. "Sometimes he would push the importance of being a field staff member and how vital it was for celebrities to talk about Scientology to their friends," recalled Karen Pressley. "Other times he would challenge them to engage in important personal projects."

This included spreading Scientology's message beyond Hollywood. It helped that the church's roster now included the legal analyst Greta Van Susteren and her husband, the powerful Washington lawyer John Coale, as well as the singer Sonny Bono, who had studied Scientology in the 1970s and 1980s and was elected to Congress in 1994. Having a presence in Washington had always been a priority of the church, and Bono became a vocal advocate for Scientology-related causes in the House of Representatives. He was particularly instrumental in helping the Church of Scientology fight a number of copyright-infringement cases, notably one against the Internet service provider Netcom, on which a Scientology critic had posted some of the church's secret doctrine.

Bono also joined several other members of Congress in appealing to the U.S. trade representative, Charlene Barshevsky, to put pressure on Sweden, which had allowed public access to Scientology doctrine, costing the church millions of dollars in lost income, its leaders claimed. Swedish law permitted free access to any published work, regardless of copyright. Nonetheless, Barshevsky threatened to put Sweden on a U.S. government watch list of countries that violated international trade agreements unless it complied. In October 1997, under pressure from Congress, the Office of the U.S. Trade Representative, the State Department, and the Commerce Department, Sweden agreed to pass tougher copyright-protection laws that would stop the infringement of Scientology's secret doctrine.

But if anyone helped get the church's message across in Washington it was John Travolta. No longer the reticent star, Travolta had spent much of the 1990s promoting Scientology outright. ("I never defended Scientology," he told an interviewer from *Playboy*, adding that he felt more of an urge to "enlighten others about it.") By the late 1990s, Travolta had become an outspoken supporter of Scientology's ongoing campaign against the German government, which had been investigating the Scientology movement since the early 1990s. Germany was notably hard on groups it suspected of cultlike activities, and it viewed Scientology as a threat to its system of democracy. German Scientologists claimed to have been fired from jobs and prevented from joining political parties because of their affiliation with the church. Some claimed their children had been turned away from local kindergartens.

In response to these reports, Travolta's attorney, Bertram Fields, wrote an open letter to Chancellor Helmut Kohl, which was published in January 1997 in the *International Herald Tribune* and reprinted in several U.S. papers, including Hollywood's own *Daily Variety*. It was signed by thirty-three other well-known entertainment and industry figures, including Dustin Hoffman, Goldie Hawn, Oliver Stone, Gore Vidal, and the chief of Warner Bros., Terry Semel, and drew an analogy between the mistreatment of Scientologists in Germany and the Nazi persecution of the Jews.

Several weeks later, the U.S. State Department released its annual human rights report, which, in careful language, detailed German Scientologists' claims of "government-condoned and societal harassment." Though the report did not directly take the German government to task for human rights abuses, it was notably in-depth, dedicating six paragraphs to describing the various measures that had reportedly been taken against German Scientologists.

That April, Travolta met President Bill Clinton at a volunteerism summit in Philadelphia, where Travolta was stumping for Scientology's Applied Scholastics program. As the actor later recalled, Clinton — possibly to curry favor with Travolta, who was preparing to play a Clintonesque character in *Primary Colors* — offered his help with Scientology's problem in Germany.

In the months ahead, Clinton deputized his national security advisor, Sandy Berger, to serve as the administration's point person for Scientology. In a meeting with Travolta and Chick Corea, Berger, according one former administration official, briefed them on the administration's position regarding Germany "in exactly the same manner he would a senior senator."*

But this flurry of promotion — surely what L. Ron Hubbard would have envisioned for his "opinion leaders" — was only a prelude. Miscavige had a vision far more comprehensive than Hubbard's and a Hollywood star willing and able to see it through. This was a celebrity whose Scientologist beliefs and, ultimately, his public persona, were shaped not by Hubbard but by David Miscavige. What happened would bring unprecedented attention to both the star and to Scientology, though not in the way either would have hoped.

---

* When asked about it several months later on *Meet the Press* (February 15, 1998), Berger said he'd met with the celebrities "to indicate that we would continue to discuss with the German government our belief that one should not be discriminated against on the basis purely of belief," adding that the only ulterior motive he had for the meeting was to get an autograph for one of his children.

CHAPTER 14

The Seduction of Tom Cruise

O N THE FACE of things, Tom Cruise, who joined the Church of Scientology in 1986, was an unusual recruit. Twenty-four years old, he was certainly not "up-and-coming" or insecure, the two qualities that had defined John Travolta when he joined the church in 1974. To the contrary, Cruise was already a movie star, fresh off *Top Gun* fame and soon to be one of the most bankable actors in Hollywood. Handsome, wholesome, with his big-toothed grin, he exuded the sort of thumbs-up self-confidence that made him both a sex symbol and a role model — "guys want to be like him and girls want to be with him," the *Top Gun* producer Jerry Bruckheimer said.

Privately, however, Cruise was a seeker. A devout Catholic for most of his life, he'd lived an itinerant and at times semi-impoverished childhood, moving frequently with his mother and three sisters after his parents divorced when Cruise was twelve. Cruise's father, Thomas Mapother III, was an abusive "bully," as Cruise later called him, prone to drunken, and often violent, tirades. As he grew up, Cruise struggled with dyslexia. A diligent worker, he'd managed to overcome his disability, but in Hollywood friends wondered if Cruise's intense drive was a foil for something deeper. Cruise's costar in *Rain Man,* Dustin Hoffman, later recalled that the actor hated to be alone. "I think he desperately needed a family," he said.

Cruise found it, and much more, through Scientology. His introduction to the church came through the actor Mimi Rogers, whom Cruise met in 1986 and married a year later. Five years older than Cruise, Rogers was the daughter of one of the church's most powerful mission holders, Phil Spickler, and was herself a highly trained auditor who, prior to launching her acting career, had opened what is known as a "field auditing" practice in the San Fernando Valley with her first husband, Jim Rogers.

Field auditors are licensed to use Hubbard's technology by a Scientology group called I-HELP, which, like the WISE business association, charges its members a fee and also receives 10 percent of their gross profits. Like psychotherapists, field auditors charge by the hour. Many have created thriving practices outside the organized church.

The Rogerses' practice, called the Enhancement Center, was based in Sherman Oaks, California, and was seen as an exclusive and discreet setting for initiates to learn about Scientology. It employed auditors with the highest level of training, people who "didn't go in for the high-pressure sales tactics that were common at orgs like Celebrity Centre," said Nancy Many. Not surprisingly, many actors and other celebrities preferred this environment, and among the Enhancement Center's clients were Sonny Bono, who'd been introduced to Scientology by Rogers, and Kirstie Alley, who was one of Rogers's closest friends.

By the time Rogers met Cruise, she and her husband had divorced, and Frances Godwin, a friend and longtime Scientologist, was running the Enhancement Center, which maintained an air of exclusivity. But as the 1980s wore on and David Miscavige solidified his hold, small groups like Godwin's came under pressure to feed clients to Celebrity Centre, where the church could reap more of a profit from their involvement.

Cruise, described by former Enhancement Center employees as "very intense and very bright," was also fiercely private. "He came to resolve some personal problems and he was uncomfortable with the idea of people knowing — as I think most people would be when they're trying to discover something," recalled one former auditor. Cruise enrolled at the center under his real name, Thomas Mapother IV, and for a year no one outside the field auditing group knew of his involvement. But word eventually leaked out, at which point tremendous pressure was put on the Enhancement Center to "turn him over," as this auditor put it, to Celebrity Centre. Ultimately, the group did, about two years after he first joined, said Karen Schless Pressley, president of Celebrity Centre at the time. In accordance with Miscavige's policy, Pressley reported this development to her superiors, who reported it to the officials in the RTC.

According to Miscavige's onetime aide-de-camp Mark Fisher, when the leader learned that Scientology had landed the biggest celebrity whale in its history, he immediately focused on what this could mean for the church. As Fisher recalled, Miscavige told his staff, "This guy is so famous, he could change the face of Scientology forever."

Miscavige called for Cruise's auditing folder. When it arrived, he declared Cruise's field auditor had made certain "errors." To fix them, Cruise would need to go through an "auditing correction program" administered by the Religious Technology Center, through Celebrity Centre, where every aspect of Cruise's experience would be controlled, a not uncommon situation for high-level stars. Though the celebrities remain unaware of it, their entire involvement in Scientology is scripted, former officials say, to ensure the stars see the movie, so to speak, that Scientology wants them to see.

In Cruise's version of this drama, Greg Wilhere, one of Miscavige's senior lieutenants, was dispatched to Los Angeles to serve as Cruise's new auditor. Wilhere was also Cruise's handler, hanging out with him and easing him into the world of Scientology while shielding him from any negative information — "entheta" — about the church.

The tall, confident Wilhere, a Scientologist since the early 1970s, was the ideal choice for the job. He had worked as a steward for L. Ron Hubbard aboard the *Apollo* and had a wealth of stories about the Commodore. He was also, like Cruise himself, something of a clean-cut jock: prior to joining Scientology, Wilhere had played football for Villanova.

"Greg isn't an intellectual heavyweight," said Chuck Beatty, a former Scientologist who'd worked under Wilhere, "but he's an ultra-smooth communicator. He knew the Hubbard viewpoint, he knew all the ways to handle black propaganda against Scientology, he was impeccably dressed, polite to a fault — he was like a J. Crew model, a real sports-hero type, but also a walking showpiece for Scientology. So he was someone a guy like Tom Cruise would look up to."

Furthering the plot, Pat Gualteri, an official at Celebrity Centre, was assigned to be Cruise's course supervisor. Gualteri too had worked with L. Ron Hubbard. He was also a decorated Vietnam vet. This came in handy, as Cruise was beginning to prepare for his role as the wounded Vietnam veteran Ron Kovic in *Born on the Fourth of July.*

"Celebrities, and certainly someone like Tom Cruise, are completely ignorant of the strategy that has been put in place to hook and control them," said Nancy Many. "And the manipulation is different for everyone. With Tom Cruise, here was a guy who needed to portray a Vietnam vet; Pat survived the Tet Offensive. Who better to help Tom get through his basic courses? From the church's perspective, it was a win-win."

After a few months, Wilhere invited Cruise to Int. This, noted Fisher, had been the plan all along, but Miscavige hadn't wanted to overwhelm Cruise too soon. The Gilman Hot Springs compound was still so secret that many ordinary Scientologists didn't know of its existence, let alone its location.* Sea Org members recruited to work at the base were sworn to maintain confidentiality; a stint on the Rehabilitation Project Force was the punishment if they divulged the compound's clandestine location.

Extensive planning and preparation went into Cruise's first visit in the summer of 1989. The base had been given a mini-facelift: buildings painted, bushes pruned, walkways cleared. Staffers, briefed that a "special VIP guest" was coming through, were instructed to be on their best behavior, refrain from smoking and cursing, and work on projects that could easily be explained, were the special guest to ask. Those who were aware that the visitor would be Tom Cruise were instructed not to talk to the star nor look at him, and to respond to any question he might ask by addressing him as "Mr. Cruise."

Miscavige and Cruise met over lunch on the *Star of California,* a three-masted, rudderless clipper ship the Sea Org had built for L. Ron Hubbard, which was situated in the scrubby hills overlooking the Int campus. The actor was a "cool guy," Miscavige told his staff afterward, and seemed dedicated to Scientology, if also nervous about how this might affect his reputation. Cruise was so uncomfortable with being "known" as a Scientologist, in fact, that he walked around

* Those who knew of it believed it to be Scientology's production facility.

in sunglasses and a baseball cap at the base. Miscavige sought to reassure him. Over the next several days the movie star and the leader of his church, twenty-eight and thirty years old respectively, hung out together, touring the base on dirt bikes, watching movies at the base's screening room (Miscavige was an avid *Top Gun* fan), and going skeet shooting.

It had come up in Cruise's auditing, explained Fisher, that Cruise, the action hero, was afraid of guns. To remedy the problem, Miscavige ordered Fisher to prepare the rifle range, where L. Ron Hubbard used to enjoy taking target practice. "DM brought him up there and they hung out and shot skeet for a few hours until Tom got more and more comfortable with guns," he recalled. Cruise was so grateful, Fisher said, he later sent Miscavige an automated clay-pigeon launcher to replace the handheld one he ordinarily used.

Miscavige then ordered the entire rifle range redone in preparation for Cruise's next visit. For three days prior to it, said Fisher, members of the Sea Org worked around the clock, landscaping the grounds, installing the skeet shooter, and building a bunker. "All so that Tom Cruise would be impressed," Fisher added. "And he was."

That Miscavige seemed so smitten with the actor was shocking to longtime associates like Fisher, who noted that although the leader of Scientology had always recognized the strategic value of bringing celebrities into the church, "he'd never cared about them personally. His view toward these people was that they were dilettantes," said Fisher. "They didn't work for the church; they didn't promote the church aggressively. They weren't 'real' Scientologists, like we in the Sea Org were. But something in DM changed after that meeting with Cruise."

Miscavige soon convinced the actor to do all of his Scientology courses, training, and auditing at the base, which, encircled by high stone walls and protected by armed guards — including one known as "Eagle," who was installed as a lookout on a hilltop — offered Cruise a clandestine environment in which to study Scientology away from the glare of Hollywood. Before long, he'd begun keeping his Porsche and his Range Rover SUV at the base, flying back and forth in a helicopter from Los Angeles on weekends. "From A to Z his entire experience was orchestrated so that he'd have the best time possible in

Scientology, and you could tell he bought into everything," said the ex–Sea Org member Bruce Hines, who worked with Cruise on his basic communication drills. "He had that dedicated glare you get after reading *Keeping Scientology Working* dozens of times, and getting tested on it."

To the Sea Org, it seemed obvious that Miscavige hoped to make Cruise an "ideal" Scientologist — not a "floundering" Scientologist, as he'd often perceived Travolta to be, with his years of disaffection in the 1980s. One step in this direction was to teach Cruise to audit. Many Scientologists, including celebrities, never bother to pursue this route on the Bridge to Total Freedom. But a "true" Scientologist, in both L. Ron Hubbard's and David Miscavige's estimation,* was a person who had received and given counseling: indeed, Hubbard had maintained that 50 percent of the gains one got through Scientology were achieved through training as an auditor.

To ensure that Cruise's training went off without a hitch, Bruce Hines set up a special course room in the base's music studio. Then Hines and other officials combed through the personnel files of the base's nine-hundred-person staff to find an appropriate candidate to serve as Cruise's "preclear." After reviewing the paperwork on numerous candidates, Hines settled on Marc Headley, then a teenager newly arrived at the base. The child of Scientologists, Headley had grown up in Hollywood and was recruited into the Sea Organization when he was just fifteen. A year later, he was selected to come to Int, where he labored in the tape and CD manufacturing plant on the base, as a quality control officer. He was a hard worker, with a clean ethics record, and he was also a blank slate: he had received almost no auditing before.

Though not as a rule star-struck, Headley admitted that it took him a while to get over what he called the "wow factor" of being audited by the hero of *Top Gun*. He'd been sworn to secrecy by Marty Rathbun himself: a cardinal of the Church of Scientology in Headley's eyes, Rathbun had warned the sixteen-year-old that severe punishment lay in store for him were he to speak of this top-secret auditing to anyone.

---

* Though Miscavige hadn't audited anyone personally for decades, he routinely spoke of his teenage years when he audited officials at Saint Hill.

The following day, Headley reported to the music studio, where Cruise was waiting outside the course room. "Hello," Cruise said, grasping the teenager's arm in a double handshake. "I'm Tom."

After leading him into the room, Cruise sat Headley down in front of the E-meter for what is known as a "metabolism test." In this procedure, the subject grasps the metal cans, or probes, of the meter while taking a deep breath, which ostensibly indicates whether the subject is rested and has had enough to eat. Headley's test showed his metabolism to be "off." Cruise looked concerned. Did he eat enough at dinner? Headley nodded. "Did you take your vitamins?"

Headley never took vitamins. "No?" Cruise looked surprised and then got up and ushered Headley into a kitchen area off the auditing room to see if he could find some vitamin packets. A cornucopia of edibles was spread on the table. "There was more food in that kitchen than I had seen all year," Headley recalled. "Sandwiches, snacks, drinks, three types of entrées, rice, vegetables, fruit." And this was just snack food. "Who knows what they were feeding him for dinner?"

Headley, like the other staff on the base, lived in a cramped apartment in Hemet. He ate the food served at the base's dining hall, which usually consisted of bland, high-carbohydrate selections, and when punishment was meted out, rice and beans alone. He slept five hours per night, often less, depending on his production schedule. Cruise, on the other hand, was given carte blanche service at the base, including his own bungalow in a private area near the golf course, a personal valet, and meals prepared by the executive chef, Sinar Parman.

For the next several years, as long as he served as Cruise's preclear, Headley was ordered to get at least eight hours of sleep per night and to eat well-rounded meals, with vitamin supplements. "I even got meals brought to me to make sure I was eating properly," he said. "All so that Tom Cruise could learn how to be an auditor and nothing would go wrong."

For Miscavige, having Cruise at the base offered the leader exclusive access to, and ultimately control over, the man whom he hoped to mold into the ur-Scientologist. But it also seemed to provide Miscavige with something more. "I think DM lived vicariously through Tom Cruise," said Karen Pressley, who was working at Int by the time Cruise started coming to the base. "I remember David's father, Ron Sr., telling me that hanging out with Tom was a dream come true for David, and I thought that seemed very true. He'd lived a very isolated life with no social interactions except with other Scientologists."

Now Miscavige began traveling to Los Angeles to visit Cruise at his Pacific Palisades mansion. In January 1990, when Cruise was in Florida filming *Days of Thunder*, he invited Miscavige to join him at the Daytona 500. Afterward, Cruise took the leader skydiving. "DM was so proud of that trip," Mark Fisher recalled, noting that when Miscavige returned from the Daytona 500, sporting a "Days of Thunder" leather jacket, he gathered his senior executives together and showed them a video of his jump from the plane with his instructor.

Though Cruise was still married to Mimi Rogers when he made *Days of Thunder*, he had fallen in love with his Australian costar, Nicole Kidman. Miscavige approved the match — he had never been a fan of the first Mrs. Cruise. Rogers was disaffected with Scientology's new management, which had purged her father in the early 1980s. Such estrangement threatened the foundation David Miscavige was building with Cruise. "David couldn't wait to get rid of her," said Mark Fisher.

Divorce is not forbidden in Scientology, but it is heavily frowned upon.* In theory, explains Fisher, "the only reason you'd want to leave your marriage is if you had overts or things you were withholding from your partner." To remedy this, couples go through what is called a "marriage co-audit," a form of marriage counseling done with the assistance of the E-meter, in which each party is encouraged to confess any transgressions against the other.

With Tom Cruise and Mimi Rogers, it didn't work this way, said Fisher, who was there when the couple showed up for their counseling. Twenty-four hours after the session, they'd decided to split up. The church reportedly handled the arrangements free of charge, assigning the senior financial counselor, Lyman Spurlock, to negoti-

---

* Sea Org staffers, who divorce at an alarmingly high rate, are an exception to this rule. Jeff Hawkins, for example, had three wives during the time he was in Scientology.

ate a settlement with Rogers, who was reportedly paid $10 million and signed a confidentiality agreement. By February 1990, the couple had divorced.

Now Cruise was able to openly pursue Kidman. To help in the blossoming romance, Miscavige and Greg Wilhere arranged for Cruise's VIP condo, located on a remote corner of the five-hundred-acre property, to be thoroughly renovated. To make Kidman happy, Sea Org members filled the place with balloons. When the couple wanted to take up tennis, the Sea Org built tennis courts for them on the property, at the Church of Scientology's expense.

"Millions of church dollars were spent so that Tom Cruise could regularly visit the Scientology base and be friends with Miscavige," said the former Int security chief Andre Tabayoyon. The tennis court alone cost more than $200,000, he said. And the people who built that tennis court — and landscaped the property, built and renovated Cruise's apartment, and performed all other menial and labor-intensive tasks for the actor's benefit — were Scientology staffers, and many of them, Tabayoyon added, were doing time on the RPF, which meant they worked without even the paltry wage Sea Org staffers usually made.

Amy Scobee, a onetime head of Celebrity Centre and a former church "watchdog," or overseer of international management, recalled the day in 1991 when she was abruptly taken off her post at Int and sent to Los Angeles to assist the Cruises in hiring household help. Her assignment, given to her personally by Miscavige's wife, Shelly, was to find and do video interviews of "upscale Scientologists in the L.A. area" who might agree to work as Cruise's housekeeper, cook, and nanny.

It was understood, at least by the person employed to work for a celebrity, that his or her first loyalty was to the church. "Everyone who was on celebrity lines would have to write a daily report about their activities that would go into the celebrity's PC file," said Karen Pressley. "Any conversations you'd have with the star, anything you did with him, what the star read, watched, who he talked to, what he was hearing . . . all of that would be reported, and the reports were sent up to Int," where Miscavige often read them personally.

In Cruise's household, Andrea and Michael Doven, the actor's personal assistants, wrote these reports. Andrea, the daughter of the actor Robert Morse, had been introduced to Scientology by Cruise; her husband, a professional photographer, had joined Cruise's staff later and was known within Scientology — and increasingly in Hollywood — as Cruise's "communicator," the person who spoke and ran interference for the star. Scientology had by now taken over every aspect of Cruise's life, and also his wife's: Kidman, though a lifelong Catholic, had tentatively begun studying Scientology at Int.

"Nicole was willing to try Scientology, but my opinion was always that she was doing it because Tom was involved," said Bruce Hines, who was Kidman's auditor. "But because of the treatment she received at Int, she had a very good experience." In fact, said Hines, thanks to the personal attention she received, Kidman reached OT 2 in just a year, an extraordinarily fast rise even by the standards of celebrities, who tend to ascend the Bridge more quickly, Hines noted, because of their ability to pay.

Cruise, in the meantime, had reached OT 3, the vaunted Wall of Fire. For seven years, he'd waited to discover the hidden truths that he'd been promised would change his life. When he did, he had what many former Scientologists say is not an atypical reaction "He freaked out and was like, *What the fuck is this science fiction shit?*" as Marc Headley put it — and he took a step back.

"From my recollection, Tom went kind of crazy when he reached that level," said Karen Pressley. "You have to remember that this was before the Internet became popular, and everything about Scientology was still veiled in secrecy. So as a dedicated Scientologist, following the rules, he would have never heard of Xenu, body thetans — any of that stuff. Finding out that this was what Scientology was about I'm sure came as quite a shock."

Scientology maintains that OT 3 is not what Scientology is about, that it is simply one process, one tiny particle, in a great oeuvre of material, most of which has nothing to do with Xenu or body thetans: indeed, despite the fact that Hubbard's handwritten notes for OT 3 have been posted on the Internet and authenticated in court, the Church of Scientology refuses to acknowledge the OT 3 myth as true. But those who have done OT 3 and are critical of it say that it is a process that can, and does, destabilize many people, as it requires that a member suspend disbelief in order to audit invisible entities stuck to various parts of the body.

"The way to look at the OT levels is as a form of exorcism," explained Glenn Samuels, a former Scientologist who now counsels other ex-members, including many, he said, who've been severely traumatized by OT 3 and the subsequent advanced levels. "Some people disassociate and suddenly hear voices not their own chattering away at them, saying things like 'You're going to die' or 'I'm giving you cancer, I'm your worst nightmare.' Just imagine the startling reality of having to think your body is loaded full of other people with voices, desires, emotion, and feelings separate from and different than your own."

Those members who are more philosophical about OT 3 explain it as a "handling" for the unknown factors inside every human being that are hampering their ability to progress. Cruise, though, did not see it this way, and he and Kidman stopped coming to the International Base.

For the next several years, other celebrities would front the church's agenda while Cruise pursued his career, making films that many Scientologists recognized as out of step with Scientology's ethics: notably his 1994 performance as the sexually ambiguous Lestat in *Interview with a Vampire* and his role as Dr. Bill Harford, a man flirting with infidelity, in Stanley Kubrick's *Eyes Wide Shut*, in which Cruise and Kidman played a married couple.

Cruise and Kidman spent two years working on the film in London, during which time the Dovens filed regular reports on their activities to the Int Base. "Every once in a while, Michael Doven would get pulled to the base to get sec checked [about the Cruises]," recalled Marc Headley's wife, Claire, who worked for the RTC. Miscavige, she said, was looking for any way to recover the star, but the couple was on a new path: Tom took on the role of the predatory self-help guru Frank T. J. Mackey in *Magnolia,* and Nicole starred in a risqué play by David Hare, *The Blue Room.*

The couple's edgier new course symbolized an act of defiance for Scientologists taught to look upon marital infidelity, not to mention any form of sexual deviance or exhibitionism, as sinful. Miscavige began to take a hard line toward Cruise, denigrating him as "off-purpose" and "out-ethics" in communications with Scientology staff. "I saw the social interaction between Dave and Tom grow less and less personal until it was down to the formalities of sending Christmas and birthday gifts only," said Tanja Castle, then an RTC staffer who would soon become Miscavige's secretary. "There was no live communication at all."

But Miscavige was even more upset with Kidman, whom he blamed for Cruise's growing detachment from Scientology. Miscavige had initially put aside the fact that Kidman's father, Dr. Antony Kidman, was a psychologist — a hated SP — but he'd become dismayed that Kidman, who'd refused to move on to OT 3 after finishing OT 2, remained extremely close to her father. Now Kidman and Cruise had purchased a house in her hometown of Sydney, where they began to spend an increasing amount of time.

The story told within the private world of the Sea Organization is that David Miscavige, aided by Marty Rathbun and several other deputies, engineered the dissolution of Tom Cruise's marriage to Nicole Kidman and Cruise's subsequent emergence as the Most Famous Scientologist in the World. No one still a member of the Church of Scientology has ever admitted to this, and Kidman has never discussed the reasons why her marriage abruptly ended in January 2001, shortly after the couple's tenth wedding anniversary. But those who have left Scientology since the early 2000s recall that it was widely understood in the combative, rigorously single-minded world of David Miscavige's Church of Scientology that Nicole Kidman was an SP.

SPs were much on the church leader's mind by the late 1990s, as Scientology, still enmeshed in the Lisa McPherson case, became even more embroiled in the ongoing battle with its critics, whose number now included a legion of former members who'd become disillusioned by Scientology's high prices and authoritarianism. This "quiet mutiny," in the words of Sandra Mercer, who would ultimately leave herself, was not always reflected in Scientology's income, which continued to receive a boost from frequent fundraising events. However, according to Jeff Hawkins, who as the church's marketing chief kept careful track of such data, virtually every other indicator showed a church on the decline. This devastating piece of information was widely known but never discussed outside the executive suites at Int, where Miscavige scrambled to reverse the trend, to no avail. At Flag, which as Scientology's chief financial engine was a good indicator of the church's overall health, members had completed 11,603 courses and auditing services in 1989, the year Miscavige assumed full control of the church. That number had decreased to 5,895 in 1997, the year that the Church of Scientology was first implicated in the death of Lisa McPherson.*

That year, hoping to drum up new members and counteract the bad press, the church launched what it called the "largest and most comprehensive" public relations campaign in its history, producing a series of thirty-eight television advertisements, some of which promoted Hubbard's books while others emphasized aspects of his philosophy. Miscavige unveiled the campaign during the June 1997 "Maiden Voyage" event on the *Freewinds*, a gala celebration attended by church dignitaries and high-rollers, such as Bennetta and David Slaughter. And yet, as recalled by Steve Hall, the copywriter who created most of these ads, within months of this event, Miscavige had pulled the funding from the campaign.

"This was his pattern," said Hall. "He'd have these events, where they'd show these ads that would get everyone excited and everyone eager to give money to help spread Scientology around the world." After the event, Hall said, Miscavige would generally run the ads for a few months but never did a serious ad buy. "Then he'd cut the funding: he found fault either with the person doing the ads or with the ads themselves, but he'd shut it all down and so the whole thing would quietly die." By then, Miscavige would have moved on to a new event and fundraising campaign, which often was coordinated with the release of a new product: audiotapes or CDs of Hubbard's lec-

---

* Scientology's course completion lists, published in the back of many church magazines, pertain strictly to programs, not individuals. The 1989 figure thus does not suggest that over 11,000 people were at Flag—indeed, according to the website www.truthaboutscientology.com, which keeps track of these statistics, just 5,515 people completed courses at Flag in 1989, and just 3,155 in 1998, some taking multiple courses. These numbers are consistent with anecdotal reports from Scientology members and onetime officials who say the number of people at Flag decreased in the 1990s, along with the number of courses or other programs they signed up for and completed.

tures, for example, or a handsomely packaged set of Hubbard's policy letters or other books, which the public would be encouraged to buy on the spot.

But nothing, said former executives, grew the church. At the orgs, members continued to slip away. Others languished on the Bridge. For Miscavige, who'd been raised to believe in Hubbard's management technology, the fact that it didn't seem to be working was unthinkable—indeed, it was a point of doctrine that the tech "works every time." The idea that *he* was not doing things right was even more unthinkable, noted Jeff Hawkins. "The only conclusion he was left with was that someone was working against him, some SP."

In fact, Miscavige was right. A broad network of individuals were working against Scientology, united by a new and even more daunting enemy, the Internet. The online world was a powerful weapon in the hands of critics of the Church of Scientology, including many free-speech advocates who built websites dedicated to exposing and analyzing Scientology's secrets. Some sites were dedicated to "scholarship" related to the OT documents; others were devoted to shining a light on L. Ron Hubbard's war record, scientific claims, correspondence with the FBI, and the various lies he told about his youth. Much of Scientology's legal archive—dozens of highly contentious cases, with accompanying court transcripts and affidavits, as well as analysis—were now easily viewable online. Even Lisa McPherson's grotesque autopsy photographs were scanned and posted on several different websites, with accompanying captions that accused the Church of Scientology of murder.

For Miscavige, who'd spent most of the past twenty years deftly shifting the spotlight away from the scandals that dogged the church, the sheer glut of negative information about Scientology now available through a simple Google search was disastrous. Nothing the leader had previously dreamed up, certainly no weapon in his legal arsenal, could counter the deluge of data—scanned copies of L. Ron Hubbard's handwritten OT 3 materials, for example—that was spreading across the Internet.

At gatherings of the flock, Miscavige beseeched his followers to beware of the "lies" posted in cyberspace. At the orgs, officials urged the membership to create personalized Scientology webpages to flood the Internet with positive promotion. To help them do this, the church issued a compact disk with both a web design program and a special Internet filter program, which censored particular search terms, sites deemed to be using the trademarks or writings of Scientology or Dianetics in an unauthorized fashion, and sites that, according to the CD's licensing agreement, were seen as "improper or discreditable to the Scientology religion."

But the filter was effective only in households with a single computer and soon proved obsolete. And even if members did avoid reading such criticism, nothing prevented other people — the potential recruits that the church so badly needed — from discovering these unsavory reports when they researched Scientology. Negative stories posted on the Internet dealt a particularly devastating blow to the church because they reached young people under the age of thirty — the population whose idealism, and naiveté, had built the church in the first place. Facing perhaps the biggest crisis in its history, Scientology needed a new kind of symbol: someone whose star power could deflect, even transcend criticism.

And so, in early 1999, Marty Rathbun, who'd been spending most of his time in Florida handling the Lisa McPherson case, was called back to Los Angeles by Miscavige and assigned a new task: "recover" Tom Cruise, in earnest. Neither Rathbun nor Cruise has ever spoken about the details of this "recovery," but over the next two years, Rathbun steered Cruise back to the OT levels. By 2002, he'd reached OT 4. That year, during Cruise's publicity tour for his film *Vanilla Sky*, he and his new girlfriend, the actress Penelope Cruz, lobbied the U.S. ambassadors in France, Greece, and Germany, countries where Scientology was under investigation, to support the church in its cause of "religious freedom." This lobbying was not unlike Travolta's efforts, begun in the late 1990s, but Cruise took up the cause with even more passion. In June 2003, for instance, he secured a meeting with Deputy Secretary of State Richard Armitage to further press his concerns about the Church of Scientology's treatment in Germany. The next day, Cruise met with Scooter Libby, Vice President Cheney's chief of staff, to discuss the same topic.

Cruise also took on the cause of education, hoping to win government funding for Scientology's Applied Scholastics supplemental education program. Over lunch with Secretary of Education Ron Paige and his chief of staff, John Danielson, Cruise, according to a report in the *Washington Post,* asked numerous questions about the No Child Left Behind Act of 2001, the Bush administration's mandate that schools found to "need improvement" must set aside 20 percent of the annual budget to provide students with supplemental education. By the summer of 2003, Applied Scholastics, now headed by Bennetta Slaughter, had been approved in the state of Missouri as one such provider and soon met with similar endorsement in Florida, California, Louisiana, and Washington, D.C.

During this phase of Cruise's activism he began to float a story that became a key part of the rewritten script of his life: that his dyslexia had rendered him a "functional illiterate" until he was "cured" by Hubbard's study technology. By the summer of 2003, Cruise was openly promoting Scientology as a cure for learning disabilities, often plugging a Scientology-backed tutoring program, the Hollywood Education and Literacy Project (H.E.L.P.), that he'd helped found.

By the fall of that year, Cruise garnered even more publicity for his sponsorship of the New York Rescue Workers Detoxification Project, a Scientology-endorsed clinic in lower Manhattan that used Hubbard's controversial Purification Rundown to treat first responders at the World Trade Center on 9/11, who now, two years later, suffered from health problems related to the disaster. In an interview with Larry King on November 28, 2003, Cruise, who donated more than $1 million to the effort, defended the clinic, whose techniques some physicians had criticized. "Doctors do not know how to diagnose chemical exposures, because it can actually have mental ramifications," he said. "You go to a doctor and now he's going to put you on more and more drugs, steroids, things that are ineffective." But Scientologists, he suggested, had far more potent solutions. "I've actually helped people that have been diagnosed with ADD, ADHD," Cruise said, giving a plug for Hubbard's study technology.

"I watched Tom promoting those causes and I just felt a shiver," said Karen Pressley, who'd left Scientology in 1998, disillusioned with David Miscavige's leadership. "He had that same passion I'd once had when I was convinced that I had found the only thing that worked. It's a phase you go through in your development as a zealot."

But Cruise was a special kind of zealot: he was the biggest movie star in the world. His intense personality lent fervor to his new role as a one-man Scientology promotion machine. "At Int," recalled Marc Headley, then the head of production at Golden Era, Scientology's in-house film studio, "they put together a media reel each week of everything being said about Scientology that everyone on the base had to watch, so people who saw it thought Scientology was *the* biggest thing that was happening right now in the world." Cruise's effectiveness as a spokesman was the most exciting thing to happen to the church since it was granted a tax exemption in 1993. "They thought it was awesome," said Headley.

As Cruise was getting ready to embark on an overseas tour to publicize his film *The Last Samurai,* Warner Bros. reportedly became concerned about how his advocacy of Scientology would play. According to numerous reports, the actor's longtime publicist, Pat Kingsley, often credited with carefully constructing Cruise's "Teflon" persona, advised her client that, for this trip, he should leave the Scientology talk at home. Instead, it was Kingsley who stayed behind: when Cruise began his European tour, his publicist was noticeably absent.

Two months later, Cruise ended his fourteen-year affiliation with Kingsley and her company, PMK, and hired his older sister and fellow Scientologist, Lee Anne DeVette, as his new publicist; Marty Rathbun later said that David Miscavige encouraged Cruise to make this move. Now, free of Kingsley's moderating influence, Cruise and DeVette embarked on a plan to educate journalists about Scientology. Whereas Kingsley had often scolded certain reporters for asking about Cruise's religious beliefs, and even banned some from doing so, the actor now insisted that journalists tour the Celebrity Centre before he'd sit down for an interview. Scientology was "the shit, man," Cruise told *Rolling Stone*'s Neil Strauss in the summer of 2004. "Some people, well, if they don't like Scientology, well, then, fuck you." "Really," he added. "Fuck you. Period."

David Miscavige, by all accounts, was thrilled by the emergence of Tom Cruise, Proselytizer. It fully realized his strategy. To Scientologists who knew the men, it seemed as if a complete transference had taken place. "Tom talked and acted as if he were a clone of David Miscavige," said Mark Headley. And in fact Miscavige, the chairman of the board, or COB, of the church, often told his staff that Cruise was the "COB of celebrities."

During one meeting on the base, Headley recalled, Miscavige told the assembled Scientologists a revealing story. In late 2003 or early 2004, Cruise invited a group of Scientologist celebrities to a meeting in Hollywood. About twenty or thirty reportedly showed up to hear Cruise offer a powerful rallying call to activism; Cruise read the actors the riot act about what it meant to be a "real" Scientologist. Headley said, "Now this is a guy who didn't say shit about Scientology for ten years — but now he is telling them they were 'out-ethics' for not being vocal enough about Scientology."

Miscavige, said Headley, used this story to illustrate Cruise's dedication. "He'd done it totally unsolicited, and called Dave *afterward* and told him what he did. Dave loved it. And I'll tell you one thing," he added. "Right after that meeting supposedly happened, Jenna Elfman showed up at the opening of a Scientology mission in San Francisco, and then another one in Buffalo."

Elfman wasn't the only one spurred to advocacy. The second-generation Scientologist Ericka Christensen, a young actress who'd starred in Steven Soderbergh's *Traffic*, told the New York *Daily News* that she counted Scientology as one of her "secret weapons," as the newspaper put it, and considered Cruise a mentor. The actor Jason Lee, who'd costarred with Cruise in *Vanilla Sky* but had kept mum about his involvement in Scientology, now showed up for the opening of a Scientology mission in Los Feliz. Perhaps the most surprising new spokesperson was the pop singer Beck. His father, the composer David Campbell, is a Scientologist, and Beck, as he once said, "grew up in and around" Scientology; but like Lee, the singer had never spoken openly about the group. Now in an interview he reported that the faith had "strengthen[ed]" his outlook on life and inserted a small anti-prescription-drug message in the video for his single "Girl."

Cruise, meanwhile, had recruited James Packer,* the son of the

---

* According to several reports, Packer is no longer affiliated with the church.

richest man in Australia, Kerry Packer, to Scientology. Sea Org staffers, who'd long ago been instructed to refer to Cruise as "sir," were
now ordered to salute the actor as if he were their superior officer.*
When Cruise visited Int, as he did with more frequency after 2003,
he was no longer accommodated in his standard condo, but rather
in the guesthouse of L. Ron Hubbard's $10 million mansion, Bon-
nie View. One reason for this treatment was that Cruise, at least according to Miscavige, was now Scientology's main cash cow. In 2004,
Cruise gave close to $3 million to Scientology, with much more prom-
ised. Miscavige frequently bragged to his staff that Cruise intended to
use some of that money to help build hundreds of new churches and
boom Scientology beyond anything Miscavige had previously imagined. In the leader's mind, Cruise could be a one-man "war chest," the
sole funder of the church's expansion.

Cruise's strategic value to the church was so crucial that nothing
was too good for the actor. Miscavige even created a special award for
him, the International Association of Scientologist's Freedom Medal
of Valor, which he presented to Cruise at the IAS's twentieth anniversary gala in October 2004. When Cruise, in a black velvet jacket,
walked onstage to receive his medal, a platinum disc encrusted with
diamonds, the audience gave him a standing ovation as the actor and
the Scientology leader saluted each other, hugged, and then clasped
hands in a victory gesture. Miscavige called Cruise "the most dedicated Scientologist I know."

Other Scientologists cringed at that statement. "All I thought
about was the dedicated Sea Org members who'd sacrificed and given
their lives to Scientology," said one member who was in the audience
that evening. But to Miscavige, Cruise was better than all of them.
The leader had even begun to tell his staff that he wished that Cruise
could be his second-in-command, recalled Jeff Hawkins. "He'd say
that Tom Cruise was the only person in Scientology, other than himself, that he would trust to run the church."

All the other Scientology executives, even such esteemed officials
as Ray Mithoff, Greg Wilhere, and Mike Rinder, were "degraded" in

---

* Once, recalled Marc Headley's wife, Claire, Cruise came down with food poi-
soning at Int, prompting the immediate departure of the unfortunate Sea Org
member who had unwittingly fed the actor bad shrimp.

Miscavige's eyes; their repeated failures — Rinder and Marty Rathbun's inability to protect Miscavige from personal involvement in the Lisa McPherson case, for example — made them unworthy.

Zealously embracing the role of Scientology's chief proselytizer, by the spring of 2005 the actor was presenting himself as a "helper" who'd assisted "hundreds of people" to get off drugs. "In Scientology, we have the only successful drug rehabilitation program in the world," he told a reporter from Germany's *Der Spiegel,* who replied by calling Hubbard's techniques "pseudoscience." Cruise also maintained he could help criminals reform their lawless ways. "You have no idea how many people want to know what Scientology is," he told the German newspaper.

According to the *Los Angeles Times,* Cruise spent so much time proselytizing about Scientology during his spring 2005 promotional tour for *The War of the Worlds* that the director, Steven Spielberg, became concerned that Cruise was drawing attention away from the movie. But the actor was by now sealed so tightly within Scientology's protective shell that he barely took notice.

The next step was a new wife. Sandra Mercer, the onetime Scientologist of Clearwater, Florida, watched Cruise declare his love for Katie Holmes on *The Oprah Winfrey Show* in the spring of 2005 and chuckled when she saw him jumping enthusiastically on Winfrey's couch. ("Enthusiasm is very high on Scientology's tone scale," she said.) It was not unheard of for single members at Cruise's level to be "ordered" to get married in order to continue to progress in the church, she explained. Hubbard stressed that a truly successful Scientologist would be successful on all the dynamics of existence, including the "2nd Dynamic," which is marriage and family. "I can't say that happened with Tom, but I've heard it said to others; I've said it to people myself. And in Tom's case, he would have been told: 'If you find someone who can help us reach more young people, wow, what a win that would be!' That is what's promoted. Everything you do, every action you take should be done from the standpoint of gaining worldwide acceptance of Scientology."

Eventually, however, Cruise's increasingly strident advocacy began to backfire, notably after he lambasted the actress Brooke Shields, a onetime friend, for using the antidepressant Paxil to treat postpartum depression. Then, a few days after his *Oprah* appearance, Cruise sat for an interview on the *Today Show,* where he lectured Matt Lauer on the dangers of antidepressants. "Do you know what Adderall is? Do you know what Ritalin is? Do you know now that Ritalin is a street drug? Do you *understand* that?" Cruise asked Lauer. "You see, here's the problem. You don't know the history of psychiatry. I do."

It was, as many television critics noted, spectacular TV. It was also proof to many observers, including many former Scientologists, of just how dangerously out of control Cruise's zealotry had gotten. Though Miscavige by all accounts viewed Cruise's advocacy as a win, former Scientologists and even some current ones were shocked by his tone-deaf approach. The Church of Scientology, which for decades had deftly morphed in response to society's latest interests, now seemed wholly oblivious to the effect Cruise's performance was having not only on the actor, whose career took an irreparable hit, but on his church.

By the end of 2005, Scientology had been lampooned on virtually every late-night talk show and, most memorably, on *South Park.* By 2006, a spate of magazine articles* had examined Scientology's teachings and scrutinized its more controversial practices. As the church spokesman Mike Rinder went on television to deny Scientology's policy of making its members disconnect from family and friends who had fallen away from the church, Tom Cruise receded into the background, although by all accounts, his friendship with Miscavige, who served as best man at his wedding to Holmes and even accompanied the couple on their honeymoon, remained strong. "Dave probably told Tom to cool it a little bit and not be so aggressive in fighting people like Matt Lauer, but he wouldn't go, 'Oh my God, this really backfired,'" said one former Scientology executive who worked with Miscavige. To the contrary, he said, Miscavige would simply think that those outside of Scientology were wrong "and Tom Cruise had been 'black PR'ed.'"

For a short while, John Travolta stepped back into the promo-

* This spate includes my own article, "Inside Scientology," published on February 23, 2006, in *Rolling Stone.*

tional spotlight, albeit unsuccessfully. In February 2007, Travolta told the media that Scientology's Narconon program might have helped save the former Playboy Playmate Anna Nicole Smith, who died of a drug overdose. "Google Narconon for a minute," MSNBC's Willie Geist suggested to the talk-show host Tucker Carlson, in response to this statement. "If I wasn't so completely terrified of Scientology, I would," Carlson quipped.

By the end of 2007, Scientology's public image was worse than at any other time in Miscavige's tenure. It was a "joke" how bad it was, a onetime senior church official told me when I interviewed him in the spring of 2008. "Between Cruise and Miscavige, they absolutely destroyed Scientology's PR," he said. "I've never seen it like this."

And yet Miscavige seemed almost oblivious to this problem, a quality that set him notably apart from L. Ron Hubbard, who'd reacted to negative press with hurt feelings, blaming the "wog world" for his problems and isolating himself and his followers. According to many observers, Miscavige was unfazed ("Dave doesn't care if people like him," an official noted) and blamed his staff when things went wrong.

It was a tendency Miscavige had shown since taking over the church: an example, said many of his former executives, of the leader's poor management. But Miscavige's imperviousness was also wholly understandable. He had lived immersed in Scientology since the age of eight. He'd become the leader of the church at the tender age of twenty-five. He'd had no experience living in the non-Scientology world, much less in running a Scientology org or mission, or even counseling people in any significant way. Indeed, Miscavige's dealings with the flock had always been limited — according to Marty Rathbun, the leader frequently sent emissaries like Rathbun to interface with prominent members while he remained at a distance. In his twenty-odd years at the helm, Miscavige did one television and one print interview. After 1998, he did no interviews at all.

Scientology too had become more insular. And this, noted Steve Hall, made it even harder to promote Scientology to mainstream Americans. "That has got to be the hardest assignment in the world," he said. "By this point, Scientology is a culture. Inside the church you can go on completely unaware, really ignorant of how to connect to people, because you live and breath Scientology twenty-four hours a day. But outside of the church, people know all about the lawsuits, they've heard it called a 'mafia' or a cult, they've gone on the Internet to read the OT materials . . . so how do you sell Scientology to new people? You don't."

CHAPTER 15

The Bubble

L
UCKILY FOR THE CHURCH, a growing majority of today's Scientologists are, like David Miscavige, people who were born or raised in the movement. This makes the marketing of Scientology far easier. Children who grow up in Scientology have a limited worldview: they are integrated into mainstream society, yet in many ways are totally isolated from its standards and norms. The degree of this isolation may differ, but the general rigor of a Scientology upbringing holds true whether members live in a sleepy community like Clearwater or in Los Angeles, the second-largest city in the United States. Many church-raised kids refer to their childhood as a "bubble." Some children thrive in this environment; others, chafing against its dogma, rebel; still others are consumed by it entirely.

Natalie Walet falls into the first category. She is part of Scientology's third generation: both of her parents, a few aunts and uncles, and her paternal grandmother are Scientologists, and Scientology is the only religion she's ever known. When I met her for the first time, in August 2005, she was seventeen, just out of high school and living with her parents in Dunedin, outside Clearwater. We met at the Starbucks on Cleveland Street, around the corner from the Fort Harrison.

This, she realized, was a daring move. Scientologists are discouraged from speaking to journalists; those who do — indeed most of those I met — do so with the church's permission and are often chaperoned by church officials. Natalie hadn't asked anyone's permission. A pretty girl with shiny dark hair, she was tremendously self-assured, which was something I'd find true for many Scientologist kids. She had agreed to talk to me "without a filter," as she later said, "because quite frankly I wanted to stand up for the rest of us Scientologists that get globbed in with the crazy people."

We watched from the wide front patio of the Starbucks as a blue and white bus, adorned with the word FLAG in elaborate script, discharged what looked like a small army of Sea Org members. Each was dressed in a preppy uniform of khaki, black, or navy blue trousers and a crisp white, blue, or yellow dress shirt.* "Most people think that all Scientologists look like that," Natalie said. She was dressed in a low-cut black T-shirt and jeans. "I meet people all the time who say, 'Oh my God, you're a Scientologist?'" She rolled her eyes in teenage exasperation. "I mean, dude, you see them every day. Your clerk at the 7-11 could be a Scientologist. Your neighbor may be a Scientologist. You just don't know. And that's because we're not that different from you! We're all just people," she said.

Of course there were some differences, she acknowledged. Like all Scientologists, Natalie saw herself as a thetan, and her physical, or "meat," body one of many she'd had on life's continuum. In the end, her body was unimportant. She lit a cigarette. She'd started smoking when she was eleven, she said, which she realized was "kind of bad," but then again, L. Ron Hubbard chain-smoked Kools for most of his life. "LRH never said we were supposed to be perfect."

Natalie idolized Hubbard. I noticed that she often prefaced her sentences with the phrase "LRH says," and she could quote him, chapter and verse. But unlike many older Scientologists, who describe the Founder in almost godlike terms, Natalie saw Hubbard as simply "a brilliant person who came up with a fascinating technology, a lot of which is common sense." She spent a lot of her free time studying Hubbard's ideas, which, she explained, were primarily about learning how to take better control of one's life and handle problems in a rational way. "For me, Scientology is about finding out the 'why' for whatever it is you want to apply it to. But you have to find that out for

---

* The Sea Org had abandoned its navy-style uniforms as day-to-day attire in Clearwater by 1996, as part of the church's ongoing effort to make friends in the community. This would soon become standard practice throughout Scientology, though the Sea Org dons the formal uniform on special occasions.

yourself," she said, and quoted Hubbard: "What's true for you is what you observe to be true."

Natalie was born in Arlington, Virginia, and spent her early life in the suburbs of Washington, D.C., where her father, John Walet, ran the church's large organization on Dupont Circle. Natalie's mother, Emily, also worked at the D.C. Org, and as an only child, Natalie virtually grew up there. Despite her father's official-sounding title — he was the executive director — her parents were part of the church's rank and file, not Sea Org members, but paid staff who worked long hours. Loyal Scientologists, they were also independent. "My mother is very outspoken; she'll tell you exactly what she thinks," Natalie said, recalling one instance when Emily Walet staunchly defended a church member whom officials had wanted to declare suppressive — and prevailing. "That guy is still a Scientologist, in D.C., and doing really well," Natalie said. "There's a lot of pressure when you work in the org. I know my parents got in arguments with higher-ups from time to time. But if they saw something they felt was wrong, they said something."

Scientology is an extremely doctrinaire faith, yet it does not necessarily produce robots. Natalie, an extremely poised and articulate teenager, was an example of just how independent some Scientologist kids can be. She explained it was due to the unique way Scientologist children are raised, which is in accordance with Hubbard's dictum that all people, regardless of age, be granted their own "beingness," or self-determinism. The Walets took this directive seriously and rarely yelled at or talked down to their daughter, unlike the parents of non-Scientologist kids she'd later meet. "I was never treated like a little kid, even when I was a little kid," she said, and thought about that for a minute. "I guess I never really felt like a little kid either," she added.

Natalie began school, upon her own insistence, she said, when she was four, skipping kindergarten. She attended a private school, the Chesapeake Ability Academy in northern Virginia, which was run by Scientologists. There are nearly fifty such schools in the United States, and for those who can't afford them, scores of private tutoring programs to help Scientologist kids in public schools supplement their education with Hubbard's techniques. All are sponsored by Applied Scholastics, which licenses Hubbard's study technology to independent schools and tutors in the same manner that WISE licenses his management technology to independent businesses.

Though they are not considered "parochial" (though they are tax-exempt), Scientology schools, according to the church's own literature, are meant to educate children into L. Ron Hubbard's philosophy, with larger goals in mind. "By educating a child into one's own beliefs, one gradually takes over a whole new generation of a country and can thus influence, in the long term, the development and growth of that country," stated a 1986 issue of *Impact*, the magazine published by the International Association of Scientologists. The Jesuits, for example, "were very successful at this strategy."

Natalie never saw Chesapeake as "religious" in any way. "They just used study tech," she explained. The kids learned at their own pace; used physical examples — clay models, marbles, or diagrams — to help them work out complex concepts; and focused intensely on vocabulary, never skipping a word they didn't understand; instead, they looked it up in the dictionary. Natalie described this education as "awesome" because she was never allowed to just ignore things she did not fully comprehend. "If I got a ninety-eight on a test, they would go to that two percent I did wrong and help me figure it out." An intelligent and highly motivated girl, she stayed at Chesapeake through fifth grade and then transferred to a public middle school, where she was an accelerated student. At thirteen, she started high school.

The next year, her parents moved to Dunedin, in part to be closer to Flag, but also, Natalie said, because Washington had become too expensive. For Natalie, it would prove to be both a social and spiritual awakening.

The Walets arrived in the Clearwater area just two years after the Lisa McPherson criminal case had been thrown out, an event that had angered many people in the community. For the next several years, the case was kept alive as the McPherson family's civil lawsuit against the church continued,* and the public's resentment of

---

* The family ultimately settled with the church in 2004 for an undisclosed amount, estimated at $20 million.

Scientologists, or "Scienos," as many derisively called them, was palpable. Some twelve thousand Scientologists were living in or around
Clearwater by the early 2000s, according to church estimates* — the
greatest number in any city except Los Angeles. The Church of Scientology was one of the largest owners of property in Clearwater;
half of their holdings were located in or around downtown Clearwater, where, in response to years of protests fomented by church critics, an extensive security system was installed. Some 150 surveillance
cameras are posted on or around all buildings associated with Scientology, some disguised as streetlights or hidden inside lampposts,
but most perched quite openly on rooftops and window ledges. Some
cameras face in, toward the buildings themselves; others are aimed
at the street.

Natalie thought this was normal — "It's the twenty-first century;
who doesn't have a security camera?" — but many other people found
the cameras disconcerting. Scientologists, many locals complained,
had "taken over" downtown; indeed, just a year before I met Natalie,
the *St. Petersburg Times* had dubbed Clearwater, a city of more than
100,000 people, "Scientology's Town."

Natalie's religion had never caused problems for her in Virginia — it had almost never come up among her friends and teachers in middle school, in fact. But at the public high school she began
attending in Dunedin, some of her teachers advised her that certain
faculty members might lower her grade if they knew she was a Scientologist. The parents of several of her classmates, upon learning of
Natalie's faith, refused to allow her in their homes. Several even sent
letters to one of her teachers, saying they didn't want her to have contact with their children at school.

Kids asked Natalie if she was an alien. She didn't know what they
were talking about. Like all Scientologists, Natalie had been instructed not to read about Scientology in any source except a Scientology-sponsored website or publication, and she believed that much
of what was posted on the Internet or written in the newspapers
about her religion was "entheta." Though the church might have insisted that the OT levels remain secret until its members had earned,

---

* The city of Clearwater has never conducted its own survey to test Scientology's claims.

and paid for, the right to have those mysteries revealed, the kids at school had no such restrictions and garnered more from a simple web search than Natalie would learn for years.

Natalie was miserable. "I started hanging out with the wrong kids," she said, with a flick of her cigarette. "You know, the typical story." Yearning to fit in, she made friends with the drug crowd — "basically the only people who were nice to me" — and began smoking pot. Before long, she'd entered what she called a "pretty heavy drug phase" that would last for two years. "Looking back, I see it was an interesting experience," she said. "I'd taken a lot of things for granted because I'd lived in that bubble of Scientology — I didn't know anything else. But when I went to high school I started hanging out with these kids and seeing the way they lived and how different their lives and families were from mine . . . it blew me away."

Some of Natalie's new friends came from broken or dysfunctional homes; others were underachievers and struggled in school. Natalie, who'd managed to do well in school despite partying on weekends, would look at them and think, God, this is so horrible. But what could she do? "These kids didn't know how to, you know, look up a word in a dictionary," she said. "They didn't know why they didn't understand things. They didn't know why they would fail tests." Some kids she knew had been diagnosed with ADD and took Ritalin or Adderall. "They would fail and fail, and they wouldn't pay attention in class because they didn't understand, and so they'd be prescribed these drugs. Meanwhile, nobody was actually helping them." (In one desperate effort to help a friend who was failing a science class, Natalie said she grabbed a dictionary and made her friend look up everything she didn't understand, which she said ultimately helped the girl pass that class, and several others.)

Like that of many teenagers, her rebellion lasted only a few years. Drugs, she realized by her sixteenth birthday, were not only unhealthy, they were "counter-intentioned": Scientologists not only eschew mind-altering substances but cannot be audited if they have imbibed. They are also expected to maintain a high level of ethics, which, quite obviously, ruled out taking cocktails of pills and staying out all night. This is not who I am, she thought. Why am I doing this?

She had no idea. With great trepidation, Natalie went to her father, a dedicated Scientologist for thirty years, and told him that she had a drug problem. Her dad's reaction, as she recalls it, was not atypical for Scientologists. "He just sat there and he looked at me. He didn't freak out. He didn't even ground me. Nothing. He just said, 'We are going to fix you.'"

The next day, Natalie started the Purification Rundown. Every day for the next three weeks, she went to a local field auditing group that offered the program and spent up to five hours a day in the sauna, alternating lengthy sweat sessions with half-hour runs on the treadmill. The experience, as she recalled, was almost mystical, far more intense than any other detox program she'd ever heard of, and way beyond what friends experienced doing juice fasts or high colonics. "I used to feel like I could never see the real colors of the world because I was so dulled out," she told me. But during the Purification Rundown, she began to see things clearly, with almost psychedelic vividness. Afterward, Natalie felt renewed. "It was amazing how much better I felt. I could think faster, process things faster. I was more *there*."

This was step one of Natalie's fix. The second phase was the Life Repair auditing program, which she did the summer after her junior year. It began with a complete purging of her transgressions, which Natalie found tremendously therapeutic; the entire package of auditing sessions similarly impressed her. "I had some really amazing revelations in auditing," she said. "I got a much clearer idea of who I actually was."

By Christmas, she'd gotten rid of her drug-using friends, "disconnecting" from them in the way she felt L. Ron Hubbard intended: she'd realized they were bad influences and no longer wanted them in her life. She also began auditing in earnest, eager to ascend the Bridge to Total Freedom. She approached her Scientology study as a form of spiritual healing as well as self-help. "I really wanted to figure out why I had done some of the things I had done, and find answers for some of my problems, and I found them," she told me. That spring, she graduated with honors from high school.

Now Natalie was preparing to go to college, though several of her Scientologist friends, and some Scientologist adults, including her boss at her summer job, thought it was unnecessary. What could a person learn that couldn't be picked up simply by studying L. Ron Hubbard? "I said excuse me, and I left," Natalie said, and she moved to a position with more supportive supervisors. "*Keeping Scientology Working* never says you shouldn't be educated in other things," Natalie said. "I mean, LRH obviously knew other things." Was he as educated as he claimed to be? Natalie confessed that she had gone on the Internet and read a bit about Hubbard's biography. She doubted the truth of everything she found there, but whatever his education had been, she liked what he said about learning. "I don't think LRH would be okay with people thinking that all you have to learn is Scientology." She referred to one of the Founder's statements, a personal favorite of hers: "One doesn't learn about life sitting in an ivory tower, thinking about it. One learns about life by being part of it."

Natalie was determined to live Hubbard's words. Over the next few years, she would — at the University of Tampa she joined a sorority, majored in economics, and graduated summa cum laude in May 2010. Her world had broadened with each step out of the Scientology bubble, a development that her parents supported. And she continued to remain a dedicated Scientologist, perhaps even more dedicated, she said, because of her diverse experience. "One thing I've noticed," she said recently, "is that there are kids who've grown up in Scientology and have never really seen anything else. I think that bubble can be a problem."

Kendra Wiseman grew up in Scientology's bubble in Los Angeles. A few years older than Natalie, she left the bubble — and Scientology — during her teens. Kendra is the daughter of two of the most prominent Scientologists in Los Angeles. Her father, a former president of the U.S. branch of the Citizens Commission on Human Rights, is an outspoken anti-psychiatry activist, and her mother was one of Scientology's most successful FSMs during the 1990s. Kendra's uncle is another key Scientology figure: the president of Narconon International, which now operates more than 120 drug rehabilitation and education centers around the world.

The church caters to Scientologists of this elite stature and they receive treatment much like that of celebrity members. Indeed, as "opinion leaders," which Hubbard defined as "any person important in their field," they are considered "celebrities" by the Scientology rank and file. Many of them have been in Scientology for decades, contributing steadily to most of its key campaigns. Because they are Scientology's most dedicated, great care is taken to ensure they have a positive, not a punitive, experience.

In exchange for this treatment, all opinion leaders are expected to promote Scientology in the secular world, and many do by talking about the church to non-Scientologist acquaintances or business associates. But unlike the Hollywood celebrities, who often maintain independent social networks (according to the journalist Lawrence Wright, who has written about the screenwriter-director Paul Haggis for *The New Yorker*, some of Haggis's friends maintain they had no idea he was a Scientologist, despite his affiliation with the church of more than thirty years), Scientology opinion leaders, and their children, tend to live in a world rigidly focused on their faith. In Kendra's case, all of her childhood friends were Scientologists, as were her parents' friends, her uncles, aunts, nieces, nephews, cousins, and half brother. The dancing school she attended was run by a Scientologist, as were the stables where she took horseback riding lessons. The school she attended, the Delphi Academy in Los Angeles, is one of the most prestigious Applied Scholastics–backed schools in the country. During the summer, she enrolled in programs at the Celebrity Centre or another Los Angeles church, or at Flag, where her parents visited frequently. "I was in a completely isolated community," Kendra told me. "I had no contact with non-Scientologists — none. That kind of thing just didn't exist."

And yet Kendra spent her childhood in one of the most diverse metropolitan regions of the United States. Kendra lived in a spacious home in an upper-middle-class neighborhood of Glendale, and later in Burbank. Growing up there in the 1990s, Kendra had what she considered to be a typical suburban life. "I rode my bike, I used the computer, I watched TV, just like any other kid," she said. On weekends, she and her friends rented videos, shopped at the Glendale Galleria, ate at In-N-Out Burger, and went to the multiplex (Kendra was a diehard fan of *The Lord of the Rings*). No matter what day it was, they communicated via their pagers and chatted on AOL.

But her everyday reality was Scientology and the teachings of

L. Ron Hubbard, whose framed portrait hung in her home, much as a Christian family might display an image of Jesus Christ. Hubbard's maxims arose frequently in her family conversations and those of their friends, and his theories and policies affected every facet of their lives. When Kendra misbehaved, she was assigned a condition — "danger," for example — for which she would have to do amends, like cleaning her room. When she skinned her knee or bumped her head, Kendra's mother would give her a "contact assist," a holistic healing technique that involves repeatedly touching a wounded area of the body until it feels better. Like all Scientologist children, Kendra was raised to believe that, as a thetan, she had not only lived before, but had chosen her own body. "When I was little, my mom would tell me a story about how she was playing the piano one day when she was pregnant, and felt my thetan inhabit her," said Kendra. "She said there were lots of other thetans kind of hovering around, but I was strongest: I picked her." Kendra's family unfailingly followed church policy so that they would be "sessionable"; they stocked their home with vitamins, organic vegetables, and fruit and slept for at least eight hours every night, a prerequisite for auditing.

Kendra's parents spent a part of each day auditing, hooked up to their own personal E-meters, which cost around $4,000 apiece. Because they were at the top of the Bridge to Total Freedom, they could "solo audit," or audit themselves. Kendra never knew what went on in her parents' auditing sessions, just that they would sequester themselves in a room and hang a little sign on the door reading IN SESSION. During these periods, Kendra would tiptoe around the house. "You weren't supposed to make a peep," she explained; according to Hubbard, disturbing someone's auditing session was not only damaging to that person's spiritual well-being but also was a suppressive act.

Kendra worshiped her parents, who she believed had extraordinary psychic powers as OTs. She was particularly fascinated by their claim that they could remove the pain of death from the spirits of friends or family who'd recently died; they could telepathically connect with their thetans and give them a supernatural auditing session. As a child, she would watch, transfixed, as her mother sat on the living room couch, silently communicating with the spirits of the dead. When Kendra was six, her favorite great-aunt died. Reassuringly, her mother told her daughter that she had spoken to this great-aunt's thetan, which had agreed to go to hospitals and look for pregnant women who were Scientologists, so that it could be born again. The same was true when it came to the death of Kendra's favorite dog.

Kendra felt better. She thought to herself, Okay, I'm six now, so when I'm ten, I should look for a four-year-old who's a Scientologist, and that'll be my dog. She did that quite a bit when people died, made that mental calculation, though she never really followed it up. But she had a general notion that the world was going to be full of Scientologists soon, each one reincarnated from the last, and that one day, in the cycle of one of her lifetimes, she would again meet everyone she ever loved. "It was comforting, and it helped you get over death," she said. "I guess it's parallel to the idea of heaven."

Heaven, though, was a concept Kendra never knew much about. Like the idea of God or the messiah, it belonged to the world of wogs, who Kendra believed were evil at worst, but simply helpless at best, caught in what Hubbard called the "labyrinth"; only Scientology provided a clear route out of this confused state. Unlike Natalie, who was once reprimanded for referring to a non-Scientologist as a wog, Kendra's family and their acquaintances used the term liberally.

Frightening concepts about the wog world permeated Kendra's childhood. Wog society, she believed, was a place where psychiatrists, whom she was raised to fear and considered "the devil," had total control, particularly over children. In wog schools, she was told, kids, particularly the smart and active ones like her, were force-fed medication to calm them down. The fear that she might be sent to a dreaded public school, where she'd be diagnosed with a learning disability and given Ritalin, loomed over her every time she got in trouble. "I remember hearing, 'If you went to public school you'd have to tiptoe around being too smart in case they try to drug you,'" she recalled. "That totally freaked me out, since there was no protection from psychiatry in public school. I even heard that sex ed was taught in public school with a psychiatric agenda."

Kendra's own school ran much differently. Scientology schools all claim to be secular but replicate the org experience to a greater or lesser extent. At Delphi, a formal "org board" hung on the wall, list-ing many divisions and job titles found in a Scientology church; the school ran so much like a Scientology organization, former students say, that it mirrored the experience almost completely.

Teachers were known as "supervisors," as they also were at church. Counselors were called "ethics officers." Those who administered dis-cipline were "masters at arms." When it came time to be tested, stu-dents would report to a separate division known as Qualifications, or "Qual," where, to make sure kids were being honest about how fully they understood what they had learned, they were quizzed verbally while hooked up to an E-meter. The exact same procedure is used for students in courses at Scientology orgs.

Socially, Delphi worked like an org as well, maintaining ethics files on every student, which included reports of every rules violation a child ever committed. From the time that they can write their name, Scientologist children, like their parents, are taught to report on one another, as well as on themselves, if they have taken part in a "crime," such as chewing gum when it wasn't allowed or stealing a kiss with a classmate, which is considered "out-ethics" behavior.

Located in the foothills of the Angeles National Forest, Delphi looks like any private school in southern California, with grassy play-ing fields; expensive facilities for art, music, and computer work; and a research library, which includes all of the classics as well as nu-merous history and foreign language texts and a great number of encyclopedias and dictionaries. The school, which enrolls about 175 students, most of them Scientologists, offers a standard academic curriculum as well as a Scientology curriculum.

At the primary school level, students begin their encounter with the basics of Hubbard's study tech through a book called *Learning How to Learn*. As they progress, they are introduced to other Sci-entology concepts, such as ethics and the "conditions of existence," which they learn through an abridged version of Hubbard's *Introduc-tion to Scientology Ethics*, a core Scientology text. Other books teach them about the harmful effects of drugs and the basics of "money and exchange," the Hubbard concept that nothing worth having comes for free, which is the principle upon which all churches of Scientol-ogy operate.

Because study technology is based on the idea that it's possible to teach oneself anything simply by following Hubbard's core precepts, there is often no actual "teaching" in Scientology schools; indeed, many teachers at Delphi, as at similar schools, have earned no accreditation outside the Church of Scientology. There is also no classroom discussion. Instead, students work alone, following individualized "check sheets" that list the books or tasks required to finish the course. Maggie Reinhart, the former director of the Delphi Academy, told me that this technique forces a student to take an active role in his or her education.

Natalie Walet was educated this way at Chesapeake, and thrived. And so did Kendra, a voracious reader, who spent most of her time reading and writing papers. But her best friend, a girl I'll call Erin,* yearned for a more rigid academic structure. "I'd look at the supervisor and think, 'Why can't you just teach me?' But they never did," she said. "All they did if you had a question about anything was tell you to refer to the materials, or find your misunderstood word." A bright and articulate girl, Erin nonetheless finished high school unable to name the two houses of the U.S. Congress.

But this training is vital if a child is to become a Scientology parishioner, something all children raised in Scientology are expected to become. Natalie went "on course," or enrolled in classes at the church, at the age of seven. Kendra started even earlier — around five, she believes. There was no refusing: it was expected of Scientologist children and their parents too, so the adults would not seem "off-purpose" to the goals of the church. In a vast array of programs, children learned alongside adults, and Kendra, like Natalie, enjoyed them. "You played with dolls or made little figures out of clay," she said, recalling one course, Overcoming the Ups and Downs in Life, which required that she learn the twelve "anti-social personality types" in society by memorizing the definitions and then demonstrating the principles using dolls as actors. Another course, known as Key to Life, taught aspects of study tech with the help of picture books.

One course that kids particularly enjoyed was Success Through

---

* A pseudonym.

Communication, the entry-level rung on the Bridge, which teaches both children and adults the basic training routines. To children, staring at a partner without blinking or making funny faces to try to break the other's composure feels like a game. But some of the other TRs, notably the drill known as "bull-bait," in which one partner heckles the other mercilessly in an attempt to shake the other person's resolve, can be excruciating for sensitive adolescents.

Erin, a slender, somewhat shy blonde girl, was thirteen years old when she did her bull-bait TR. Her partner was a teenage boy. "I'd just gotten boobs and I was wearing a tight shirt, and he made fun of me," she said. "Then, at one point he started to unzip his pants. I was *horrified*, but I just had to sit there. It was mortifying. But since it was part of bull-baiting, it was okay. The whole idea is that you're supposed to be able to handle anything that comes at you with no reaction, just totally self-contained."

These drills, particularly bull-bait, are a crucial part of auditor training, which children also begin at a young age. Kendra was being audited by the time she was in kindergarten and learned to audit others when she was around eleven or twelve years old, working with a partner who'd play the role of the preclear. Her job was to ask her partner questions, and then, using the techniques she learned in her TR drills, repeat them if her partner didn't answer or refused to give her the answer she sought. If the preclear got up, she would force the person back into the chair, something she was taught was for the subject's own good, as it might be harmful to leave the session before the person was deemed "ready" to do so. If a subject still refused to do what he or she was told, Kendra, using another technique she'd learned, would yell to show her "intent," as Scientologists put it. A tall, naturally assertive girl, Kendra had no trouble doing as she was trained to do, which was to "be in control of the session one hundred percent of the time," she said. "Even if it meant blocking the door if the person wanted to leave the room."

Kendra learned her TRs at church; Erin learned hers at school. Some kids learned them in both places. This is by design; a Scientology education provides a natural flow between the two institutions. The idea, noted Sandra Mercer, the former Scientology registrar from Clearwater, Florida, is to create a seamless world through which children can travel without any outside influence. But the Scientology world is viable only as long as a member agrees with its precepts. Natalie Walet, despite her independent spirit, never doubted these ideas. Kendra Wiseman did.

In 1997, when Kendra was fourteen, she developed a fascination with a bookstore across the street from the Celebrity Centre, where she was then on course after school. The shop, a Hollywood landmark known as the Daily Planet, sold eclectic books on different subjects as well as an assortment of New Age products: candles, crystals, tarot cards. Kendra had peeked in the window and thought it "looked really cool inside" but was afraid to go in. "The Scientologists at church said it was very degraded and woggy," she said. "I can still remember that feeling. I was fourteen, and I was afraid of going into a bookstore."

One day, on her lunch break from a course, Kendra and a friend mustered their courage and ventured into the Daily Planet. Entranced by the bohemian atmosphere, Kendra picked up a vial of incense, something she had never smelled before, and inhaled deeply. Immediately, she began to worry that she was "out-ethics," and fearing that the girl she was with would write a report on her, Kendra left. But the next day she returned, alone. She bought a vial of gardenia oil and furtively hid it in a T-shirt inside her gym bag. When she got home, she carefully unwrapped it and stowed the vial in the back of a dresser drawer. "I'd just take it out sometimes and smell it," she said. "It was like my little secret."

Before long, she'd shared her secret with Erin, who then sneaked into the Daily Planet and bought her own vial of gardenia oil. This initiated a period of exploration. The girls began to read about other philosophies—Buddhism and Taoism. When the singer Madonna famously embraced Kabbalah, they explored that too. Then Kendra and Erin discovered Wicca. And like many teenage girls at the time, they fell in love with the occult.

They collected books with mysterious Wiccan symbols on the cover. They grew herbs, lit candles, and recited spells. They baked "mooncakes" and hiked into the hills to eat them. "It was a phase," Kendra said, "but at the time I thought it was so cool—it was like an entire religion for *Lord of the Rings* fans."

Kendra's Scientology counselors, however, were not sympathetic. Feeling guilty that she might be breaking church rules, Kendra admitted to her auditor that she'd been lighting incense and meditating. At once, she was sent to a tiny room in the basement of the Celebrity Centre, where she was grilled about her newfound interest in "other practices." And, to her horror, the same thing was done to her at school. "The thing about Scientology is that everything is connected," she explained. "So if you're skeptical about something or don't agree with something, you get this entire society coming down on you: your school will call the church, the church will call your parents, or your work, or both; your parents will call somebody — you're locked in."

At school, students, teachers, and even the school's headmaster avoided her. Finally after several days, a friend confided that he'd been ordered not to speak to her. Kendra's phone then began to ring off the hook, with parents of her friends calling to tell her that she was unwelcome in their homes and not allowed to spend time with their children. She would continue to be unwelcome, they said, until she came to her senses and was back "in good standing" with the church.

At home, Kendra's parents, with whom she'd always been close, believed their daughter's rejection of Scientology was a phase. When Kendra insisted it wasn't, they quoted Hubbard's sayings related to sin: one single wrong act—an overt—could result in a series of events that would make a person want to leave a group. What was it? What was her sin? Kendra countered by citing L. Ron Hubbard's most famous statement: "What's true for you is true." She'd done nothing wrong, she said. Scientology just wasn't true for her any longer.

Fearful that Kendra was losing her chance at eternity, her parents turned to the church itself, which dispatched members of the Sea Organization to their home to handle the problem. Kendra hid in her room. "They'd cluster in little groups around the coffee table, discussing my case, while I made my point by blasting Rage Against the Machine at full volume from behind the closed door," she said. The church officials came day after day. Kendra's parents begged her to talk to them. Finally, she agreed.

"I was so angry, I just wanted these people to drop dead and leave me alone," she recalled. "But on the other hand I was really scared." For weeks, she said, one Sea Org official after another would take her aside and "use Scientology on me," as she put it. When Kendra didn't answer their questions, they'd ask them again, just as they'd been trained to do in their TR drills. If she was sulky or defiant, her interlocutor, following Scientology teachings, would try to "raise her tone" by hitting a note just above hers — "antagonism," one tone higher than hostility, was the most common note they struck.

"After a while I'd want it to end so much, I'd end up crying and agreeing to whatever" — which was usually to talk to yet another Sea Org member, Kendra said. "But I knew what I wanted, and I so didn't want to have that conversation, because all they did was break me down. They'd throw things back at me until I felt like *I* was the guilty one for not wanting to stay in Scientology. Every conversation I'd had with the Sea Org for years had been like that."

The Sea Org had, in fact, once targeted Kendra for recruitment. The same held true for virtually every one of her friends. Scientology children are raised to not only respect and defer to Sea Org officials, but to envision themselves in a Sea Org uniform. Since David Miscavige became the leader of the church, the Sea Org ranks had swelled with the children of church members. Recruiters patrol the orgs and also show up at schools like Delphi, looking for possible candidates. Once they've isolated a target, who can be as young as eight years old, they may make frequent visits to the child's home, sometimes, as Kendra witnessed, almost forcing their way in to talk to the kid. They present an image of the Sea Org as one part humanitarian mission and one part "cool, space-age army," in the words of one young Scientologist from Los Angeles, who recalled Sea Org promotional materials filled with military imagery like swords and shiny uniforms, as well as pictures of spaceships. It is a powerful pitch for kids raised in the insular bubble of the church.

If that angle doesn't work, there are other lures. Some kids are assured that they will still be able to become an archaeologist, or a ballet dancer, if they join the Sea Org. Others are encouraged to think about the independence they'll have, living away from parents. One of Kendra's friends, who swore for years that he would never join, changed his mind after he was presented with an offer he simply couldn't refuse. "You're not supposed to have sex unless you're married," said Kendra. "So they pulled him into a room with seven beautiful Sea Org girls and said, 'Join the Sea Org and you can get married.' After being harassed over and over again, he signed."

Kendra estimated that 25 percent of her Delphi class joined the Sea Org. Like her friend Erin, she resisted and ultimately did succeed in leaving Scientology, to her family's dismay. Natalie Walet also chose not to join the Sea Org, though she said she seriously considered it. "I was too young—I think I was thirteen when I was approached, and even though I was really mature, I was still a kid." Her parents also had a hand in her decision, she added. "They made me understand that if I signed up, it would be like the military; I wouldn't be able to come home whenever I wanted." So Natalie decided to finish her education. "I think everyone at some point gets spoken to about the Sea Org," she said. "It can be really tempting."

One Scientologist who was tempted, and succumbed, was Claire Headley. Claire was nine years old when she spoke to her first Sea Org recruiter, although it wasn't until she was thirteen that she began hearing from the org regularly. She was a seventh-grader living in Burbank with her parents, Gen and Hugh Whitt, both dedicated Scientologists who had moved to California from Scientology's British hub, Saint Hill, just a few years earlier. Lacking the finances to send their daughter to Delphi, where tuition was over $10,000 per year, they home-schooled Claire, a well-scrubbed-looking girl with a cascade of long red hair, adding an extra layer of isolation to an already sheltered childhood.

This made her a particularly easy target for Sea Org recruiters, who approached her at church with a warning about the dangers of the wog world. Then they asked her what she wanted to do with her life—Claire didn't know. So they appealed to her idealism by saying if she joined the Sea Org, she'd be "helping people." Who wouldn't want to help people? The recruiters called her on the phone: the planet was in desperate trouble, they told her; there were only five years left to clear the planet—she needed to do something about it *right now*.

Unlike most of her friends at church, Claire was intimately familiar with the Sea Org: she'd grown up in the order, which her mother had joined when Claire was four years old. Divorced from Claire's biological father, Gen had taken her daughter to Saint Hill, where they spent the next four years. As Gen worked and pursued her own spiritual goals, Claire saw her mother for one hour a day, around dinnertime, and then for three hours on Saturdays.

Children of Sea Org members, notably those whose parents serve at large Scientology installations, were given their own organization, called the Cadet Org.* They lived apart from their parents, in dormitory-style accommodations, with little adult supervision. At Saint Hill, the Cadet Org was housed in a dilapidated country mansion known as Stonelands. When Claire arrived, in 1979, there were about forty kids between the ages of four and sixteen, supervised by a single adult, a Scientologist in her sixties.

Few provisions were made for the education of the kids in the Sea Org (aside from putting them to work, Hubbard never figured how to accommodate actual children in his organizations). At Saint Hill, which had no school, some children joined the Commodore's Messenger Organization, which they could do at age eight. Claire, still too young, was bused to a local elementary school in East Grinstead, whose residents, like those in Clearwater, were notably unfriendly.

Yearning to make friends with the "normal kids"— Claire and her Cadet Org friends were, in her mind, the "weirdo kids"— she learned how to speak two languages: one for Scientology, the other for school. When she slipped up and started talking about things like overts or withholds, the other kids laughed. She'd been relieved when her mother met Hugh Whitt, an American Scientologist working at Saint Hill, and decided to marry him. Whitt had taken LSD in his youth and was prevented from joining the Sea Org because of it. As Sea Org members are not allowed to marry non–Sea Org members, Claire's mother had to petition Scientology to leave the Sea Org, and was granted permission.

"To me, it was like a dream come true: I was finally going to get to live in a house with my parents and be like a normal kid," Claire said.

---

* The Cadet Org was abolished in the mid-1990s.

But the years she spent at Saint Hill stayed with Claire even after her family moved to Los Angeles, where Hugh ran the Scientology mission of Beverly Hills. She said, "The world outside of Scientology just seemed like this vast unknown: how could I possibly live in it?"

In 1989, when Claire was fourteen, she and her father went to Clearwater, where a friend of her father's named Richard Reiss, the base's highest-ranking auditor,* told her that joining the Sea Org would be the "right thing to do." Momentarily inspired, Claire decided she would join. But she changed her mind once she got back to Los Angeles, particularly as her mother, according to Claire, "flipped out" when her fourteen-year-old daughter told her she'd signed a billion-year contract to serve Scientology for the rest of her life. Gen understood the rigors of Sea Org life. Claire was intelligent and attractive — there were plenty of things she could do, Gen believed, and still remain true to the church.

The reaction of Claire's mother illustrates a common dilemma for Scientologist parents, who are supposed to feel honored that their child has been selected for the Sea Org in the same way a Catholic parent is supposed to swell with pride if their child joins the priesthood. But many parents are not eager to give their son or daughter to the church, which requires signing away all legal rights to the child's welfare. "You get a lot of parents who are just beside themselves," says Sandra Mercer, whose youngest son was approached as a ten-year-old, and without either of his parents present, signed a contract — with crayon, she said — though he was not formally approached to activate his contract until he was thirteen. Mercer refused to allow her son to join until he finished high school (by which point, she added, he'd lost interest), and since she was a prominent Scientologist in Clearwater, church officials didn't push. "But I was an exception," she noted. "If you're just a rank-and-file member, you can't complain or say no."

The scrutiny that unwilling parents receive — they may be condemned for being "counter-intentioned" to Scientology, an act of

---

* Richard Reiss was the senior case supervisor at Flag who was out of town on training in 1995, when Lisa McPherson was receiving counseling — her care fell to Reiss's deputy, Alain Kartuzinski.

treason, if they prevent their child from joining the Sea Org — forces many into silence and even leads some to encourage their kids to make the commitment. Gen Whitt managed to delay Claire's enrollment for two years with a pledge that her daughter would help out at the Beverly Hills mission. But in 1991, when Claire was sixteen, Gen finally gave her consent. Richard Reiss reminded the Whitts that were they to refuse to let Claire go, they might be put before a church ethics board. Reiss himself might face a Scientology tribunal for his failure to recruit her unless Claire agreed to enlist.

And so began Claire's immersion into the tightly wound, paramilitary world of the Sea Organization, where she would spend the next fourteen years of her life.

CHAPTER 16

Int

S CIENTOLOGY'S PUBLICITY MATERIALS portray the Sea
Organization as similar to the U.S. Marines. "The toughest, most dedicated team this planet has ever known," says
one recruiting brochure. "Against such a powerful team the opposition hasn't got a chance." Though these are L. Ron Hubbard's words,
the vision they invoke has been fully realized only in the era of David
Miscavige. Today it is impossible to understand the Church of Scientology without understanding the Sea Org, which over the past forty
years has evolved from Hubbard's private navy to Scientology's man-
agerial elite, to its current incarnation: an executive body but also a
low-paid workforce that can run the church's engines without im-
pacting its overall revenue.

Induction into the Sea Org begins with a boot camp known as the
Estates Project Force, or EPF. In Los Angeles, the EPF is located at
the Pacific Area Command Base (PAC Base) on Sunset Boulevard.
Here, Claire Headley learned to march, salute, and perform manual labor. Physical work is a key training technique for new Sea Org
recruits. Among the chores given people on the EPF are scrubbing
pots, washing garbage receptacles, and cleaning roach- or rat-in-
fested ducts. Claire described the work as "nasty" but ultimately noble in purpose. "The idea," she told me, "is that you do this for a few
weeks and you can do any task given to you and do it right."

After graduation, inductees are assigned a post at one of Scientology's organizations. Many kids hope to work at Celebrity Centre,
where staffers are outfitted in custom-made uniforms and have a
chance to mingle with movie stars. Claire was even more ambitious:

she wanted to work at Int, the most exclusive Scientology facility on land. Like all public Scientologists, she'd known of the base as "Gold," the home of Scientology's film studio, Golden Era Productions, which sounded glamorous. She heard rumors that Tom Cruise was a regular there. And she'd been shown pictures of the five-hundred-acre property and its large swimming pool and golf course. There were grassy meadows, winding paths, and a small lake where swans and ducks roamed freely. With its neat white buildings with blue tiled roofs, she thought it looked like Disneyland — and in fact, this comparison with Disneyland was often used to promote the place to potential teenage recruits.

Only the most qualified and privileged Sea Org members were posted to Gold; often they were the children of Scientology's elite. Among them were L. Ron Hubbard's granddaughter Roanne and the sons and daughters of some of Scientology's top attorneys and money managers. Claire was told she'd need to score at least 125 on an IQ test, which she did, and that she would also have to score high on a variety of leadership and personality tests. The rules were very strict: no one with family members in government or media could work at the International Base; no one with friends or family who'd left Scientology on bad terms could be assigned there either. A wholesome, virginal girl with a "clean" drug history, Claire sailed through the process, and two months after joining the Sea Org, she got her wish and was assigned a clerical position at Gold.

At first glance, Gold did look a lot like Disneyland. Driving in through the main gate, Claire saw a beige estate house, known as the Castle, which looked like an actual castle. This housed Scientology's film wing. Nearby was a stone carriage house called the Tavern, which was where visiting VIPs often ate their meals. It was decorated in the style of King Arthur's court, complete with a sizable round table and even a stone with a sword embedded in it, like Excalibur. Across the road, rising up from the hills, was the *Star of California* clipper ship, which was done up in "Pirates of the Caribbean" style, with mermaid figurines and plastic crabs.

But there were also many other buildings, most of them utilitarian looking, scattered around the property, and Claire had to memorize the names and locations of all of them, and their abbreviations.

Her new home, she learned right away, was far more than the film and production studio most Scientologists thought it was. This was a ruse, or "shore story," the church told the public in order to maintain the security of the base. Int was Scientology's nerve center, where every policy, legal strategy, advertising campaign, and event was planned and launched.

Virtually everything about the Int Base was different than Claire had imagined. It was run and organized like a covert military installation. The base's location was a secret — Claire had to pledge never to divulge it to her friends or family, under the threat of treason. Leaving the compound with any documents or paperwork was forbidden. Similarly, she was not allowed to speak of her job nor of any goings-on at the base to anyone, not even to a Sea Org friend. She was banned from riding in local taxis or taking any form of public transportation; instead, she traveled on special Scientology buses or in a private vehicle driven by a staff member who'd completed a special driving course designed by L. Ron Hubbard. Every Sea Org member who wants to drive is required to attend this "car school," even if the person already has a driver's license and a car.

Writing home from Int was an ordeal. Letters could not be sent through regular mail or Fedex, but had to instead go through the base's internal mail system, where screeners read everyone's incoming and outgoing correspondence. In a similar vein, staffers were given Nextel phones that doubled as walkie-talkies to communicate on the base, but with very few exceptions, they were not allowed to use the phones to make outside calls. They were also banned from using pay phones in town, and could make calls only from special base phones, which were monitored by censors. To get permission to do this, one had to fill out a formal request, citing the reasons for making the call.

"All of this was so freaky, especially for a sixteen-year-old," said Claire, who immediately began to wonder if she'd made a mistake by working there. But on the other hand, the Int Base was the very heart of the whole Scientology organization, whose mission was to save the world. Every training and orientation film, every marketing strategy, every bit of technical material — dictionaries, instruction manuals, recorded Hubbard lectures, even every E-meter — all were born of the efforts of the staff members at Int, the most "on-policy," ethical, ideal organization on the planet, or so Claire believed. How could she call herself a Scientologist and *not* be a part of it?

Plus, David Miscavige was at Int. Like all young Scientologists, Claire was in awe of Miscavige, who, at the events she'd attended with her parents, came across as a handsome, charismatic, youthful, tanned (thanks to a personal tanning bed aides said he utilized before every Scientology event), and most of all, totally in control. To Claire, he (she was instructed to call him "sir") appeared to be the most dedicated Scientologist on the planet.

Like L. Ron Hubbard, Miscavige moved with an entourage, the two constants being his wife, Shelly, and his personal assistant, or "communicator," a dark-haired New Zealander named Laurisse Stuckenbrock, who was called Lou. The three of them always dressed identically, in white or black, and Shelly and Lou also carried tape recorders to take down Miscavige's every word, much as Hubbard's personal aides had scribbled his directives with paper and pen. The tapes were then rushed to Miscavige's office in the RTC building, which was located at the far north side of the base in a modern structure called Building 50. There, a pool of secretaries set to work transcribing them; then they issued transcripts so that staff could read Miscavige's thoughts and directions just as they had L. Ron Hubbard's, and, as with the Founder's, follow them exactly.*

Stories of Miscavige's lifestyle abounded at Int, where the leader rode his customized Yamaha motorcycle around the base, leaving huge dust clouds in his wake. A car aficionado, Miscavige owned a Mazda Miata, a forest-green Range Rover, and a BMW M6, among other vehicles. He also had a custom-made, armored GMC van with bulletproof windows, which was set up as a "mobile office" with a computer, a fax, a wireless hookup, and a surround-sound audio system and satellite TV. He lived lavishly, by base standards, in private

---

* Miscavige's missives, unlike L. Ron Hubbard's, are generally not for public consumption. With the exception of the occasional RTC Executive Directive, such as one of 1991 wherein Miscavige announced that the church was winning its campaign against the IRS, the leader's written words are confined to the base, where staffers maintain thick binders of his utterances. Miscavige speaks to the Scientologist public at events, and his speeches are often reprinted in Scientology magazines.

quarters, with a screening room and a $100,000 stereo system. On his birthday, each April 30, everyone at Int was required to chip in part of his or her salary to buy him a present. One year staffers got him a fancy golf cart,* another year a titanium frame mountain bike, and another, a handcrafted acoustic guitar.

A workout fanatic, Miscavige, who rarely wore the same garment twice, was fond of extra-snug T-shirts that showed off his buff physique. On more formal occasions he wore a Hermès tie, a monogrammed Egyptian cotton shirt (handmade for him by Turnbull & Asser), and a $5,000 suit; the suit was custom-made by his Beverly Hills tailor, Richard Lim, who also made suits for Tom Cruise. Lim visited the base regularly to do the leader's fittings. Miscavige was quite particular about distinguishing himself from all others: on days when his staff dressed in uniform, the leader wore civilian clothes. On weekends, when the Sea Org was allowed to wear "civvies," Miscavige wore his navy blue Sea Org uniform, trimmed with gold braid.

There were hundreds of kids on the Int Base in the 1990s, some even younger than Claire. Boys were often sent to work in the technical areas, building computer systems or working in the lighting department. Girls worked as secretaries, quality control officers, and, as Claire did for a time, "program operators," charged with making sure other base staffers were meeting their targets. This meant she was expected to exert her power by roaming the base and descending upon unsuspecting officials to demand compliance. A soft-spoken, angelic-looking girl who was well-drilled on the training routines, Claire quickly learned to scream at staffers who questioned an order, refused to address her as "sir," or in any other way challenged her authority, or "command intention."

The base followed a protocol L. Ron Hubbard had devised called the Team Share system. Upon arriving at Int, each staffer was given five cards: one for social activities, one for pay bonuses, one for "chow," one for salary, and one for berthing. Hubbard had designed it

---

* According to several former staffers, including Marc Headley, Miscavige rejected the golf cart, which was used instead by the base's public relations officials to give tours to visiting VIPs. When I visited Int in the winter of 2006, the OSA chief at the time, Mike Rinder, drove me around the base in the golf cart.

as a motivational tool, explained Jeff Hawkins, who was also at Int, to make each staffer feel as if he or she had a stake in the organization.

In practice, the Team Share system was a form of punishment. When a worker committed an infraction, the supervisor or ethics officer was entitled to take away a card. "If you lost your social card, you could not take any liberties"—the rare day off, awarded only to staff whose statistics were up—"or attend any events or parties," said Hawkins. "If you lost your bonus card, you would not be paid any bonuses. This was kind of a null card as we weren't paid any bonuses anyway," he added. "If you lost your pay card you could not collect your pay. If you lost your chow card you had to eat beans and rice only. And if you lost your berthing card you had to sleep outside, or in your office—you could not go home. We used to joke about having an 'air card,' and when that card was pulled, you weren't allowed to breathe."

Virtually any executive, seeing an actual infraction, or more commonly, wishing to advance a personal vendetta, could "pull cards" on a subordinate. As a result, staffers were routinely deprived of things like money or balanced meals. Sometimes entire divisions had their berthing or pay cards revoked, meaning they'd all have to sleep at their desks or go without their weekly $50 salary.

Even under the best of conditions, Claire's day began at seven-thirty in the morning and went until midnight, seven days a week. She had fifteen-minute meal breaks, sometimes half an hour if she was producing well. On Thanksgiving, the staff got an hour for dinner; otherwise, the schedule was the same.

Exhausted, the staff gave in to the paranoia that was a constant at the base. They were required to report any critical statements, reports, or casual asides they'd hear, even if it meant turning in their spouse or best friend. That person would then be hauled into security checking to uncover the "crime." Only when the person confessed, recanted, and in some cases publicly retracted whatever critical statement he or she had made, would the process end. This was called a "viewpoint shift." And what it meant, Claire quickly understood, was that everyone at the Int Base lived in fear of everyone else and what they might be saying, or reporting, about one another.

• • •

In 1992, about a year after she arrived at Gold, Claire met nineteen-year-old Marc Headley. He too was the son of Scientologists from Los Angeles and had been recruited into the Sea Org at the age of fourteen. Unlike her, though, Marc joined immediately. Signing a billion-year contract, he'd decided, was an excellent way to get out of school — Marc attended Delphi, which he hated. Joining the Sea Org also offered the chance to make money, or at least that's what his recruiters told him, promising he'd make at least a few hundred dollars a week.

A handsome kid with light brown hair and large blue eyes, Marc, as everyone knew, was Tom Cruise's preclear, and he was excellent at gaming the system. Though the rules on the base were always tight, Marc and his friends still managed to break them to act like teenagers: renting movies at Blockbuster, pooling their money to hold late-night pizza parties in their rooms, racing around the base on their motorcycles, and even going into the town of Hemet, a small community with several strip malls, to hang out from time to time.

Claire fell for Marc right away. And Marc fell even harder. But the couple knew they had to be careful. Sex, even kissing, before marriage is strictly prohibited in the Sea Organization. After a few months, in August 1992, they decided to get married. Because Claire was only seventeen, and thus not able to be legally married in California, the couple went to Las Vegas to get married, then returned to Los Angeles to have a more formal wedding at the Celebrity Centre in Hollywood. Dressed in a white, off-the-shoulder gown and tulle veil she'd purchased the day before, Claire promised Marc that, in addition to being true, she would always "maintain communication" as a sign of her commitment. Marc, in a tuxedo, vowed the same. The next morning, they returned to Gilman Hot Springs.

Day-to-day life there was grueling. Though she loved her husband, Claire frequently thought about what she'd given up by joining the Sea Org. Her stepsister was planning to go to college. Claire, who'd looked at Scientology as the only education she'd ever need, would never have that chance. She also knew that she'd probably never have children, because it would mean leaving the Sea Org. This rule had not been in place when Claire was a child at Saint Hill, but by the mid-1980s, rules had changed. So that the Sea Org could dispense with providing child care for the very young, parents who had children under the age of six were no longer allowed to join. Also, women were not allowed to have babies while serving in its ranks. In the 1980s, those who became pregnant had to leave the order and work at lower-ranking Scientology organizations while raising young children.

By the early 1990s, however, a new, even stricter policy was coming into force to prevent such departures. Members of the Sea Org were pressured to terminate their pregnancies.* Having kids was seen as bad for business, and at Int, Claire learned from casual conversation, a good 60 to 80 percent of the married women on the base had had at least one abortion, even several, often claiming indigence to force the county to pay for the procedure. If a woman resisted (and few did), she would be separated from her husband, put on heavy manual labor, and vigorously "sec checked." If she still refused to get an abortion, she would be sent from the base in disgrace, alone.

Claire had never thought much about having children, but that changed when she married Marc. "I would often have these fleeting thoughts of how much I would love to have a family with him — not that I could ever express them. And not that we ever discussed it either."

Such conversations were strictly forbidden; after all, a discussion of that nature was considered tantamount to a discussion of wanting to leave. And leaving, Claire knew from the moment she arrived at Int, was not an option. Though it was against the rules to physically prevent a person from departing, tremendous security measures were set up to keep staffers on the base. Anyone suspected of "disaffection" would be immediately reported to a collective security force known as the Perimeter Council. This group maintained lists of "suspects" who were seen as security risks. Those individuals were forced to do manual labor and endure long hours of interrogation. Some were put on a twenty-four-hour security watch, during which

---

* The church denies that it pressures people into having abortions. In 1996, a formal policy was enacted, banning Sea Org members from having children. Youngsters were seen as "interfering with the productivity" of the staff, according to the current Scientology spokesman Tommy Davis. See Joe Childs and Thomas Tobin, "No Kids Allowed," *St. Petersburg Times*, June 13, 2010.

staff members shadowed them as they went about their day. A security guard slept outside their door, sometimes with wrists tied to the doorknob, to prevent them from escaping in the middle of the night.

Electric fences ringed the property, topped by razor barriers that were said to be for the staff's protection — a deterrent to intruders — but in fact they faced inward, to prevent the staff from escaping. If a person got too close to the exit, underground motion sensors would activate a series of alarms and searchlights. In addition, electronic monitors, concealed microphones, and hidden cameras were installed throughout the property, and even outside the base itself. Security guards were outfitted with night-vision goggles.

If a person did manage to escape, a special "blow drill" was launched. Ethics and security officers combed through the files of the escapee to determine where he or she might go. Then teams of Scientologists would fan out to the local bus and train stations, the airport, and area hotels to "recover" the truant, using information gleaned from the ethics files to convince the person to return. Back on base, heavy labor and intense interrogation awaited the recovered staff member. The defeated look of those who had blown and been recovered was enough to discourage Claire from attempting the same course of action.

In 1994, Claire's "worst nightmare," as she said, became reality. She was nineteen, and pregnant. "Birth control was expensive," she admitted. She'd done her best to prevent conception, but having had no sex education as a child, she said, "I guess I failed miserably."

Devastated and terrified, she told Marc, and they agreed that she should go through with the abortion at the local Planned Parenthood clinic in Riverside, where Scientologists from the base went regularly. A base staff member drove her to the appointment. "Every ounce of me was screaming no, and yet I felt like a cornered cat . . . there was absolutely nothing I could do about it," she said. "If I tried to keep it, they'd put me on manual labor, which might hurt the baby. Not to mention that I had no money, no insurance, and I knew that I would be cut off from Marc completely if I didn't go through with it. So I did it."

Two years later, Claire found herself pregnant again. This time, she didn't have to think about what she should do. Obediently, she had an abortion and then returned to work, training for her new job as a member of the Church of Scientology's police force. Claire had been given a promotion. She was now working for David Miscavige's Religious Technology Center, by then the most prestigious organization in Scientology. To even be considered for this exclusive order, Claire had to pass a battery of security checks and be deemed superior intellectually, ethically, and also physically: "COB," as everyone knew, loved having pretty women around him.

The RTC is Miscavige's honor guard — some might even say a Praetorian Guard — comprised of a few dozen staffers at the base as well as maybe a dozen or so RTC representatives at key Scientology outposts like Flag. Their job, in addition to controlling the rights to all of Scientology's intellectual property, is to patrol Scientology for wrongdoing of any kind. No one else in Scientology has such absolute authority.

Accordingly, no one else in Scientology, or the Sea Organization, is treated with such deference. The majority of RTC officials are young women, not unlike L. Ron Hubbard's original Commodore's Messengers. While the "crew," or regular Sea Org staff, queue up for meals in the dining hall, stewards wait on RTC staffers. Housekeepers tidy their rooms. The clothes they wear — in the 1990s, a simple blue suit with a white cotton shirt; by the 2000s, a black suit and shirt — are made of high-quality material and are purchased by the church. Other staffers shop for clothes at Wal-Mart and pay for them with their meager earnings.

For the first few years, Claire worked at the RTC as a "corrections" officer, assigned to "fix" whatever was wrong with management executives who were not performing up to standard. Most of her job consisted of interrogating executives on the E-meter, investigating them for abusing drugs or alcohol, viewing pornography, or making financial errors. She also pressed them for details about their sexual proclivities: masturbation, a sin in Scientology, was a frequent problem for some men on the Int Base, she said. Claire was twenty-two when she started this job. Other women were as young as fifteen. "I remember being so embarrassed by some of the things I had to ask, but I think that was the idea of having someone like me do the check," said Claire. "How much more humiliating could it be, if you're a forty-year-old man, to be asked by some young girl if you've been masturbating?"

Working for the RTC meant working directly for David Miscavige, who, like L. Ron Hubbard, smoked constantly and worked tirelessly — well into his forties, the leader bragged about staying up until 4 A.M. He frequently called officials at all hours of the night, demanding that they work round-the-clock shifts as well. Those who couldn't handle the exhaustion were routinely attacked for not being "tough enough." Toughness was an ideal that L. Ron Hubbard had promoted as "a distinctive SO attribute," suggesting that a Sea Org member was capable of handling any challenge. Miscavige, however, made it the definitive criterion, indicating whether a person could cut it in the Sea Org.

To harden his staff, Miscavige brought back Hubbard's practice of "overboarding," which had been largely abandoned in the 1970s. Sometimes the base's swimming pool stood in for the Mediterranean, and its diving board served as the gangplank; at other times, the muddy lake on the property was used and staffers were pushed off a bridge. Many of these events took place at night, in the desert chill, without regard for the season. Miscavige, recalled a number of former Base staff, seemed to enjoy the spectacle; he'd often watch officials submerge themselves and resurface, freezing, while he sipped tea or cocoa, wearing a fuzzy bathrobe.

This behavior was of a piece with L. Ron Hubbard's in the late 1960s. The Commodore, as his former aides recalled, also was captivated by the drama of overboarding: dressed in his naval uniform, he would watch, and sometimes make a film, from the deck of the *Apollo* as his crew members were tossed into the sea with feet and wrists bound. But few at Int, save men like Jeff Hawkins, Mike Rinder, and Norman Starkey, the former captain of the *Apollo*, had any recollection of those days, nor in fact of L. Ron Hubbard at all — who, it should be noted, also surrounded himself with young people, believing them to be the only Scientologists whom he could trust.

Miscavige preferred an entourage of young staffers for somewhat different reasons. The leader of Scientology, the head of a multinational religious corporation, had assumed power with virtually no prior executive experience. Within a very short time of his takeover, it became obvious to longtime Scientology officials that Miscavige, while an able warrior, lacked the maturity of a stable manager. What's more, he had very little administrative ability. A micromanager, but famously impatient, he involved himself in nearly ever detail of church business, from legal strategies to carpet samples. If a project didn't deliver immediate results, he'd scrap it and blame his staff's inadequacies.

Deeply paranoid — so much so that he ordered his water glass be covered with cellophane, for fear that someone might poison him — Miscavige trusted virtually no one and was openly contemptuous of anyone whose experience in Scientology predated his own. "I think he was panicked that someone who knew more than him might try to usurp power," said Jeff Hawkins, who saw in Miscavige a "manic desperation" that drove him to surround himself with naive young people who would never question his authority. Surely none of the pretty girls at the RTC would challenge the system.

One of the most pliant girls was Tanja Castle, the daughter of prominent British Scientologists. A few years older than Claire, Tanja, a willowy blonde, was one of Miscavige's secretaries. There were more than one dozen such women in Miscavige's personal office, in addition to the ordinary RTC staff, and most were, like Tanja, beautiful, even-tempered, and under the age of twenty-five.

Tanja was a favorite of the leader and his wife, Shelly. She went to the movies and out to dinner with the Miscaviges. At the conclusion of a particularly grueling work cycle, she and her colleagues might be rewarded with a day at the beach, a ski trip, or even a few days of vacation. There were trips to Europe and Caribbean cruises aboard *Freewinds;* Miscavige's entourage sometimes enjoyed scuba diving or jet skiing. "In terms of a Sea Org life, I had a great life," said Tanja. "I couldn't really complain, especially given how everyone else was treated."

Tanja's husband, Stefan, for instance, never enjoyed the perks his wife received; this was also true for Marc Headley (Miscavige was notably uncharitable to the husbands of the women who worked for him). A wiry, handsome, and extremely headstrong young man, Stefan had married Tanja in June 1988, about a year after she arrived at Int. He was twenty at the time and a department head in the Commodore's Messenger Organization — nearly the same position Miscavige himself had once held at about that same age. Tanja and Stefan had begun what appeared to be a perfect Sea Org life, though like the Headleys, they wrestled with disappointment over not being able to have children. But they resigned themselves to that fate as faithful servants of the Church of Scientology. Raised by his Scientologist mother in Washington, D.C., Stefan had joined the Sea Org when he was twelve. He had every intention of spending his life at Int, as did his wife.

But as the couple began advancing in their careers, things changed. Stefan became a producer of Scientology's technical films and live events; Tanja was promoted to the RTC. This made Tanja a "sir" to Stefan — just as Claire was a "sir" to Marc. It was weird, the girls thought, but they accepted it. Far less comfortable, however, was the unspoken rule that staffers in David Miscavige's organization should distance themselves from anyone not in the RTC, including a spouse. Of course many people ignored this — Claire was married to Marc, Tanja was married to Stefan, and many of their friends were married to men in other organizations. But there was always a subtle pressure to *stop* being married to that person.

Tanja felt this pressure profoundly. For all of his initiative, Stefan would never ascend to the same echelon as his shy and retiring wife, who became a companion of "COB Assistant" Shelly Miscavige, a tough woman with very few friends. Shelly demanded that Tanja keep her company on Saturday nights. While the women ate popcorn and watched movies at the Miscaviges' condo on the base, Stefan spent the night alone.

Before long, Stefan's resentment began to show. In 1998, while in England producing a live event, he knocked heads with Miscavige — over what, Stefan does not exactly recall. But Shelly Miscavige approached him immediately after the altercation. "What kind of beef do you have with Dave?" she asked.

Stefan considered his answer: what beef did he have with DM?

"You know what?" he said. "I hate that I don't see my wife. And when I do," he added, bluntly, "she's too exhausted to have sex."

Shelly blanched. "Oh," she said. "Okay."

This criticism would be Stefan's undoing. He was subjected to the False Purpose Rundown, put on the E-meter, and asked about his crimes. Why did he hate COB? What had he done to hurt him? Stefan maintained he'd done nothing. But Shelly was suspicious. As Tanja later explained, "Shelly was extremely serious about protecting Dave. She was like his bodyguard, doing whatever she had to in order to stop anyone or anything getting to him. She honestly believed that there were numerous people out to intentionally harm or destroy him — suppressives were all around." Those working closest to Miscavige, such as Stefan when he was managing the events, "were under constant surveillance," she added.

Miscavige himself had always had mixed feelings about Stefan, as he did about most of his employees. It was only a matter of time before he would find fault in Stefan's performance. In early 1999, Stefan booked a venue for the church's Millennium New Year's Eve event, in Los Angeles, only to be told later that it wasn't available. Miscavige was furious about this logistical mishap. Major events like this one had become his chief fundraising tool; a perfectionist, he was often dissatisfied with some aspect of their planning or production. After this problem occurred, both Tanja and Stefan recalled, he began to look more closely at Stefan's management of the budgets, apparently convinced that Stefan had hidden crimes.

To uncover them, Stefan's co-workers were audited in hopes they'd inform on him, he said, and he himself underwent an even more stringent form of interrogation, known as the Truth Rundown. Like the False Purpose Rundown, the Truth Rundown is a security-checking process specifically targeted at "black propaganda." Under duress during this interrogation, Stefan admitted to harboring deep resentments about the leader's lavish lifestyle, particularly given how parsimonious Miscavige could be in concerning truly pressing needs within the church. The leader seemed to think nothing of purchasing first-class plane tickets to attend Scientology events in England, for example, but he would fly into a rage if a few extra workers were flown over, in coach class, to help on the project. He would approve demanding plans for lavish new buildings, then become tremendously angry about the money being spent to construct them, almost always insisting that staffers were being wasteful. "It made no sense," Stefan said.* "But once those criticisms were known, my life was over. And because my wife worked for DM, my life with her was over as well."

In June 1999, Miscavige, now believing himself fully aware of Stefan's "black propaganda," sentenced him to an indefinite period of reeducation on the Rehabilitation Project Force, which was located in a remote camp at the edge of the base known as Happy Valley. On its website, the church describes the RPF as a voluntary rehabilitation program offering a "second chance" to Sea Org members who have become unproductive or have strayed from the church's codes. It is not, in the strictest term, a "prison," if only because Scientologists agree to do the RPF of their own free will. There is tremendous psychological pressure to consider oneself fortunate to receive this chance of redemption.

"The way the RPF works is you agree to leave your day-to-day life and go through the program to explore all the areas of your life and what types of transgressions you've been committing," Stefan said. Upon arrival on the RPF, each person is given a partner, or "twin," with whom to spend virtually the whole time there, whether auditing each other, working side by side on a gardening or construction project, or watching to make sure the partner does not try to escape. Meals are scant, often just rice and beans, and communication is controlled: just as in Hubbard's day, people on the RPF are not allowed to speak to anyone who is not also on the RPF, which means that wives and other family members are not allowed to visit or call. The only communications allowed to and from RPFers are handwritten letters, which are screened.

Stefan was entering his ninth month on the RPF when the church

---

* During my last interview with Stefan, in September 2010, he noted that he ultimately came to understand that Miscavige feared appearing to be too much "in control" of the church, as that might violate the church's agreement with the IRS regarding its tax exemption. According to this agreement, Scientology's Mother Church controls the budgets and the RTC simply oversees copyrights and trademarks.

closed Happy Valley* and moved its fifteen-odd RPF inmates to the fortress-like Cedars of Lebanon building in Los Angeles, where they merged with more than a hundred other disgraced Sea Org staffers, including a number of high-ranking executives such as Brian Anderson, the former commanding officer of Flag's Office of Special Affairs, who had been sent west for rehabilitation after the Lisa McPherson debacle.

Work consisted of cleaning, maintenance, and various construction projects: fixing leaking roofs, sanding doors, repairing air-conditioning units, hauling garbage. Five hours a day consisted of mandatory study and routine auditing and security checking. Like most of the people he knew on the program, Stefan had been promised the RPF would take six months. Two years later, he was still there (though that was nothing compared to the ordeal of some worn-down souls who had endured a far longer stretch — six to eight years).

Tanja, meanwhile, remained at Int, where she faced daily pressure to divorce her husband. Steadfastly she refused, even after it was made clear to her that Stefan might never return to Int, which, after all, was a privileged post. An edict prevented Sea Org members from being married to staffers on other compounds, Tanja knew; to stay with Stefan she'd have to give up her job, and her life, at Int. From Shelly Miscavige on down the ranks, the RTC women reminded Tanja that she had the best job in Scientology, working for "the most ethical person on the planet," Miscavige. How could there even be a contest? Finally, after months of coercion, she agreed to initiate divorce proceedings.

Shortly afterward, in February 2002, Stefan completed the rehabilitation program laid out for him by his auditor. Aware that his wife had filed divorce papers, he submitted a request to begin the process of reacceptance into the Sea Organization. If he could just return to

---

* Though Scientologists are not supposed to know the location of the Int Base, nor that it is the seat of international management, the base's location has been public since the 1980s, and maps of its various buildings have been posted on the Internet. Happy Valley, however, was a true "secret" until 2000, when a German documentary team revealed its location. The church, seeking to avoid negative publicity, closed it down.

the base before the final papers were signed, he thought, he might still have a chance to save his marriage.

But the RPF refused to let him go. Another year passed. Stefan remained imprisoned. Every day his auditor worked on him: why was he still so in love with his wife? "It was like this Machiavellian thing had been unleashed against me — I didn't know who was doing this to me, or why," he said. "All I knew was that somebody really wanted to make sure that I got divorced."

More months went by. His auditor told him that Tanja had signed divorce papers. Stefan began to understand that he would never leave the RPF unless he agreed to let go of Tanja completely. "And so I let go," he admitted to me.

Accordingly, he forced himself to stop talking about Tanja. He told himself to stop thinking about her. He agreed not to write or in any other way try to communicate with Tanja. He pledged himself to serve the Church of Scientology in whatever way it asked. Finally, in June 2003, Stefan "graduated" from the RPF, a broken man. He emerged from the Cedars of Lebanon building as cleansed as Winston Smith, in the book *1984*. "I felt just like him," he said. "Everything's great, the organization is great, the propaganda is great, the technology is great, it's all wonderful. I'm divorced."

Less than twenty-four hours after Stefan got off the RPF, Tanja's mother, who worked at the PAC Base, approached him and gave him a cell phone. Soon Stefan received a call. "I still love you," Tanja whispered into the phone. She'd never signed divorce papers. They were still married.

For all the years that they had been separated, and in spite of all the pressure she'd endured, Tanja had never let go of Stefan. By the summer of 2003, she'd even begun wearing her wedding ring again. "It was my little statement," she said. "I didn't care what anyone said; the only thing that mattered was what was between him and me."

To understand just how dramatic this quiet act of defiance was, consider that during her thirteen years of working for Miscavige, Tanja had never voiced an opinion about anything that happened on the base, from her husband's banishment to Miscavige's increasingly brutal behavior, let alone express opposition to any of them.

Certain officials and inner-circle members like Tanja report that in addition to routine tongue-lashings, Miscavige from time to time physically attacked executives who angered him.* One frequent target was Mike Rinder, his unflappable Australian deputy and the head of the OSA, whose job was to manage lawsuits and do damage control. One time, Miscavige, furious over the negative press coverage of the Lisa McPherson case, called the OSA chief to his villa; then, grabbing Rinder around the neck, he swung him into a small tree. "[Then he] started kicking him," said Marty Rathbun, who'd been called to "witness" the attack.

On other occasions, the leader of Scientology is said to have publicly slapped, kicked, punched, or shoved executives who angered him, including Jeff Hawkins, who said he was attacked by Miscavige on five separate occasions, beginning in 2002. "It wasn't like he did it everywhere — it was usually in meetings or when he was inspecting an area," said Hawkins. Only those present saw what went on, "and they did not talk about it to other staff." The lowest-ranking workers on the base, for the most part, were exempt from the leader's abuse. The rest took what came to them silently. No one reported these beatings to the police.

"After twenty-eight years in Scientology, you blamed yourself for what was happening. *I* must be a real scumbag to pull that in," explained Tom De Vocht, who said he was attacked several times by Miscavige. He never fought back, nor did he expect anyone else to put up a challenge. "You're talking about the pope of Scientology beating on his staff, the man who controls your eternal salvation," he said. Besides, De Vocht added, many people, including him, had been conditioned to act exactly as Miscavige did.

Indeed, this toxic environment metastasized to such a degree that Miscavige's underlings, unprovoked by the leader, would similarly descend upon one another, ganging up on whoever seemed weakest. Group confessions, referred to as "séances," had become regular occurrences at Int. At these events, executives who'd angered Miscavige in some way were made to sit at the front of a large room, such as the base dining hall, and one by one stand up and confess their "crimes."

---

* The Church of Scientology denies that Miscavige has ever physically attacked anyone.

De Vocht witnessed numerous séances, including those where Miscavige himself would stand up and reveal someone's crimes, having combed through their auditing folders. "In front of seven hundred people, he'd say, 'It came up today that so-and-so was jerking off,' or 'Sam, here, in another life molested a child.' Well, people had very little sleep, they were eating rice and beans, they were half psychotic from working such long hours, and they'd go into a frenzy." Often the attacks were made in defense of the chairman of the board himself. *"What have you done to Dave?!"* the people would shout, and they'd jeer while the accused racked his brain to think of an appropriate response.*

Somehow, Tanja told herself, all of this must be for the greatest good. But doubt had begun to eat away at her. "Please try to get back here — you have to," she told Stefan one night on the phone. "I don't think I can handle it here alone."

But Stefan remained in Los Angeles, no closer to leaving the PAC Base than when he'd arrived four years earlier. Miscavige had refused to sign his release papers. The leader now decreed that those recently finished with the RPF were not to be seen as "rehabilitated" until they'd made up for the damage they'd caused the organization. How they were to do this was never explained. Meanwhile, Miscavige had grown suspicious of his secretary. One day in Los Angeles, the leader confronted Tanja. "Tell me the truth," he said. "Have you spoken to that scumbag husband of yours?"

Mustering all of her courage, Tanja admitted it: yes, she had. It was the last conversation she and Miscavige would have.[†]

---

* During the late 1990s, Miscavige spent most of his time in Clearwater. However, according to Marty Rathbun, the leader would often monitor the "séances" remotely, by instructing an RTC staffer to put a conference phone into the room so he could listen in. "When he heard something that piqued his interest, he would have his assistant reach one of those RTC staffers through a separate phone, and then bark his instructions. Many times this had to do with making the confessing person give more details about his or her transgressions, particularly alleged sexual ones. Miscavige would then continue to listen surreptitiously through the conference phone to ensure that his order was complied with satisfactorily."

† Eighteen months later, Miscavige did acknowledge Tanja's presence one more time, with a single sentence. He otherwise never spoke to nor acknowledged her again.

The following day, August 14, 2004, Tanja was sent back to the Int Base, where she was ordered to the Old Gilman House, a ramshackle, two-story building on the far edge of the property, which was used as a detention center for staff who'd expressed disaffection with the current management or a desire to "blow." There she would begin a program of "correction," a less structured, and more isolated, version of the RPF. She picked vegetables, lived in a trailer off the main house, and ate her meals, delivered by a security guard, alone. She was audited daily. None of her friends or former colleagues in Miscavige's office were allowed to have anything to do with her; indeed, her name would never be uttered among the regular staff at Int, as if she had literally been wiped from the collective memory there. From her once-lofty position as the favored communicator of the chairman of the board, Tanja had fallen to the level of, as she put it, "scum."

Three months passed before Tanja was summoned to a private room to meet with the Sea Org executives Warren McShane and Mike Rinder. Stefan had left the Sea Org, they told her. He'd walked off the PAC Base in broad daylight a few weeks earlier, slipping past his minder during a shift change. Then, they said, he'd sought legal advice from Ford Greene, a well-known attorney of the San Francisco Bay Area who'd successfully litigated against Scientology in the Larry Wollersheim case. That Stefan had contacted this sworn enemy made him unredeemable in the eyes of the church.

Tanja will never forget how coolly Rinder delivered the news about Stefan's defection. He had her divorce papers folded under an envelope on the table in front of him. There was one set of documents left to finalize her split with Stefan. "He thought for sure I was going to sign the papers and end it right there," she said. Instead, Tanja stood her ground. "Well, if he left, then I guess I'm going to leave too," she announced to the men. Rinder, she added, was "furious."

For the next week or so, Tanja endured "intense pressure" to change her mind. Rinder in particular couldn't fathom Tanja's stubbornness: her husband had committed some of the worst sins imaginable, and she *wanted* to be with him? She aimed to leave behind her family, her group, her religion, everything? According to Scientology's teachings, Stefan Castle was just one husband in a long string

of husbands Tanja had already had, and would have, as a spiritual being over many lifetimes. "What is the big deal?" Rinder said.

Tanja was then subjected to another ten days of constant auditing.
Then once again she met with Rinder, for what was called an "ethics interview." This time, he informed her, she wouldn't be allowed to
leave the room until she confessed. When she insisted that she'd already told him everything, Rinder began to berate her. "He was just
wide-eyed and red in the face, spitting and spraying me with his fury
. . . He painted this whole picture of what it would be like if I went out
and found Stefan." Rinder, she said, gave the couple six months. "He
kept saying, 'You have no money, no experience. You won't be able to
talk to your family,' and he kind of played on my uncertainty. How
could I know what I would be walking into if I were to leave?" Tanja
had never had a credit card, didn't drive a car, didn't have a bank account. How could she possibly survive?

For years, Tanja had thought that one day she might be interrogated, and wondered how she would hold up. She'd assumed that she
would be strong and make it through. But as Rinder's harangue continued, she felt herself weakening. She found it unbearable that Stefan, wholly unaware of her punishment and possibly believing she'd
soon follow, had defected. Now he'd lost his spiritual salvation — his
eternity. Even if he begged, he would never be able to return to the
church. "These were things I couldn't bear the thought of," she said.
After a while, "I was just dead. I wasn't crying, I wasn't showing any
emotion, I was feeling kind of numb."

After more than twelve hours of interrogation, Tanja was given
a piece of paper and a pen and told to write a "disconnection" letter
to Stefan. She read the letter aloud while Rinder recorded the event
with a video camera. Then Tanja was presented with divorce papers
one last time. Through tears, she signed her name.

CHAPTER 17

Exodus

D AVID MISCAVIGE BURST into the conference room on the International Base one afternoon in the late fall of 2004, looking as if he was going to explode. "You guys are all shit-heads," he barked. The leader ran through his usual litany of complaints: the overall organizational board was a mess; no one was doing their job; he was working himself to death just to counter the laziness and incompetence of those around him. All of the senior executives were SPs who might as well spend the rest of their lives cleaning septic tanks and breaking rocks. In fact, he might just make sure that some of them did that.

Suddenly, he asked, "Who knows what 'musical chairs' means?"

Several people raised their hand and stammered out Scientology's particular definition: "A constant transfer of workers from one job to another."

"No, fuck you," Miscavige said. "What else?"

"It's a game," someone finally said.

Miscavige, it turned out, had called them all to this meeting to play musical chairs, albeit with a twist. He explained that when the music stopped, whoever didn't get a chair would be offloaded from the base.

The officials went silent.

"You guys have fucked with me for the last time," Miscavige said.

The leader ordered that a large boom box be brought into the conference room, and when it arrived, he popped in a CD of Queen's *Greatest Hits*. Freddie Mercury's operatic tenor led off with "Bohemian Rhapsody": *"Is this the real life? Is this just fantasy?"* Slowly, people began walking around the circle of chairs. Marc Headley, now an executive, couldn't believe he was doing this. He took a quick survey of the players: among the nearly seventy officials were Miscavige's onetime deputy Greg Wilhere, and another top lieutenant, Mark Ingber; there was the OSA chief, Mike Rinder, and also Marty Rathbun and the CMO executive Tom De Vocht. The music stopped. An old-time member of the Sea Org who probably hadn't left the base in twenty years lost his chair. Then the game continued and a second person was gone.

What did Miscavige really mean by "offload"? Headley, who was eliminated after a few rounds, decided it could mean a number of things: Some people, the lucky ones, might be moved to another organization; those whom Miscavige considered more serious offenders might be sentenced to a remote Rehabilitation Project Force in, say, New Zealand. Others might be handed a few hundred dollars, put on a bus, and kicked out altogether. Most of the people on the base had no family outside Scientology. Where would they go? What would they do? Few had credit cards or bank accounts; even fewer owned vehicles. The base was all they knew.

Headley watched as friends who'd worked together for years battled it out for a chair. By the time the number had dwindled to twenty, people were throwing one another against the walls, ripping seats from one another's hands, wrestling one another to the floor.

Finally, just four players remained. Miscavige changed the music to Mozart's Requiem Mass. Greg Wilhere grabbed Mark Ingber and threw him aside — one down. Lisa Schroer, one of Marc Headley's colleagues, bested Wilhere in racing for a seat — now he was gone too. It was between Schroer and Wilhere's wife, Sue. The women walked around a single chair for what struck Headley as an eternity. The music stopped. Schroer won. The game was over.

"Do any of you animals have anything to say?" Miscavige asked. No one did. It was 3 A.M. The leader confined all seventy people to the conference room and ordered them to sleep under the tables. Food was delivered from time to time. A few days later, they were told that Miscavige had decided not to offload anyone after all.

• • •

For Marty Rathbun, who'd spent the game of musical chairs quietly looking out the window "trying to distract myself," as he said, Miscavige's threats were nothing new. After twenty years as the leader's deputy, Rathbun, like Tom De Vocht and several other senior officials of the Church of Scientology, had grown almost used to DM's bizarre behavior. Virtually every meeting with Miscavige involved an element of fear: the initial summons required that those called to it drop whatever they were doing and sprint to the assignation place; there they would wait until the leader, who'd often be playing Nintendo in his private lounge, decided to show up.

He would arrive flanked by his wife and Lou Stuckenbrock, a retinue of aides, and, often, his beagles. He had five dogs, two of which, Jelly and Safi, wore tiny blue sweaters with commander's bars. Miscavige was known to make his staffers salute the dogs, who held ranks higher than those of many people on the base. The meeting room would have been thoroughly white-gloved and set with an ashtray, an air purifier, and an assortment of the leader's favorite snacks — Balance or Pure Protein energy bars were a notable passion, as were raspberry sour candies and Penta ultra-purified water, which Miscavige ordered by the case.

Then Miscavige would open the meeting with an accusation or, more often, a comment about someone's sexual peccadilloes, which he seemed to relish discussing at great length. If anyone else in the room was to snicker or even blink, the leader would threaten him or her with expulsion. "You'll be flipping burgers at McDonald's," he frequently said, before launching into the main thrust of his meeting, which was usually, according to Jeff Hawkins, "a dissertation about how everything was wrong and how terrible and suppressive everybody was."

The once-vast org board, which at Int had originally listed hundreds of posts, was now irrelevant. Its purpose, to ensure that a particular organization worked like a well-oiled machine to achieve the goals of Scientology, was moot at Int. Distrusting many of his associates, Miscavige had sidelined them to be punished or rehabilitated, so that important efforts were understaffed. He forced his remaining executives, an ever-dwindling number, to endlessly revise the organizational charts; because he was perpetually displeased with their strategies, the task had dragged on for four years — since 2000. He micromanaged each facet of the work done at Int, demanding that every marketing plan, event proposal, and film script be submitted to him instantly. Then he sat on the documents for days or weeks, or even months, only to reject each one, with a scathing putdown of the person who'd submitted it. In this atmosphere, little productive activity could occur.

The leader's impatience and disgust with Int Base personnel eventually escalated into a full-blown purge. During group confessions, often daylong affairs, hundreds of people were evicted from the base and sent to the RPF; dozens more waited at the former Happy Valley, now called the Int Ranch, to be offloaded, Scientology's equivalent of a dishonorable discharge.* Virtually all of the Church of Scientology's senior managers and technical officials were denounced as SPs and locked in the large, doublewide trailer that housed the conference room where the game of musical chairs had taken place. The trailer had been designated "SP Hall," or simply "The Hole." The condemned would remain there for months — some for years — sleeping under their desks, showering in a garage, unable to get even a change of clothes unless it was to do work Miscavige had specifically ordered, such as squiring around visiting VIPs or appearing at church events (for example, the OSA chief, Mike Rinder, and Guillaume Lesevre, head of the Church of Scientology International, would be released, outfitted in tuxedos, and sent to promote Scientology to the membership, then reinstalled in The Hole upon their return).

Even the grand new RTC building Miscavige built on the base in 1999, a fifty-five-thousand-foot structure of imported sandstone, now stood empty. The only people who worked there were Miscavige and his personal staff, which by the time of the infamous musical

---

* Albeit with a price attached: offloaded Sea Org members are presented with "freeloader bills" for the years of training and auditing they've received as church employees. All "blown" staffers must reimburse the church to clear this debt before they can resume auditing and other services and be considered members in good standing. But those who wish to permanently leave Scientology and risk disconnection from their families generally do so without paying their freeloader bill.

chairs had reportedly dwindled to just half a dozen people; the rest had been demoted or declared SPs.*

Such purges had, of course, happened before. In the early 1950s Hubbard had denounced and expelled those in the Dianetics movement who opposed him; by 1959, the Founder would declare his own son an SP. But Hubbard, while a tyrant in his worst moments, also had the capacity to forgive. "Once he got over his tirades and tantrums, he'd follow it up with some justice measure" — often by granting sweeping "amnesties" to those he'd committed to the RPF, said the former Scientologist Glenn Samuels, who was purged from Scientology in 1982.

But Miscavige didn't seem to believe in absolution, nor, as many saw it, in justice. By the mid-2000s, the leader's way of denouncing staffers as Suppressive Persons had become staggeringly random. No longer was a defection, a leaked document, or some other treasonous act a prerequisite for being deemed an SP, though only serious offenses like those would seem to merit such severe condemnation. It meant, after all, expulsion from the church and the loss of salvation — a severe penalty. But now anyone who expressed even the smallest criticism of church policy or leadership was in danger of being cast out.

For people like Marty Rathbun, the promise of eternal freedom, Scientology's core doctrine, kept them hanging on during Miscavige's oppressive regime. But ultimately, even Rathbun decided he'd had enough. One afternoon in December 2004, having witnessed Miscavige physically attack Tom De Vocht during a meeting, Rathbun felt himself hit an invisible wall. If he didn't remove himself from the situation, he realized, he might kill Miscavige out of pure hate. Later that evening, Rathbun retrieved his Yamaha 650 motorcycle from the bushes where it was parked, wheeled it downhill, and waited for the back gate to open. When it did, just as a car drove through, "I gunned it and headed out down the road." That was the last he'd ever see of the base.

---

* By 2006, one of those abruptly "disappeared" from the RTC, and from Int, would be Miscavige's wife, Shelly, who was reportedly exiled to a Church of Scientology compound near Big Bear, California.

Within a few weeks, De Vocht was gone as well, in much the same manner. By that spring, so was Jeff Hawkins. Not one of these executives, nor those who followed, including Mike Rinder, who departed Scientology in 2007, made a move to suggest that Miscavige should be the one to leave, though both Rathbun and De Vocht later said they thought about it. "We had a tacit agreement that something needed to be done about this guy . . . but you couldn't go there, because if you got caught going there, you'd be declared [an SP] forever," said Rathbun, who would never relinquish his belief in L. Ron Hubbard's technology, despite losing faith in the management of his church.

Hawkins knew that opposing Miscavige would be futile. He'd been in the Church of Scientology for thirty-eight years, had seen the movement's leadership evolve from idealistic to authoritarian to, as he saw it, Orwellian in mindset. Through it all, he'd fought to maintain his own integrity in what became a permanently hostile and intimidating environment. Finally, Hawkins accepted as pointless his hopes that things might change. What was happening at the base, said the onetime marketing chief, "was an irreversible trend. And when I realized that, I said, 'I'm out of here.'"

Throughout the Sea Org rank and file, many other members were making the same decision.

On January 10, 2005, Stefan and Tanja Castle were legally divorced. Five months later, Tanja left the trailer by the Old Gilman House that had become her home and returned to Int proper, where she was given a bed in a dormitory and a new job: helping to build sets for Golden Era Productions. The internal struggle she'd gone through for nine months, poring over LRH's teachings to see if she could find some justification for what had happened to her, was over. Stefan was an SP. Nothing else mattered. "Once the group has agreed that something is a certain way, one person can't change it on her own," she said.

It had been five years since Stefan had been separated from his wife, and less than one year since he had fled from the PAC Base, a far easier place to leave, he knew, than Int. He had tried everything he could think of to communicate with Tanja, even filing a missing person's report with the Hemet police department; nothing had worked. The detectives couldn't prove that Tanja was being held against her will. His lawyer informed him that there was no legal way to force Tanja to speak to him, unless it could be proved that she was being held captive. Desperate, Stefan contacted the church a few weeks after he fled, offering to come back to Scientology if they would let him be with Tanja. Maybe there was a place where they could go. Australia, he offered. Even the RPF, provided they could do it together.

But Scientology didn't want him back. Instead, Stefan received a call from the Office of Special Affairs, summoning him to Scientology's large Mother Church building on Hollywood Boulevard. When he arrived, Elliot Abelson, the Church of Scientology's general counsel, handed Stefan a thirty-page document stating that he would never sue or denounce the church to the press, and asked him to sign. Then Abelson wrote a check for $25,000. "This will help you get started," he said.

The money petrified Stefan. Scientology often made cash settlements with its defectors, particularly those the church worried might speak to the press or testify against it in court. Several of these former officials, after reportedly receiving payments, had in fact retracted the negative statements they'd previously made. But no one, to Stefan's knowledge, had ever been offered as much as $25,000 to simply keep quiet, unless the person posed a particular threat.

What the fuck is going on? he wondered. Then he realized what it was: his wife had been Miscavige's secretary. *What does she know?* Stefan didn't have a clue. Tanja had never shared RTC secrets with him.

But clearly the church feared that she had. Stefan tried to bargain with Abelson: what if he and Tanja stayed in the movement and simply minded their own business? Abelson said it was too late. "Take it." He pushed the check toward Stefan. "We'd like to rest at ease that you aren't going to talk to anyone."

"I didn't think I had a choice," Stefan said. So he signed the agreement and took the check, but didn't cash it. The following day, his lawyer, Ford Greene, sent a strongly worded letter to the church, accusing its leaders of coercion and demanding that they rescind the agreement. The church, remembering the tenacity with which

Greene had successfully litigated against them on behalf of Woller-sheim and several other Scientologists, agreed. Then all went quiet.

Stefan tried to move on with his life. He found a job working in production design and soon started his own company. He began to read the critical material about Scientology on the Internet. He reached out to former Sea Org members he met online, many of whom, he discovered, had been hauled into OSA headquarters, confronted by lawyers, and offered sizable monetary inducements to keep their mouths shut, just as he had.

Toward the end of 2005, Stefan reconnected with Marc and Claire Headley, who'd escaped from the Int Base shortly after the musical chairs incident. Marc had gone first, in the early hours of January 5, 2005, on his motorcycle, ultimately making his way to Kansas City, Missouri, where his father, who had long ago left Scientology, now resided.

Claire followed a few weeks later, having finagled a trip into town to refill a contact lens prescription. From there, she'd called a taxi and hightailed it to the nearest bus station.

Sitting with the Headleys in the back garden of their snug, bungalow-style house in Burbank, Stefan knew he had to rescue Tanja. He'd continued to dream about her, which was reaffirming. There was still a connection. She was the only woman he'd ever loved. If she had moved on, he believed he would have sensed it.

And Tanja felt this too. "All this time I'd been wondering, 'Is Stefan surviving, is he doing okay, what's happened to him?'" she said. "There was always a side of me that was out there with him. I never stopped thinking about it."

In her former life as an obedient RTC staffer, Claire Headley had helped convince Tanja to file for divorce. Now she was plagued with guilt. "I felt like the shittiest person," she said. "I thought to myself, anything I could do to somehow make things right I had to do."

The answer came to her in a dream. She had sent Tanja a letter in a Victoria's Secret box. Lingerie items, which RTC women ordered online, were the only packages that were never opened by security staff at the base — a rule that was passed after some security guards had gotten in trouble for opening several Victoria's Secret packages. Excitedly, Claire shook Marc awake. "I know how we can free Tanja."

The following day, Stefan ordered Tanja some items from the Victoria's Secret catalog. Then he sat down and composed a letter. "I love you and know you still have love for me too," he wrote. "Regardless of everything, I have no regrets of having left the Sea Org. I am free. I have my dignity."

Stefan then tucked the letter into a pair of jeans and put a cell phone in the box as well. He taped the package securely and, for good measure, "kicked it around to make it look like it was coming from Ohio. And then I sent it by UPS." Then he waited.

A few days later, Tanja received the package. Knowing she hadn't ordered anything, she took it as a message. "It was surreal," she said. "But there was a calmness about me." She opened the package and read her husband's letter. *"Call me!"*

Tanya wavered. She wanted to be with Stefan, of course. But after all she'd been through, how could she leave? She considered all the ways in which people had escaped from the base: They'd driven off in a car or motorcycle — Tanja didn't have either. They jumped the fence — exhausted from working long hours and eating rice and beans, Tanja was too weak. Simply walking down the highway would be easiest, but that hardly ever worked: only three people she'd ever heard about had successfully blown using that technique.

She wrote Stefan a letter telling him she didn't see how it would be possible. But she couldn't stop thinking about her husband. "I knew once I had sent the letter I had crossed a line," she said. One night, summoning every ounce of her courage, she called him.

Overjoyed, Stefan urged Tanja to communicate with him by voice mail and text message, methods he knew would be hard to trace. Through these furtive exchanges, Tanja learned about her husband's new life. He was making over $100,000 per year as a production designer. He had a house in the San Fernando Valley and a car. Were she to join him, they could have children, he promised her. Finally, after several weeks, Stefan convinced his wife to risk escape.

On August 5, 2006, Tanja took a ladder and walked toward the wall near the Castle, the only spot on the base not surrounded by an electric fence. It was just after midnight. Outside the wall, Stefan sat in his dark blue Mustang, waiting. His friend John, in a separate vehicle, drove down the road to an area where it was possible to pull onto the base. This, they knew, would alert the security guard, who would immediately go to investigate, at which point Tanja would jump over the wall. Even if she happened to trip the wire at the top, setting off an alarm, she would still have at least two minutes to run.

Stefan had painstakingly organized the plan. He and John stayed on the phone as John parked on the base. A few minutes later, a roving security guard walked toward his car. John hung up — the agreed-upon signal. Then Stefan called Tanja. "Go baby, go!" he said. "Now!"

"I'm going!" Tanja said, and taking a deep breath, jumped over the wall into the darkness. She saw her husband's waiting car and ran toward it. Then, with no one behind them, they sped off down Highway 79, out of the dust-choked San Jacinto Valley, and toward Los Angeles, and freedom, unleashed from the bonds of Int, David Miscavige, the Sea Organization, and the Church of Scientology.

The Scientologists who have left the church since the mid-2000s, a group from all strata of the organization, form part of what some have called the Second Great Exodus. There is a significant difference between this generation and those who were part of the exodus of the 1980s, largely thanks to the Internet, which has enabled former members, both Sea Org and public, to find one another and unite over their shared experience. "You don't tend to blame yourself when you see that others went through the same thing," commented Jeff Hawkins, who has become an outspoken critic of Scientology's current management. "It's made for a strong, well-informed, and co-ordinated group of ex-members, which the church has never had to face before."

Hawkins has helped this group develop, writing about his personal experiences in a memoir and blog, called Counterfeit Dreams, and creating a second website, Leaving Scientology, intended to help current, as well as former, Scientologists see beyond the church's hyperbolic speeches and marketing strategies. He advised his readers to look at their local org. "How many people are in the org? Are there more people in the org than there were ten years ago? Twenty years ago? Or are there less? What about events? Are there many more people now at events than there were ten years ago? You would think that if Scientology had been experiencing 'unprecedented expansion' for the last 10 years" — as the church often claims — "they would need bigger and bigger event venues. But the LA Events are still at the Shrine, as they were 20 years ago. And they have trouble filling that. So *where* is this expansion?"

One answer is Scientology's real estate portfolio. Since the early 2000s, Scientology has been running what former church executives say is a very profitable building and renovation scheme called the Ideal Org program. Indeed, according to numerous reports from within and outside of the church, real estate may now be Scientology's principle cash cow.

A comparable model for the Ideal Org program would be one used by another franchise-based operation, McDonald's, which is also one of the most successful real estate corporations in the country. McDonald's earns most of its income not from the sale of Big Macs, but from the money its franchise owners pay in rent on their properties. Scientology too has used this formula, assigning a special division of church management, the International Landlord Office, to purchase choice buildings around the world, often through third-party corporations, and paying for them in cash, with IAS money raised from Scientology's parishioners.

In some cases, these buildings have reportedly been leased to the local orgs, which are expected to raise the money for rent, and for renovations, from their congregation. This buys the Church of Scientology, as a business enterprise, significant autonomy. No longer is the church dependent on services — sales of auditing and course packages — for income; the onus is now on the local organizations to succeed, and if they don't, the Church of Scientology, whose investment in the Ideal Org was minimal, is none the poorer.

The New York Org, which I visited in 2005, was one of the original Ideal Orgs. As the Church of Scientology already owned the West 46th Street property, it did not need to purchase a new building, but the church nonetheless spent $18 million on renovating the structure, installing skylights, building a full-service spa for its Purification Rundown program, redoing the ornate lobby, and adding other plush features. Tom De Vocht, who'd run similar building projects in

Florida, was tasked with overseeing the renovations, which, he said, were far from complete as the grand opening ceremony, slated for September 25, 2004, approached. To address the problem, some four hundred Sea Org members descended upon midtown Manhattan the day before the ribbon cutting, to finish the cosmetic renovations.

After the ceremony, said De Vocht, many of the refurbishings had to be redone, having failed to meet certain building codes, which drove the local organization only further into debt. "It was a disaster. The org already owed $1.8 million to contractors who were banging on the door every day, saying, 'Where the hell's my money?' They had not paid the building off as yet, and so they were regging the public like crazy. But hey, on the face of things, it looked like a beautiful new organization." (In Scientology parlance, *regging* means "soliciting money from members.")

The theory behind the Ideal Org program is "If you build it, they will come." By most accounts, however, it hasn't worked out that way. Montreal, for example, has always had a small congregation and roughly fifteen people on staff. Yet the Church of Scientology recently decided to open an Ideal Org there. Members were convinced to donate $4 million to purchase the building and then another $4 million to renovate it. While the membership was pressured for the money, sometimes holding all-night fundraising sessions, the new building sat empty, and the original organization struggled with debt, because the parishioners had spent all their money on the building and thus could no longer afford to pay for services.

But it is likely that this problem did not affect the Church of Scientology as a corporate entity. "As a money-making scheme, the Ideal Org plan is pretty good," said Mat Pesch, a former Sea Org official who was an executive in the International Landlord Office. Though he lacks current financial data, which remain confidential (Pesch left Scientology in 2005), he said, "What I would expect to find based on the indicators and data that I have is that cash and real estate are growing by leaps and bounds. On the other hand, the staff and public and structure of the church, other than real estate, are breaking down . . . even the best PR will not be able to cover it up or slow it down."

In the summer of 2010, Mike Rinder conducted an online survey of former Scientologists to find out what had motivated them to leave the church. Of the hundreds of respondents, most cited the unremitting pressure, sometimes called "crush regging," to donate to various Scientology causes, like the Ideal Org program. Rinder dubbed it the "vulture culture."

Mike and Donna Henderson, onetime Scientologists from Clearwater, were victims of this culture. OT 7 and OT 8 respectively, they were nearly bankrupted by their involvement with the church. Today they are two of a growing number of ex-Scientologists who predict that in these dark economic times, Scientology's "unvarnished demand for money," as Mike puts it, may lead to its demise.

Mike joined the Church of Scientology in 1971, as a nineteen-year-old in Los Angeles. By 1973, he'd signed a billion-year contract with the Sea Organization and was sailing with L. Ron Hubbard aboard the *Apollo*. When Hubbard moved onshore, Mike, eager to strike out on his own, went through the appropriate steps to leave the Sea Org. He moved back to L.A. and became a public Scientologist, ultimate reaching the very top of the Bridge to Total Freedom, as did Donna, his second wife, whom he married in 2003.

Along the way, Mike contributed to a wide range of causes and programs, ranging from the Golden Age of Tech to the release of a sophisticated new E-meter. To further Scientology's "planetary dissemination," he and Donna bought extra copies of *Dianetics* and other books by Hubbard to send to libraries all over the world. They helped fund a project to translate the Founder's writing and lectures into languages spoken by relatively few people, such as Lithuanian. To preserve Hubbard's technology for eternity, the couple gave money to the Church of Spiritual Technology, a special entity that has spent the past twenty years preparing and storing all of the Founder's handwritten notes, policy letters, and science fiction in secret, underground vaults spread across three remote locations in California, as well as one near Trementina, New Mexico. The Hendersons also regularly took cruises, costing $10,000 to $20,000, aboard *Freedwinds,* and they gave generously to groups such as Narconon, Applied Scholastics, and the Citizens Commission on Human Rights; they were listed in church publications as patrons of the International Association of Scientologists, signifying they had contributed at least $50,000 to the church's legal war chest.

Joining the IAS was not optional. Every Scientologist must be a member, though when people first become interested in Scientology they are offered a free six-month membership. After that, members are prohibited from taking further Scientology services until they buy either a yearly or a lifetime membership. A yearly membership costs $300 and a lifetime membership costs $3,000. "The thing is, you are pretty much expected to become a lifetime member, and they hit you up for money all the time," Mike said during an interview in Clearwater in 2010. "Every few months, or weeks, there's some kind of event that they get you to go to, and then ask you for this and that. And eventually, you wind up being an IAS sponsor, which is $5,000, and then you get up to where you've paid $40,000 or $50,000, and now you're a patron."

During his thirty-four years as a member of the Church of Scientology, Mike, who once ran a profitable contracting business, estimated he "donated" roughly $600,000. Donna, a veterinarian, was a member for just ten years but spent well over $1 million in that time. The Hendersons also claimed over $100,000 in tax deductions in the decade or so after donations to the Church of Scientology became tax-exempt, though as with most parishioners, the money they saved was plowed back into the church.

"The money that keeps this church going comes from professionals like my wife," Mike explained. "People think it's the celebrities" — the actress Nancy Cartwright, the voice of *The Simpsons'* Bart Simpson, for example, donated $10 million to the IAS in 2007 — "but a big, big part of Scientology has nothing to do with celebrities; it has to do with dentists, vets, chiropractors, podiatrists, accountants, professional people who have six-figure incomes and who can afford to drop everything, come to Flag twice a year, and spend some serious money because it won't make a dent in their life."

Ultimately, however, even Scientology's wealthiest benefactors have found themselves running out of money, as the Hendersons did in 2005. By then Mike, whose business had suffered a downturn, had committed so much money to the Church of Scientology that he was reduced to borrowing from his elderly divorced mother to recompense Flag for past debts. Donna was in such bad financial straits that she sold her thriving veterinary practice to help pay off some of what she owed. Left with no work and little choice, but still loyal to Scientology, the couple made what to them seemed the logical decision at the time: they joined the Sea Organization to defray costs.

But rather than indoctrinate them more deeply, Donna Henderson, a plainspoken woman, said the Sea Org experience served to "wake us up." Public members, and notably those who've paid enough to become Operating Thetans, are assiduously kept in the dark about how the Sea Org, and the overall church hierarchy, actually functions. "You truly have no idea that things are as bad as they are within the organization," said Donna. "But once you're in, it's like the curtain just drops, and all of a sudden there's absolutely no pretense. You're not there to save the planet, you're not there to help anybody — you're there to get money from people. And you don't have money anymore, so you're a slave."

Four months after joining the Sea Org, in July 2005, the Hendersons packed their belongings in a Ryder truck and drove away. They refused to submit to the coercive exit interview process, known as "routing out," by which disgruntled staffers are often (albeit after days or weeks of pressure) convinced to stay. They thus became SPs. Shortly afterward, Mike's sisters, brother, nieces, nephews, his children, and his ex-wife — roughly thirty-five people in all* — disconnected from him. So did many of his business associates, and almost all of the couple's friends.

Today the Hendersons live alongside the water in a quiet middle-class neighborhood of St. Petersburg, just south of Clearwater. Slowly, they have rebuilt their lives: Mike has worked odd jobs and currently sells furniture; Donna opened a new veterinary practice.

---

* One of Mike's sisters, an OSA executive, is the president of the Church of Scientology of Los Angeles; the other, also in Los Angeles, is the headmistress of the upper school at Delphi. Two of Mike's nephews are in the Sea Org, posted at Int, and Mike's son is also in the Sea Org, posted at the American Saint Hill Organization, on the PAC Base.

They have become vocal critics of the church and its administration, and their fear of harassment is palpable. Their ranch-style home is a fortress not unlike a Scientology org, Mike said with a laugh. "We have a twenty-four-hour alarm system, plus fire protection, glass-break protection, forced-entry and burglar protection, and security lights around the house, with motion detectors."

In many other ways, leaving Scientology has not been easy. During my visit to Clearwater, Mike and Donna took me to dinner at a water-front restaurant just off the Memorial Causeway between Clearwater and Clearwater Beach, a resort community that is home to many Scientologists. Mike is a tall man, six foot six, with a loping gait that makes him hard to miss, even amid dozens of people. Shortly after we sat down, a couple and their teenage children were seated at the table next to us. Glancing over, they became visibly uncomfortable. The woman took out her cell phone and walked a few feet away. Her daughter began craning her neck, looking for the hostess.

"They're Scientologists," Donna whispered.

"Just wait," Mike said.

"Maybe we should go." Donna looked chagrined.

"No, let's see what they do." A few seconds later, the woman returned and everyone at her table got up and left. "Wow," Mike said. He looked around at the other well-dressed people eating on the patio. "I guess they know we're declared."

"But we haven't seen anything in writing," Donna protested. When Scientologists are formally excommunicated, a written declaration known as a "goldenrod" is issued, stating their crimes against the organization. It is printed on a piece of golden parchment and sent to both the member and his or her church, where it is often posted on the wall. The Hendersons had not received their goldenrod.

"Oh, we're definitely declared." Mike reminded his wife of another Scientologist friend they ran into at a local Dillard's department store. Upon seeing them, she'd turned and walked in the other direction. "If she walked away from us and wouldn't talk to us, then it's known among Scientologists in Clearwater that we're declared." Mike seemed regretful about this.

In their prior, flush life as OTs, Mike and Donna owned a Bellanca

Viking airplane, which they sold to help recoup some of their financial losses. After dinner, Mike took me to the hangar where they had
kept the plane. He'd repurposed it as a storeroom for a floor-to-ceil-
ing assortment of boxes and stacking shelves filled with Scientology
books, tapes, CDs, DVDs, E-meters, and other paraphernalia.

"This is probably one of the best collections ever put together,"
Mike said, handing me a leather-bound, gold-leaf-edged copy of *Dianetics*. He was selling it on eBay. "This is a special edition. You'd
probably get a hundred, maybe a hundred and fifty dollars for something like that." He picked up another book. "This is a transcript of
a taped lecture that Hubbard gave on the *Apollo* in 1968." It forms
the basis of Hubbard's book *Mission into Time*, in which Hubbard
discussed his past life in ancient Greece. I opened the book, with its
fraying dust jacket, and read the inscription: *We hope the reading of
this book is only the first step of a personal voyage of discovery into
the new and vital world religion of Scientology.*

Mike reached over to a shelf and took down an emerald green
Planetary Dissemination Meter, a special-edition E-meter that came
in a silk bag embroidered with gold thread. "My wife owns five of
these. Each one cost ten grand. And that isn't even the most expensive one." He lifted an E-meter plated in twenty-four-karat gold.
"This one is worth twenty thousand dollars." Mike estimated that he
was one of just one hundred people who owned a gold E-meter. He'd
used it to audit body thetans — millions of them, he figured. But the
exorcism and indeed the entire OT experience, he admitted, hadn't
really worked.

"I've had to come to grips with the fact that, yes, I've raised a family, and yes, I've had a successful business and all that, but a lot of my
energy and my impetus as a person was channeled toward Scientology," he said sadly. "It's been a real letdown, letting go of that. But I
just couldn't keep lying to myself any longer."

He looked around in the hangar, where virtually everything was
for sale. "Maybe at some point in human evolution, people will be
able to do some things we can't do now, but you're not going to have
the ability to use every ounce of your intelligence, and develop psychic powers, and be able to leave your body at will. And that's what

we thought when we got into Scientology. We thought we were going to be able to do all these things that the yogis taught, that the maharaja talked about. Immortality. Real freedom. I wanted the certainty that I would live and die and live again, and remember everything, and be okay, forever."

Instead, Mike Henderson had doubts and fears, just like every other mortal. "I don't know what's in store for me down the road, but I know I won't get there with Scientology," he said, with resignation. "And after thirty-four years, and six hundred thousand dollars, that is the saddest thing I can say about my life."

EPILOGUE

What Is True for You

S IX THOUSAND SCIENTOLOGISTS and their guests turned out to christen the new Church of Scientology of Los Angeles on Saturday, April 24, 2010. It was a crystal-clear afternoon, and for the believers who'd gathered at Scientology's West Coast headquarters on Sunset Boulevard — those people for whom the sixteen-foot, illuminated SCIENTOLOGY sign atop the landmark Cedars of Lebanon building is a testament to Scientology's claim of being the "fastest-growing religion of the twenty-first century" — here was the final manifestation of their hard work.

Amid the faceless commercial towers and stucco bungalows installed in this section of East Hollywood, Scientologists and a number of Los Angeles city officials, as well as the Los Angeles County sheriff, Lee Baca, a vocal supporter of Scientology's anti-drug program, gathered before an outdoor stage decorated, as all church functions are, with a huge portrait of L. Ron Hubbard. A dance troupe, attired in glittery top hats and tails, performed a routine. The band played "Hooray for Hollywood." Before the entrance to the new building — which, as everyone there knew, was actually the old building, with a multimillion-dollar facelift and a fresh coat of blue paint — bobbed an arc of blue and gold balloons. "Today marks a milestone step in our planetary crusade to bring on our help on a truly global scale," said David Miscavige, looking out from the podium. Dressed in a sharp navy suit, he commended the Los Angeles Scientologist community for its dedication in creating this new Ideal

Org, the fourth such organization to open in 2010 and the most historic, for here, in 1954, is where the first church of Scientology was born.

Now there are countless churches. From London to Nashville, Las Vegas, Los Angeles, and Washington, D.C. — and also Quebec City, Brussels, Seattle, Pasadena, Mexico City, Madrid, Rome, and Johannesburg — Ideal Orgs have opened throughout the world over the past several years. By the end of 2011, according to the church's predictions, seventy new organizations will be opened or under construction from Atlanta to Battle Creek, Michigan, and from Caracas to Tel Aviv.

In Clearwater, the landmark Fort Harrison Hotel has been given a $40 million upgrade.* Just next door, connected to the Fort Harrison by a glass-enclosed sky bridge, is a facility referred to as the "Mecca" or "Super Power" building, which is still, more than a decade since ground was broken for it, under construction.†

The Super Power building — named for a highly classified, and expensive, new rundown intended to enhance Scientologists' perceptions — is an enormous white Mediterranean revival–style edifice occupying a full square block of downtown Clearwater. The largest building in all of Pinellas County (church officials call it Scientology's "Sistine Chapel"), it stood as an empty shell for six years, while it underwent a number of redesigns. When it is finally completed, at an estimated cost of $90 million, the seven-story, 380,000-square-foot building will have 889 rooms, 142 bathrooms, 2 kitchens, a 1,140-

---

* Because the Fort Harrison serves as both hotel and "religious retreat," all of the renovations, which include gold-leaf crown moldings and a chandelier made of twelve thousand crystals, were installed tax free, under the church's 501c3 tax exemption. This exemption has saved the church roughly $1.2 million in property taxes in Clearwater. Still, Scientology paid $800,000 in property taxes on nonreligious, revenue-generating property in 2008, which church officials maintain makes the Church of Scientology the largest single property taxpayer in the city, as well as the largest property owner.

† As it is recognized as a crucial partner in the city's downtown development scheme, the church has so far been spared the collection of more than $300,000 in liens that has been levied against the church by the city of Clearwater over Scientology's "Mecca" building.

seat dining room, an indoor running track and sculpture garden, and 2 Scientology museums. The crowning touch will be a two-story illuminated Scientology cross that, perched atop a fifteen-story tower, will shine across the city of Clearwater like a beacon.

What this says about the church, according to its leaders, is that Scientology is a growing, vital movement — far from the dying organization its detractors contend it has become. "It certainly creates this incredible illusion of success and expansion," conceded its onetime finance officer Mat Pesch. "But it's like the housing market of 2005 — 'Things have never looked better.'"

But behind this façade, say people like Pesch, members are fleeing the organization in droves. How many? "This is as hard to estimate as it is to count how many people are 'in' Scientology, as it depends entirely on your definition of 'in,'" said one former senior church official. Perhaps forty thousand people have contributed to the IAS, Mike Rinder and other ex-officials noted. But indeed millions — perhaps even Scientology's current figure of eleven million — may be counted as Scientologists if, as the church does, you include in that number everyone who has ever read a Hubbard book or signed up for an introductory service. I myself, having once bought a book on Dianetics and completed an auditing session, am by that measure a "Scientologist."

The truth, as I noted at the beginning of this book, is not an easy thing to discern when it comes to the Church of Scientology. One thing is clear, however: for all of the charges leveled against the church by its current defectors, similar, if not worse, allegations were leveled against it in the past.

Yet throughout its history, Scientology has shown a remarkable ability to both survive scandal and deflect many hard questions. For the church to do that today will be daunting, given the breadth of negative information about it available on the Internet. But it may not be impossible.

Over the past decade, the church has been notably proactive with regard to what was until recently a largely untapped market: African Americans. This happened thanks in part to the late musician Isaac Hayes, a Scientologist and passionate advocate of Hubbard's study technology, who started a number of small storefront tutoring programs to help inner-city youth. Early in 2000, Hayes met with Marty Rathbun, then the inspector general of the RTC, and proposed that the church consider a new financial strategy to make Scientology more affordable, and thus accessible, to the black community.

As Rathbun later wrote of the meeting, Hayes struck both an idealistic and pragmatic note. If Scientology's management was averse to making Scientology affordable to poor people on a simple humanitarian level, then perhaps it might consider how such an investment might pay off. "All that is hip and cool comes from the black ghetto," he told Rathbun. From a marketing perspective, Scientology was "shooting itself in the foot" by ignoring the black community. "Help Black America," Hayes said, "and you help yourself."

Miscavige seized upon this idea — less for idealistic reasons than for the prospect of Scientology becoming "hip," according to Rathbun — and three years later announced plans to open two new Ideal Orgs: one in Harlem and another in the Inglewood section of South Central Los Angeles.

For the next half dozen years, Scientology greatly stepped up efforts to reach out to the black community, notably through its ministers, courting such prominent leaders as the Reverend Johnny Ray Youngblood, who is the former head of the ten-thousand-member St. Paul Community Baptist Church in Brooklyn, New York. At Flag in June 2010, the church sponsored the three-day Clear African Americans awards banquet and convention, which included a seminar on how to disseminate to African Americans and a session called "Religious Influence in Black Life and How to Help Religious People Reach for LRH Tech." Guest speakers included Alfreddie Johnson Jr., a Baptist minister and the founder and executive director of the World Literacy Crusade, a Scientology-backed tutoring program based in Compton, California, and Tony Muhammad from the Nation of Islam.

Louis Farrakhan, the founder of the Nation of Islam, was a recipient of a Scientology Friends of Mankind award in 2006, cosponsored by the Church of Scientology and Ebony Awakenings, an African American nonprofit organization with ties to the church. Since then,

Farrakhan has become notably enamored of Hubbard's philosophies, promoting Scientology's drug awareness and literacy programs and embracing its management technology. The Nation of Islam now has a national and regional "org board." It has also held Dianetics training seminars for its followers. In August 2010, the Nation held one such seminar in Rosemont, Illinois, at which Farrakhan announced that this training would soon be mandatory for every leader of the Nation's U.S. and international operations.*

Farrakhan did not, however, mention the key terms associated with the brand — *Scientology, Dianetics, L. Ron Hubbard* — an irony for a church that has spent so much money and human capital promoting itself and its name. But Miscavige, nothing if not pragmatic, would surely approve this tactic if it served to drive up Scientology's enrollment statistics, just as he has appeared to endorse the quiet ways that Scientology-sponsored front organizations are now disseminating Scientology's message into society.

Over the past decade or so, Scientologists have forged bonds with state and local lawmakers in cities across the United States, some of whom may not be fully aware of the Scientology connection. One example is the church's close ties to the National Foundation of Women Legislators, which counts more than eight hundred members in state and federal government. Since the late 1990s, Scientologists have held key positions in the organization, which they have used to reach out to lawmakers on issues pertaining to drugs and social reform, notably psychiatry.

In the spring of 2010, this link became notably clear after it was revealed that the Nevada Republican Sharron Angle, a Tea Party candidate for the U.S. Senate and a member of the NFWL, had backed a bill to implement a Hubbard-inspired drug rehabilitation and re-

---

* Whether the black community will truly take to Scientology is anyone's guess. Proselytizing to the poor through missionary efforts and other activities is the work of modern churches. Scientology, however, is a corporation; the sustainability of its connection with Farrakhan or any other black leader will ultimately rest on whether such leaders are willing to embrace Scientology's Bridge to Total Freedom, which is a pay-as-you-go endeavor.

form program known as Second Chance in Nevada state prisons. The president of Second Chance, Joy Westrum, sat on the NFWL board and had reportedly been instrumental in linking Second Chance, which uses the Purification Rundown, with a drug awareness program known as Shoulder to Shoulder, which has nothing to do with Scientology but happens to be supported by the NFWL.

Angle, a Southern Baptist, was clearly enamored of Second Chance, appearing in a promotional video for the program. Angle also became an advocate of CCHR's agenda — though she did not publicly endorse CCHR — and in 2001 and 2003 tried to introduce legislation that would prohibit school nurses or psychologists (though not licensed physicians) to require that certain students take psychotropic drugs like Ritalin. These efforts failed, but in 2003, Angle did manage to convince the Nevada senator John Ensign to introduce a similar bill in Congress. (According to the *Las Vegas Sun*, Angle's website at one point contained a reference, later scrubbed, to her partnering with actresses Jenna Elfman and Kelly Preston, who joined her in lobbying Ensign.)

"The Church of Scientology has been excellent at taking well-established social problems and capitalizing on them for its own good," noted the Canadian sociologist Stephen Kent, who has studied Scientology's tactics and practices for twenty years. The devastation caused by Hurricane Katrina, for example, provided Applied Scholastics — along with many other for-profit educational systems — with the opportunity to introduce Hubbard's study technology into the schools, and it was highly successful at implementing the program in one middle school in Baton Rouge, Louisiana, which was notorious for its poor performance record. Similarly, in Washington, D.C., Applied Scholastics International is now one of twenty-nine tutoring services listed in the Title I Supplemental Educational Services Guide provided to parents of children attending D.C.'s failing public schools.

The attacks of 9/11 also gave Scientologists a chance to introduce Hubbard's Purification Rundown to skeptical New Yorkers, and first responders continue to receive help from the New York Rescue Workers Detoxification Project, which critics decry is Narconon by another name. WISE has a number of management consultancy groups that specialize in teaching small business owners L. Ron Hubbard's management technology—indeed, Mike Henderson's wife, Donna, was introduced to Scientology through a WISE-affiliated company that had promised to help her better manage her veterinary practice.

Where Scientology has not been wary of using its name has been in its humanitarian work. After the Haiti earthquake of January 12, 2010, for example, teams of Scientology missionaries, known as "volunteer ministers," flocked to Port-au-Prince, where they established a semi-permanent base, along with several other relief organizations such as Catholic Relief Services and Doctors Without Borders. Wearing the signature yellow T-shirts that identified them as members of the Church of Scientology's volunteer minister program, they brought food, water, medical supplies, and also plentiful Scientology literature. They served as surgical assistants and orderlies at the makeshift hospitals set up in the wake of the disaster, and also offered their own holistic healing techniques, known as "touch assists," to wounded children.

John Travolta flew his private plane to the island, bringing with him a team of doctors, more volunteer ministers, and a reported six tons of ready-to-eat military rations and medical supplies. The project won Travolta, and Scientology, tremendous media coverage. And, as with every church initiative, Scientologists were encouraged to donate to the cause. "We need to get as much Scientology technology into the hands of the Haitian people," noted one fundraising letter promising members that a $3,000 gift or more would win the donor a "very special commendation" in their ethics file.

The appeal likened the tragedy in Haiti to the attacks of September 11, 2001, which Miscavige had described as a "wake-up call" to Scientologists to proselytize.

Since leaving Scientology, Marty Rathbun has become the chief thorn in David Miscavige's side. On his blog, and in several key interviews with the *St. Petersburg Times,* CNN, and other media, he has railed against Miscavige's policies and accused him of human rights abuses. But Rathbun is still a Scientologist, as are a number of former Int staffers mentioned in this book, among them Dan Koon, Steve Hall, and Mike Rinder. They are part of a new "Independent Scientology" movement: people who've remained true to the original theories and teachings of L. Ron Hubbard, though not to the current management of the church.

Such splintering is not unusual for religions — Protestantism, after all, was originally a splinter movement — and indeed, dissension has been a hallmark of Scientology since its earliest days, when Dianeticists like Helen O'Brien split with Hubbard over the very creation of a religious movement called Scientology. In the 1980s, the so-called Free Zone movement attracted a few thousand members but was ultimately hounded out of existence — ironically, by Rathbun and the church's legal department. Now Rathbun's own movement (which is largely, but not entirely, comprised of former Sea Org members) is facing similar attacks leveled by the Church of Scientology, which claims, among other things, that Rathbun, not Miscavige, was responsible for the culture of violence that developed on the base.

After leaving the Sea Org, Rathbun moved to south Texas, where he spent several years staying assiduously under the radar. Many former Scientologists, including Marc and Claire Headley, believed he was dead. Then, in 2008, he emerged, posting on an ex-Scientologist message board that he was open for business as an auditor. Since then, hundreds of former church loyalists have reportedly availed themselves of his services at his Corpus Christi home.

But Rathbun's "church," if it could be called that, is still largely a virtual church, located on his website, where the former RTC inspector general sermonizes on everything from David Miscavige's abusiveness to the inspiration he draws from the rapper Nas, who, on his album *Hip Hop Is Dead* criticized the music industry — and America — for, as Rathbun saw it, "degraded values."* Rathbun similarly

---

* Nas himself never used this term. In an interview shortly before his album was released, in October 2006, the rapper explained, "When I say 'Hip-hop is dead,' basically America is dead . . . There is no political voice. Music is dead . . . Our way of thinking is dead, our commerce is dead. Everything in this society has been done." See Shaheen Reid, "Nas Previews 'Hip Hop Is Dead . . . the N,'" MTV.com, October 10, 2006.

judged Miscavige's church to be degraded. Indeed, he has likened himself, in vague terms, to Martin Luther, challenging a corrupt and megalomaniacal pope.

Such tactics have their price, and since the summer of 2009, when Rathbun gave several lengthy interviews to the *St. Petersburg Times,* he has been hounded by private investigators. "My wife and I can't even have a quiet meal at the local Chuck Wagon without some[one] plopping down beside us, straining his ear," Rathbun wrote on his blog in September 2010. His home, he said, is under constant surveillance, and investigators have dug into his personal life. One of them, Rathbun claimed, has suggested to authorities that Rathbun was somehow involved in the 1981 murder of his brother, Bruce, a charge he unequivocally denied. "I joined Scientology for the sole purpose of helping my troubled brother," Rathbun has said.

Marc and Claire Headley too have been followed by church-funded P.I.'s, although for different reasons. The Headleys, who disavowed Scientology, sued the Church of Scientology in 2009 for violations of labor law, human trafficking, and forced abortions. On August 5, 2010, the suits were dismissed by the U.S. district judge Dale Fischer, who ruled that as the ministerial arm of the church, the Sea Organization was protected by the First Amendment. "Inquiry into these allegations would entangle the court in the religious doctrine of Scientology and the doctrinally motivated practices of the Sea Org," Judge Fischer wrote.

In response to the ruling, the Scientology spokesman Tommy Davis said succinctly, "Scientology wins."

The Church of Scientology in the twenty-first century may be very different from the therapy group L. Ron Hubbard founded in 1954, but its core tenets have not changed. Scientologists continue to see tax collectors and government officials as "criminal elements," largely because of Hubbard's belief that these groups take money from the public and deliver nothing in return. They view journalists with distrust and disdain as "merchants of chaos" and believe that psychiatrists, in cahoots with drug companies like Eli Lilly and GlaxoSmithKlein, are part of a broad, government-endorsed, global conspiracy to subjugate the human race. Scientology continues to use the legal system as a weapon, just as Hubbard intended; its lawsuits aim to "harass and discourage" as well as, in myriad cases, "ruin" its opponents utterly: since the Operation Snow White investigation of the late 1970s, the U.S. government has been loath to investigate the Church of Scientology despite numerous charges of wrongdoing, ranging from human rights abuse to financial corruption. According to several reports, the FBI is currently investigating Scientology over the abuse allegations made by numerous Sea Org staff; the agency is also reportedly investigating David Miscavige for "inurement," or allegations that he has personally enriched himself with church funds.

A fiercely doctrinaire religion, Scientology has always required that its adherents follow L. Ron Hubbard's edicts to the letter. Dissent or opposition to any of Hubbard's views or technologies has never been tolerated. Throughout the church's history, those who challenged Hubbard's authority, including several early members of his Sea Organization, were immediately cast out. Debating church tenets in any context that would foster the free exchange of ideas and, ultimately, adaptation has never been looked upon favorably. While members are expected to take responsibility for one another — which would include reporting abusive Sea Org members, as Natalie Walet's mother once did — comporting oneself in any way that could be seen as contrary to church goals, including expressing curiosity about other philosophies, or about people or aspects of life that might be independent of the church's immediate purview, is considered subversive: punishable, in its most egregious cases, by excommunication.

Scientology, in other words, is and has always been a fundamentalist faith. And like other fundamentalist groups, it will have its factions and its apostates. Whether it will endure in spite of that rests on whether its basic mission — to "clear" the planet and thus create a Scientology world — remains vital to its flock, and to their children.

After Kendra Wiseman left Scientology in 2000, she spent a few years in Los Angeles, searching for meaning. Her passing interest in Wicca was over; now she explored Kabbalah, Buddhist meditation, yoga, and Pilates. She worked for Food Not Bombs, took part in anarchist conventions, protested the impending war in Iraq, and tried to become obsessed with various rock-and-roll bands. Nothing filled the void left by her abandonment of the church. "One of the most addictive things about Scientology is the constant feeling that you are part of the Universal Struggle," she later wrote in an essay, "Growing Up a Scientologist." This feeling is not unique to her; it is an integral feature of the movement's success. "You *personally* are giving the universe real hope . . . simply by existing, by the mere fact that you are Moving Up the Bridge." A science fiction fan, Kendra compared L. Ron Hubbard to Yoda and everyone else she knew to Luke Skywalker. "Imagine feeling that big, that important, that powerful every day of your life," she said. "I challenge anyone to look into their heart of hearts and tell me that if they ever found a cause that they considered worthy, as we considered that cause worthy, that they wouldn't join it."

Now, Kendra realized, leaving Scientology was about much more than simply deciding not go to church or use language developed by L. Ron Hubbard. It was about learning to live in a world that hadn't in some way been designed by L. Ron Hubbard. In 2004, having dropped out of Delphi and gotten a GED, Kendra went to college. She chose a school as far away as she could imagine: in Beijing, a city where Scientology, like most religions, is outlawed.

From there, she began posting to anti-Scientology websites. The church soon became aware of this, and in the spring of 2006, Kendra's name was entered onto what she called a church "blacklist" of Scientology critics. As a result, her parents disconnected from her. "They have abandoned me here," she wrote me from China. "But it's okay," she added. "I'm doing fine."

She'd become a writer and a web designer. Warily, she continued to post her thoughts on anti-Scientology message boards. Then, in January 2008, Kendra and many other former Scientologists were given a tremendous boost by a loose affiliation of Internet hackers, free-speech advocates, and critics who, calling themselves "Anonymous," began attacking Scientology websites and holding large anti-Scientology rallies in cities around the world. Emboldened by the safety in numbers on the Internet and at the rallies, Kendra and two friends, Jenna Miscavige Hill, a niece of David Miscavige, and Astra Woodcraft, the daughter of one of Lisa McPherson's former caretakers, launched Ex-Scientology Kids, a website offering "non-judgmental support for those who are still in Scientology" as well as "discussion and debate for those who've already left." Their motto: "I was born. I grew up. I escaped."

But Kendra hadn't spoken to her parents in more than two years. "I write them letters sometimes," she told me in an e-mail. "I haven't heard from them in so long, writing the letters is like writing in a diary, or talking to myself." She had recently gotten engaged and was planning her wedding, which she knew her family wouldn't attend. "I don't hate them. I don't resent them. I don't want to see them punished, or forced to not be Scientologists, or anything like that. I just want to talk to them again." If she could say one thing to her family, "I'd tell them I love them. I wish they'd given me a chance to show that I've grown up, and that I'm happy."

A few months later, these sentiments, which Kendra posted on Ex-Scientology Kids, abruptly disappeared from the site. By the end of 2008, Kendra's name had also disappeared from that website, save one small reference, which identified her as a founder. Scientology had not forced this to happen; Kendra herself had decided to do it.

As it turned out, her parents had attended her wedding after all. Afterward, the family agreed to come to a sort of détente. Kendra would stop publicly voicing her opposition to church policies, which would make it easier for her parents to keep her in their lives. Both parties would maintain their own views, but they simply wouldn't talk about them. "I guess it's like don't ask, don't tell," Kendra told me. "We basically agreed that the only way it would work out was if we totally kept Scientology out of each other's lives."

If the Church of Scientology — not Scientology as a philosophy, but the church as an institution — is to survive, it will have to find a way to reconcile itself, and its policies, with people like Kendra Wiseman. Reform is not an idea that sat well with L. Ron Hubbard, who preached that Scientology was the only way out of the maze of the human condition, and, moreover, that its message and practices could be delivered only through Scientology organizations or individuals controlled by them and licensed to provide "100 percent standard tech." But reform may nonetheless be what is needed. "LRH's real mission was to teach people to look for themselves: into themselves, into others, into the world around them," said Dan Koon, who is one of a number of former Scientologists who believe that Hubbard's original philosophy differed vastly from the policies and ideology imposed by his organization. Because of this, Koon estimated that there may now be more people practicing Scientology outside the organized church than inside.

Those people have had to make a choice: should they speak out and be declared heretics or keep silent and maintain their ties with family and friends? It is a bitter and, for many, an impossible choice, and because of it, the Church of Scientology, controlled as it is by authoritarian and image-conscious leaders who appear to have invested far more in the look than the substance of the faith, may not, as its detractors predict, survive as it exists today.

I have no doubt, however, that for as long as people yearn for the answers to eternal questions, as well as to their own immediate problems, some vestiges of L. Ron Hubbard's philosophy will remain, provided the movement's second and third generations lead the way.

Natalie Walet, for instance, has stayed true to Scientology, and to the organized church. She is also applying to law schools. On her list: Stanford, Georgetown, Columbia, Tulane, and the University of Michigan. While she waits, she is living in Tampa, working as a waitress, and taking Scientology courses at Flag. "I go there every week," she says. "I love it there."

Which is not to say that Natalie is unaware of Scientology's problems. Like many young Scientologists, she has broken church rules and gone on the Internet to read the OT levels and peruse critical websites. Over the past years, she has read all the stories published in the *St. Petersburg Times* detailing the accounts of human rights violations at the Int Base. "I don't doubt that some of those things happened," she said. "I'm well aware of what it's like inside the Sea Org, and there is definitely truth to every bit of bad PR you hear."

On the other hand, she wondered, why did officials let this happen? "All the people who've come out and told the press these things were in a position to do something about it — to change things. Instead, they stood there and watched. Why? It's so beyond what the church — any church — should stand for."

She rejected the defectors' claims that the environment was too corrosive — too "cult-like," in the words of men like Jeff Hawkins and Tom De Vocht — for them to do anything more than take the abuse, and run. "If you know there's a problem, it's your responsibility to fix it — that's what LRH says," she noted. "When you look at the doctrine, it's not all that free-thinking, but the auditing is all *about* freedom of thought. If orders are coming down that you know are wrong, it's your responsibility as a Scientologist to handle them. So it really floors me that people saw DM doing this, *if* he did this, and didn't do anything. Shame on them for not fixing it."

It is a fairly revolutionary thing to say: to shame not only the defectors, but the loyalists; to admit that the overwhelmingly negative reports about Scientology are not all "lies," as Scientology has claimed; to muse on whether or not David Miscavige is guilty — and yet, to still love the church. "I don't look at COB and think he's my Jesus Christ and can never be wrong," said Natalie — though if one were to suggest that LRH did the things Miscavige is accused of doing, she added, "I'd think you're on drugs because I can't imagine a man who was as brilliant as he was, and who wrote what he did, being like that."

Hubbard, by all accounts, *was* to a degree "like that." But twenty-five years since his death, which is two years longer than Natalie has been alive, does it matter? Scientology, like all religions, accepts even grave imperfection as part of the human condition and, like all religions, seeks to transcend it. In Judaism, this is called justice. In Buddhism, it is called seeking nirvana. In Christianity, it is absolution from sin.

In Scientology, the route from flawed to faultless is called "going Clear." Natalie hasn't reached that point as yet; she hopes to. She also hopes the same for the church. "I am a Scientologist because when I read LRH, it helps me. So when I hear these terrible things, it makes me want to stand behind my organization that much more and change it. And I know so many young Scientologists who feel the same way. We are the going to be the new face of Scientology."

Some of these people, she noted, have gone into politics, or medicine. Natalie hopes to become a judge. There are some who've become management consultants. Others have joined the Sea Organization.

"There are as many different kinds of Scientologist as there are different kinds of people," she said. "But you can only change things by changing the way people think or operate; by educating them." That, she believes, is something LRH would highly approve of. "I want to make sure Scientology is the best it can be, and that *we're* the organization *we* want it to be. It's my personal responsibility."

NOTES

Secrecy and control are hallmarks of the Church of Scientology. Writing a book about such an organization thus poses myriad challenges to a journalist trying to construct a truthful narrative. Though the early history of Scientology has been documented, virtually no credible, unbiased books, scholarly or popular, have been written about the past twenty-five years of church history. Also, very few documents pertaining to this period have surfaced publicly because David Miscavige's orders and directives are almost always kept confidential, circulated only to officials at the International Base.

Sourcing for a book like this is particularly difficult, first, because the Church of Scientology harasses critics and defectors who speak about it, and second, because Scientology has a highly effective self-censorship mechanism, in that members must confess their transgressions prior to auditing. As journalists are, by L. Ron Hubbard's definition, "potential trouble sources," unauthorized contact with them is something to which a person would have to confess, and thus members who do speak to reporters almost always do so with the permission of the church.

For example, in 2005 I interviewed Kelly Preston and Kirstie Alley in Clearwater, Florida; in both cases, Scientology's Office of Special Affairs provided them with equipment to record our conversation. In early 2006, I interviewed the actor Doug Dohring and several other young Scientologists in a conference room outfitted with recording devices at Scientology's Mother Church in Los Angeles. Every other Scientologist I have interviewed has been personally chaperoned by at least one and sometimes three church officials. The sole exception was Natalie Walet, who spoke to me freely, on the record, in person, on the telephone, and through e-mails dozens of times over the past few years. I applaud her courage and honesty.

Because of the Church of Scientology's history of harassing and discrediting its critics and defectors, the vast majority of people who leave the church do so quietly. This book began as a magazine assignment for *Rolling Stone* and could not have been completed without the help of a former Scientologist whom I have promised not to name but who has served as my Virgil since the earliest days of my reporting, painstakingly explaining not only Scientology's language, beliefs, practices, and moral codes, but also the mechanisms of control by which the church suppresses or discredits the words of its former members.

I felt it was imperative to this book's credibility that it be based largely on the accounts of "quiet defectors" such as my Virgil: people who had neither sued the church nor spoken publicly about their involvement with Scientology in any way. Finding the right individuals took months. Gaining their trust took just as long. And getting them to agree to go on the record was, in many cases, an almost Herculean task.

One cost of a book like this one is the time it takes to complete. Over the years I was reporting, a number of my sources, emboldened by the Internet, decided to become more public. These include Jeff Hawkins, Marc and Claire Headley, Nancy Many, Steve Hall, Kendra Wiseman, Mark Fisher, Amy Scobee, and several others who, since I first began talking to them, have posted their stories on the Internet and talked to other journalists; Many, Hawkins, Scobee, and Marc Headley have also self-published memoirs about their years in Scientology.

Though I would be remiss in not mentioning this, I must also stress that not a single one of these people had ever spoken publicly prior to my interviewing them, nor had any of them pursued legal action against the church or written a book. Except where specifically noted, all references to these people, their stories, and their quoted words come from my own interviews and conversations with them.

Every bit of information in this book has been checked and cross-checked with multiple sources, and where I have found discrepancies, I have erred on the side of caution and toned down certain accounts whose veracity I do not feel I can comfortably prove. While this book relies almost wholly on named sources, there were a few people who, fearing retribution against themselves and their family members still in Scientology, requested I give them pseudonyms or total anonymity. Those few cases are clearly identified. I am particularly grateful to the Church of Scientology officials who spent time with me during my first year of research. This book benefitted greatly from their tremendous help.

Piecing together the complex history of Scientology is extremely difficult, and I could not have done it without the tremendous expertise and research of others, whose work I will try to acknowledge here. The early history of Scientology has been documented in two highly critical books: Russell Miller's *Barefaced Messiah*, which remains the best and most comprehensive biography of L. Ron Hubbard, and Jon Atack's *A Piece of Blue Sky*, which offers a remarkably thorough insider account of the founding and development of the Scientology movement through the 1980s. Though biased, these books are nonetheless essential reading for anyone interested in Scientology, and taken together they supply excellent insight into the mind of L. Ron Hubbard and the creation of his church.

Helen O'Brien's *Dianetics in Limbo* is regarded as the seminal book on the early Dianetics movement, as is Dr. Joseph Winter's *A Doctor's Report on Dianetics*. Paulette Cooper's *The Scandal of Scientology* was one of the first journalistic examinations of Scientology and is particularly helpful in describing the movement in the 1960s, as are George Malko's *The Now Religion* and Stephen Kent's *From Slogans to Mantras: Social Protest and Religious Conversion in the Late Vietnam Era.* For a sociological analysis of Scientology, Roy Wallis's *The Road to Total Freedom* is invaluable for its objectivity, though it covers Scientology only through the 1970s; more recently, J. Gordon Melton's *The Church of Scientology*, Stephen Kent's *From Slogans to Mantras* and his numerous studies of Scientology's Rehabilitation Project Force, and James Lewis's collection of scholarly essays, *Scientology,* provide the best, and right now some of the only, academic writing on the movement. I also found tremendous insight and much-needed interpretation of the Church of Scientology's practices and protocols in Cyril Vosper's *The Mind Benders* and Margery Wakefield's *Understanding Scientology,* first published in 1991 by the Coalition of Concerned Citizens, and later as an e-book (www.religio.de/books/wakefield/us.html).

David Halberstam's *The Fifties* and Stephen Whitfield's *The Culture of the Cold War* helped me understand the sociopolitical environment in which Scientology was born, as did Hugh Urban's excellent paper "Fair Game: Secrecy, Security, and the Church of Scientology in Cold War America." I was hugely grateful to those who worked with L. Ron Hubbard who suggested I read Vance Packard's *The Hidden Persuaders* and Napoleon Hill's *Think and Grow Rich* to glean an understanding of the business psychology mindset of the 1950s and how that may have played into Hubbard's thinking. Scientology has been called by more than one critic the McDonald's of religion — I found this to be true, not only in terms of its real estate strategy but also in its overall franchising concept. To gain a better understanding of franchising, I found John F. Love's *McDonald's: Behind the Arches* to be a fascinating corporate study.

Phillip Jenkins's *Mystics and Messiahs* and Anthony Storr's *Feet of Clay* are excellent references on the development of cults and new religious movements, as well as the personality traits of gurus. I would have been lost without Jon Krakauer's *Under the Banner of Heaven*, which provided both inspiration and in many ways an ideal model for how to tell the story of a little-understood religious movement. George Pendle's *Strange Angel: The Otherworldly Life of John Whiteside Parsons* was invaluable in providing research into the life of John Whiteside "Jack" Parsons and the culture of physics in southern California. For historical and sociological perspectives on the birth and development of Los Angeles in the first half of the twentieth century, my first and best resource was the journalist Carey McWilliams's *Southern California: An Island of the Land;* I also appreciated Mike Davis's *City of Quartz* and Kevin Starr's *The Dream Endures: California Enters the 1940s,* which devotes a chapter to Pasadena and Caltech.

Some of the very best coverage of the Church of Scientology has appeared in the *St. Petersburg Times,* the *New York Times,* and the *Los Angeles Times* — Pulitzer Prize winners all, for their reporting on the church in the 1980s and 1990s. Additionally, the investigative reporter Richard Behar did some of the bravest and most groundbreaking reporting on the move-ment, first for *Fortune,* and then for *Time* magazine. The reporting of jour-nalists at the *Boston Herald* and the *Wall Street Journal* provided great help in my research into the Church of Scientology's social betterment organiza-tions and its IRS tax battle and secret agreement; the Lisa McPherson case might have never come to light were it not for the reporting of Cheryl Wal-drip from the *Tampa Tribune,* who broke the story of Lisa's death in 1996. I also owe a tremendous debt of gratitude to Robert Farley at the *St. Peters-burg Times* for his continued assistance and research, and to his colleagues, Tom Tobin and Joe Childs, whose 2009 and 2010 reporting on abuse at the International Base confirmed many of the stories I had been told by former staffers and officials for several years prior. The thoroughness of the *Times*'s recent coverage, particularly the paper's video interviews with Marty Rath-bun, which were posted on the paper's website, were invaluable to me in piecing together the very complex story of Scientology's current leadership.

Though Rathbun, for reasons known only to him, chose not to be inter-viewed for this book, he provided a wealth of information on the church's recent history and the mindset and behavior of David Miscavige on his blog, Moving On Up a Little Higher (markrathbun.wordpress.com). Simi-larly, the former Scientology spokesman Mike Rinder, whom I interviewed at length early in my reporting, has also helped fill in those blanks through his frequent posts and, while still a church official, was hugely helpful in shining a light on some of the more positive aspects of Scientology, L. Ron Hubbard, and the movement's early history.

Finally, L. Ron Hubbard's own books, policy letters, and other directives informed almost every page of this book and were made available to me through a variety of former Scientologists, through the Church of Scientol-ogy itself, and through the assistance of numerous researchers, notably Pro-fessors Stephen A. Kent at the University of Alberta and J. Gordon Melton and the J. Gordon Melton Collection at the University of California, Santa Barbara, Library's Special Collections; I also appreciate the work of the re-searcher Chris Owen and, most crucially, Gerry Armstrong, whose tremen-dous contribution to the historical record of Scientology I have detailed in the notes for chapter 2.

Though there has been a profound lack of unbiased scholarship on Sci-entology, there is plentiful critical information about the church for those who seek it. Dozens if not hundreds of websites, with new ones popping up all the time, are devoted to debunking various aspects of Scientology and critiquing L. Ron Hubbard and David Miscavige. These sites, most of which have been created by former Scientologists or free-speech activists, with names such as Scientology-cult, Scientology Lies, and Operation Clambake, do not pretend to be neutral. Nonetheless, many could be characterized as an independent, if biased, research library: a repository for troves of Scien-tologist documents, newspaper articles, letters, affidavits, and other materials that might otherwise take a researcher months to acquire. Because scans of those documents have been freely posted on these sites, I have turned to many of them as a secondary source of information, keeping in mind their anti-Scientology bias. In every case, I have been extremely careful which documents to use; whenever possible, I acquired the originals or original photocopies of all historical materials.

All quotes are sourced in these notes except in the case of a subject who was interviewed by me and was speaking to me. Unless specified, it should be assumed that all quotes by a single source within a single paragraph come from the same page or document noted.

Scientology's policy letters and bulletins are voluminous, so when citing them in the notes, I have used the church's standard abbreviations. Hubbard Communication Office Bulletins and Policy Letters are referred to by the acronym HCO.

Introduction

The description of the New York Church of Scientology, and the people who work there, comes from my own observation and notes from several visits I made to the organization in July 2005 while on assignment for *Rolling Stone*. In order to get a sense of what a newcomer might experience upon simply walking into a Scientology organization, I concealed my identity as a journalist (though not my name or any other important details of my life) and was thus availed of the typical "orientation package" offered to newcomers: lectures, films, and introductory auditing. As this would amount to an "undercover" bit of research, I could not take notes while in the New York church. However, I wrote copious notes just after leaving it each day, recalling every part of my conversations and other important information gleaned from my interaction with Scientologist greeters and registrars. Many of these observations first appeared in an article I wrote for *Rolling Stone*, "Inside Scientology," in February 2006.

The statistics on Scientologists' previous religious affiliations found in this chapter come from Scientology's primer *What Is Scientology?* and from the church's website, www.scientology.org.

page

xiii　*In Germany, where the church:* Kate Connolly, "German Ministers Try to Ban Scientology," *The Guardian*, December 8, 2007.
　　in May 2008, for example: Anil Dawar, "Teenager Faces Prosecution for Calling Scientology 'Cult,'" *The Guardian*, May 20, 2008.
　　one outspoken member: Anne Wright, "Senator Nick Xenophon Brands Scientology a 'Criminal Organization,'" *Herald Sun*, November 18, 2009. Xenophon, an independent senator from South Australia, began receiving letters from former Scientologists after ques-

tioning the organization's tax-exempt status during a 2009 television interview. Those letters, he said, detailed "a worldwide pattern of abuse and criminality." Since then he has become one of the most vocal critics of Scientology, repeatedly calling for inquiries into the church's activities and the repeal of its tax exemption. In September 2010, at his urging, Australia's Senate initiated an investigation into Scientology and other nonprofit organizations; it then created a committee to ensure that such groups deserve their charity status. (Its work is ongoing at the time of writing.)

xiv   *"I don't think that's going"*: "Scientology: Former Scientologist," *The Current*, Canadian Broadcasting Corporation, October 30, 2009.

xv   Roughly a quarter of them: Church of Scientology, *What Is Scientology?*, p. 463.

xvi   *"If it isn't written"*: Hubbard, "The Hidden Data Line," HCO Policy Letter, April 16, 1965.

"growing faster now than": Church of Scientology, "Frequently Asked Questions," www.scientologynews.org/faq/frequently-asked -questions-introduction.html.

1. The Founder

The true story of L. Ron Hubbard was unknown to Scientologists, and to the public at large, until the early 1980s, when a onetime Hubbard acolyte and church archivist named Gerald Armstrong left Scientology after eleven years in the church's inner sanctum, taking with him a trove of private letters, journals, files, and other materials that, as he said, "documented that Hubbard had lied about virtually every part of his life, including his education, degrees, family, explorations, military service, war wounds, scientific research, the efficacy of his 'sciences' — Dianetics and Scientology — along with the actions and intentions of the organizations he created to sell and advance these 'sciences.'"

This material, deposited with several attorneys for safekeeping, became the basis of a 1984 lawsuit, *Church of Scientology of California v. Gerald Armstrong*, brought by Scientology against its former archivist for theft and breach of trust. (The church did not dispute the authenticity of the documents themselves.) During the course of the trial many pages of previously unknown biographical data about L. Ron Hubbard, including his infamous affirmations, were read into the record, ultimately helping to form a counternarrative to the official life of Hubbard that the church promulgates.

This chapter, which covers the first forty years of L. Ron Hubbard's life, relies heavily on Jon Atack's *A Piece of Blue Sky* and Russell Miller's *Barefaced Messiah*, both of which drew extensively on the Armstrong materials. Unless otherwise noted, quotes from Hubbard's childhood journals come largely from *Barefaced Messiah*. To supplement this biographical research,

I did my own interviews with Armstrong about these materials, and interviewed him at length about the authenticity of the affirmations, which Scientology viewed as confidential. I also used documents presented in the 1984 Armstrong case. In addition, and where at all possible, I quote from Hubbard's own writing, some of which the Church of Scientology has made available on its websites www.aboutlronhubbard.org and www.ronhubbard.org prior to the spring of 2010; it is also published in Scientology's series of *Ron* magazines (Bridge Publications, 1991).

For background on the life and times of John Whiteside Parsons, I referred primarily to George Pendle's excellent biography, *Strange Angel,* which offers a detailed portrait of L. Ron Hubbard's relationship with Parsons and the underground world of Aleister Crowley's Ordo Templi Orientis in Los Angeles, as well as an excellent analysis of the development of aeronautics and the inspiration it took from science fiction. I also drew from Parsons's own writing, notably "The Book of Babalon," or "Liber 49," available online at hermetic.com/wisdom/lib49.html. Unless otherwise noted, all quotations from Parsons regarding Hubbard's behavior are from these sources. I gained invaluable insight into the Western esoteric tradition that gave birth to Crowley's Thelema, and a fascinating explanation of Scientology as a religion with esoteric roots, from Professor J. Gordon Melton of the Department of Religious Studies at the University of California, Santa Barbara, and his archive at the UCSB Special Collection.

The history and development of science fiction as a literary genre has been documented extensively. For background on the pulp fiction world of New York during the 1930s, I turned to Frank Gruber's *The Pulp Jungle,* which gives an excellent portrait of both the key players and the overall scene. Jack Williamson's *Wonder's Child;* Isaac Asimov's *In Memory Yet Green* and *I.Asimov: A Memoir;* L. Sprague De Camp's *The Science Fiction Handbook;* and the unparalleled *John Campbell Letters* give a more detailed analysis of the science fiction world and its golden age, as well as recollections of L. Ron Hubbard from the late 1930s.

For historical and sociological perspective on the birth and development of Los Angeles, Mike Davis's *City of Quartz* and Carey McWilliams's *Southern California: An Island of the Land* were outstanding resources, as were Kenneth Starr's *The Dream Endures: California Enters the 1940s* and Harry Carr's *Los Angeles: City of Dreams.* Complete publication information for all books mentioned here is given in the selected bibliography.

4   *When I was very young":* L. Ron Hubbard, "A First Word on Adventure," from "Letters and Journals, Early Years of Adventure," circa 1943, www.lronhubbard.org.
    "a lovely, vicious lonely thing": Ibid.
    "a deeply conservative plodder": Russell Miller, *Barefaced Messiah: The True Story of L. Ron Hubbard,* p. 97.

5   *"as if he were a well-traveled man"*: Ibid., p. 44.
"which had a faculty for ground-looping": Hubbard, "Tailwind Willies," *The Sportsman Pilot*, 1931.
L. Ron "Flash" Hubbard: "Controversial Author–Stunt Flier Landed in Gratis 52 Years Ago," *Preble County News*, July 21, 1983. Reprint of original article, "Here and There," September 17, 1931.
"adventurous young men": "The Caribbean Expedition," 1932 advertisement, "The Caribbean Motion Picture Expedition," www.lronhubbard.org/biography/adventures-explorations/caribbean-motion-picture-expedition.htm.

6   *"worst trip I ever made"*: Jon Atack, *A Piece of Blue Sky*, p. 62.
a crucial bit of wisdom: Hubbard claimed to have met Thompson, a navy surgeon and psychoanalyst, at the age of twelve while sailing with his mother through the Panama Canal en route to Washington, D.C. The story of Hubbard's friendship with Thompson, including his assertion that Thompson took him to the Library of Congress as a boy and explained Freudian theory to him, is part of Scientology lore, first asserted during Hubbard's lecture of October 18, 1958, "The Story of Dianetics and Scientology."
"If there is anyone in the world": Ibid.
"a bit too long on the ambrosia": L. Sprague De Camp, "Elron of the City of Brass," *Fantastic*, August 1975; also "Modern Imaginative Fiction," in *The Science Fiction Handbook*, p. 93.
"I seem to have a sort of personal": Letter from Hubbard to Margaret Ann "Polly" Hubbard, 1938. Polly was also known as "Skipper."

7   *"He had been in the United States Marines"*: Frank Gruber, *The Pulp Jungle*, p. 80.

8   *"one of aviation's most distinguished"*: *The Sportsman Pilot*, editorial by H. Latane Lewis, July 1934.
"Corn flakes could": This letter, addressed to "General Manager, The Kellogg Company," was posted by the Church of Scientology on www.lronhubbard.org, in a section containing some of Hubbard's literary correspondence.

9   *"I have high hopes of smashing"*: Letter from Hubbard to Polly Hubbard, 1938.
"We were all exploring": Jack Williamson, *Wonder's Child*, p. 131.

10   *"Given one slim fact"*: Hubbard, "Search for Research," www.lronhubbard.org.
"Some thought him a Fascist": De Camp, "Elron of the City of Brass," and *The Science Fiction Handbook*, p. 94.
"offer my services in whatever": Letter from Hubbard to the War Department, September 1, 1939.

11   *with a propensity for having:* Notice of Hubbard's posting to U.S. Naval Training School (Military Government), January 17, 1945, www.cs.cmu.edu/~dst/Cowen/warhero/1944/441004B.gif.

"*The Great Era of Adventure*": Hubbard, "A First Word on Adventure."

12   "*conjured into existence*": Carey McWilliams, *Southern California: An Island in the Sun*, p. 134.

13   "*Do what thou wilt*": Aleister Crowley, *The Book of the Law*, p. 9.

15   "*He was a fascinating storyteller*": Russell Miller's interview with Nieson Himmel, August 14, 1986, www.cs.cmu.edu/~dst/Library/Shelf /miller/interviews/himmel.htm.
     "*From some of his experiences*": Letter from Parsons to Aleister Crowley, January 1946, cited in John Carter, *Sex and Rockets: The Occult World of Jack Parsons*, p. 106.

16   "*the most profitable ecclesiastic*": H. L. Mencken, *The American Mercury*, April 1928.
     "*good friend*": Hubbard, "Conditions of Space/Time/Energy," Philadelphia Doctorate Course cassette tape #18 5212C05.

17   "*crippled and blinded*": Hubbard, "My Philosophy," 1965; also Hubbard, *Ron — Letters and Journals*, published by the Church of Scientology, 1997.
     No evidence has been found: The Scientology researcher Chris Owens has written extensively on Hubbard's war record, using Hubbard's navy records and other data acquired through the Freedom of Information Act. Most of his findings are contained in the e-book *Ron the War Hero: L. Ron Hubbard and the U.S. Navy, 1941–50*, www.cs.cmu .edu/~dst/Cowen/warhero/contents.htm.
     "*Have served at sea*": Telegram from Hubbard to Chief of U.S. Naval Personnel, October 12, 1945, www.cs.cmu.edu/~dst/Cowen/war hero/1945/451012.gif.

18   "*flood of copy*": Letter from Hubbard to agent Lurton Blassingame, December 29, 1945, as cited in *Ron: Journals and Letters*.
     "*capabilities and crafts*": *Parsons v. Hubbard and Northrup*, Dade County, Florida, July 11, 1946, as cited in George Pendle, *Strange Angel*, p. 267.
     "*writing material*": Letter from Hubbard to Chief of Naval Personnel, file number 113392, April 1, 1946, as cited in Pendle, *Strange Angel*, p. 268.

19   "*near mental and financial collapse*": Letter from Parsons to Aleister Crowley, 1947, as cited in Kenneth Grant, *The Magical Revival*, p. 168.
     "*broke, working the poor-wounded*": Letter from De Camp to Isaac Asimov, August 27, 1946, as cited in Pendle, *Strange Angel*, p. 271.

20   *quietly writing a series:* Hubbard's affirmations have been a point of controversy since they were revealed during the 1984 Armstrong case. During his trial, Armstrong read portions of them into the record, and the Church of Scientology authenticated them. More than fifteen years later, in 2000, Armstrong received an e-mailed copy of the affirmations, which he posted on his website, www.gerryarmstrong.org,

vouching for the authenticity of the document. "I don't have any desire to profit monetarily by posting Hubbard's unpublished affirmations," he noted. "My desire is that these writings help everyone, Scientologist and wog [non-Scientologist], to make informed and better choices about L. Ron Hubbard and Scientology."

2. Dianetics

For the story of the rise and fall of the Dianetics movement, I relied primarily on Helen O'Brien's insider account, *Dianetics in Limbo,* as well as Dr. Joseph A. Winter's *A Doctor's Report on Dianetics* and Martin Gardner's *Fads and Fallacies in the Name of Science,* all cited in the bibliography. Of these three, O'Brien's offers the best personal account of Hubbard's movement, Winter's book provides a more critical analysis, and Gardner's book takes the position of a skeptic. Unless otherwise cited, all references to Winter, including quotations, come from *A Doctor's Report;* all references to Helen O'Brien come from *Dianetics in Limbo,* as do quotations. The account of the Shrine Auditorium event draws from Gardner's *Fads and Fallacies* and from Russell Miller's *Barefaced Messiah.*

For general historical and biographical information on Hubbard, I relied upon Atak's *A Piece of Blue Sky* and Miller's *Barefaced Messiah,* as well as Sara Northrup's account of her marriage as told to the Los Angeles Superior Court during her 1951 divorce proceedings and to the writer and former Scientologist Bent Corydon for his book *L. Ron Hubbard: Messiah or Madman?,* written with Brian Ambry.

For correspondence from Hubbard, I relied on scans of original letters published by the Church of Scientology International at several websites, notably "Ron the Philosopher: The Birth of Dianetics," which is published at www.ronthephilosopher.org. I also received assistance from Gerry Armstrong and Caroline Letkeman, who have published many of Hubbard's letters, speeches, and other communiqués on their website Refund and Reparation (www.carolineletkeman.org).

This chapter also contains numerous statistics and notes on psychiatry and psychotherapy during the 1950s and its role in American society. Unless noted, these come from *The Collected Works of C. G. Jung;* Morton Hunt's *The Story of Psychology;* Lauren Slater's *Opening Skinner's Box;* Jack El-Hai's *The Lobotomist: A Maverick Medical Genius and His Tragic Quest to Rid the World of Mental Illness;* Stephen Whitfield's *The Culture of the Cold War;* and Hugh Urban's article "Fair Game: Secrecy, Security, and the Church of Scientology in Cold War America."

In addition, I relied on a tremendous number of newspaper and magazine stories from the 1950s, notably those that appeared in *Time, Newsweek,* and *Look* magazines, all of which have been cited below or in the bibliography.

22 *"rape women without"*: Letter from Hubbard to Forrest Ackerman, January 13, 1949, carolineletkeman.org/sp/index.php?option=com_content&task=view&id=387&Itemid=116.

Hubbard offered the APA: Letter from Hubbard to the American Psychological Association, April 13, 1949, www.ronthephilosopher.org/phlspher/page16.htm.

The society turned him down: Hubbard also wrote to the American Medical Association, the American Gerontological Association, and the American Psychiatric association, with a similar offer to share his research. He later maintained that the AMA responded with a single word — "Why?" — and that the APA wrote him a curt response: "If it amounts to anything I am sure we will hear of it in a couple of years." From "Ron the Philosopher: The Birth of Dianetics," www.ronthephilosopher.org, by the Church of Scientology International.

24 *"My response to this information"*: Joseph Winter, *A Doctor's Report on Dianetics Theory and Therapy*, www.xenu.net/archive/fifties/e510000.htm.

26 *"Many traumata were so unimportant"*: C. G. Jung: Collected Works, volume 4: *Freud and Psychoanalysis* (1961), "Some Crucial Points in Psychoanalysis," from the Jung-Loy Correspondence, paragraph 582.

"cures and cures without failure": Hubbard, *Dianetics: The Modern Science of Mental Health [DMSMH]*, p. 482.

Hundreds of people: In his original article, "Dianetics," published in the May 1950 issue of *Astounding Science Fiction,* Hubbard wrote that "to date, over two hundred patients have been treated; of those two hundred, two hundred cures have been obtained."

about six thousand psychiatrists: Albert Maisel, "Dianetics: Science or Hoax?" *Look* magazine, December 5, 1950.

Only six hundred or so: Morton Hunt, *The Story of Psychology,* p. 660. This number accounts for "medical" analysts, meaning licensed physicians with psychoanalytic training. In addition, Hunt notes there were "about 500 lay analysts in the country and perhaps a thousand in training in some twenty institutes for physician analysts and a dozen for lay analysts."

27 *"The trail is blazed"*: Hubbard, *DMSMH*, p. 1.

28 *"You are beginning an adventure"*: Ibid., p. 4.

"empirical evidence of the sort": Lucy Freeman, "Psychologists Act Against Dianetics," *New York Times,* September 9, 1950.

twenty to thirty: Hubbard, *DMSMH*, p. 198.

29 *"poor man's psychoanalysis"*: "Poor Man's Psychoanalysis," *Newsweek,* October 16, 1950. The article, addressing the medical community's view of Dianetics, also makes the point that while most physicians "maintain their haughty silence, the dianetics vogue flourishes."

"lunatic revision of Freudian psychology": Williamson, *Wonder's Child*, p. 183.

"I considered it gibberish": Isaac Asimov, *In Memory Yet Green*, p. 587.

"any engram command": Hubbard, *DMSMH*, p. 494.

30   *A five-week course, priced:* All information on prices is derived from "Dianetics: Science or Hoax?" *Look* magazine, December 5, 1950; see also Williamson, *Wonder's Child*, p. 84. The description of the five-week course at the Elizabeth Foundation is drawn from *Look* as well as from "After Hours," *Harper's*, June 1951.

A one-on-one session: Look magazine, December 5, 1950, notes that Dianetics sessions started at $25 per hour; a typical psychiatrist's fee at the time, the article noted, started at $15 per hour.

"fifteen minutes of Dianetics": Williamson, *Wonder's Child*, p. 84.

31   *"a personality, a national celebrity": Los Angeles Daily News,* September 6, 1950, as cited in Russell Miller, *Barefaced Messiah*, p. 162.

"full and perfect recall": Ibid., p. 165.

"I thought he was a great man": Ibid., pp. 182–83.

32   *"You could practically see the AMA"*: Helen O'Brien, *Dianetics in Limbo*, p. 8.

"People had breakdowns": Miller, *Barefaced Messiah*, p. 169.

33   *"Looking back, it is hard"*: Ibid., p. 10.

"I became a Dianetic preclear": Ibid., p. 12.

"It nearly floored my auditor": Ibid., p. 15.

"The violence of that sight": Ibid., pp. 19–20.

34   *"I never was the same again"*: Ibid., p. 20.

Sara Hubbard would later estimate: Sara Northrup Hubbard v. L. Ron Hubbard, filed in Los Angeles Superior Court, April 23, 1951.

One official of the Elizabeth: O'Brien, *Dianetics in Limbo*, p. 27.

By the end of 1950: Atack, *A Piece of Blue Sky*, p. 118.

"The tidal wave of popular interest": O'Brien, *Dianetics in Limbo*, p. vii.

35   *"The only thing I ever saw"*: Ibid., p. 33.

The New Jersey Board: Bulletin of the Hubbard Dianetic Research Foundation, Elizabeth, NJ, January 1951; *Elizabeth Daily Journal,* January 15, 1951, and March 28, 1951.

the head of the famous Menninger: In the *Look* article, which compared "dianetic hocus-pocus" to voodoo, Dr. Will Menninger said of Dianetics: "It can potentially do a great deal of harm. It is obvious that the mathematician-writer has oversimplified the human personality, both as to its structure and function. He has made inordinate and very exaggerated claims in his results." In addition, Dr. Jack A. Dunagin, of the Menninger Foundation, made the point that while patients may experience some temporary relief, "the greatest harm to a person would come, not because of the vicious nature of dianetic therapy, but because . . . it will lead them away from treatment which they may badly need."

resigned from the foundation: Another reason Winter resigned was his frustration that no research was being done at the foundation. Ceppos joined him as support. Campbell, however, did seem to cite money as a key concern. According to Russell Miller (*Barefaced Messiah*, p. 181), "In Campbell's view, Hubbard had become impossible to work with and was responsible for the ruinous finances and complete disorganization throughout the Dianetics movement."

He also accused Ceppos: Letter to the director of the FBI from the special agent in charge of its Newark field office, March 21, 1951, FBI file #100, www.xenu.net/archive/FBI/table.html.

in 1951, Hubbard: Letter from Hubbard to the director of the FBI, Washington, D.C., March 3, 1951, FBI file #89.

36 *"Many manics are delightful":* Miller, *Barefaced Messiah*, p. 175. Miller referred to Klowden by the pseudonym "Barbara Kaye."

"insert a fatal hypo": Ibid., p. 175.

37 *Sara . . . signed a statement:* Bent Corydon and Brian Ambry, *L. Ron Hubbard: Madman or Messiah?*, p. 305. During his research, Corydon wrote Sara a letter, asking her why she'd signed the document. "I thought by doing so he would leave me and Alexis alone," she responded. "It was horrible. I just wanted to be free of him!"

3. The Franchised Faith

For the early history of Scientology, I relied upon the recollections of Jana Daniels and Alan Walter, whom I interviewed personally, as well as Helen O'Brien, as found in her book *Dianetics in Limbo*. For a less subjective view, I relied upon Atack's *A Piece of Blue Sky* and Miller's *Barefaced Messiah*. The Australian *Report of the Board of Enquiry into Scientology*, while certainly not objective, proved to be a quite insightful study of Scientology in Australia, enabling me not only to glean the practices the board found objectionable but also to discern the hatred and fear that Scientology inspired.

I was particularly interested in Scientology's place in Cold War America and found great insight in Stephen J. Whitfield's *The Culture of the Cold War*, as well as Hugh Urban's paper "Fair Game." I also relied on Hubbard's FBI files, accessible through the Freedom of Information Act; his correspondence, made available by Armstrong and Letkeman; and particularly his myriad Hubbard Communication Office (HCO) bulletins and policy letters of 1954–65, which are too many to be mentioned here, but which are cited in the notes and collected in *Technical Bulletins of Dianetics and Scientology* and *The Original LRH Executive Directives*.

Much can be said about Scientology as a business, and for help in understanding Hubbard's overall strategy, I relied upon personal interviews with Hubbard's former aide Ken Urqhart, with Alan Walter, and with the later Scientology executives Chris and Nancy Many, as well as with Sandra Mercer, a longtime Scientologist and onetime church staff member. For fine-grain detail in legal matters, I read articles in the *Washington Post* pertaining to Scientology's lawsuit against that newspaper, concerning violation of trade secrets. To understand Scientology's own view, I read stories on the protection of trade secrets published in the church's magazine *Freedom*.

39   *"important new material"*: O'Brien, *Dianetics in Limbo*, p. 49.
"deep and marvelous insight": Ibid., p. 55.
It was, essentially, a lie detector: Scientologists routinely deny that the E-meter bears any relationship to the lie detector. Nonetheless, like lie detectors, E-meters register the "electrodermal response," or changes in the conductivity of the surface of the skin, in people undergoing emotional stress, conscious or unconscious. Lie detectors, however, are much more sophisticated and also monitor changes in heartbeat and perspiration.
"Knowing How to Know": *What Is Scientology?*, Church of Scientology, 1978 ed.; also "Frequently Asked Questions" at www.scientology .org, which states, "Scientology, which means 'knowing how to know,' is a religion based on the works of L. Ron Hubbard."
"exact anatomy of the human mind": Hubbard, *DMSMH*, p. 590.
"theta beings": Atack, *A Piece of Blue Sky*, p. 129. A full description of "theta beings" can be found in chapters 2 and 3 of Hubbard's *Scientology: A History of Man.*

41   *Hubbard had begun:* "The Story of Dianetics and Scientology," lecture by L. Ron Hubbard, delivered on October 18, 1958.

42   *Even Hubbard's onetime lieutenant:* Charles Platt's interview with Van Vogt, as cited in Charles Platt, *Dream Makers: The Uncommon People Who Write Science Fiction*. In fact, Van Vogt was president of the California Association of Dianetic Auditors.

43   *"Perhaps we could call it":* Letter from Hubbard to Helen O'Brien, April 10, 1953.
"Churches were by far": Stephen J. Whitfield, *The Culture of the Cold War*, pp. 83–84.
the most popular therapist: Ibid., p. 84.
Peale's best-selling book: New York Times Best-Seller List; Publisher's Weekly Best-Seller List.

44   *religious fellowship: The Aberee* (a newsletter published ten times a year from 1954 to 1965 by Dianetics followers Alphia and Agnes Hart), July and August 1954. A later reference to the HASI as a religious fellowship can be found in Hubbard, "Religion," HCO Policy Letter, October 29, 1962.
"Hubbard had learned from": Atack, *A Piece of Blue Sky*, p. 139.

45 *"If advertised products don't have":* Hubbard, HCO Policy Letter, August 14, 1963.

Hubbard instructed one of his: Miller, *Barefaced Messiah*, p. 226. Hubbard also described his "three methods of dissemination," including the "I will talk to anyone" technique, in HCO Operational Bulletin No. 14, January 24, 1956.

A similar ad was used: Hubbard, HCO Operational Bulletin No. 14, January 24, 1956.

Another technique Hubbard advocated: Ibid.

46 *"The law can be used":* "The Scientologist: A Manual on the Dissemination of Material." This text first appeared in Scientology's magazine *Ability* in March 1954 and was later reprinted in Hubbard, *Technical Bulletins of Dianetics and Scientology.*

Congresses could be highly lucrative: Paulette Cooper, *The Scandal of Scientology*, p. 108.

In 1956, the Church of Scientology's gross receipts: Founding Church of Scientology v. U.S. No. 226–61, U.S. Court of Claims, July 16, 1969.

47 *"The prosperity of any organization":* Hubbard, HCO Policy Letter, February 6, 1968.

From the 10 percent tithe: Founding Church of Scientology v. U.S. No. 226–61, July 16, 1969.

"the McDonald's hamburger": Atack, *A Piece of Blue Sky*, p. 138.

48 *"a symbol which assures":* Church attorney Laurence E. Heller, in a transcript of the Mission Holder's Conference, San Francisco, CA, October 17, 1982, as issued by Executive Director Guillaume Lesever, Church of Scientology International, Inc., sc-i-r-s-ology.com/documents/1982-10-17missionholders.html.

"trade secrets": The crux of Scientology's various lawsuits against its critics on the Internet and against such publications as the *Washington Post* has been media publication of its confidential OT (Operating Thetan) doctrine, which Scientology has called one of its "trade secrets." A 1995 article titled "Freedom of Speech at Risk in Cyberspace," in Scientology's *Freedom* magazine (volume 28, issue 1), asks, "When was the last time the formula for Coca-Cola ran in the morning paper?" and goes on to equate the secret soft-drink formula with Scientology's "sacred and confidential religious scriptures," which, it notes, "are also subject to legal protection under copyright and trade secret law." For more information on Scientology's trade secrets argument, see *Religious Technology Center v. Netcom On-Line Communication Services, Inc., 907 F. Supp. 1361* (NDCal. 1995).

"The body is normally sweet-smelling": Hubbard, *Science of Survival*, p. 146.

49 *"a cold-blooded and factual account":* Hubbard: *A History of Man*, p. 3.

"Can you imagine a clam": Ibid., p. 33.

"One such victim, after hearing": Ibid., p. 28.

He explained that thetans: For Hubbard's description of "implant stations," including those on Mars, and what happens there, see *A History of Man,* pp. 78–79.

50 *"Communist-connected personnel":* Letter from Hubbard to the FBI, July 29, 1955, FBI file #131.

In one 1955 missive: Letter from Hubbard to the FBI, September 7, 1955, FBI file #132.

"Appears mental": FBI memo of October 11, 1957, as cited in Miller, *Barefaced Messiah,* p. 221.

"appeared to be a Communist manual": Letter from Hubbard to the FBI, December 16, 1955, file 133.

"since it lacks documentation": Letter from FBI SAC in Los Angeles to J. Edgar Hoover, April 17, 1956, file 141.

It was widely assumed that: "All About Radiation, by a Nuclear Physicist and a Medical Doctor," Publications Organization, East Grinstead, 1957, 1967.

The text promoted a vitamin: Ibid., p. 124.

In 1958, the FDA: Roy Wallis, *The Road to Total Freedom: A Sociological Analysis of Scientology,* p. 190.

54 *"holes appear in [the soap] bubble":* O'Brien, *Dianetics in Limbo,* p. 70.

"The tremendous appeal": Ibid., p. 72.

55 *"the joy and frankness":* Ibid., p. vii.

"As soon as we became responsible": Ibid., p. 73.

"one of the best auditors": Atack, *A Piece of Blue Sky,* p. 147.

57 *"A Scientologist is heavily":* Corydon, *L. Ron Hubbard: Messiah or Madman?,* p. 149.

"incredible dynamism, a disarming, magnetic": Cyril Vosper, *The Mind Benders,* p. 42.

58 *"Scientology flourished":* Miller, *Barefaced Messiah,* p. 3.

59 *"Man is now faced":* Hubbard, *DMSMH,* p. 488.

"the Santa Claus pack": *Saturday Evening Post,* March 21, 1964.

60 *One year earlier, in 1963:* Wallis, *The Road to Total Freedom,* p. 191; also, George Malko, *Scientology: The Now Religion,* p. 75.

61 *"represent, suggest and imply":* Wallis, *The Road to Total Freedom,* p. 192, and Malko, *Scientology,* p. 76.

"Scientology is a delusional belief": Kevin Victor Anderson, Q.C., "Conclusion," in *The Report of the Board of Enquiry into Scientology,* chapter 30. The Anderson Report can be read in full at www.xenu .net/archive/audit/andrhome.html.

"For some, . . . Scientology's conflict": Wallis, *The Road to Total Freedom,* p. 214.

62 *"From that moment on":* Hubbard, "Keeping Scientology Working," HCO Policy Letter, February 7, 1965.

4. The Bridge to Total Freedom

A great deal of this chapter relies on the recollections of Jeff Hawkins, a member and official of the Church of Scientology for close to forty years. To tell the story of Jeff's growing involvement in Scientology in the 1960s, and of Scientology's overall evolution and cultural outlook during the 1960s, I relied primarily on four lengthy in-person interviews with Hawkins in the spring of 2007, as well as numerous follow-up phone calls and well over two hundred e-mail exchanges through the summer of 2010. Other essential sources of information on Scientology in the 1960s were Nancy and Chris Many, Jim Dinalci, Mike Henderson, and Dan Koon, all of whom I interviewed personally, and with whom I also conducted subsequent, and lengthy, e-mail exchanges.

For a less subjective view on the era, I referred primarily to Paulette Cooper's *The Scandal of Scientology,* George Malko's *Scientology: The Now Religion,* Stephen Kent's *From Slogans to Mantras,* Roy Wallis's *The Road to Total Freedom,* and L. Ron Hubbard's own copious writing and taped lectures, notably his policy letters and executive directives. As in prior chapters, biographical and narrative history pertaining to Hubbard and his adventures was drawn from *A Piece of Blue Sky* and *Barefaced Messiah,* among other sources.

The description of Scientology's attempted takeover of the National Association of Mental Health is drawn primarily from C. H. Rolph's *Believe What You Like,* as well as Wallis's *The Road to Total Freedom.*

70 *"Wherever you go":* Malko, *Scientology: The Now Religion,* p. 7.
STEP INTO THE WORLD: Cooper, *The Scandal of Scientology,* p. 47.
"drugless psychedelic": Malko, *Scientology: The Now Religion,* p. 9.
"After drugs comes Scientology": Recollection by the ex-Scientologist Jim Dinalci of a poster he saw near the University of California, Berkeley, circa 1969, told to me in an interview, September 20, 2007.
"be a member of Scientology": Wallis, *The Road to Total Freedom,* p. 162.

71 *"raw meat":* Hubbard, HCO Bulletin, January 16, 1968.
"Beautiful": Cooper, *The Scandal of Scientology,* p. 14, and interviews with Hawkins, Many, and others.

72 *"step into the exciting world":* Cooper, *The Scandal of Scientology,* p. 13; Malko, *Scientology: The Now Religion,* p. 7.
More recently, the Kabbalah: Ruth La Ferla, "Objects of Jewish Devotion Evolve into a Fashion Fad," *New York Times,* June 29, 2004.

73   *Leonard Cohen, Cass Elliot:* Malko, *Scientology: The Now Religion,*
p. 6.
even Jim Morrison: Ibid., p. 7.
"Scientology can do more": William Burroughs, *Naked Scientology,* p.
72, citing a statement made in the *Los Angeles Free Press,* March 6,
1970.
Charles Manson, for one: Vincent Bugliosi, *Helter Skelter: The True
Story of the Manson Murders,* pp. 176–78, 318, 610.

77   *At the close of 1967:* The $1 million figure is an approximation taken
from what Atack, in *A Piece of Blue Sky* (p. 170), writes was a sum
of £457,277 for the year ending April 1967 (or roughly £9,000 per
week).
averaged $80,000: Atack, *A Piece of Blue Sky,* p. 171. By August 1967,
"Saint Hill was taking in as much as £40,000 a week, almost five
times its income of the previous year."
"run-of-the-mill, garden-variety": Lecture, "Creative Admiration Processing," January 10, 1953; Saint Hill Special Briefing Course-82
6611C29.

78   Enturbulated *was a word:* Hubbard, *Scientology and Dianetics Technical Dictionary,* p. 144.
"rationality toward the greatest": Ibid., p. 146.
"Conditions of Existence": Ibid., p. 86. This refers to the so-called ethics conditions. In a more general sense, Scientology defines three basic "conditions of existence" that define life: "beingness," "doingness,"
and "havingness" (ibid., p. 87).

80   *He had resigned:* Atack, *A Piece of Blue Sky,* p. 167; Miller, *Barefaced
Messiah,* p. 263; Cooper, *The Scandal of Scientology,* p. 110.
He was "Fabian": On the recording of "Ron's Journal '67," Hubbard
advised his followers that "so long as we are Fabian — elusive — we
grow strong." Jon Atack, in an online essay, "General Report on Scientology" (home.snafu.de/tilman/j/general.html#JCA-84), takes it a bit
further: "Hubbard asserted that the Sea Org is 'fabian,' and redefined
that word to mean 'using stratagem and delay to wear out an oppo-
nent.' Hubbard wanted the Sea Org to be seen as 'a determined but
elusive and sometimes frightening group.'"
To ingratiate himself: Miller, *Barefaced Messiah,* p. 259.
he had come to Africa: Atack, *A Piece of Blue Sky,* p. 166; "Millionaire
in Bumi Hills Hotel Deal," *Sunday Mail Reporter* (Rhodesia), May 22,
1966.

81   *refused to renew his visa:* "U.S. Financier Is Refused Residence Per-
mit," *Bulawayo Chronicle,* July 14, 1966; "Financier Must Quit Rhodesia," *Rhodesia Herald,* July 14, 1966.
David Ziff, an heir: According to Hawkins and other former Scientologists, Ziff was the son of William B. Ziff Sr., founder of Ziff-Davis,
and a brother of William Ziff Jr., who built the company into an em-

pire, publishing such titles as *Car and Driver* and *Popular Mechanics.*
Ziff's 2006 obituary in the *New York Times,* however, made no men-
tion of David Ziff, nor has his name come up in other references to the
Ziff family, possibly due to his long estrangement over Scientology.

83　*"We are rolling up":* Hubbard, Executive Directive 42 INT, November
4, 1968.
had isolated the enemy: Hubbard, "Stability," Executive Directive 51
INT, November 24, 1968.

84　*"In all the broad Universe":* "Ron's Journal '67."
"undesirable alien" . . . *"pseudo-philosophical cult":* Atack, *A Piece of
Blue Sky,* pp. 182–83; *Enquiry into the Practice and Effects of Scientology* (The Foster Report), by Sir John Foster, 1971, www.cs.cmu
.edu/~dst/Cowen/audit/fosthome.html.
carrying banners that said: Wallis, *The Road to Total Freedom,* p.
204; C. H. Rolph, *Believe What You Like,* pp. 52, 102.

85　*"We are masters of IQ":* Hubbard, "The Special Zone Plan: The Scien-
tologist's Role in Life," HCO Bulletin, June 23, 1960.
"If attacked on some vulnerable": Hubbard, "Dept. of Govt. Affairs,"
HCO Policy Letter, August 15, 1960.
"To take over absolutely": Hubbard, CS-G "Confidential: Intelligence
Actions, Covert Intelligence, Data Collection," December 2, 1969.

86　*"safeguard Scientology orgs":* Hubbard, "The Guardian," HCO Policy
Letter, March 1, 1966.

87　*"riots and disaffection":* Order of the Day, November 18, 1970. Hubbard accused *Time's* medical and health editor of being a member of
the World Federation of Mental Health, and also went on, in this issue, to accuse much of the American press of being Communist.

5. Travels with the Commodore

The primary sources for this chapter were Jeff Hawkins, Neville Chamberlin, Alan Walter, Mike Henderson, Glenn Samuels, Gerry Armstrong, Gale
Irwin, DeDe Reisdorf, and Karen Gregory, who provided personal recollections of life in the Sea Org and aboard the *Apollo.* For a less personal view of
Hubbard's years at sea, I turned to Miller's *Barefaced Messiah* and Atack's *A
Piece of Blue Sky,* as well as to L. Ron Hubbard's policy statements and bulletins issued in the 1960s and 1970s, his book *Mission into Time,* and several other Scientology publications.

I gleaned a fuller understanding of the Xenu and OT 3 myth through discussions with J. Gordon Melton at the University of California, Santa Barbara, and through lengthy conversations with Jeff Hawkins, Chris Many,
and several other former members, as well as with Mike Rinder. James
Lewis's book *Scientology* also offered an excellent scholarly perspective.

For insight into Scientology's marketing strategy, I relied upon Scientology's "sales bible," *Surefire Sales Closing Techniques* (Parker Publishing

Company, 1971), and L. Ron Hubbard's compilation of sales-related bulletins, contained in the Church of Scientology's "Hard Sell Reference Pack." I also had the good fortune to have access to a trove of Scientology ads, circulars, brochures, and other written material made available to me primarily through the J. Gordon Melton Collection at the University of California, Santa Barbara.

90   *a three-story, 3,278-ton behemoth:* Hubbard, *Modern Management Technology Defined* (referred to as *"The Admin Dictionary"*), p. 25; Cooper, *The Scandal of Scientology*, p. 51.
"aristocracy of Scientology": Flag Order 137, The Sea Organization, September 12, 1967.

91   *"My crew were sixteen men":* Sunday Mirror, December 24, 1967, as cited in Atack, *A Piece of Blue Sky*, p. 174.

92   *"My first thought was, this":* Miller, *Barefaced Messiah*, p. 283.

94   *"Don't explain. Penetrate":* Hubbard, "Dissemination Tips," HCO Bulletin, September 15, 1959.

95   *a technique he'd picked up:* Hubbard was particularly captivated by so-called super-salesman Les Dane, whose 1971 book, *Surefire Sales Closing Techniques*, became required reading for all Scientology registrars and other sales staff. Included in the book are instructions on how to use applied psychology when dealing with customers and how to "tag team" or "double team" a prospective buyer, which is a common tactic used in Scientology organizations, particularly with reluctant prospects.
"more or less in a hypnotic daze": Hubbard, HCO Policy Letter, September 26, 1979.
"We have learned the hard way": Hubbard, "Handling the Public Individual," HCO Policy Letter, April 16, 1965.

96   *In 1967 when Jeff joined: The Auditor,* numbers 24 and 25, 1967.
Four years later, that number: There were forty-three Scientology organizations worldwide in 1971. *The Auditor,* number 69, 1971.
"The supreme test of a thetan": Hubbard, "The Supreme Test," HCO Bulletin, August 19, 1967.
"MAKE MONEY. MAKE MORE MONEY": Hubbard, "Income Flows and Pools: Principles of Money Management," HCO Policy Letter, March 9, 1972.
in contrast to other gurus: "Sect Recalled as 'Bad Dream'; Bhagwan's Deserted Buildings in Oregon Sold to Another Church," *Washington Post*, June 27, 1987; "Rolls-Royce Guru Who Set Up Commune in Oregon Is Dead at 58," Associated Press, January 19, 1990.

97   *the Religious Research Foundation:* Bill Driver, "Scientology on Trial," *Willamette Week*, May 30–June 5, 1985; Robert Lindsey, "Scientology Chief Got Millions, Aides Say," *New York Times*, July 11, 1984.

"*It was fraud*": *New York Times*, July 11, 1984.

100 "*Hubbard's noting that human souls*": "Aspects of Scientology's Founding Myth," cited in James R. Lewis, *Scientology*, p. 375.

101 *Hubbard's announcing OT 3:* Interview with Neville Chamberlin.

"*help Ron clear the planet*": This phrase, cited in the "Foster Report," part of a 1970 report on Scientology and Dianetics by Professor John A. Lee in Ontario, Canada (*Sectarian Healers and Hypnotherapy*, e-book chapter 4 at www.cs.cmu.edu/~dst/Cowen/audit/lee.html), is also present in numerous Scientology publications of the time, and was told to me by many former members.

"*just a shade above Clear*": *Certainty* magazine, volume 5, number 10.

102 *The Scientology magazine: Advance*, December 1974, March 1975, and May 1975.

"*What would Ron do?*": Hubbard, "Post, Handling of," HCO Policy Letter, September 12, 1967. Hubbard encouraged his followers to think this way. In this policy letter, he stated that every Scientology staff member was wearing the Founder's "administrative hat" at their post.

103 *He'd been a racecar driver*: Miller, *Barefaced Messiah*, pp. 279–80.

He'd sailed with the Carthaginian: Hubbard, *Mission into Time*, p. 33.

had served as a tax collector: Atack, *A Piece of Blue Sky*, p. 178.

troves of gold and jewels: Hubbard, *Mission into Time*, p. 59. Neither the crew of the *Enchanter* nor of the other two ships ever found any treasure — though many would swear they found evidence of ancient temples and other ruins that Hubbard promised would be there. "Ron would make little clay models for us," explained one of Hubbard's most dedicated followers, Yvonne Gilham, in 1968, after returning from a five-week voyage through the Sicilian Channel, which Hubbard dubbed the Mission into Time. In Hubbard's clay renderings — he'd also occasionally draw pictures, Gilham said — he would depict, for example, a set of hills, where on one side, he said, would be a temple. "Sure enough we'd go over and there would be two hills and there on the left would be the temple. Then he'd say, 'On the hill, there will be a tower.' And we'd go along and, sure enough, there would be the tower. We just followed the models and followed his drawings and we'd hit the target. It was like that all the time."

"*I am literally petrified*": Letter to J. Edgar Hoover, February 13, 1973, FBI File #264, names redacted.

"*If your parents or friends*": Hubbard, "Order of the Day," distributed to the *Apollo* staff, May 2, 1969. Provided to author by a former Sea Org member.

104 "*The red chair to us*": Miller, *Barefaced Messiah*, p. 320.

107 "*emissaries of the Commodore*": "Commodore's Messengers," Flag Order 3729, September 15, 1978.

110   *One Trinidadian newspaper:* Robert Gillette, "Scientology Flagship Shrouded in Mystery," *Los Angeles Times*, August 28, 1978.

6. Over the Rainbow

To understand the intricacies of the Operation Snow White case, and the government response, I relied upon court documents, primarily the transcript of the government's 1979 case, *United States v. Mary Sue Hubbard et al.*, 493 F. Supp. 209; *United States v. Mary Sue Hubbard et al.*, Stipulation of Evidence for Criminal Case No. 78–401; *United States v. Mary Sue Hubbard et al.*, Sentencing Memorandum for Criminal Case No. 78–401; and *United States of America v. Jane Kember, Morris Budlong aka Mo Budlong*, Sentencing Memorandum in Criminal Case 78–401 (2) & (3). I also found great insight and detail in Atack's *A Piece of Blue Sky*, which was supplemented by reporting on the raid and subsequent legal battle in the *Washington Post* and the *Los Angeles Times*, notably Robert W. Welkos and Joel Sappell, "Burglaries and Lies Paved a Path to Prison" (*Los Angeles Times*, June 24, 1990).

For the personal recollections pertaining to Operation Snow White and other Guardian's Office intelligence operations, I interviewed Nancy Many, Gerry Armstrong, several former members of the Guardian's Office who wished to remain anonymous, and the author Paulette Cooper, who provided tremendous personal insight. I also referred to Cooper's journal and other writings pertaining to her harassment under Operation Freakout.

With regard to Hubbard's years at the Winter Headquarters ranch and in hiding in Sparks, I relied primarily on interviews with former Messengers Gale Irwin, DeDe Reisdorf, and Julie Holloway, and former Sea Org members Sinar Parman and Dan Koon.

113   *"If Hubbard screamed":* Terry Colvin, "L. Ron Hubbard Likened to Howard Hughes," *Riverside Press–Enterprise* (Riverside, CA, April 14, 1980), B-1.
      "A truly Suppressive Person": Hubbard, "Suppressive Acts — Suppression of Scientology and Scientologists — the Fair Game Law," HCO Policy Letter, December 23, 1965.

114   *"may be deprived of property":* Hubbard, HCO Policy Letter, October 18, 1967.
      "fanatical Scientologist": Atack, *A Pierce of Blue Sky*, p. 221.

116   *"For months, my anxiety":* *Byline*, June 2007, reprinted on Cooper's website: www.paulettecooper.com/scandal.htm.
      tasked with the theft: Testimony of Robert Dardano, City of Clearwater Commission hearings re the Church of Scientology, Tuesday, May 6, 1982.

7. DM

David Miscavige is in some ways as enigmatic a figure as L. Ron Hubbard was: very little can be conclusively proven about the man, as he rarely, if ever, grants interviews and reportedly exerts tremendous control over all who know and work with him. As has been true for every journalist since 1998, Mr. Miscavige refused my requests to interview him and thus did not contribute to the information presented in this book nor in the original *Rolling Stone* magazine article. Piecing together his story, then, poses a significant challenge. For a broad view of "DM," his basic history, and rise to power, I relied heavily on the few stories that have appeared about Miscavige in the *St. Petersburg Times* and the *Los Angeles Times*, notably Joel Sappell and Robert W. Welkos, "The Man in Control" (*Los Angeles Times*, June 24, 1990), Thomas Tobin, "The Man Behind Scientology" (*St. Petersburg Times*, October 25, 1998), and three stories by Thomas Tobin and Joe Childs: "Change of Plans" (*St. Petersburg Times*, November 15, 2009), "What Happened in Vegas" (*St. Petersburg Times*, November 2, 2009), and "The Truth Rundown" (*St. Petersburg Times*, June 21, 2009) . But my primary, and best, sources were Gale Irwin, DeDe Reisdorf, Julie Holloway, Mark Fisher, Larry Brennan, Dan Koon, Sinar Parman, Marty Rathbun, and several others who, in a series of interviews and many exhaustive e-mail exchanges, helped me piece together and confirm the narrative of Miscavige's rise and ultimate takeover of the church.

For background on the purges of the early 1980s, I relied upon these sources as well as on Atack's *A Piece of Blue Sky* and transcripts from the 1984 Gerry Armstrong case, as well as declarations and affidavits used in the 1984 case *Tonja C. Burden v. Church of Scientology of California, et al.* Alan Walter and Melanie Stokes gave me insight into the mission holders conference and the dismantling of the mission network. Larry Brennan provided an excellent, and overwhelmingly thorough, explanation of the corporate restructuring of the Church of Scientology, which I address in both the text of the chapter and in the notes.

To tell the story of the last years of L. Ron Hubbard's life, and the days immediately following his death, I relied on interviews with Julie Holloway, Sinar Parman, and Steve "Sarge" Pfauth, as well as on accounts from *Barefaced Messiah* and *A Piece of Blue Sky*, from Robert Vaughn Young's extensive write-up "RVY Update by RVY" (September 2, 1998, published on the alt.clearing.technology message board: groups.google.com/group/alt.clear ing.technology/msg/ac775c2dc5a0646c), and a comprehensive report of Hubbard's final years: Colin Rigley, "L. Ron Hubbard's Last Refuge" (*New Times*, May 29, 2009). The event announcing Hubbard's death was videotaped and has been made available on YouTube; I was also given a DVD of this event, and provided a description of it, by Jeff Hawkins and Mark Fisher.

125   *"a trusted associate"*: "Declaration of L. Ron Hubbard," probate document of May 15, 1983.

126   *"It was the reactive mind"*: Thomas Tobin, "The Man Behind Scientology," *St. Petersburg Times,* October 25, 1998.

129   *"Don't ever feel weaker"*: Hubbard, HCO Policy Letter, February 12, 1967.

   This reorganization seemed like: Even though Scientology had a labyrinth of separate entities, Brennan explained, the church had nonetheless been controlled "as if it were one big, international unincorporated association." The tithes by lower organizations were sent to Scientology management in a fairly transparent manner that left little doubt as to where the money went. Because of this, "there was always a danger that management would be pulled into legal suits and other actions because of their obvious unbridled control of not only the lower organizations but of the money they took weekly at will," he said. The new corporate structure would, crucially, separate Scientology management from the organizations that were drawing most of the income, making it harder to pierce the myriad veils separating the smaller organizations and even the larger Mother Church from L. Ron Hubbard, who still controlled Scientology in absentia.

133   *"It lasted from about ten"*: *Church of Scientology v. Gerald Armstrong,* testimony given on Tuesday, June 5, 1984, case no. C420153, Superior Court of the State of California for the County of Los Angeles.

139   *He liked to shoot:* "Scientology: The Road to Total Freedom?" *BBC Panorama,* April 27, 1987.

140   *"I am not a missing person"*: Declaration of L. Ron Hubbard, May 15, 1983, Case No. 47150, re: the Estate of L. Ron Hubbard, Superior Court for the County of Riverside.

141   *"a small hardcore group"*: Atack, *A Piece of Blue Sky,* pp. 317–18.

143   *"weren't white enough"*: Joel Sappell and Robert W. Welkos, "The Scientology Story: The Making of L. Ron Hubbard," *Los Angeles Times,* June 24, 1990.

   A few days later, Hubbard: Ibid.

8. Power Is Assumed

David Miscavige's ouster of Pat Broeker as anointed successor to L. Ron Hubbard has been one of the most contentious issues in Scientology history. For help in putting together a coherent narrative of this takeover, I relied on interviews with Dan Koon, Amy Scobee, Mark Fisher, and Julie Holloway, and the tremendous amount of information provided by Marty Rathbun on his blog and in several interviews conducted by Joe Childs and Tom Tobin of the *St. Petersburg Times.*

A number of articles were crucial to my understanding of where Scientology found itself just after L. Ron Hubbard's death: Richard Behar, "The Prophet and Profits of Scientology" (*Forbes*, October 27, 1986); Richard Behar, "Scientology: The Thriving Cult of Greed and Power" (*Time*, May 6, 1991); and Joel Sappell and Robert W. Welkos, "The Scientology Story" (*Los Angeles Times*, six-part series, June 24–29, 1990). For help in understanding Scientology's Religious Freedom Crusade and the Christofferson Titchbourne and Wollersheim cases, I found numerous stories to be enlightening, notably Peter H. King, "Rally Against Huge Damage Award; Scientologists Cast Protest as Defense of All Religion" (*Los Angeles Times*, May 25, 1985); Mark O'Keefe, "The Church of Scientology Is No Stranger to Criticism" (*Oregonian*, September 26, 1996); Jan Klunder, "Scientologists Converge on Portland for Protest; Thousands to Assail Award of $39 Million to Ex-Member in Suit" (*Los Angeles Times*, May 18, 1985); Bill Driver, "Scientology on Trial" (*Willamette Week*, May 30–June 5, 1985); Alan Prendergast, "Hush-Hush Money; An Anti-Scientology Activist Said the Church Made Him an Offer He Had to Refuse: $12 Million" (*Denver Westworld*, August 14, 1997); Marita Hernandez, "Scientologists Vow to Demonstrate Until Damage Award Is Overturned" (*Los Angeles Times*, September 10, 1986); and Jay Mathews, "Scientology Winning in Court: Mainstream Groups Help Support Church's Fight for Legitimacy" (*Washington Post*, December 1, 1985).

For the story of Scientology's long road to tax exemption, there was no greater source than Douglas Frantz's Pulitzer Prize–winning article "Taxes and Tactics: Behind an IRS Reversal — a Special Report; Scientology's Puzzling Journal from Tax Rebel to Tax Exempt" (*New York Times*, March 9, 1997). For details of Scientology's controversial settlement with the IRS, my primary source was Elizabeth McDonald's article "Scientologists and IRS Settled for $12.5 Million" (*Wall Street Journal*, December 30, 1997), as well as the text of the IRS-Scientology closing agreement, "Closing Agreement on Final Determination Covering Specific Matters" (*Wall Street Journal*, March 25, 1997).

146 *"Power in my estimation":* Thomas C. Tobin, "The Man Behind Scientology," *St. Petersburg Times*, October 25, 1998.

147 *Miscavige made a side agreement:* Declaration of Jesse Prince in Support of Mr. Erlich's Motion for Reconsideration of September 30, 1998 Summary Judgment Order, Case No. C-95-20091 (EAI), U.S. District Court, Northern District of California, San Jose Division. According to the former Scientology official Jesse Prince, who accompanied Miscavige to this meeting, Mary Sue signed this agreement under significant duress. As well as browbeating her, Miscavige also informed Mary Sue that L. Ron Hubbard hadn't mentioned her in his final months, leading her to believe that he didn't care about her at all.

151 *"I was kind of afraid":* St. Petersburg Times video interviews with Marty Rathbun. The full interview can be seen online at www.tam pabay.com/specials/2009/reports/project/rathbun.shtml.

152 *"finally broke under the pressure":* Ibid.

153 *"worked like a charm":* Joe Childs and Thomas C. Tobin, "The Truth Rundown, Part I," *St. Petersburg Times*, June 21, 2009.

155 *"Of course, DM never provided":* Robert Vaughn Young, "RVY Update by RVY," essay posted on the alt.clearing.technology message board, September 2, 1998 (groups.google.com/group/alt.clearing.technol ogy/browse_thread/thread/973264cc2f3e7850/ac775c2dc5a0646c? #ac775c2dc5a0646c).
"For the rest of my stay": Ibid.

156 *"Nobody gives you power":* Tobin, "The Man Behind Scientology," October 25, 1998.

157 *"continuously changed":* Ron Curran with Jennifer Pratt, "The Other Side of the Looking Glass," *LA Weekly*, April 4, 1986. This article noted the presence of the wanted poster on the wall of the Los Angeles Org, offering $500 rewards for information on church "enemies."
in the tens of millions: Scientology never paid its dissidents nearly the amount judges ordered. In virtually every case, Scientology followed up each judgment with an appeal, followed by an out-of-court settlement for much, much less than was originally ordered.

158 *"DM became infuriated":* Jesse Prince, "No conscience, no church," post to alt.religion.scientology message board, September 29, 1998. Currently archived at www.lermanet.com/jesseprince.htm.
denouncing Mayo as a squirrel: "The Story of a Squirrel," Sea Org Executive Directive #2344 INT, August 20, 1983. This directive was sent to the entire Scientology mailing list.
the help of other ex-cops: Los Angeles Times, June 29, 1990.

159 *the defectors were "heretics":* Though *squirrel* was the term most often used, officials referred to some defectors as heretics in the "Pledge to Mankind," the founding document of the International Association of Scientologists, dated October 7, 1984.

160 *a "major religion":* Curran with Pratt, "The Other Side of the Looking Glass," April 4, 1986.
"He'll have a hard time": Joel Sappell and Robert W. Welkos, "The Scientology Story: Courting the Power Brokers," *Los Angeles Times*, June 27, 1990.
"right to compete for converts": Jay Matthews, "Scientology Winning in Court: Mainstream Groups Help Support Church's Fight for Legitimacy," *Washington Post*, December 1, 1985.

161 *"Larry Wollersheim will never":* Catherine Gewertz, "Scientologists Vow Never to Pay $30 Million Judgment," United Press International, July 24, 1986.
"dissident group": Church of Scientology of California v. Commis-

sioner of Internal Revenue, Docket No. 3352-78, United States Tax Court, filed on September 24, 1984. According to this decision, the "IRS established the Special Service Staff (SSS) to insure that dissident groups were not violating the tax laws." One of the ninety-nine groups the SSS monitored was Scientology.

"selling religion": Ibid.

162 *"suck the blood":* David Miscavige, "The War Is Over," speech announcing the victory over the IRS, delivered in Los Angeles on October 8, 1993, transcribed from DVD of the event.

"But most importantly": Ibid.

163 *"cookie cutter suits":* Childs and Tobin, "The Truth Rundown, Pt. 1," June 21, 2009.

164 *"the whole idea was to create":* Douglas Frantz, "Scientology's Puzzling Journey from Tax Rebel to Tax Exempt," *New York Times,* March 9, 1997.

"startling congressional hearings": Edward Mezvinsky and Bill Adler Jr., "Blackmail, Bribery, Corruption: The File on the IRS," *New York Times,* July 24, 1989.

Miscavige wrote an editorial: David Miscavige, "Abolish Income Tax: We'd All Benefit," *USA Today,* April 16, 1990.

166 *the IRS definition of* church: *Church of Scientology International v. C. Philip Xanthos and 16 other agents,* No. 91-4302 SVW, U.S. District Court in the Central District of California, August 12, 1991.

Miscavige proposed meeting with: The story of DM's meeting with Goldberg, and all quotations allegedly reflecting his statements, come from Marty Rathbun's recollection of events, as told to the *St. Petersburg Times* for its Truth Rundown series, June 21, 2009.

168 *"required by the I.R.S. to disclose":* Frantz, "Scientology's Puzzling Journey," March 9, 1997.

"Instead of tough tax law": "Exempted, Not Vindicated," editorial, *St. Petersburg Times,* November 21, 1993.

9. Lisa

In 2004, the estate of Lisa McPherson settled its seven-year civil lawsuit against the Church of Scientology. As a condition of the settlement, both sides agreed not to discuss the case, or the terms of the settlement, in the future. As the facts of the civil case were nearly identical to those of the criminal case, as Lisa's mother and several other relatives are now deceased, and as the majority of Scientologists referred to in this and subsequent chapters are still involved in Scientology, bound by the agreement or otherwise unwilling to talk about Lisa, much of the information contained in this chapter, as well as chapters 10–12, comes directly from the Clearwater Police Department's investigative file, which was made available by the department in a CD format.

This file is made up of more than six thousand pages of documentary evidence, including Lisa's handwritten notes and letters to friends, write-ups of her overts and withholds, a life history report and other confessions, Church of Scientology internal reports and documents including Lisa's ethics files, and scores of interviews, sworn statements, and depositions taken by Clearwater law enforcement officials from Lisa's family, friends, colleagues, and Scientology staff. Unless otherwise noted, all quotations come from these records.

In addition, for background and insight on the environment at the Dallas Mission of the Southwest, and on Bennetta Slaughter, I relied on personal interviews with Steve Hall, Melanie Stokes, and Greg Barnes. Sandra Mercer and Nancy Many were two key sources of information about WISE, the experience of working for a WISE company, and the FSM program.

176   *"They were a time of unease":* David Frum, *How We Got Here: The 70s, the Decade That Brought You Modern Life (for Better or Worse),* p. xxiii.

180   *skeptical of Scientology:* Boss, in fact, wanted Lisa to ask for a refund after she committed some $3,000 to pay for Scientology's Life Repair package; he was so irate, according to church records, that he phoned the Dallas mission numerous times, threatening legal action if they didn't return the money. Succumbing to pressure from her husband, Lisa did ask for a refund but made it clear to the staff at the mission that she was happy in Scientology and did not intend to abandon it. Rather, as she explained to several staffers, she planned to use the refund money to file for divorce and then, once free of Boss, to do "amends" to get back into the church's good graces. Though this might have sounded reasonable, it set off alarms. In Scientology, the inability to resist another person's wishes signifies a lack of "certainty" about one's commitment to the church. "Never let anyone be half-minded about being Scientologists," Hubbard wrote in *Keeping Scientology Working.* "When somebody enrolls, consider he or she has joined up for the duration of the universe — never permit an 'open-minded' approach." To counter "open-mindedness," Hubbard advocated control, which registrars like Greg Barnes were encouraged to exert over their clients, for, as Scientologists called it, the "greatest good" of the particular individual and of the organization. Hubbard wrote extensively about control: "Control equals income," he said in an HCO policy letter dated February 21, 1961. "As any control we exert upon the public brings about a better society, we are entirely justified in using control . . . One must discover what is best for the applicant and then control them into obtaining it." Ultimately, Lisa changed her mind and did not ask for any money back; instead, she moved ahead with disconnecting from her husband.

"automatically and immediately": Hubbard, *Dianetics and Scientology Technical Dictionary*, p. 415, originally stated in the St. Hill Special Briefing Course 1973, tape #6608CO2.

181 *Originally conceived of in the 1960s:* According to the Church of Scientology, Hubbard came up with study technology after attempting to study photography via a correspondence course (see the Ron series, "The Humanitarian: Education," at education.lronhubbard.org /page34.htm). However, in an interview with Alan Walter in 2007, I learned that the Berners, loyal Scientologists, had in fact brought their ideas of "study technology" to Saint Hill, where, prior to meeting with Hubbard, they explained much of it to Walter over dinner. "They were excited about it and wanted to give it to Hubbard," he recalled. "That next day, Hubbard gets up and during a lecture introduces them to the [group], and then claims *he's* discovered this technology and has done this and that, and the two of them were in shock. They got no recognition, nothing. And from that moment on, nobody discovered anything but L. Ron Hubbard."

"word clearing": Hubbard, *Basic Study Manual*, Effective Education Publishing, 2004, pp. 157–59.

182 *nine distinct types of word:* A critical analysis of word clearing can be found at the "Scientology v. Education" site (www.studytech.org). Scientology's own explanation of word clearing can be found in HCO Bulletin, January 30, 1973, revised December 19, 1979: "Method 9 Word Clearing the Right Way," HCO Bulletin, July 1 1971, revised January 11, 1989; and "The Different Types of Word Clearing," *Basic Study Manual*, pp. 188–95.

184 *"aggressive without being obnoxious"*: Clearwater Police Department interview with Craig Burton, March 10, 1997.

187 *called "blowing"*: Church of Scientology staff or Sea Org members (with the exception, reportedly, of those at the International Base) are allowed to quit their jobs, provided they complete the proper steps, a process known as "routing out." The standard procedure is to submit to a security check, followed by "lower conditions," the formulaic process Hubbard designed by which the staff member evaluates the harm he or she may have done to the group. They are also required to do a written assessment of their transgressions — overts and withholds. This process can take months, and even years, reportedly. To ensure that a Sea Org member does not "blow," which connotes an unauthorized or sudden departure, other Sea Org members are often recruited to sleep outside such a person's door, sometimes with wrists tied to the doorknob, to prevent an unauthorized departure during the night. Even though a true "blow" is defined as "leaving without permission," the term tends to be used colloquially for *anyone* who leaves the Scientology staff. Departure is generally seen as negative,

caused by overts and withholds, or hidden crimes. To inform anyone other than a superior that you desire to leave is considered suppressive.

"freeloader's bill": According to Hubbard, any staff or Sea Org member who fails to complete a contract is considered a "freeloader." This includes those who "blow."

10. Flag

For the story of Scientology's infiltration of Clearwater, I relied on personal interviews with Larry Brennan and Sandra Mercer, as well as with the journalist Richard Leiby, who was both an eyewitness to events and a reporter of them. He was tremendously helpful in assisting me in separating the wheat from the chaff and also served as a crucial check on history. The seminal news coverage of Operation Goldmine, as Scientology's takeover of Clearwater was called, was done by the *St. Petersburg Times*, notably in a series of investigative stories by the reporter Charles Stafford, published on December 16–30, 1979, and later compiled in a special report, "Scientology: An In-Depth Profile of a New Force in Clearwater" (*St. Petersburg Times*, January 9, 1980). In addition, myriad subsequent stories in the *Times* as well as in the now-defunct *Clearwater Sun* newspaper informed this chapter, as did Mike Wallace's investigative report on *60 Minutes*, "The Clearwater Conspiracy."

Tom De Vocht was tremendously helpful in providing information on David Miscavige's strategy in Clearwater and his connection to Bennetta Slaughter. Caroline Brown and Sandra Mercer also gave me detailed insight into Slaughter and took pains to explain "safe pointing" and Scientology's overall strategy in Clearwater after 1990. Michael Pattinson, Sandra Mercer, and Greg Barnes spoke to me about Lisa McPherson's declining emotional state in 1994 and 1995. I relied once again on the CPD files for most other details of Lisa's story, from her quest to go Clear, her initial Introspection Rundown at the Fort Harrison, her experience at the Orlando trade show, and then her ultimate breakdown and brief hospitalization. In addition, for insight and explanation of Lisa's auditing experience, I referred to depositions and affidavits given by Hana Whitfield and Jesse Prince during the McPherson civil investigation.

192 *"I am discomfited by"*: Charles Stafford, "Scientology: An In-Depth Profile of a New Force in Clearwater," *St. Petersburg Times*, December 20, 1979.

193 *threatened to sue*: Though the Church of Scientology didn't sue the *Times*, in February 1976 the *Times* sued the church and L. Ron Hubbard for conspiring "to harass, intimidate, frighten, prosecute, slander, defame" *Times* employees. The paper dropped the suit early in 1977. According to a report in the *St. Petersburg Times* (January 9,

1980), those at the paper had decided to do so "rather than present evidence that could have harmed an innocent third party."

194 *"Church functionaries were directed"*: Ibid.

195 *"politically fascist organization"*: *Clearwater Sun*, March 11, 1979.

196 *"Scientology is going to be part"*: *Clearwater Sun*, October 31, 1980.
"I'm not here to complain": Transcript of *City of Clearwater Commission Hearings re: The Church of Scientology*, May 8, 1982 (www.lermanet.com/82cwcommission/4-001-077.htm).
"the person you work with": As quoted by the programming director of a local radio station, *St. Petersburg Times*, December 23, 1988.
"the largest community of Scientologists": "Destination," the Flag promotional brochure, Church of Scientology International, 1993.

198 *"stable, reliable, expert"*: Hubbard, HCO Policy Letter, January 12, 1973.
In 1993, she earned more: *St. Petersburg Times*, October 31, 1997.

200 *"The rundown is very simple"*: Hubbard, HCO Bulletin, January 23, 1974, revised April 25, 1991.

202 *She was having trouble*: *Tampa Tribune*, December 15, 1996.
"extremely foreseeable": *Estate of Lisa McPherson v. Church of Scientology Flag Service Organization*, Case No. 97-01235: First Amended Complaint, December 4, 1997.

11. Seventeen Days

For information about the Introspection Rundown, I relied on L. Ron Hubbard's own description of the process, as well as on interviews with several former Scientologists who are familiar with it: Nancy and Chris Many, Maureen Bolstad, and Jesse Prince, primarily. Nancy Many also helped me analyze Lisa's seventeen-day internment and treatment at the Fort Harrison, as did Teresa Summers, a former commanding officer of the Flag Land Base; Patricia Greenway, an assistant to the attorney Ken Dandar, provided further background. The rest of this chapter is based entirely on the notes of Lisa's caretakers and on transcripts of interviews, conducted by Clearwater law enforcement, with caretakers and other church officials.

208 *"Insanity," wrote L. Ron Hubbard*: Hubbard, "C/S Series 22: Psychosis," HCO Bulletin, November 28, 1970.
"sometimes has ghosts about him": Hubbard, HCO Bulletin, December 31, 1978.
"Scientology was not researched": Hubbard, "Psychotics," *Certainty* magazine, February 1966.

209 *"Policy is that we assign any case"*: Hubbard, HCO Policy Letter, June 29, 1971.
"I have made a technical breakthrough": Hubbard, "The Technical

Breakthrough of 1973! The Introspection RD," HCO Bulletin, January 23, 1974.

"isolate the person wholly": Ibid.

"destimulate and . . . protect them": Hubbard, "Introspection RD: Additional Actions," HCO Bulletin, February 20, 1974.

"build a person up": Hubbard, "The Technical Breakthrough of 1973! The Introspection RD," HCO Bulletin, January 23, 1974.

"of a very unbrutal nature": Hubbard, "Level IV, Search and Discovery," HCO Bulletin, November 24, 1965.

"You have in your hands": Hubbard, "The Technical Breakthrough of 1973! The Introspection RD," HCO Bulletin, January 23, 1974.

210 *"a small, square opening"*: John Lee and John Johnson, "Captivity Case May Be Tied to Faith," *Los Angeles Times*, January 13, 1990.

213 *"He's watching live"*: Thomas Tobin and Joe Childs, "Death in Slow Motion," *St. Petersburg Times*, June 22, 2009.

"buzz off": Thomas Tobin and Joe Childs, "Miscavige's Spiral of Violence," *St. Petersburg Times*, June 21 and November 1, 2009 (online video of interviews with Marty Rathbun), www.tampabay.com /specials/2009/reports/project/rathbun.shtml.

12. The Greatest Good

For the story of the McPherson criminal investigation, I relied on several lengthy interviews with Detective Lee Strope, formerly of the Florida Department of Law Enforcement, as well as interviews with Florida State Attorney Bernie McCabe and several other Clearwater law enforcement authorities who have requested anonymity. I also relied on the tremendous reporting of Cheryl Waldrip of the *Tampa Tribune* and Thomas Tobin of the *St. Petersburg Times*, whose coverage of the McPherson case was outstanding, and constant. In addition, several other articles were particularly helpful, notably Richard Leiby, "The Life and Death of a Scientologist" (*Washington Post*, December 6, 1998), Douglas Frantz, "Distrust in Clearwater — a Special Report: Death of Scientologist Heightens Suspicions in a Florida Town" (*New York Times*, December 1, 1997), and Joe Childs and Thomas Tobin, "Death in Slow Motion" (*St. Petersburg Times*, June 22, 2009).

For the saga of the McPherson family's quest for the truth, I relied upon the CPD files, and for insight and background on David Miscavige and his handling of the case, I relied on personal interviews with numerous former Scientologists, notably Don Jason, Tom De Vocht, Jason Knapmeyer, Marc and Claire Headley, and Stefan and Tanja Castle. I also relied extensively on the interviews with Marty Rathbun conducted by Tom Tobin and Joe Childs of the *St. Petersburg Times*, which were published in the paper and online on June 22, 2009.

For information about Scientology's approach to mental illness since McPherson's death, I relied upon interviews with Nancy and Chris Many, Sandra Mercer, Teresa Summers, and Maureen Bolstad, and upon the correspondence of the late Greg Bashaw. For details about Bashaw's life and involvement in Scientology, I referred to Tori Marlan, "Death of a Scientologist" (*Chicago Reader*, August 16, 2002).

228   *"like vultures"*: Cheryl Waldrip, "Scientologist's Death: A Family Hunts for Answers," *Tampa Tribune*, December 22, 1996.

231   *"Mystery Surrounds Scientologist's Death"*: Cheryl Waldrip, "Mystery Surrounds Scientologist's Death," *Tampa Tribune*, December 15, 1996.

232   *There had been at least eight cases:* Lucy Morgan, "For Some Scientologists, Pilgrimage Has Been Fatal," *St. Petersburg Times*, December 7, 1997.

234   *"Lisa at first didn't want"*: Cheryl Waldrip, "Mystery Surrounds Scientologist's Death," *Tampa Tribune*, December 15, 1996.

235   *"This is the most severe case": Inside Edition*, January 21, 1997.

238   *"Lose 'em"*: Joe Childs and Thomas Tobin, "Death in Slow Motion," *St. Petersburg Times*, June 22, 2009.
      "forward an agenda of hate": Elliot Abelson, letter, *St. Petersburg Times*, March 19, 1997.
      "lying" on Lisa's autopsy report: Cheryl Waldrip, "Doctor Details Scientologist's Death," *Tampa Tribune*, January 23, 1997. Specifically, the church attorney Elliot Abelson called Dr. Joan Wood "a hateful liar."
      "extortion attempt": Thomas Tobin, "Family Sues Scientology in '95 Death of Woman," *St. Petersburg Times*, February 20, 1997.

239   *"What the documents demonstrate"*: Jeff Stidham and William Yelverton, "Documents Detail Woman's Final Days," *Tampa Tribune*, July 10, 1997.

241   *"I take a great deal of pride"*: Thomas Tobin, "The Man Behind Scientology," *St. Petersburg Times*, October 25, 1998.
      "No. No . . . That doesn't come": Thomas Tobin, "Scientology Leader Named Defendant in Suit," *St. Petersburg Times*, December 15, 1999. In this article, Tobin noted that Miscavige said this during the 1998 interview for "The Man Behind Scientology," but it was not published then, for some unstated reason.

242   *"surprising calm"*: Thomas Tobin, "Scientology Responds with Surprising Calm," *St. Petersburg Times*, November 15, 1998.
      "now, tomorrow, and forever": Thomas Tobin, "Scientology Breaks Ground with Lasers, Fireworks, Music," *St. Petersburg Times*, November 22, 1998.
      "as a sign of its commitment": Letter from David Miscavige to Ber-

nie McCabe, January 22, 1999, whyaretheydead.info/lisa_mcpherson
/legal/dm-let.htm.

a "holy war": Letter from David Miscavige to Bernie McCabe, February 4, 1999, www.xenutv.com/blog/?p=2797.

243   *The purpose of a lawsuit:* Hubbard, "The Scientologist: A Manual on the Dissemination of Material," *Ability,* March 1955.

"complex" and "voluminous" motions": Thomas Tobin, "Scientology Promises Long Fight," *St. Petersburg Times,* December 16, 1998.

"bring a peaceful resolution": Letter from David Miscavige to Bernie McCabe, January 22, 1999.

McCabe again rejected: Letter from Bernie McCabe to David Miscavige, February 4, 1999.

245   *"Nobody investigates":* Patty Ryan, "Scientology Perspective on Tragedy Rarely Seen," *Tampa Tribune,* April 2, 2000.

"very real possibility": Memorandum from Douglas Crow to Bernie McCabe, "Review of Evidence in *State v. Church of Scientology Flag Service Organization, Inc.,*" June 9, 2000.

246   *"to prove critical forensic":* Douglas Frantz, "Florida Drops Charges Against Scientology in 1995 Death," *New York Times,* June 13, 2000.

"taken a toll far greater": Patty Ryan, "Medical Examiner: Case Has Taken a Toll," *Tampa Tribune,* June 14, 2000.

247   *"pep drinks":* Letter from Greg Bashaw to Debbie Cook, captain of the Flag Service Organization, April 29, 2001.

248   *"accept and assume all":* Church of Scientology Flag Service Organization, "Agreement and General Release Regarding Spiritual Resistance," 2001.

"a Flag Ship Class XII": Hubbard, "Word Clearing Series 23: Trouble Shooting," HCO Bulletin, September 13, 1971.

13. The Celebrity Strategy

My primary sources for this chapter were Nancy and Chris Many, Karen Pressley, Bruce Hines, Art Cohan, Amy Scobee, and several other former Scientologists, including one former Celebrity Center official, whom I interviewed extensively about the "Get High on Yourself" and "Friends of Narconon" campaigns, but who wished to remain anonymous. The Church of Scientology's love affair with celebrities has been covered extensively; in addition to relying on Scientology's own doctrine on the subject, some notable sources were John Richardson, "Catch a Rising Star" (*Premiere,* September 1993); Joel Sappell and Robert W. Welkos, "The Courting of Celebrities" (*Los Angeles Times,* June 25, 1990); Douglas Frantz, "Scientology's Star Roster Enhances Image" (*New York Times,* February 13, 1998); Joseph Mallia, "Inside the Church of Scientology: Stars Wield Celebrity Clout" (*Boston Herald,* March 5, 1998); and Dana Goodyear, "Chateau Scientology" (*The New Yorker,* January 14, 2008).

For background on Scientology's war with Germany, and its use of celebrities to further that agenda, I referred to numerous articles, notably Mary Williams Walsh, "Celebrity Group Takes on Germany Over Scientology" (*Los Angeles Times*, January 11, 1997); Stephen Kent, "Hollywood's Celebrity-Lobbyists and the Clinton Administration's American Foreign Policy Toward German Scientology" (*Journal of Religion and Popular Culture*, vol. 1, Spring 2002); Russ Baker, "Clash of the Titans: Scientology vs. Germany" (*George*, April 1997); and Frank Rich, "Show Me the Money" (*New York Times*, January 25, 1997).

253 *"There are many to whom America":* Hubbard, "Project Celebrity," *Ability*, 1955.

254 *But if Scientologists succeeded:* Ibid.
   the most successful org in Los Angeles: The term *org*, though technically a term for a Scientology "organization," or church, is often used colloquially to describe lesser groups such as missions. Celebrity Centre was always an org, but other Scientology centers, including numerous missions in the greater Los Angeles area, were also known, by members at least, as orgs.

255 *"reflected glory":* John Richardson, "Catch a Rising Star," *Premiere*, September 1993.
   "One day, in L.A., we got into": Alanna Nash, *Elvis Aaron Presley: Revelations from the Memphis Mafia*, New York: HarperCollins, 1995, p. 562.

256 *"Remember twenty years ago":* Malko, *Scientology: The Now Religion*, p. 7.
   "At that point I realized": Richardson, "Catch a Rising Star," *Premiere*, September 1993.
   Chick Corea, who joined: Fred Jung, "A Fireside Chat with Chick Corea," *All About Jazz*, September 7, 2004.
   Scientology helped her portray: "Celebrities Testify for Scientology," *St. Petersburg Times*, March 20, 1976.

257 *"My career immediately took off":* Hubbard, *What Is Scientology?*, p. 233.
   "when it's appropriate": Cameron Crowe, "John Travolta," *Playgirl*, March 1977.

258 *"about the pleasure, and glamour":* William Henry III and Martha Smilgis, "Video: Get High on Yourself," *Time*, September 21, 1981.

260 *"the largest anti-drug media blitz":* Robert Evans, *The Kid Stays in the Picture*, New York: Hyperion, 1994, p. 320.
   Over the next year, the foundation: Paul Fishman Maccabee, "The Narconon Sting: Scientology's Minnesota Drug Scam," *Twin Cities Reader*, October 17, 1981.

263 *"I don't agree with the way":* Nancy Collins, "Sex and the Single Star: John Travolta," *Rolling Stone*, August 18, 1983.

263 *"It is very important for me"*: Katherine Gewertz, "Scientology Loses Mistrial Motion," United Press International, May 10, 1986.

265 *"Want to Make It in the Industry?"*: Richardson, "Catch a Rising Star," *Premiere*, September 1993.

268 *"saving her life"*: Steve Weinstein, "Look Who's Funny," *Los Angeles Times*, August 26, 1990. Alley has continued to voice her claim: Narconon "saved my life."

269 *"I never defended Scientology"*: Judson Klinger, "Playboy Interview: John Travolta Interview," *Playboy*, March 1, 1996.

270 *Bertram Fields, wrote an open:* Bertram Fields, "An Open Letter to Helmut Kohl," *New York Times* (advertisement), January 9, 1997.
"condoned and societal harassment": U.S. Department of State, "Country Report on Human Rights Practices for 1996, Germany," January 30, 1997, www.state.gov/www/global/human_rights/1996_ hrp_report/germany.html.

14. The Seduction of Tom Cruise

My primary sources for this chapter were Mark Fisher, Bruce Hines, Karen Pressley, Nancy Many, Maureen Bolstad, Marc Headley, Claire Headley, Sinar Parman, Jeff Hawkins, Amy Scobee, and several other former Scientologists, all of whom I interviewed extensively. In addition, Marty Rathbun provided invaluable insight and confirmation of many facts through interviews he gave to the *St. Petersburg Times* and postings on his blog (markrathbun.wordpress.com).

In addition, I referred to numerous magazine and newspaper articles for information on Tom Cruise and his involvement in Scientology. Among the most helpful were Claire Hoffman and Kim Christensen, "At Inland Base, Scientologists Trained Top Gun" (*Los Angeles Times*, December 18, 2005); Neil Strauss, "The Passion of the Cruise" (*Rolling Stone*, September 2, 2004); James Verini, "Missionary Man" (Salon.com, June 27, 2005); Sharon Waxman, "Tom Cruise's Effusive 'Oprah' Appearance Raises Hollywood Eyebrows" (*New York Times*, June 2, 2005); and Alessandra Stanley, "Talk Show Rarity: A True Believer's Candor" (*New York Times*, June 25, 2005).

Insight into David Miscavige's views on promotion comes from interviews with Jeff Hawkins, Steve Hall, and Karen Pressley; for information about Scientology and the Internet, I found particularly helpful Wendy Grossman, "alt.scientology.war" (*Wired*, December 1995) as well as Janelle Brown, "A Web of Their Own" (Salon.com, July 15, 1998).

272 *"guys want to be like him"*: David Ansen, "Cruise Guns for the Top," *Newsweek*, June 9, 1986.
Cruise's father, Thomas Mapother III: Dotson Rader, "'I Can Create Who I Am,'" *Parade*, April 9, 2006.

280 *"Millions of church dollars"*: Affidavit of Andre Tabayoyon, *Church of*

Scientology International v. Steven Fish and Uwe Geertz, U.S. District Court, Central District of California, August 19, 1994.

281 *"He freaked out and was":* According to Headley, Cruise did more than "freak out." "He said, 'I'm out of here,' and he and Dave had a huge argument" during which Miscavige, citing quotations from *Keeping Scientology Working,* tried to convince the actor to stay the course. But Cruise told Miscavige he needed a "break."

282 *the couple was on a new path:* Ironically, though Cruise and Kidman apparently distanced themselves from Scientology after making Kubrick's *Eyes Wide Shut,* Kubrick's daughter, Vivian, joined the Church of Scientology. According to Kubrick's widow, Christiane, Vivian had been set to compose the score for *Eyes Wide Shut* when she abruptly left for California when the film was in post-production. "They had a huge fight," Christiane Kubrick told *The Guardian* in August 2010. "He wrote her a forty-page letter trying to win her back. He begged her endlessly to come home from California." On the day of Kubrick's funeral, Christiane said Vivian arrived with a Scientologist handler, who stayed by her side. Vivian has since disconnected from her family. "It's her new religion," her mother told *The Guardian.* "It had absolutely nothing to do with Tom Cruise, by the way. Absolutely not." Jon Ranson, "After Stanley Kubrick," *The Guardian,* August 18, 2010.

284 *members had completed 11,603:* Kristi Wachter, "Source Magazine Statistics — Analysis Summary," The Truth About Scientology, last modified February 17, 2005, www.truthaboutscientology.com/stats/source/analysissummary.html.

the "largest and most comprehensive": Thomas Tobin, "Scientology Launches Massive PR Campaign," *St. Petersburg Times,* August 10, 1997.

285 *it was a point of doctrine:* Hubbard, *Dianetics: The Modern Science of Mental Health,* p. 86.

286 *"improper or discreditable":* Janelle Brown, "A Web of Their Own," Salon.com, July 15, 1998, www.salon.com/21st/feature/1998/07/15 feature2.html.

287 *Cruise, according to a report:* Lloyd Grove, "The Reliable Source," *Washington Post,* June 15, 2003.

"functional illiterate": Tom Cruise and Jess Cagle, "Tom Cruise: My Struggle to Read," *People,* July 21, 2003.

"Doctors do not know how": Tom Cruise, interview by Larry King, *Larry King Live,* November 28, 2003.

288 *"Some people, well, if ":* Neil Strauss, "The Passion of the Cruise," *Rolling Stone,* September 2, 2004.

289 *"secret weapons":* Joe Neumaier, "Cruising to Stardom," *Daily News,* January 29, 2004.

"grew up in and around": Neil Dunphy, "A Sort of Homecoming," *Sunday Tribune,* June 12, 2005.

"strengthen[ed]" his outlook: Stephen Dalton, "Beck Is Back," *Sunday Age,* March 27, 2005.

291   *"In Scientology, we have":* Interview, Tom Cruise and Stephen Spielberg, *Der Spiegel,* April 27, 2005.

"You have no idea": Ibid.

Cruise spent so much time: Rachel Abramowitz and Chris Lee, "Control Switch: On," *Los Angeles Times,* June 6, 2005.

The next step was a new wife: According to numerous sources, Miscavige played an integral role in helping Cruise find a new mate after the actor's prior two girlfriends, Penelope Cruz and Sofía Vergara, both Catholics, rejected Scientology. Miscavige then reportedly ordered his deputies to find an appropriate mate for the newly single Cruise. The ever-faithful Greg Wilhere, Cruise's original handler, worked with Cruise's new handler, Tommy Davis, the son of the actress Anne Archer, to comb through a list of aspiring actresses already in the church. At one point, Marc Headley recalled, Wilhere's son, Darius, was charged with reviewing tapes of more than one hundred young women, all Scientologists, who'd been interviewed about their feelings toward Tom Cruise and their place on the Bridge. No one fit the bill, however. The duo then turned their attention to actresses Cruise might find more immediately appealing, among them Jessica Alba, Kate Bosworth, and Scarlett Johansson. As the story has been told, these three actresses, all starlets who, like Cruise, were promoting big summer movies, were among a number of women phoned by Cruise's office and asked to meet with the star about a possible role in *Mission Impossible III.* According to some accounts, Johansson's audition went so well that she met with Cruise at the Celebrity Centre but quickly left, sensing the ulterior motive.

Katie Holmes, who'd once confessed in a magazine interview that she'd fantasized as a girl about marrying Tom Cruise, was one of the actresses "auditioned," and according to the couple, when they finally met their mutual attraction was instant.

292   *"Do you know what Adderall?":* Interview with Tom Cruise, by Matt Lauer, *Today,* June 24, 2005.

293   *In February 2007, Travolta:* Jeannette Walls, "Travolta: Scientology Could Have Saved Smith," MSNBC.com, March 1, 2007, today.msnbc.msn.com/id/17031909.

"Google Narconon for a minute": Tucker Carlson and Willie Geist, *Tucker 1800,* March 1, 2007.

15. The Bubble

The experience of children in Scientology is unlike that of their parents, and to understand this, I spent several years interviewing second- and third-generation Scientologists. Though my main sources for this chapter were Natalie Walet, Kendra Wiseman, and Claire and Marc Headley, I benefited tremendously from the insight of numerous others, including Astra Woodcraft, Jenna Miscavige Hill, Jeffrey and Anthony Aylor, and a young man who appeared in my *Rolling Stone* story under the pseudonym "Paul James."

The website Ex-Scientology Kids proved a tremendous resource and go-to guide for information on Scientology schools. Additionally, my own trip to Delphi Academy in Los Angeles, and also to the Delphi Academy of Florida, located in Clearwater, shaped my ultimate impressions of this form of education. For information pertaining specifically to study technology and Applied Scholastics, Dr. David Touretsky of Carnegie Mellon University has provided a valuable resource in his website, Scientology v. Education (studytech.org/home.php).

For insight into how Scientology TRs are used as indoctrination for children, I talked extensively with Sandra Mercer and Stephen Kent, as well as with a number of Scientology kids, notably Kendra's friend "Erin," whose name was changed to protect her family.

298   *"By educating a child":* Impact, issue 7, 1986, p. 49.
299   *Some twelve thousand Scientologists:* Robert Farley, "Scientology Expands Tampa Presence," *St. Petersburg Times*, March 28, 2003.
       except Los Angeles: Jesse Katz and Steve Oney, "The List: The Power Issue 2006," *Los Angeles Magazine*, December 1, 2006. In 2006, the author stated, Scientology had "470,000 members in Los Angeles and owns 60 buildings here, making the city the church's Rome."
       the St. Petersburg Times *had dubbed:* Robert Farley, "Scientology's Town," St. Petersburg Times, July 18, 2004.
302   *as "opinion leaders":* Hubbard, "Celebrities," HCO Policy Letter, May 23, 1976.
305   *what Hubbard called the "labyrinth":* Hubbard, "Keeping Scientology Working Series 4: Safeguarding Technology," HCO Policy Letter, February 14, 1965.

16. Int

The main sources for this chapter were Marc and Claire Headley, Tanja and Stefan Castle, Jeff Hawkins, Tom De Vocht, Steve Hall, Dan Koon, Amy Scobee, Jason Knapmeyer, Maureen Bolstad, Marty Rathbun, Chuck Beatty, and numerous other former Scientologists whom I interviewed personally, with the exception of Rathbun. Because of the contentiousness of many claims contained in this chapter, all of these sources were interviewed separately, in some cases numerous times, and their allegations were triple-checked against one another. Joe Childs and Thomas Tobin of the *St. Petersburg Times* further confirmed stories I'd long heard through their in-depth reporting on Scientology and the abuses within the upper echelon of the Sea Organization. Of specific note are "Ecclesiastical Justice" (*St. Petersburg Times,* June 23, 2009), "Chased by Their Church" (*St. Petersburg Times,* November 1, 2009), and "No Kids Allowed" (*St. Petersburg Times,* June 13, 2010).

Physical descriptions of the Int Base come from my own observations while touring the property in February 2006 and from accounts from others. Jeff Hawkins and Marc Headley supplied details about the appearance of the base during the 1990s and 2000s.

322   *they decided to get married:* Teen marriages were, for many years, widespread in the Sea Org, as were quickie divorces. Virtually all of the second-generation Sea Org members I interviewed told me they'd been married in their teens, if only so they could have sex. One of these former staffers, Jeffrey Aylor, who began work on the PAC Base when he was fourteen and left the Sea Org five years later, reported knowing at least a hundred people who married in their teens, half of whom were divorced and remarried by the age of twenty. Like the Headleys, many of these kids were married in Las Vegas. "It's common knowledge in the Sea Org," said Aylor, "that the fastest place to get married is Vegas and the quickest place to get divorced is Mexico."

324   *Electric fences ringed:* According to Marty Rathbun, from the mid-1990s forward, "The entire organization of RTC had taken on the first and foremost job of protecting and forwarding the image and power of David Miscavige." A top priority for the RTC was making sure there were no staff departures from the base, he said in a sworn statement in July 2010. Those who did succeed in "blowing" were to be immediately returned, by force if necessary. This policy was to be strictly enforced, Rathbun said, with regard to anyone who worked closely with Miscavige. "The Miscaviges made it very clear that if anyone posed a heightened security threat to Miscavige personally, by virtue of having close working contact with him over time, such persons were to be returned to the Int Base by any means necessary."

326   *"a distinctive SO attribute":* Hubbard, "Toughness," Flag Order 2802, April 9, 1971.

330   *On its website, the church:* "What Is the Rehabilitation Project Force?" The Church of Scientology International, faq.scientology.org/rpf.htm.

336   *Rinder began to berate her:* Since leaving Scientology, Tanja has reflected on what happened between her and Mike Rinder, and in 2009, agreed to speak with him on the phone. Rinder, having left Scientology by that time, apologized for his behavior and, according to Tanja, asked her forgiveness.

17. Exodus

Marc Headley first described the musical chairs game to me during several in-depth interviews I conducted with him and his wife in 2007; Amy Scobee also provided an account. Headley later sent me a written version, which he ultimately published in his memoir, *Blown for Good*. Tom De Vocht confirmed Headley's account in an interview with me, and Marty Rathbun further confirmed the events during his interview with Thomas Tobin and Joe Childs of the *St. Petersburg Times* in June 2009.

As with the prior chapter, the bulk of this chapter is based on interviews with key sources, notably the Headleys, the Castles, Jeff Hawkins, Tom De Vocht, Steve Hall, Dan Koon, Mike and Donna Henderson, and numerous others. Stefan Castle provided me with the text of his letter to Tanja, correspondence between himself and his lawyer, Ford Greene, and a copy of the missing person report he filed with the Hemet Police Department.

346 *"How many people are in the org?":* Jefferson Hawkins, "Statistics," Leaving Scientology, accessed September 13, 2010, leavingscientol ogy.wordpress.com/doubt-formulas/statistics.
349 *"vulture culture":* Mike Rinder, "Survey: What Impinges — Results," Moving On Up a Little Higher, August 24, 2010, markrathbun.word press.com/2010/08/24/survey-what-impinges-results.
350 *the actress Nancy Cartwright:* David K. Lin, "The Church of $impson-tology," *New York Post*, January 31, 2008. According to Scientology's *Impact* magazine, Cartwright was awarded the status of IAS Patron Laureate for her donation. Kirstie Alley, who reportedly donated $5 million in 2007, was awarded a Diamond Meritorious medal.

Epilogue: What Is True for You

For the opening of the Scientology Ideal Org in Los Angeles, I relied upon the Church of Scientology's own report of the event, plus video footage provided on the church website; similarly, all information about past and future Ideal Orgs is from the Church of Scientology's own publicity materials. Mat Pesch, Tom De Vocht, and several former Scientologist finance and legal officers (who wished to remain anonymous) provided critical analysis of the Ideal Org program.

Though I had been aware of Scientology's interest in appealing to African Americans, Marty Rathbun was the first to draw my attention to Scientology's current friendship with the Nation of Islam, and Rathbun also provided the text and a PDF file of the Clear African Americans conference schedule on his blog.

Kendra Wiseman has been a source since the earliest days of this project, and the remainder of her story told in this chapter is derived from perhaps two dozen or so lengthy telephone calls and e-mail exchanges over the past five years. Similarly, Natalie Walet, the very first Scientologist I met, has been a constant source, and the quotes that end this chapter come from several long telephone interviews conducted in 2009 and 2010.

355   *"Today marks a milestone step":* "Los Angeles Cuts the Ribbon on a New Ideal Church of Scientology," Church of Scientology International, September 13, 2010, www.scientology.org/david-miscavige /churchopenings/church-of-scientology-los-angeles.html.

358   *Hayes struck both:* Mark Rathbun, "Funeral for a Friend," Moving On Up a Little Higher, May 3, 2010, markrathbun.wordpress. com/2010/05/03/.
      less for idealistic reasons: Ibid.
      At Flag in June 2010: Brochure titled "Clear African Americans Convention at the Flag Land Base," Clearwater, Florida: Church of Scientology Flag Service Organization, 2010.

359   *Farrakhan did not, however:* Louis Farrakhan, "Put On the New Man: Address by the Honorable Minister Louis Farrakhan," Nation of Islam, August 22, 2010, www.noi.org/webcast/ug-22-2010.

360   *According to the* Las Vegas Sun: David McGrath Schwartz, "Sharron Angle Campaign Working to Quiet Scientology Question," *Las Vegas Sun,* May 26, 2010.

361   *"We need to get as much":* E-mail sent to Church of Scientology membership, January 21, 2010, markrathbun.wordpress.com/2010/01/23 /the-church-of-disaster-capitalism/.
      "wake-up call": David Miscavige, "Wake-Up Call — the Urgency of Planetary Clearing," Inspector General's Bulletin No. 44, September 11, 2001.

362   *"degraded values":* Rathbun, "Funeral for a Friend," Moving On Up a Little Higher, May 3, 2010, markrathbun.wordpress.com /2010/05/03/.

363   *he has likened himself:* Rathbun, "The Reformation," Moving On Up a Little Higher, February 17, 2010, markrathbun.wordpress .com/2010/02/17/the-reformation/.
      "My wife and I can't": Rathbun, "Miscavige Black Ops Squad Hits Corpus Christi," Moving On Up a Little Higher, September 10, 2010, markrathbun.wordpress.com/2010/09/10.
      "I joined Scientology for": Rathbun, "Murder Outs," Moving On Up a Little Higher, August 13, 2010, markrathbun.wordpress.com /2010/08/13.
      "Inquiry into these allegations": Memorandum, *Claire Headley v. The Church of Scientology International et al.,* Case No. CV 09-3987 DSF, filed in U.S. District Court Central District of California, August 5, 2010.

"Scientology wins": Thomas Tobin and Joe Childs, "Judge Dismisses Two Lawsuits Aimed at Scientology," *St. Petersburg Times,* August 6, 2010.

364 *According to several reports:* Personal interviews with Amy Scobee and Mat Pesch, Jeff Hawkins, and others; Lawrence Wright, "The Apostate," *New Yorker,* February 14, 2011.

"One of the most addictive": Kendra Wiseman, "Growing Up a Scientologist," Ex-Scientology Kids, February 8, 2008; removed from the website; hard copy provided to author by Kendra. Also available at Ex-Scientologist Message Board, exscn.net/content/view/39/52/.

SELECTED BIBLIOGRAPHY

Adams, Bluford, *E Pluribus Barnum: The Great Showman and the Making of U.S. Popular Culture*, Minneapolis: University of Minnesota Press, 1997

Anderson, Kevin Victor, Q.C., *Report of the Board of Enquiry into Scientology*, the State of Victoria, Australia, 1965, www.cs.cmu.edu/~dst /Library/Shelf/anderson/index.html

Asimov, Isaac, *In Memory Yet Green: The Autobiography of Isaac Asimov*, New York: Avon Books, 1980

———. *I.Asimov: A Memoir*, New York: Bantam Books, 1995

Atack, Jon, *A Piece of Blue Sky*, New York: Carol Publishing Group, 1990

Bolitho, William, *Twelve Against the Gods*, New York: Modern Age Books, Inc., 1937

Burroughs, William S., *Naked Scientology*, St. Louis: Left Bank Books, 1985

Campbell, John Wood, *The John W. Campbell Letters*, Franklin, TN: AC Projects, 1985

Carr, Harry, *Los Angeles: City of Dreams*, New York: Grosset & Dunlap, 1935

Cooper, Paulette, *The Scandal of Scientology*, New York: Tower Publications, 1971

Corydon, Bent, and Brian Ambry, *L. Ron Hubbard: Messiah or Madman?* New York: Barricade Books, 1995

Crowley, Aleister, *The Book of the Law*, Boston: Weiser Books, 1987

David, Mike, *City of Quartz*, New York: Vintage, 1992

De Camp, L. Sprague, *The Science Fiction Handbook*, New York: Hermitage House, 1953

Del Rey, Lester, *The World of Science Fiction, 1926–1976: The History of a Subculture*, New York: Ballantine Books, 1979

El-Hai, Jack, *The Lobotomist: A Maverick Medical Genius and His Tragic Quest to Rid the World of Mental Illness*, Hoboken, NJ: John Wiley & Sons, 2005

Eshbach, Lloyd Arthur, *Over My Shoulder: Reflections on a Science Fiction Era*, Hampton Falls, NH: Donald M. Grant Publishers, 1982

Evans, Dr. Christopher, *Cults of Unreason*, New York: Farrar, Straus and Giroux, 1974

Ewen, Stuart, *Captains of Consciousness: Advertising and the Social Roots of the Consumer Culture*, New York: Basic Books, 2001

Ferguson, Charles, *A Confusion of Tongues: A Review of Modern Isms*, New York: Doubleday, Doran & Co., 1928

Foster, Sir John, K.B.E., Q.C., M.P., *Enquiry into the Practice and Effects of Scientology*, London: Her Majesty's Stationery Office, 1971, www .xenu.net/archive/audit/fosthome.html

Fromm, Erich, *Psychoanalysis and Religion*, New Haven, CT: Yale University Press, 1950

Gardner, Martin, *Fads and Fallacies in the Name of Science*, New York: Dover Publications, 1957

Garrison, Omar V., *The Hidden Story of Scientology*, Secaucus, NJ: Citadel Press, 1974

Gruber, Frank, *The Pulp Jungle*, Los Angeles: Sherbourne Press, 1967

Halberstam, David, *The Fifties*, New York: Ballantine Books, 1994

Hassan, Steven, *Combatting Cult Mind Control: The Number-One Best-Selling Guide to Protection, Rescue, and Recovery from Destructive Cults*, Rochester, VT: Park Street Press, 1990

Hawkins, Jefferson, *Counterfeit Dreams*, Portland, OR: Hawkeye Publishing Co., 2010

Headley, Marc, *Blown for Good: Behind the Iron Curtain of Scientology*, Oakton, VA: BFG, 2009

Hill, Napoleon, *Think and Grow Rich!*, San Diego, CA: Aventine Press, 2004

Hoffer, Eric, *The True Believer: Thoughts on the Nature of Mass Movements*, New York: Harper & Row, 1951

Hunt, Morton, *The Story of Psychology*, New York: Anchor Books, 2007

Jackall, Robert, and Janice Hirota, *Image Makers: Advertising, Public Relations, and the Ethos of Advocacy*, Chicago: University of Chicago Press, 2003

Jenkins, Phillip, *Mystics and Messiahs: Cults and New Religions in American History*, New York: Oxford University Press, 2000

Jung, C. G., *The Collected Works of C. G. Jung*, Sir Herbert Read, ed., volume 4, *Freud and Psychoanalysis*, London: Routledge & Kegan Paul Ltd., 1993

Kent, Stephen A., *From Slogans to Mantras: Social Protest and Religious Conversion in the Late Vietnam Era*, Syracuse, NY: Syracuse University Press, 2001

Kin, L., *Scientology: More Than a Cult?* Wiesbaden, Germany: VAP Publishers, 1991

Krakauer, Jon, *Under the Banner of Heaven*, New York: Anchor, 2003

Lattin, Don, *Following Our Bliss: How the Spiritual Ideals of the Sixties Shape Our Lives Today*, New York: HarperCollins, 2004

Lamont, Stewart, *Religion, Inc.: Church of Scientology*, London: Harrap, 1986

Lewis, James R., ed., *Scientology*, New York: Oxford University Press, 2009

Lifton, Robert Jay, *Thought Reform and the Psychology of Totalism: A Study of Brainwashing in China,* Chapel Hill: University of North Carolina Press, 1989

Love, John F., *McDonald's: Behind the Arches,* New York: Bantam, 1995

Malko, George, *Scientology: The Now Religion,* New York: Delacorte Press, 1970

Marchand, Roland, *Advertising the American Dream: Making Way for Modernity, 1920–1940,* Berkeley: University of California Press, 1986

Mathison, Richard R., *Faiths, Cults, and Sects of America: From Atheism to Zen,* Indianapolis: Bobbs-Merrill, 1960

McWilliams, Carey, *Southern California: An Island on the Land,* Salt Lake City, UT: Peregrine Smith Books, 2009

Melton, J. Gordon, *The Church of Scientology Studies in Contemporary Religions Series,* volume 1, Salt Lake City, UT: Signature Books, 2000

——, ed., *Encyclopedia of American Religions: A Comprehensive Study of the Major Religious Groups in the United States,* Tarrytown, NY: Triumph Books, 1991

Miller, Russell, *Barefaced Messiah: The True Story of L. Ron Hubbard,* New York: Henry Holt and Company, 1987

O'Brien, Helen, *Dianetics in Limbo,* Philadelphia: Whitmore Publishing Company, 1966

Pendergrast, Mark, *For God, Country, and Coca-Cola: The Definitive History of the Great American Soft Drink and the Company That Makes It,* New York: Basic Books, 2000

Pendle, George, *Strange Angel: The Otherworldly Life of Rocket Scientist John Whiteside Parsons,* New York: Harvest Books, 2005

Pope, Daniel, *The Making of Modern Advertising,* New York: Basic Books, 1983

Rolph, C. H., *Believe What You Like: What Happened Between the Scientologists and the National Association for Mental Health,* London: Andre Deutsch Limited, 1973

Sargant, William, *Battle for the Mind: A Physiology of Conversion and Brainwashing,* Cambridge, MA: Malor Books, 1997

Slater, Lauren, *Opening Skinner's Box,* New York: W. W. Norton & Co., 2004

Stark, Rodney, and William Sims Bainbridge, *The Future of Religion: Secularization, Revival, and Cult Formation,* Berkeley: University of California Press, 1986

Starr, Kevin, *The Dream Endures: California Enters the 1940s,* New York: Oxford University Press, 2002

Storr, Anthony, *Feet of Clay: Saints, Sinners and Madmen: A Study of Gurus,* New York: Free Press, 1997

Sutin, Lawrence, *Do What Thou Wilt: A Life of Aleister Crowley,* New York: St. Martin's Griffin, 2002

Vosper, Cyril, *The Mind Benders*, London: Neville Spearman Limited, 1971

Wakefield, Margery, *Understanding Scientology*, 1991, www-2.cs.cmu
.edu/~dst/Library/Shelf/wakefield/us.html

Wallis, Roy, *The Road to Total Freedom: A Sociological Analysis of Scientology*, New York: Columbia University Press, 1977

Whitehead, Harriett, *Renunciation and Reformulation: A Study of Conversion in an American Sect*, Ithaca, NY: Cornell University Press, 1987

Whitfield, Stephen J., *The Culture of the Cold War*, 2nd ed., Baltimore: The
Johns Hopkins University Press, 1996

Williamson, Jack, *Wonder's Child: My Life in Science Fiction*, Dallas, TX:
Benbella Books, 1984

Wilson, Bryan Key, and Bruce Ledford, *The Age of Manipulation: The Con
in Confidence, the Sin in Sincere*, Boulder, CO: Madison Books, 1992

Winter, Joseph A., *A Doctor's Report on Dianetics: Theory and Therapy*,
New York: Julian Press, 1951

Young, Paul, *LA Exposed: Strange Myths and Curious Legends in the City of
Angels*, New York: St. Martin's Griffin, 2002

Zablocki, Benjamin, and Thomas Robbins, eds., *Misunderstanding Cults:
Search for Objectivity in a Controversial Field*, Toronto, Ontario:
University of Toronto Press, 2001

Academic Papers, Periodicals, and Other Media

Abel, Jonathan, "New Foe Emerges Against Scientology," *St. Petersburg
Times*, February 8, 2008

Baker, Russ, "Clash of the Titans: Scientology vs. Germany," *George*, April
1997

Barnes, John, "Sinking the Master Mariner," *Sunday Times Magazine*, October 28, 1984

Brassfield, Mike, "Scientology Church Gives Fort Harrison a $40M Make-
over," *St. Petersburg Times*, March 22, 2009

Brill, Ann, and Ashley Packard, "Silencing Scientology's Critics on the Internet: A Mission Impossible?" *Communications and the Law*, December 1997

Brown, Janelle, "A Web of Their Own," Salon.com, July 15, 1998

Cagle, Jess, and Tom Cruise, "Tom Cruise: My Struggle to Read," *People*,
July 21, 2003

Childs, Joe, and Thomas Tobin, "The Truth Rundown," *St. Petersburg Times*,
June 21, 2009

———. "Death in Slow Motion," *St. Petersburg Times*, June 22, 2009

———. "Ecclesiastical Justice," *St. Petersburg Times*, June 23, 2009

———. "Chased by Their Church," *St. Petersburg Times*, November 1, 2009

———. "What Happened in Vegas," *St. Petersburg Times*, November 2, 2009

———. "Caught Between Scientology and Her Husband, Annie Tidman
Chose the Church," *St. Petersburg Times*, November 14, 2009

———. "OT VII," *St. Petersburg Times,* December 31, 2009

———. "He Wants His Money Back," January 24, 2010

———. "No Kids Allowed," *St. Petersburg Times,* June 13, 2010

Dibbell, Julian, "The Assclown Offensive," *Wired,* October 2009

Farley, Robert, "Scientologists Settle Death Suit," *St. Petersburg Times,* May 29, 2004

———. "Scientology's Town," *St. Petersburg Times,* July 18, 2004

———. "Striving for Mainstream, Building New Connections," *St. Petersburg Times,* July 19, 2004

———. "Edifice Sits Empty, but Why?" *St. Petersburg Times,* December 19, 2004

———. "Tom Cruise Is So Hot — That Is, for Scientology," *St. Petersburg Times,* July 10, 2005

———. "Spiritual Symbiosis a Surprising One," *St. Petersburg Times,* October 30, 2005

———. "Scientology Awards Reach Out to Black Community," *St. Petersburg Times,* February 18, 2006

———. "Scientology Nearly Ready to Unveil Superpower," *St. Petersburg Times,* May 6, 2006

———. "The Unperson," *St. Petersburg Times,* June 25, 2006

———. "Scientology Makes It in Classroom Door," *St. Petersburg Times,* May 20, 2007

———. "Group Fights Church Policies," *St. Petersburg Times,* March 16, 2008

Fisher, Marc, "Church in Cyberspace," *Washington Post,* August 19, 1995

Frantz, Douglas, "Taxes and Tactics: Behind an IRS Reversal — A Special Report: Scientology's Puzzling Journey from Tax Rebel to Tax Exempt," *New York Times,* March 9, 1997

———. "An Ultra-Aggressive Use of Investigators and the Courts," *New York Times,* March 9, 1997

———. "Distrust in Clearwater — a Special Report: Death of Scientologist Heightens Suspicions in a Florida Town," *New York Times,* December 1, 1997

———. "Scientology's Star Roster Enhances Image," *New York Times,* February 13, 1998

Gewertz, Catherine, "Scientology Loses Mistrial Motion," United Press International, May 10, 1986

Goodstein, Laurie, "Anti-Cult Group Dismembered as Former Foes Buy Its Assets; Network Forced into Bankruptcy After Long Legal Battle," *Washington Post,* December 1, 1996

Goodyear, Dana, "Chateau Scientology," *The New Yorker,* January 14, 2008

Gorney, Cynthia, "Scientology: Money Maker or Religion?: Scientology Controversial in Many Lands," *Washington Post,* July 24, 1977

Grossman, Wendy, "alt.scientology.war," *Wired,* December 1995

Hoffman, Claire, and Kim Christensen, "At Inland Base, Scientologists Trained Top Gun," *Los Angeles Times,* December 18, 2005

Jacoby, Mary, "High-Profile Couple Never Pairs Church and State," *St. Petersburg Times,* December 13, 1998

Kent, Stephen A., "The Globalization of Scientology: Influence, Control, and Opposition in Transnational Markets," Revised Version of a Paper Presented at the Society for the Scientific Study of Religion, November 1991, www.apologeticsindex.org/s04a13.html

——."Brainwashing in Scientology's Rehabilitation Project Force," in *Behörde für Inneres—Arbeitsgruppe Scientology und Landeszentrale fur Politische Building,* 2000

——. "Hollywood's Celebrity-Lobbyists and the Clinton Administration's American Foreign Policy Toward German Scientology," *Journal of Religion and Popular Culture,* volume 1, Spring 2002

Klinger, Judson, "Playboy Interview: John Travolta Interview," *Playboy,* March 1, 1996

Kroll, Jack, "Nicole Takes Off," *Newsweek,* December 14, 1998

Leiby, Richard, "Scientologists Plot City Takeover," *Clearwater Sun,* March 11, 1979

——. "Cult Tried to Control Newspaper," *Clearwater Sun,* November 24, 1979

——. "Cover Blown, 2 Spies Came in from the Cold," *Clearwater Sun,* November 27, 1979

——. "Sect Courses Resemble Science Fiction," *Clearwater Sun,* August 20, 1981

——. "Psychiatrist: Sect Drove Man Insane," *Clearwater Sun,* August 25, 1981

——. "The Church's War Against Its Critics—and Truth," *Washington Post,* December 25, 1994

——. "John Travolta's Alien Notion; He Plays a Strange Creature in a New Sci-Fi Film, but That's Not the Only Thing Curious About This Project," *Washington Post,* November 28, 1999

Maisel, Albert Q., "Dianetics: Science or Hoax?" *Look,* December 5, 1950

Mallia, Joseph, "Inside the Church of Scientology," *Boston Herald,* nine-part series, March 1–5, 1998

Meiszkowski, Katharine, "Scientology's War on Psychiatry," *Salon,* July 1, 2005, www.salon.com/news/feature/2005/07/01/sci_psy/?sid=1361000

Miller, Laura, "Stranger Than Fiction," *Salon,* June 28, 2005, www.salon.com/books/review/2005/06/28/dianetics/index.html

Nakaso, Dan, "In a Town with No Secrets, L. Ron Hubbard Died a Man of Mystery," *St. Petersburg Evening Independent,* February 1, 1986

Neuffer, Elizabeth, "Scientology Under Siege in Germany: Church Members Face Surveillance for Roles in 'Antidemocratic' Group," *Boston Globe,* June 7, 1997

"Of Two Minds," *Time,* July 24, 1950

"Poor Man's Psychoanalysis," *Newsweek,* October 16, 1950

"Remember Venus?" *Time*, December 22, 1952

Richardson, John, "Catch a Rising Star," *Premiere*, September 1993

Rigley, Colin, "L. Ron Hubbard's Last Refuge," *New Times*, May 29, 2009

Ronson, Jon, "After Stanley Kubrick," *The Guardian*, August 18, 2010

Sappell, Joel, and Robert W. Welkos, "The Courting of Celebrities: Testimonials of the Famous Are Prominent in the Church's Push for Acceptability," *Los Angeles Times*, June 25, 1990

Smith, L. Christopher, "Scientology's Money Trail," *Portfolio*, December 2008–January 2009

Sommer, Dave, "State Drops Scientology Charges," *Tampa Tribune*, June 13, 2000

Stafford, Charles, "Special Report: Scientology, an In-Depth Profile of a New Force in Clearwater," *St. Petersburg Times*, January 9, 1980

Stanley, Alessandra, "Talk Show Rarity: A True Believer's Candor," *New York Times*, June 25, 2005

Strauss, Neil, "The Passion of the Cruise," *Rolling Stone*, September 2, 2004

Strupp, Joe, "The Press vs. Scientology," *Salon*, June 30, 2005, www.salon.com/news/feature/2005/06/30/scientology/

Swiatek, Jeff, "Lilly's Legal Tactics Disarmed Legions of Prozac Lawyers," *Indianapolis Star*, April 23, 2000

Tobin, Thomas, "David Miscavige Speaks," *St. Petersburg Times*, October 25, 1998

——. "The Man Behind Scientology," *St. Petersburg Times*, October 25, 1998

——. "A Place Called Gold," *St. Petersburg Times*, October 25, 1998

Urban, Hugh, "Fair Game: Secrecy, Security, and the Church of Scientology in Cold War America," *Journal of the American Academy of Religion*, volume 74, number 2, June 2006, pp. 356–89

Verini, James, "Missionary Man," *Salon*, June 27, 2005, www.salon.com/entertainment/feature/2005/06/27/cruise/index.html

Vick, Karl, and David Dahl, "Scientologists Profit from New Members," *St. Petersburg Times*, October 15, 1993

Waldrip, Cheryl, "Mystery Surrounds Scientologist's Death," *Tampa Tribune*, December 15, 1996

——. "Scientologist's Death: A Family Hunts for Answers," *Tampa Tribune*, December 22, 1996

Wallace, Mike, "The Clearwater Conspiracy," *60 Minutes*, CBS, June 1, 1980

——. "Scientology," *60 Minutes*, CBS, December 22, 1985

Waxman, Sharon, "Tom Cruise's Effusive 'Oprah' Appearance Raises Hollywood Eyebrows," *New York Times*, June 2, 2005

Wright, Lawrence, "The Apostate: Paul Haggis vs. the Church of Scientology," *The New Yorker*, February 14, 2011

Scientology Publications, Tapes, and DVDs

Church of Scientology International, *Scientology: Theology and Practice of a Contemporary Religion*, Los Angeles: Bridge Publications, 1998

———. *What Is Scientology?* Los Angeles: Bridge Publications, 1998

Hubbard, L. Ron, *Advanced Procedures and Axioms*, Los Angeles: Bridge Publications, 2007

———. "All About Radiation," Los Angeles: Bridge Publications, 1990

———. *Clear Mind, Clear Body*, Los Angeles: Bridge Publications, 2002

———. *Dianetics: The Modern Science of Mental Heath*, Los Angeles: Bridge Publications, 2007

———. *Dianetics and Scientology Technical Dictionary*, Los Angeles: Bridge Publications, 1975

———. *The Freedoms of Clear*, VHS tape, Golden Era Productions, 1987

———. *The Hymn of Asia*, Los Angeles: L. Ron Hubbard Library, 1974

———. "An Introduction to Scientology," taped lecture, Los Angeles: L. Ron Hubbard Library, 1966

———. *Introduction to Scientology Ethics*, Los Angeles: Bridge Publications, 1968

———. *London Congress on Dissemination and Help and the London Open Evening Lectures, Lectures 1–7*, Los Angeles: L. Ron Hubbard Library, 1978

———. *Mission into Time*, Los Angeles: The American Saint Hill Organization, 1968

———. *Modern Management Technology Defined*, Los Angeles. Bridge Publications, 1976

———. "Opinion Leaders," *Hubbard Communications Office Policy Letter*, May 11, 1971

———. *The Organizational Executive Course*, volumes 1–7, Los Angeles: Bridge Publications, 1991

———. *The Original LRH Executive Directives*, Series 1–3, Los Angeles, Bridge Publications, 1983

———. *Philadelphia Doctorate Course Transcripts*, volumes 1–8, Los Angeles: Bridge Publications, 1982

———. *The Phoenix Lectures*, Los Angeles: Bridge Publications, 1968

———. *Science of Survival*, Los Angeles: Bridge Publications, 2007

———. *Scientology: 8–8008*, Los Angeles: Bridge Publications, 2007

———. *Scientology: The Fundamentals of Thought*, Los Angeles: Bridge Publications, 1983

———. *Scientology: A History of Man*, Los Angeles: Bridge Publications, 1988

———. *Scientology: A New Slant on Life*, Copenhagen: New Era Publications

——. "The Story of Dianetics and Scientology" (lecture), Los Angeles: L. Ron Hubbard Library, 1978

——. *Technical Bulletins of Dianetics and Scientology*, volumes 1–16, Los Angeles: Bridge Publications, 1991

WISE: Your Guide to Membership, membership packet; WISE International, 1990

ACKNOWLEDGMENTS

This book would not have been possible without the support and encouragement of Jann Wenner and Will Dana, my editors at *Rolling Stone,* who first assigned me a story about Scientology in 2005 and then gave me the time and resources to develop it in a way few editors are willing to do. I am also indebted to the many others at *Rolling Stone* who offered their guidance and support, notably Sean Woods, Eric Bates, Jodi Peckman, Jim Kaminsky, and Coco McPherson.

My agent, Laurie Liss, was the first person to encourage me to expand my research into a book and helped shape the proposal as well as offer her tireless support and advocacy in the years since. Numerous individuals at Houghton Mifflin Harcourt made this book possible, among them Eamon Dolan and Webster Younce, who acquired the book and were early, and enthusiastic, supporters; the amazing Andrea Schulz, who saw the book from first draft to publication and worked relentlessly to make it the very best it could be; Lisa Glover, who managed production, and Susanna Brougham, who provided expert copyediting; and Christina Morgan, who took care of every other detail. In addition, an extra special thanks is due to Will Blythe, a longtime mentor and friend, for being the rare editor who can take a disorganized pile of pages and give them shape, structure, and depth. I truly could not have written this book without his help.

Of the many former and current Scientologists, academics, and researchers who spoke with me, I am most grateful to the woman I have called "Sandra Mercer"; without her insights, encouragement, and guidance, I would never have understood the first thing about Scientology. I am also deeply indebted to Nancy and Chris Many, who, over countless tuna sandwiches and cans of Diet Coke, educated me about the Sea Organization, provided me with a library of Scientology texts and other documents, and offered their house as a refuge and meeting place. A special thank-you also goes to Anne, Jeffrey, and Anthony Aylor; Chuck Beatty; Jason Beghe; Maureen Bolstad; Larry Brennan; Caroline and John Brown; Tanja and Stefan Castle; Neville Chamberlin; Art Cohan; Jana Daniels; Mark Fisher; Steve Hall; Jeff Hawkins; Marc and Claire Headley; Mike Henderson and Donna Shannon; Bruce Hines; Gale Irwin; Don Jason; Jason Knapmeyer; Dan Koon; Sinar Parman; Mat Pesch; DeDe Reisdorf; Glenn Samuels; Amy Scobee; Teresa Summers; Tom De Vocht; Natalie Walet; the late Alan Walter; Kendra Wiseman; Astra Woodcraft; and the many other former and current Scientologists who shared with me their joys, sorrows, fears, hopes, and disappointments during my five years of research into this mysterious and often incomprehensible church. That a number of them still value L. Ron Hubbard's technology, if not the organizational management of the Church of Scientology — and were eager to differentiate between the two — is a testament to the growing number of Scientologists who hope to form an independent, and free, movement. I wish them all the best of luck in doing so.

On the academic front, Drs. Stephen A. Kent and J. Gordon Melton, with their distinctly different views on Scientology, have each spent years painstakingly collecting Scientology's vast trove of doctrine, publications, and other materials; they made that research available to me. I am also deeply indebted to Kristi Wachter, who patiently scanned many of the key documents on the Lisa McPherson case and posted them online, and to Mark Bunker, of XenuTV, for his massive archive of news and video footage, articles, transcripts, and other materials. In Clearwater, Lee Strope and his colleagues in the law enforcement community proved invaluable when it came to understanding the Lisa McPherson case.

Of the many friends and colleagues who provided assistance and support, I want to particularly thank my father, Alan Reitman, a meticulous line editor and the man who inspired me to become a journalist and who never ceased to amaze me with his generosity, love, and guidance. Josh Hammer and Shannon Burke read early drafts of the book and offered valuable criticism, as did Richard Leiby, who knows more about Scientology than most journalists and shared his knowledge and insights freely. Nora Connor, my researcher, spent months synthesizing complex legal data and poring over documents and transcripts; Alex Provan fact-checked every paragraph; Amelia McDonnell-Parry transcribed my interviews and also organized my office and files — not an easy task. Chris Steffen did additional transcribing and reporting. Raney Aronson at PBS's *Frontline* and Lisa Santandrea were amazing friends and sounding boards. To all I say thank you.

Finally, Lee Smith, an amazing journalist who understands better than most the emotional and financial costs of this profession, not only insisted I write this book but stuck it out with me through all the years it took me to finish it. Key chapters could not have been completed without his editorial guidance; the entire book could not have been written without his patience, encouragement, and most of all his love. Thank you for enduring . . . and Bode, too.

INDEX